UNFREE ASSOCIATIONS

Advance praise

'It is a work of scholarship that is unparalleled in its field. Truly a magnum opus'.
— Charles Brenner, MD author of *An Elementary Textbook of Psychoanalysis* and *The Mind in Conflict*.

'Using extensive interviews and documents Kirsner has written an arresting, definitive account of the internal politics of psychoanalytic institutes and their sometimes paralysing effects on policy and research.'
– Nathan Hale, PhD, author of *Freud and the Americans* and *The Rise and Crisis of Psychoanalysis in the United States*.

'Douglas Kirsner has produced a pioneering study of the operations of psychoanalytic institutes. *Unfree Associations* traces the consequences of various organisational arrangements on their vital functions. It also presents a veritable nosology of the ills that beset analytic education. Kirsner's case studies are focused on four of the most influential institutes in North America. The database he has collected is both convincing and astonishing. His conclusions transcend the problems of psychoanalytic education, for they are equally relevant to the fate of psychoanalysis as a body of knowledge.'
— John E. Gedo MD, author of *Psychoanalysis and Its Discontents; Spleen and Nostalgia: A Life and Work in Psychoanalysis; Beyond Interpretation* and *The Languages of Psychoanalysis*.

'As a survivor of a paradigmatic split (Boston 1973), I can attest to Prof. Kirsner's sensitivity and precision, in collecting many accounts of these traumatic events. He has recorded dozens of sympathetic interviews, in which each informant reports his or her own version of what happened, and he has reviewed hundreds of documents. From these conflicting and complex details, he has woven a seamless web that is both scholarly and extremely readable.

From this brilliant historical reconstruction, the general as well as the scholarly reader will learn how complex and easily forgotten are the details of relatively recent events. As a sympathetic interviewer of the analysts who survived these traumatic experiences, each with a different view of what happened, Kirsner has created a unified narrative that makes lively and dramatic reading. Historians of psychoanalysis will also be grateful for the wealth of factual detail he has preserved.'
— Sanford Gifford, MD, Chair of the History and Archives Division of the American Psychoanalytic Association.

'I should be embarrassed about having known so little about American psychoanalysis, but I am just grateful to Douglas Kirsner for having done all the hard work which has brought up so much that is new. Kirsner is balanced and impartial; his interviewing has yielded a rich storehouse of material which makes a wonderful book.'
— Paul Roazen, PhD, author of *Freud and his Followers; Erik H. Erikson: The Power and Limits of a Vision* and *Brother Animal: The Story of Freud and Tausk.*

'Kirsner's study of the dissensions in the most expansively successful psychoanalytic culture in the world is not only an extremely impressive piece of social and historical research, but is also a revelation concerning the local causes of bitter feuds and squabbles amongst Freud's most orthodox progeny. Whether the issues were money, professional style, parochial empire-building or the future developments of clinical technique and scientific theory, Kirsner gives a clear and unbiased account of the, at times, bitter struggles. It will be absolutely indispensable to all those interested in the fate of professional societies, scientific institutions and the rise and fall of American psychoanalysis.'
— John Forrester, PhD, Reader in History and Philosophy of the Sciences, University of Cambridge. Author of *Dispatches from the Freud Wars; Truth Games* and *The Seductions of Psychoanalysis.*

UNFREE ASSOCIATIONS
INSIDE PSYCHOANALYTIC INSTITUTES

DOUGLAS KIRSNER

Process Press   'only purity of means can justify the ends'
London 2000

Published in Great Britain in 2000 by
Process Press Ltd.
26 Freegrove Road
London N7 9RQ
pp@rmy1.demon.co.uk

© Douglas Kirsner 2000

The right of Douglas Kirsner to be identified as the author
of this work has been asserted by him in accordance with the
Copyright, Designs and Patents Act 1988

A CIP catalogue record for this book is available from the British Library.

ISBN 1-899209-12-3

The motto of Process Press is a quotation from *Darkness at Noon*
by Arthur Koestler (Cape, 1940; reprinted Penguin, 1947, etc.),
Penguin ed., p. 207.

Designed and Produced for Process Press by
Chase Production Services, Chadlington, OX7 3LN
Printed in the EU

CONTENTS

	Acknowledgements	vi
	Introduction	1
1	The Anointed: The New York Psychoanalytic Institute	13
2	The Boston Split	72
3	On the Make: The Chicago Psychoanalytic Institute	108
4	Fear and Loathing in Los Angeles	139
	Conclusion: The Trouble with Psychoanalytic Institutes	232
	Notes	252
	Bibliography	286
	Interviews Cited	308
	Personal Communications Cited	311
	Index	312

ACKNOWLEDGEMENTS

This book about contemporary psychoanalytic institutional histories has relied more on people as sources and informants than on documents. Inevitably, then, there are many people I want to thank. Those I interviewed or corresponded with made this work possible. Almost all are psychoanalysts; most of them members of the American Psychoanalytic Association. They spoke freely of often painful events. Some chose to remain anonymous. I have made many friends among them through the process of working on this book. It has greatly saddened me that some of these new friends and acquaintances became ill or died during the period that I have worked on this project.

Many others helped me throughout this project. Many shared experiences of their own institutes and commented on the manuscript. Many both inside and outside the American Psychoanalytic Association were enthusiastic, even passionate, about the project. Many were warmly hospitable during my numerous field trips. I have enjoyed enormous encouragement from many friends and colleagues. I wish to thank Jacob Arlow, Charles Brenner, Ken Calder, Susan Fisher, Bob Gardner, John Gedo, Sanford and Ingrid Gifford, Ron Gilbert, Arnold Goldberg, Elizabeth Hegeman, Elliott Jaques, Elizabeth Knoll, Albert Mason, David McDonald, James McLaughlin, Anthony Molino, George Moraitis, Grace Mushrush, Leo Rangell, Arnold Richards, Herman Sinaiko, Michael Guy Thompson, Christine Ware and Diane Wieneke.

Special thanks are due to my editor, Bob Young, for his enthusiasm and belief in this book, for his abundant constructive suggestions and for his vision in launching the book into cyberspace on his remarkable human-nature.com website.

As always, I am deeply grateful to my parents, Gordon and Sadie Kirsner, who have encouraged me in all my endeavours. They have been generous and staunch supporters from the beginning. Sadly, my mother, Sadie, died while the book was in press and did not have the pleasure of seeing it in print.

My wife, Marion Lustig, has painstakingly read the manuscript and made countless excellent suggestions. Her patient and energetic support has given me time for this project over many years, including my many absences in the US.

I want to thank those listed opposite for their interviews.

ACKNOWLEDGEMENTS

Robert Akeret
The late Sol Altschul
Jacob Arlow
Gerald Aronson
Rolf Arvidson
The late Samuel Atkin
Norman Atkins
Bernard Bail
The late Michael Basch
Irwin Bieber
Bernard Brandchaft
Charles Brenner
Kenneth Calder
Sandra Cohen
Arnold Cooper
Hartvig Dahl
Robert Dorn
Marvin Drellich
The late Rueben Fine
Leonard Friedman
M. Robert Gardner
John Gedo
Ingrid Gifford
Sanford Gifford
The late Merton Gill
Peter Giovacchini
Arnold Goldberg
Leo Goldberger
The late Roy Grinker
James Grotstein
Elizabeth Hegeman
Axel Hoffer
Philip Holzman
Elliott Jaques
The late Edward Joseph
Ralph Kahana
Jerome Kavka
Otto Kernberg
Edwin Kleinman
The late Charles Kligerman
The late Heinz Kohut
Maimon Leavitt
Edgar Levenson
Robert Jay Lifton
Roy Lilleskov
The late Samuel Lipton
Peter Loewenberg
Zvi Lothane
Ivan McGuire
Roger McKinnon
James McLaughlin
Charles Magraw
The late Margaret Mahler
Melvin Mandel
The late James Mann
Don Marcus
Norman Margolis
Albert Mason
The late Rollo May
Phyllis Meadow
William Meissner
Robert Michels
Arnold Modell
George Moraitis
Grace Mushrush
William Offenkrantz
Arthur Ourieff
The late Thomas Pappadis
The late Andrew Peto
George Pollock
Robert Pyles
Leo Rangell
Joseph Reppen
Arnold Richards
M. Barrie Richmond
David Riesman
Anna-Maria Rizzuto
Arnold Rogow
Hilda Rollman-Branch
The late Leonard Rosengarten
The late Henry Rosett
Creighton Rowe
Geoffrey Rubin
Roy Schafer
Jorge Schneider
Martin Schulman
Evelyn Schwaber
Hanna Segal
Morton Shane
Daniel Shapiro
Lee Shershow
Jonathan Slavin
The late David Slight
The late Alfred Stanton
Martin Stein
Robert Stolorow
The late Leo Stone
Charles Strozier
Blumer Swerdloff
Thomas Szasz
Arnold Tobin
Sherry Turkle
Arthur Valenstein
Heiman van Dam
Robert Wallerstein
Lotte Weil
Edward Weinshel
Lisa Weinstein
Bryant Welch
Robert Westfall
The late Otto Will
Jerome Winer
Earl Witenberg
Ernest Wolf
Victor Wolfenstein
Abraham Zaleznik

INTRODUCTION

In an age of managed care and of cognitive, behavioural and biological therapies for mental illness, psychoanalysis is generally seen as a 'profession on the ropes' whose hour is up.[1] The numbers of analytic patients have been in constant decline since the 1970s when four or five times per week psychoanalysis began to disappear rapidly. Psychoanalysis became less attractive as a mode of treatment as new, less expensive and less time-consuming therapies and modern medications began to sweep the US. Analytic patient numbers declined further with the recession and changes in third party insurance – especially managed care which supports only brief therapy and medication. Psychoanalysis is no longer popular with the general public, and university humanities departments, with the exception of some interest in Lacan, have largely abandoned psychoanalysis in favour of postmodernism. Ongoing conceptual critiques of Freud and psychoanalysis have made psychoanalysis less popular as a methodology and treatment.[2]

What went wrong? External factors have, of course, played a significant part but they are not the whole story. In blaming the outside world, psychoanalysts have disregarded their own crucial role in creating this crisis. Freud's question to his patient Dora is an important one here, 'What is your part in this?' In Dora's case, Freud could say, 'A string of reproaches against other people leads one to suspect the existence of a string of self-reproaches with the same content' (Freud 1905, p. 35).[3]

This book examines an aspect of the role played by psychoanalysts themselves in the formation of the current decline and crisis. This has been played out through their own institutions, the free-standing psychoanalytic institutes. Theoretical developments are only part of the story, which is about the institutional context within which developments take place, are transmitted or impeded (see Rangell 1988a, p. 60). The body of this book does not examine all the factors that have led to the parlous state of psychoanalysis in the US and by implication much of the world, but rather how some of the problems of psychoanalysis have been manifested, reproduced and amplified in psychoanalytic institutions.

Psychoanalytic institutes have been notable as closed shops. Their solid walls have kept them sealed off and mysterious to the outside world, including the mental health professions and the academy. Authoritarian cliques, power struggles and intrigues have predominated inside the institutes. Institute life has been secret, the subject of rumour rather than knowledge. Insiders often know little about other institutes (unless they are involved in site visits to particular institutes). Sometimes, insiders have a limited view of their own institutions because they stay within their own coteries and see the institute from the vantage points of their own experience and that of some close colleagues. What goes on behind the closed doors of institutes has not until now been examined in detail. I have been privileged to interview a wide variety of participants in the often dramatic histories of some central psychoanalytic institutes in the US. There have been many speculations about the manifold problems of psychoanalytic education and institutions, about the preponderance of conflict, acrimony and splits in the psychoanalytic field but there have been no attempts to gather the necessary facts on which to base our speculations. The painstaking task of collecting and synthesising the enormous number of factual details necessary to present an institutional history of psychoanalysis as it evolved in the United States through its institutes has not been carried out before. This book recounts for the first time the intricate inside history of the primary psychoanalytic organisations, the secret life of institutes.

My detailed investigations reveal some of the ways that psychoanalytic institutes have arrested free inquiry. This book describes the group psychologies so endemic to psychoanalysis. Honorary President of the International Psychoanalytic Association, American analyst Leo Rangell has observed that in the psychoanalytic field 'rational argument and scientific discourse do not generally prevail' as they are 'lost in the face of group psychology' (Rangell 1974, p. 6). Further, he has argued that if the history of psychoanalysis does not examine sociological, political, and interpersonal elements, 'we leave out half the history of every institute in the country' (Wilson 1993a, p. 15).[4] Kenneth Eisold has argued that the base anxieties evinced in psychoanalytic life, work and culture tend to bring about the intolerance and schismatic activities so endemic to psychoanalytic institutions, because these anxieties are not contained (Eisold 1994). As Jacob Arlow has recently observed in an article about the history of the Cleveland Psychoanalytic Institute, 'In order to learn the lessons that experience teaches, every organized group has the duty to study and to try to understand its history. Otherwise important lessons and guidelines for the future may be missed' (Arlow 1998, p. 36).

Psychoanalytic institutes have been troubled everywhere and always. Whether they are medical, nonmedical, Freudian, Jungian, Kleinian, Kohutian or Lacanian, whether they are in New York, Chicago, Paris, London or Sydney, psychoanalytic institutes behave in strikingly similar ways. According to the *New York Times* (December 11, 1996), even recently formed institutes in Moscow have similar problems: two of the three psychoanalytic institutes in Moscow call themselves 'The Russian Psychoanalytic Association'. In his 1953 Presidential Address to the American Psychoanalytic Association, Robert Knight lamented the typical themes of difficulty in institutes:

> The spectacle of a national association of physicians and scientists feuding with each other over training standards and practices, and calling each other orthodox and conservative or deviant and dissident, is not an attractive one, to say the least. Such terms belong to religions, or to fanatical political movements and not to science and medicine. Psychoanalysis should be neither a 'doctrine' nor a 'party line'. (Knight 1953, p. 218)

In Knight's view, 'the most pressing issue and the one charged with the greatest emotion has always been that of training' (ibid.).

As sites for transmitting psychoanalytic ideas to the next generation, institutes are the lifeblood of the psychoanalytic movement. They are central to issues of power, prestige and knowledge. The 'private club' nature of free-standing institutes has made it close to impossible to gain access to detailed information about their functioning and history. When social institutions are not organised so as to induce confidence and trust, they become suffused with suspicion and mistrust. (see Jaques 1976, p. 34). There is no redress outside psychoanalytic institutes which claim a special expertise function for training practitioners in the therapy.

Freud hoped that the therapeutic practice of psychoanalysis would not destroy the 'science' – the field of intellectual inquiry – of psychoanalysis. But in the main, the spirit of open inquiry has been replaced by training in a therapeutic endeavour. Unlike psychology and psychiatry, psychoanalytic training does not take place in universities but in its own institutions which are supposed to serve not only training but also research functions. From the outset psychoanalysis has been organised around its own free-standing institutions, perhaps deriving from Freud's own unhappy experiences with the University of Vienna.

Psychoanalytic ideas are often perceived as being owned by Freud and his heirs enshrined in psychoanalytic institutions that have served vital gatekeeping and other political functions.

In an important article considering the nature of psychoanalytic institutions, the President of the International Psychoanalytic Association, Otto Kernberg, asserted,

> Psychoanalytic education today is all too often conducted in an atmosphere of indoctrination rather than of open scientific exploration. Candidates as well as graduates and even faculty are prone to study and quote their teachers, often ignoring alternative psychoanalytic approaches. (Kernberg 1986, p. 799)

As Robert Holt observed,

> American psychoanalysis has lived for so long within a snug cocoon of myth that it seems unable to go through the predictable pains of metamorphosis into a viably progressive discipline. The protective threads it has wound around itself include warding off all criticism as resistance, idolatry of Freud, and faithful internalisation of all his faults as a scientist and writer. (Holt 1989, p. 341)

Kernberg proposed four models for understanding psychoanalytic education, each corresponding to aims that have been seen to be primary tasks of institutes. The models, each having a related organisational structure, were: (1) an art academy training expert craftspeople and bringing artistic talents to fruition; (2) a technical trade school focused on learning a 'clearly defined skill or trade, with no emphasis on artistic creativity'; (3) a monastery or seminary model that treats psychoanalysis as a religious system; and (4) a university college model that aims at the transmission, exploration and generation of knowledge and methodological tools for the creation of new knowledge. In Kernberg's view, psychoanalytic institutes are often conceived of as a trade school mixed with a religious system on the seminary model, whereas they should be modelled somewhere between an art academy and a university (Kernberg 1986, pp. 809–10).[5]

Psychoanalysis can be seen as a method for understanding the unconscious mind as well as a psychotherapy and body of knowledge based upon the findings of this method. Institutes have generally seen their central task as training practitioners in the therapy. Of the tripartite division in analytic education that most institutes adopt – training analysis, seminars and supervision – the training analysis is normally regarded as the most important.[6] Through the medium of the training analysis, the transmission of important aspects of psychoanalysis often takes the form of an esoteric pipeline of sorts through which analytic truth is transmitted, from Freud on down, from analyst to analyst. This involves the process of the anointment of those analysts – training analysts – deemed good enough to be the 'real', *echt* psychoanalysts. Training analysts, in turn, anoint their candidates through the medium of the training analysis. Because of this, the persistence of anointment has played a significant role in most institutes. Who an analyst's analyst was signifies how good an analyst a person is – not so much whether there are good analytic results. One does not think of asking who one's heart surgeon was after an operation, at least it is secondary as to whether the operation was successful! What other profession asks for exact genealogy? As Helmut Thomä wrote, 'That the genealogical tree and the descent – legitimate when it can somehow be traced back to Freud – should count more than one's own personal achievement is a peculiarity of institutionalised psychoanalysis' (Thomä 1993, p. 50).

A training analyst has the right to conduct psychoanalyses with candidates as part of their training. Because this position normally brings such power, who is or is not appointed as a training analyst is often at the heart of psychoanalytic ideological and political disputes. As Jacob Arlow observed,

> The tensions emanating from the division of colleagues into two categories of analysts, training analysts and just plain analysts, intrude themselves into the organisational and scientific life of the institutes. This is an ever-present problem, and its impact is accentuated by the aura of special status which surrounds the position of training analyst, a position endowed with charismatic implications. The training analyst is regarded as possessing the psychoanalytic equivalent of omniscience. It is from the training analyst that candidates claim their descent. In many places the professional career of an individual may be determined by who his training analyst was. (Arlow 1972, p. 559)

Why have psychoanalytic institutions been so closed, sectarian and seminarian? Reasons can be found in personal, cultural and historical aspects of Freud and the development of the psychoanalytic movement. However, a more fundamental explanation may lie in the psychoanalytic metaphor itself. Freud wanted psychoanalysis to be 'a profession of lay curers of souls who need not be doctors and should not be priests' (Freud to Pfister, in Freud 1963). Despite many differences, psychoanalysis shares many humanistic concerns with religion and philosophy, such as the big questions of ethics, human relationships, emotions and experience. But, in addition, psychoanalysis focuses in detail on a person's life and experience. Psychoanalysis can be seen as not so much a scientific search for causes as a humanistic search for meaning and interpretation.[7] Moreover, it must be remembered that Freud was so enthusiastic about psychoanalysis that he often treated psychoanalysis as an all-inclusive world-view that, like religion, could ultimately explain everything about human reality. Perhaps Freud's antipathy to religion lay not so much in seeing it as wrongheaded, as in its occupation of some of the ground over which Freud wanted psychoanalysis to be able to have explanatory power.

This book examines the problems of a humanistic discipline that has been touted as a science on the model of the medical or natural sciences, and has been organised institutionally as a religion. Freud saw psychoanalysis as based on psychology and not medicine and was implacably opposed to excluding lay analysts as the Americans did.[8] However, the expertise of psychoanalysts lies in an entirely different direction from that of medical science, that of trying to understand the language, context and communications of the neurotic as a 'stranger in a strange land'. It can be seen as a special probe of the everyday experience, using the interactions of the patient with the analyst as ways of framing and transcending it. The psychoanalytic field began with the discovery of the 'talking cure' in the conversation between Breuer and his patient, 'Anna O'. Change could come about through a special way of talking, free association. Free association involves patients speaking candidly and being open to their experience, saying what is on their minds no matter how difficult, embarrassing or seemingly ridiculous this may seem. The special skills or 'know-how' psychoanalysts use lie in the domain of language, literature, sociology, philosophy, anthropology and art far more than in medicine or science.[9] Freud's theory of mind was, as Lionel Trilling suggested in his essay, 'Freud and Philosophy',

> the only systematic account of the human mind which, in point of subtlety and complexity, of interest and tragic power, deserves to stand beside the mass of psychological insights which literature has accumulated through the centuries. (Trilling 1951, p. 34)

As Jonathan Lear recently argued (1998), Freud continued the open investigation into the nature of mind that was so central to Plato and Artistotle. Like the Delphic Oracle, 'Know thyself' is a central aim of Freud's essentially humanistic and critical discipline based on human agency and language rather than mechanisms. As New York psychoanalyst Edgar Levenson has argued, Freud's discovery lay in using language as a therapeutic instrument, but he mistakenly attributed his success to what was talked about instead of the semiotic act. The important discovery of this semiotic act, common to all psychotherapies, became derailed by a fundamental mistake. Freud and later analysts mistakenly concluded that it was the *content* of the conversation rather than the *process of conversing* that brought about change (Levenson 1983, especially pp. 8, 55; 1991, especially p. 198).

This discovery of a new method for focusing on understanding the patient's communications and experience had institutional ramifications. Psychoanalysts believed they had found a new way of understanding that was sufficiently different from other approaches to be a special discipline of its own. While some wisdom about the human mind, behaviour, communications and experience accumulated over decades of psychoanalytic inquiry, shutting off the outside world of other disciplines, approaches and data stymied development and reinforced prejudices. Different schools developed different emphases on content. Freudian patients had sexual dreams, Jungian patients dreamt of mandalas while Kleinian patients could only dream of escaping from the bad breast. The illuminating insights of gifted founders were transmuted into doctrine by far less talented followers who disseminated psychoanalysis and ran its institutions. Psychoanalysis became stagnant as dogma replaced method.

* * *

There are currently about 20,000 analytic practitioners in the US, most of whom have trained through and remain members of psychoanalytic institutes. The major national umbrella organisations are the American Psychoanalytic Association (3,200 members), the American Academy of Psychoanalysis, the American Psychological Association's Division 39 on psychoanalysis (the number of psychologists indicating their specialty area as psychoanalysis was 4,109 in 1998), and the National Association for the Advancement of Psychoanalysis (1,700 members including seventeen accredited institutes).

The largest, oldest, most prestigious and historically the most important national psychoanalytic organisation is the American Psychoanalytic Association (APsaA) of 3,200 members. It is affiliated with the world-wide accrediting organisation founded by Sigmund Freud, the International Psychoanalytic Association. The APsaA was founded in 1911 and currently has thirty-three accredited training institutes, forty-one affiliate societies and three affiliate study groups throughout the US. The APsaA has always provided an important forum for the exchange of psychoanalytic ideas and publishes the major American psychoanalytic journal, the *Journal of the American Psychoanalytic Association*. However, its principal function has been the accreditation and maintenance of professional standards in psychoanalysis. To this end, institutes are reviewed and evaluated through regular site visits, and individual analysts are evaluated for certification as analysts belonging to the APsaA. However, the powerful and prestigious APsaA is an umbrella organisation that plays little part in the regular educational, clinical or intellectual activities of institutes.

In order to understand psychoanalytic institutional life, it is essential to examine individual institutes where training and other psychoanalytic activities are based. Institutes vary widely with their different structures, unique histories and cultures. While all institutes train candidates to become psychoanalysts, there is considerable variation in curriculum, requirements, standards, approaches, openness and flexibility. So too do the methods vary for appointment to the prestigious position of training analyst.

Psychoanalytic institutions are divided into two. First, the psychoanalytic society which consists of the graduates of the analytic training program and any other practitioners who are accepted into the organisation. This acts essentially as a forum, although it may conduct some extramural educational activities as well. Second, the institute, the training arm, consists of the faculty and candidates. The institute is often governed by an Education Committee frequently consisting of training analysts, sometimes with some others. While the institute and society are often connected in some way, the structure of the relationship varies from the institutions being totally separate to being completely unified. Institutes are often run by a Board of Trustees or a Board of Directors, mostly elected from the membership or, in the case of the Chicago Psychoanalytic Institute, consisting of lay people as well as analysts. Methods of governance vary. Although most are freestanding, others have more or less close relations with universities. (For example, the Columbia Center in New York forms part of the Department of Psychiatry at Columbia University).

Therefore, a complex picture of institutional governance emerges, even within the APsaA. When the cultures and histories are factored in, each institute can be seen as unique. In these difficult times for psychoanalysis, although there are many similarities in institutional behaviour, each is perhaps unhappy in its own particular way.

Psychoanalytic institutions are based on the transmission and advancement of psychoanalytic ideas, ideas that are not easily defined and understood in the same way by the actors in these dramas. Psychoanalysis is unmoored; it is not a science, nor a religion, not a medical specialty nor simply an art. Freud was an explorer but he also codified his ideas. His work has been taken as an inspiration to explore without presuppositions. and also as Holy Writ. Psychoanalysis deals with emotions and excites passions. Like religion, psychoanalysis asks big questions, and, like religion, is easily influenced and seduced by dogmatic answers to these difficult questions.

The early days of psychoanalysis were imbued with Freud's inspiration and the excitement of new ideas. Neither ideas nor institutions were set in stone. The new discoveries were the result of an open spirit enshrined in free association. However, the technique of psychoanalytic practice assumed a somewhat mystical status. Institutes, which trained analysts in their new discipline, became less critical and increasingly dogmatic as psychoanalysis became professionalised and more socially acceptable. Training institutes seemed to carry conviction, certainty and knowledge with them through their teachers and graduates. Qualifying as a psychoanalyst increasingly required obsessional devotion to the trappings of analysis (five times a week on the couch, and so on) and surviving the ordeal of local, and often wider, psychoanalytic politics. The training became the transmission of dogmas and received truths in the seductive illusion of knowledge rather than a method based on ambiguity, unknowing and uncertainty. Orthodoxy was rewarded as psychoanalysts became more devotional.

A distinction can be made here between what I would term 'critical psychoanalysis' and what could be termed 'professionalised psychoanalysis'. Critical psychoanalysis focuses on an open investigation of the field of the unconscious using as primary the psychoanalytic investigative procedure while professionalised psychoanalysis treats the derivatives of this procedure – the therapy and the collection of information. Critical psychoanalysis takes truth to be its only goal; Freud regarded the analytic relation as 'based on a love of truth' (Freud 1937, p. 248). 'During my whole life,' Freud said, 'I have endeavored to uncover truths.' He added, perhaps somewhat disingenuously, 'I had no other intention and everything else was completely a matter of indifference to me. My single motive was the love of truth' (quoted in Sterba 1982, p. 115). Critical psychoanalysis investigates why this goal, the love of truth, meets with most powerful often successful resistances that result in mental, theoretical and institutional formations that are based on our need to avoid the truth. The very object and tool of psychoanalytic investigation, the human mind, often produces obstacles to understanding it. Freud never wanted the therapy to stand in the way of an open perspective and was critical of what he saw as the American approach:

> Therapeutic ambition is only halfway useful for science, for it is too tendentious. Free investigation is tremendously hampered by it. Therapeutic ambition leads to a kind of pragmatism, as in America, where everything is judged by its dollar value. As a scientific investigator, one should not take therapy into consideration. (quoted in Sterba 1982, p. 111)

He even maintained: 'I have always been of the opinion that the extramedical applications of psychoanalysis are as significant as the medical ones, indeed that the former might perhaps have a greater influence on the mental orientation of humanity' (Freud to Hendrik de Man, December 13, 1925, quoted in Gay 1988, p. 310n).

However, professionalised psychoanalysis, which relies on 'false expertise', concentrates on the therapy as an end in itself and does not normally deeply question its theoretical underpinnings, regarding them as established truths. Thus, while sometimes superficially appearing empiricist and using quasi-scientific jargon, in reality psychoanalysis resembles an institutionalised secular religion. Qualified psychoanalysts, trained in a restrictive and neurotic approach, were perhaps restricted in their capacity to treat ordinary neurotics.

Most psychoanalytic institutes are unfree associations of psychoanalysts where the spirit of free inquiry has been replaced by the inculcation of received truth and the anointment of those who are supposed to possess knowledge. Through their institutions, psychoanalysts can easily become blind to the spirit of sceptical inquiry on which psychoanalysis was based. This method is rarely applied to their institutions, which are mostly unfree oligarchies, and which rewarded conformity and punished difference. The story of psychoanalytic institutions is central to psychoanalytic history, and to what has gone so wrong with psychoanalysis.

Institutions are often inimical to ideas, yet they are essential for their transmission and application. In part, organisations have their own separate dynamics apart from what they are manifestly about. Once psychoanalytic institutes were established to take on the business of the administration and training of practitioners, inevitably certain dynamics, such as the corruptive influences of power, were set in motion. Yet they traced a path conditioned by the social, economic and historical context, the nature of the field and task, as well as the personalities involved. They have been centrally influenced by factors such as substituting a 'body of knowledge' for the methodology, the psychology of anointment, and the nature of psychoanalytic professional life. How historical, social and special psychoanalytic cultural factors were played out and bolstered in the specific organisation of the institutes forms the substance of the chapters on the individual institutes.

This book reveals the inner political histories of arguably the four most important and varied psychoanalytic institutes affiliated with the APsaA. The New York Psychoanalytic Institute was the first and, for decades, the prestigious institute which set the model for many others. It became pre-eminent on a world-wide scale with the immigration of leading European analysts fleeing the Nazis. I move from the earliest psychoanalytic society in the US to the more recent, which, like the history of European settlement of the US, traced a westward path. The Boston Psychoanalytic Society and Institute, the Chicago Psychoanalytic Institute and the Los Angeles Psychoanalytic Society and Institute are quite varied in their organisation and histories. The cultures are often different, yet many of the problems will be found to be similar at base.

My examination of the detailed political history of the New York Psychoanalytic Institute provides a quintessential example of analytic anointment in practice, together with its pitfalls. I then examine a split that occurred in the Boston Psychoanalytic Society and Institute. This demonstrates some of the tensions and ambiguities that seem inherent in psychoanalytic organisations, especially where society and institute are part of the same institution. Then I move on to investigate the Chicago Psychoanalytic Institute which is quite differently organised: in Chicago, the institute with a lay Board of Trustees is quite separate from the society, and for most of its history has been headed by a powerful director. Then I look at the very complex history of the Los Angeles Psychoanalytic Society and Institute which the APsaA nearly closed down in the 1970s. The Los Angeles history is especially colourful and informative, and includes the introduction of Kleinian and object relations ideas into the institute and the reactions to them. Finally, I draw some conclusions from my research about the causes of the ubiquitous problems in psychoanalytic institutes with some suggestions for change.

This research is based on my extensive interviews with 150 psychoanalysts belonging to the APsaA who experienced the events they described at their institutes. I conducted a number of interviews with many of the same analysts over a number of years. Many of the analysts

I interviewed were prominent in psychoanalysis as established leaders and were quite often protagonists in the stories of their institutes. I transcribed a mass of oral history, over a million words from interviews. I consulted a mountain of material in libraries and archives, attended institute meetings and conferences and became conversant with the complexities of the field. A major obstacle was that institutes were less than forthcoming in releasing historical documents.[10]

These histories are unique detailed political chronicles that provide a basis for understanding the nature of psychoanalytic institutions as they develop. They provide a foundation for a critique of what has gone wrong with psychoanalysis and its institutions and for the larger conclusions I reach about why psychoanalytic institutions behave the way they do. These histories provide dramatic insights into what psychoanalysts and their institutions have contributed to what has gone wrong with psychoanalysis.

1 THE ANOINTED: THE NEW YORK PSYCHOANALYTIC INSTITUTE

> I don't think there's a major split in New York on ideological lines. We are basically in agreement. A major problem New York has had is the age-old problem of all institutes – who will have the right to train? How do you get on the ladder? Favouritism, nepotism, how to be assigned to the right analyst who had an interest in your career.
>
> New York analyst (interview 1981)

With more than forty psychoanalytic institutes, New York City boasts the highest incidence of psychoanalysts anywhere the world. The three APsaA affiliated institutes and societies comprising about 800 members make the number of APsaA analysts in the New York area vastly greater than in any other area.[1]

For the two or three decades after World War II when psychoanalysis dominated psychiatry and was very influential in the universities, membership of the New York Psychoanalytic Institute was very prestigious. To be a leader in the NY Institute conferred immense power and distinction not only within psychoanalysis but also within psychiatry and the general culture. Until now, the story has not been told about how for the four decades following World War II a small inner group controlled the New York Psychoanalytic Institute. This group felt they possessed special knowledge and acted as an anointed elite. As one analyst put it, 'New York feels annointed. They were! After the War, New York had the major analytic figures from Europe' (New York analyst interview 1981).

Anointment and genealogy fill a vacuum created by uncertainty in the field. Instead of developing through an accumulation of evidence, psychoanalytic knowledge is often assumed to develop via a pipeline to certain people with supposed knowledge. Those purported to have the truth pass on the torch to selected members the next generation. For a qualification to be conferred, a level of skill and knowledge is assumed, an assumption that is not really warranted. Therefore, the gap between real knowledge and presumed, 'pretend' knowledge is filled through particular 'anointed' people. The story of the NY Institute is an exemplary tale of anointment, of what fills the gap when there is a contradiction between the nature of the psychoanalytic field – experiential, subjective, and yet (if ever) to be established scientifically – and the assumption that qualification as an analyst reflects a high level of knowledge.

However, control by a small ruling clique has not been limited to the NY Institute.[2] Authoritarianism in psychoanalysis is not the property of the particular personalities who are in control. It may have its source in the way that Freud structured the psychoanalytic movement. In this sense, the personalities of those who have maintained authoritarianism are less important because they tried to adhere to what was given to them (Moraitis interview 1996a). Sandor Rado remarked that it is well known that people in disagreement with the group they leave reproduce that group's authoritarianism (Rado, quoted in Roazen and Swerdloff 1995).

This very New York story thus involves the coalescence of issues that are common to all psychoanalytic institutes and issues that are particular to this one. It is about an arrogant ruling clique who behaved as though they had a channel to the truth, and about the resistance of the majority of members who opposed them. It is also about a 'revolution' in the mid-1980s from within the ruling group that finally brought about more open and democratic procedures with a greater degree of tolerance and pluralism. This revolution from within was like Gorbachev's success within the Soviet elite that brought about 'openness' and 'restructuring'.

During the four post-war decades, the power structure of the NY Institute meant that candidates identified with their analysts to produce an atmosphere akin to an orthodox religious institution. A ruling coterie of principally European analysts gained control through both intellectual and political processes, and then refused to share power with anyone else. They controlled access to training analyst status and most of the major institute committees, especially the closed and all-powerful Educational Committee (EC). The EC was the central institute body that made the vital decisions about subcommittees, admission, graduation, curriculum, appointments of training and supervising analysts, in fact, everything germane to training. The inner group's control of the EC became self-perpetuating since the outgoing EC nominated the slate of training analysts standing for the election to the next EC. This oligarchy intimidated candidates and analysts alike (see, for example, New York analyst interview 1981; Galenson interview 1994).[3]

Beginnings

The 1910 Nuremberg Psychoanalytic Congress adopted a plan to set up the International Psychoanalytic Association with local branches. Freud wanted James Jackson Putnam of Boston to be the leader of institutional psychoanalysis in the US and to found the American Psychoanalytic Association (APsaA). However, Abraham A. Brill (1874–1948) formed the New York Psychoanalytic Society (NY Society) which subsequently refused to join the APsaA (Richards 1995; Hale 1971a, pp. 314–15). On February 11, 1911, fifteen psychiatrists, led by Brill and Clarence Oberndorf, founded the NY Society. Brill had met with a group of psychiatrists to discuss Freud's work since 1908. Brill lectured extensively on psychoanalysis and his translations of Freud were responsible for much of the dissemination of Freud's ideas in the US. Brill became an important leader of American psychoanalysis, as did Oberndorf. Both held firmly to the position that prevailed in the US that analysts needed to be medically qualified (a view that ruled from the 1920s to the 1980s). At its Weimar Congress that summer, the International Psychoanalytic Association accepted both the APsaA (founded three months later) and the New York Psychoanalytic Society as independent members. The NY Institute, the first American psychoanalytic training institute, was established on September 24, 1931, under Sandor Rado who was specially brought from Berlin to be its director.

The two other APsaA affiliated institutes in New York were formed from within the NY Society in 1945 and 1955. In 1945 there was an acrimonious split which led to the formation of the Columbia Institute and in 1955 the New York University Institute was formed from a group of members who also retained their NY Institute membership.[4]

The 1945 split in the NY Society centred on issues of political power and prestige far more than on theoretical differences about psychoanalytic ideology. Even in 1939, there were many complaints about an arrogant and contemptuous ruling clique at the NY Institute. Although there were not significant theoretical differences in the institute, this political situation led to several student resignations from training (Frosch 1991, p. 1045). The Columbia Center was established at Columbia University as part of the Department of Psychiatry in 1945 in protest at what its founders saw as the intolerable authoritarianism of the NY Institute. It continues to represent an important alternative to the NY Institute, and for some members of both institutes, the nemesis of the NY Institute.[5] However, its structure is far from democratic.

From its inception, the NY Society held pride of place as the first American psychoanalytic society, the model for many other APsaA institutes and, for much of its history, the largest and most powerful American psychoanalytic organisation. It has always been the chief bearer of mainstream psychoanalysis in the US.

The context that situated the development of the NY Institute is vital to understand. Training at the New York Psychoanalytic Society was very meagre even until the end of the 1920s. New York analyst Theodore Jacobs wrote,

> If interested young physicians wished to become analysts, they sought out an analyst for themselves, attended lectures, became acquainted with the members, and hoped, in time, to be asked to join the Society. There was no formal admission procedure, no set course of instruction and no criteria for progression or gradation. (Jacobs n.d., p. 7)

On October 25, 1925, the New York Psychoanalytic Society formed its first Educational Committee. For the next five years, a relatively loose curriculum of didactic analysis, supervision and courses were given in sites such as A. A. Brill's home and at the Oliver Cromwell Hotel (NYP Society and Institute [hereafter NYPS/I] 1976, p. 9). Long-time NY Institute member Charles Brenner remembered his first meeting of the APsaA in 1942 when there were about 400 members, half of whom lived in New York. He recalled his training in Boston when

> everybody knew everyone else, students and faculty alike. It was a tiny group by post-War standards. A psychoanalytic institute or society, whether in Europe or in the USA before the War, was never more than a handful of colleagues. An institute could be run very well quite informally – from someone's vest-pocket so to speak.

The European analysts who became the most influential teachers in this US after the War were accustomed to running their institutes informally. Charles Brenner saw it as inevitable that

> there would be lots of difficulty when psychoanalysis changed from what might be compared to a dame school and a cottage industry to the likes of a university campus and big business. It took a long time to make the transition from an organisation suitable for a few dozen members nationwide to one suitable for a few thousand. (Brenner pers. comm. 1997)

The Arrival of the Europeans

During the early 1940s, the New York Psychoanalytic Society and Institute (the only IPA-affiliated psychoanalytic society in New York at the time) became the premier international society. Because New York and London were the major destinations for refugee analysts fleeing Hitler in the 1930s the epicentre of psychoanalysis moved from Vienna and Berlin to New York and London.

The migration of psychoanalysts fleeing Hitler greatly boosted the growth of American psychoanalysis. Between 1933 and 1941 about forty European analysts migrated to the US, of whom sixteen became training analysts by 1941. Many émigrés filled clinical positions at Mt Sinai and Columbia Presbyterian Medical Center in New York (Talan 1998). The APsaA's Emergency Committee on Immigration helped forty-one medical analysts and thirteen lay analysts migrate to the US between 1938 and 1943 (Hale 1995, p. 126; see also Jeffrey 1989b, p. 7). Because of their standing and abilities, many Europeans assumed psychoanalytic leadership roles in the 1940s and quickly outshone the natives in journal publications. They exerted an enormous influence on the direction of American psychoanalysis, especially through the spread of ego psychology (Coser 1984, p. 42).

The immigrants were reluctant to leave New York. The city provided the opportunity of considerable support from other Europeans living there. Moreover, it was far easier to obtain the medical licence necessary for membership of a psychoanalytic institute in New York State than in other states (Hale 1995, p. 127). Psychoanalysis spread from New York across the US because of what Margaret Mahler termed the 'ambivalent if not double-edged' reception of the European psychoanalysts by the New York psychoanalytic leaders. Considering the limited population of potential analysands in New York, Mahler recalled that

> many senior analysts were less than sympathetic to the avalanche of prestigious European analysts who were then concentrated in New York. While nominally sympathetic to the plight of the refugees and helpful in expediting their relocation, these establishment figures made it plain that they would be happier if their European colleagues sank roots outside the boroughs of New York City. (Cited in Stepansky 1988, p. 102)

Mixed feelings matched a mixed reception. While many analysts were receptive (for example, Loewenstein 1962), there was also considerable resistance among prominent New York analysts. As sociologist, Lewis Coser observed, the generations responded differently to the Europeans. The older generation of American-born psychoanalysts was unreceptive to the newcomers, fearing competition. Moreover, they feared the discrepancy between their own relatively easy-going standards and what they perceived as the more rigorous standards of the Europeans. Still, the younger generation of psychoanalysts who knew many of the immigrants in Europe as fellow psychoanalysts and teachers helped the European psychoanalysts emigrate (Coser 1984, pp. 49–50; see also Hale 1995, pp. 128–9). Some feared that overcrowding the eastern seaboard with foreign physicians would induce New York State to impose licensing restrictions. That would make it impossible for foreign-trained physicians to practise there, and that other states might then follow (Jeffrey 1989b, p. 7). None the less, when the president of the NY Society was asked for affidavits to sponsor Viennese analysts to migrate to the US after the *Anschluss*, he refused, with the reply: 'What in the world would we do with all these additional analysts?' Fortunately, affidavits for the Viennese analysts could be collected outside psychoanalytic circles (Langer and Gifford 1978, pp. 42–4, 53).

Many American analysts, then, were clearly concerned about competition from the newly arrived Europeans.[6] This should be seen in the context that from the late 1930s to the early 1940s the political and economic climate changed as the Great Depression dissolved into World War II. However, in 1937–38 when times were hard for everybody, unabashed attempts were made to move the European analysts out of the major population centres. Real concerns about economic rivalry from the Europeans remained until the US became involved in the war and many analysts and psychiatrists were drafted. Even by the early 1940s, Jacob Arlow remembered charging his first analytic patients four dollars per session and feeling put off that his closest colleague, Leo Rangell, charged five dollars! (Arlow interview 1994; see also Wallerstein 1998b, p. 27).

While Bertram Lewin was opposed to sponsorship during his presidency of the NY Society (1936–39), Lawrence Kubie who followed him as president (1939–40), was very active in rescuing European colleagues. Kubie and Bettina Warburg co-chaired the APsaA's Emergency Committee on Immigration (Jeffrey 1989a; Arnold Richards, pers. comm. 1996a). However, the APsaA's Emergency Committee wrote to intending European refugee analysts in 1938 stating that they must clearly understand 'that the practice of psychoanalysis on adults without a medical license or a medical degree is a violation of the law for which severe penalties have sometimes been imposed' (American Psychoanalytic Association 1938).[7] This claim was a great exaggeration, even deception. In an isolated case, an untrained lay 'analyst' was fined $500 after a complaint by a client (Hale 1995, pp. 127–8). The analysts' claim was reminiscent of the earlier claim by the NY Society that the practise of lay analysis was in violation of New York State law. However, there was no such law.[8] Such claims were devices for population control.

At a 1939 conference of refugee psychoanalysts convened by NY Institute EC chairman Adolph Stern, senior NY Institute analysts advised the refugees to obtain New York medical licences. Then, Margaret Mahler recollected, the refugees were told to 'go "pioneering" to Buffalo, Utica, Syracuse, or some other upstate location'. Everyone was stunned by what was viewed as a preposterous directive to leave the city (Stepansky 1988, p. 102).[9] However, this directive was scarcely as wrong as the refusal to provide affidavits for Jewish analysts to be able to leave the terrors of Austria or Germany.

The Americans reacted to the influx of Europeans by going further along the road of regulation. Apart from the NY Institute's unflinching position about medical prerequisites, psychoanalytic training in the US before the arrival of the Europeans was relatively lax. During the late 1930s, the APsaA rules were made far stricter in an attempt to stop the refugees just walking in and taking over because of their seniority and perceived higher psychoanalytic skills. In 1937, the NY Institute made a training analysis prerequisite for future members. However, this requirement did not question the qualifications of the American analysts. It was a reaction to the current influx of European analysts some of whom were training analysts who had not had personal analyses. 1937 also saw the APsaA (with the NY Society as its most prominent member) declare to International and European psychoanalytic societies that it would not recognise membership of foreign psychoanalytic societies as fulfilling the membership requirements of American societies. This irritated many immigrants who had to apply for membership of the NY Society (Lorand 1969, p. 593). After a major struggle with the IPA, the Americans finally agreed in 1938 to accept as members European lay analysts who were members of the IPA (Hale 1995, p. 128). Brought up in a tradition around Freud that eschewed national considerations in favour of being psychoanalytic citizens of the world, the Europeans mistakenly expected to be appointed training analysts upon their arrival. This assumed that being a training analyst was a qualification of universal status instead of a particular position or function within a particular institute that had a certain number of students and teachers (Arlow interview 1994).

Despite the pressure to leave New York City, one-third of the European analysts remained in New York, settling in privileged areas in Park Avenue, Central Park West and around Columbia University (Hale 1995, p. 129). The immigrants, who constituted the majority of the inner group and their analytic descendants, took over the NY Institute for the next forty years.[10] Apart from their 'inside' status in the psychoanalytic movement and their status as the teachers of several of the Americans, the Europeans were formidable in their own right. As well as their analytic genealogy, their success was also based on their analytic expertise, given the extent of their perceived higher abilities as teachers, practitioners and theoreticians (Calder interview 1994c). Many were highly reputed in Europe and continued their creativity in the US to become, in the words of leading institute member, Norman Margolis, 'titans in the field' (pers. comm. 1996). The Europeans replaced those American NY Institute analysts who were drafted during World War II. From a power-political point of view, many of the Americans were understandably concerned about the arrival of the Europeans who succeeded in gaining dominance over the Americans.[11] Because of the movement to other cities, the influence of psychoanalysis spread – schools across the country acquired first class analytic teachers.[12] Finally, the Europeans prevailed throughout the US.[13]

The major European figures who came to New York included Heinz Hartmann, Ernst and Marianne Kris, Rudolph Loewenstein, Edith Jacobson, Hermann Nunberg, Annie Reich, Robert Bak, Kurt and Ruth Eissler, Otto Isakower and Margaret Mahler. A number were very close to Freud and his family. Marianne Kris was the daughter of Oscar Rie, Freud's closest friend, colleague and tarok partner who figured in the dream of Irma's injection. Marianne's sister, Margarete, was married to Hermann Nunberg who was part of Freud's circle (Young-Bruehl 1988, p. 52; Gay 1988, p. 540).[14] As part of Freud's circle and coming from the centre of international psychoanalysis, the Europeans were powerful and central characters in a unique cast who greatly contributed to the pre-eminence of the NY Institute (Atkin 1978, p. 78).[15]

With a European psychoanalysis strongly influenced by European humanism, the American psychoanalysis that the Europeans joined was rigidly medicalised and closely allied with psychiatry. Before they came to the US a number of the Europeans were left-wing intellectuals. Born around the turn of the century, the second generation of European psychoanalysts was decisively influenced by the European youth movements, World War I and the post-war workers' revolutions. These psychoanalysts never thought of psychoanalysis as a trade; instead, they saw it as a cause that would help bring sense to a disjointed world (see Jacoby 1983). That world could not have become more disjointed with Hitler and their transatlantic migration.

For the Europeans who pushed the American analysts aside, the mission of ruling the NY Institute meant far more than gaining control of a large psychoanalytic institute. For them the NY Institute was to be the repository of a cause, true psychoanalysis. Aiming at the preservation of something they saw as very precious – psychoanalysis itself – the Europeans were the keepers of the flame who ensured that they retained control of the institute by whatever means were necessary. Thus, they excluded those whom they saw as not directly linked with the Europeans who possessed psychoanalytic truth, who had not had ongoing analysis, supervision or other personal contacts with Freud or his immediate circle. That impressive legacy unfortunately allowed the NY Institute and its leadership to be commonly viewed in quasi-religious terms as a mysterious 'holy of holies' where the Grail was kept. The leadership was akin to a Council of Elders with special access to Freud and to psychoanalytic truth. Loyalty to Anna Freud, with whom several of the group remained close, played an important part in their attitudes. These cohorts of Anna Freud were partly motivated to maintain control by the success of the Kleinian movement over Anna Freud in London during the same period.

Halcyon Years

During the 1950s, the major divisions within the institute were unknown to the outside world. Perhaps these divisions did not result in splits because, as one analyst told me, the institute was always 'very careful about pushing things to the point where people leave in a group' (New York analyst interview 1992a).

The fact that the inner group's greatest ascendancy was during the 1950s and early 1960s – halcyon days for psychoanalysis – seemed to provide confirmation that its ascendancy was good for psychoanalysis. Psychoanalysis was the major psychotherapy available to the many physicians wanting training after World War II. Before the introduction and widespread use of effective psychotropic drugs, the great hope for mental illness was dynamic psychiatry.[16] Psychoanalysis was such an important part of American psychiatry after the war that William Menninger (chief of Army psychiatry in the office of the Surgeon-General during World War II) represented the prevailing view when he described psychoanalysis as 'probably the most important contribution to our technical knowledge in the history of psychiatry' (Menninger 1948, p. 6).[17] Until the 1960s analytic training was considered a necessary calling card in psychiatry, particularly in New York, with which it became enmeshed as in no other country (Kovel interview 1981). The many medical students who trained in psychiatry regarded their psychiatric residencies as interludes before going on to train at psychoanalytic institutes (Peterfreund interview 1983).

Economic factors were central to the success of psychoanalysis from the 1950s. Created in 1949, the National Institute of Mental Health (NIMH) was the fastest-growing section of the National Institute of Health. Research grants increased from $374,000 in 1948 to $42.6 million in 1962 and training grants from $1.1 million to $38.8 million over the same period. The government offered especially generous stipends to physicians who trained in psychiatry and required nothing in return – not even that physicians spend some time working in state mental hospitals (which was the intention of the original legislation. Starr 1982, p. 346). With the number of afflicted veterans, the Veterans Administration was also a major source of funding. As it was more affluent than European countries in the post-war decades, the US could afford training and treatment on a large scale. A booming economy was necessary for psychoanalytic therapy to be carried out on a large scale.

Psychoanalysis was an attractive specialty during these decades. Psychiatrists were greatly encouraged to go on to psychoanalytic training: with the clamour for medical psychoanalysts, psychoanalysis afforded a good income. Moreover, psychoanalysis permeated American intellectual life, especially in New York. With an abiding myth about the answers that psychoanalysis could provide, this cultural context, together with interest, affluence and demand for treatment set psychoanalysis on a successful path. Especially around Manhattan, this boom period for psychoanalysis from the late 1940s into the 1960s when many patients could afford analytic treatment was the era when the European émigré 'Giants' taught at the institute.

Psychoanalysis and its premier institute were so prestigious, the rewards of becoming an analyst so bountiful, and the intimidation and control of the inner group so effective that there was no challenge to those in power. Significant economic advantages accrued to being on side with the professionally well-established ruling clique who were a source of referrals for younger analysts who needed patients.[18] Without objective measures of merit a courtier culture prevailed in which members, deprived of any direct power, were forced to seek influence with the ruling group through informal connections. As psychoanalysis bloomed during the 1950s, analysts became rich and the NY Institute increasingly cliquish.

In its heyday, the NY Institute provided the premier postgraduate training centre for the many gifted students who wanted to be psychoanalysts. Immense secrecy clothed the workings of the NY Institute Admissions Committee which made or broke careers. To be rejected rendered one a second-class citizen while admission to the NY Institute promised a prestigious and wealthy career (Calder interview 1994c).

While many candidates took for granted that there were enormously gifted people at the top who must have deserved their positions, others were more critical. Some were schooled in left-wing political activities during and after World War II, such as those that achieved salaries for interns at local hospital level. Eleanor Galenson, who trained at the NY Institute during the early 1950s, arrived there accustomed to 'a rather forthright expression of our opinions and our minds. We came into an institute where the tradition was holy, looking up to the teachers – they were the elect. The first ten rows of our auditorium were always occupied by the same big people. Then the students came in the twelfth row' (Galenson interview 1994). And then came the guests, who were forced to sit in the rear section behind a red rope (see Wallerstein 1998b, pp. 70, 72). Many analysts of that generation did not participate in work outside the institute, in universities or hospital settings. However, perhaps forty American NY Institute analysts became involved at Mt Sinai as attending physicians.[19] Moreover, many candidates received their psychiatric training in the very different culture of city hospitals.

For example, a strong psychoanalytic staff was gathered by Milton Rosenbaum, founder and Chair of the Psychiatry Department at Albert Einstein College of Medicine, established in 1955 at Yeshiva University in New York. An analyst from Cincinnati (he was a geographic training analyst at the Chicago Psychoanalytic Institute), Rosenbaum strongly envisioned a psychiatry department with psychoanalysis as its leading discourse. In those financially and ideologically golden days for psychoanalysis, Rosenbaum was able to bring together a brilliant group of core faculty with a real sense of intellectual excitement. Psychoanalysis was then in such favour that Rosenbaum was able to negotiate for residents to receive NIMH Fellowships of $3,600 a year to support their personal analyses. Rosenbaum arranged the patriation of some European analysts such as Robert Bak and Andrew Peto who joined the NY Institute, resulting in a great deal of indebtedness to Rosenbaum. The NY Institute analysts came to the Bronx to give seminars and supervise in the residency training programme at Einstein. The curricula of the NY Institute and Einstein were said to be identical (Kovel pers. comm. 1995). A shuttle was set up between Einstein and the NY Institute.

Residents were taught at Einstein from an analytic viewpoint and applied immediately to the NY Institute, probably more than from anywhere else.[20]

Remarkably forceful and talented residents went on to undertake analytic training. Einstein became the most sought after US psychiatric residency because it had so many very good teachers. According to Joel Kovel who trained at Einstein between 1962 and 1965 and later taught there, Einstein residents felt sufficiently entitled and prideful to give the impression of independent thought (Kovel pers. comm. 1995). Eleanor Galenson, who taught at Einstein, recalled residents being 'encouraged to challenge us, to do their own thinking'. Galenson found what happened when they went to the analytic institute in the 1960s and early 1970s very disturbing. 'They became afraid to open their mouths, to challenge their teachers in any way.' Many candidates graduated from analytic training at the NY Institute by aping what they were taught. Those analysts, who were used to speaking their minds on political issues, Galenson recalled, 'spoke in this peculiar hush-hush way' (Galenson interview 1994). In 1976 Charles Brenner told the site visitors of a trend toward conformity among students since the polarised institute was run by a small unrepresentative group (American Psychoanalytic Association 1976a).

The Anointed

In the decades following World War II, the NY Institute was reasonably perceived by those outside it as a closed corporation and as the repository of psychoanalytic orthodoxy.

However, this orthodoxy has been almost universally misunderstood. The real situation was quite contrary to the popular view that the institute was under the control of the most well-known psychoanalytic theorists and clinicians – the founders of ego psychology – Heinz Hartmann, Ernst Kris and Rudolph Loewenstein, followed by Charles Brenner and Jacob Arlow. Although intellectually powerful, the 'holy trinity' of Hartmann, Kris and Loewenstein did not actively exercise political power as such. Their ego psychology, the NY Institute's orthodoxy for decades, challenged classical Freudianism and in turn many later repudiated their ego psychological concepts (Richards interview 1992). Far from running the institute, Brenner and Arlow opposed the ruling clique within the institute. Brenner and Arlow's views did not constitute the central approach at the NY Institute even though their *Psychoanalytic Concepts and Structural Theory* together with

Brenner's (1973) standard *Elementary Textbook of Psychoanalysis* appeared to represent the NY Institute to psychiatrists and psychoanalysts around the US. Brenner and Arlow's approaches are independent and both differ from classical psychoanalysis.[21] Both are past presidents of the APsaA and have published voluminously. Arlow has always been a particularly outspoken critic of authoritarianism in psychoanalytic training (see, for example, Arlow 1969, pp. 104–20; 1970; 1972; 1991). Charles Brenner fought hard to disregard many of Freud's ideas before *The Ego and the Id* (1923a) during the ascendancy of the inner group.[22]

In contrast, most of those Europeans who occupied the central power positions in the NY Institute published little and were not generally well-known. However, they acted as repositories of established psychoanalytic truth which, like magical transmission, could only be passed down effectively from analyst to analysand. The NY Institute orthodoxy was not so much an orthodoxy of ideas as of persons. The Europeans who came to the NY Institute did not preserve a particular set of ideas as much as a faith in the lineage from Freud. Because of their anointment, they saw themselves as entitled to develop aspects of psychoanalysis, whereas others were not so permitted. This helps to explain why Instructors at the NY Institute have always been granted a wide berth to teach as they wanted (Richards interview 1996). Training and Supervising Analysts are called 'Instructors' at the NY Institute. As Arnold Richards noted, once one became a training analyst one was almost like God and could do what one wanted. Richards had trained at the NY Institute during 1964–69 and became a NY Institute leader in the 1980s (Richards pers. comm. 1996b). Since only certain analysts were selected to teach, this was not so much 'academic freedom' as much as faith in the entitlement of particular persons who inherited the mantle ultimately from Freud and his inner circle. It was not what analysts did and thought so much as who they were, which in turn came from who trained them. Orthodoxy was defined by the current beliefs of those in control, not by a particular set of shared beliefs among the power group. It was a question of who could be trusted, and to be trusted, you had to be a protégé.

The oligarchy controlling the institute for the four decades after World War II consisted mostly of Europeans who escaped Hitler. Otto Isakower led a group of about twenty Europeans but there were divisions within that group. Most of the better-known Europeans – Heinz Hartmann, Ernst and Marianne Kris, Rudolph Loewenstein, Annie Reich and Margaret Mahler – were relatively marginal to power and to most of the rest of the group (Arlow interview 1994). However, although

Hartmann, Kris and Loewenstein were not very involved politically (Furer interview 1996; Calder interview 1996), they were essential bolsters to the ruling group.

A major division also existed between the Europeans and the Americans.[23] Europeans such as Kurt and Ruth Eissler and Anna-Marie and Fred Weil seemed to display little regard for the faculty. They would often attend faculty Meetings simply to cast their vote and then go home. Highly protective and slightly paranoid, they were especially interested in who was going to be Chairman of the EC and the Progression Committee, which oversaw the academic progress of candidates (Calder interview 1994c). The Chairman of the EC had such inordinate powers as to be, as one analyst put it, virtually 'dictator of the institute' (New York analyst interview 1994).

The core of the group of about twenty that acted as though it possessed special power and magic included its leader, Otto Isakower, together with Lillian Malcove, Kurt Eissler (who became Freud's greatest defender through his directorship of the Freud Archives and his many books mainly on cultural topics), Ruth Eissler, Nicholas Young, Lili Bussel, Hermann Nunberg, Elizabeth Gleerd Loewenstein, Robert Bak, Ed Kronold, Phyllis Greenacre. In the 1970s power passed to the next generation – all Americans – including Peter Richter, Irwin Solomon and Martin Stein. While the basic leadership of the ruling group was Viennese, there was a coalition with others – such as Phyllis Greenacre and later Martin Stein – who were willing to cooperate with it.

A number of these leaders apparently wanted their students to follow in their footsteps as disciples. Analysands divided into two groups, those remaining loyal to their training analysts and those who joined the rebel camp (Arlow 1970; Arlow interview 1994). For example, a group of five of Nunberg's analysands frequently voted the same way and did what Nunberg expected of them (Calder interview 1994a). Phyllis Greenacre analysed the greatest number of candidates over a long period. Her candidates divided into two, those who went along with her approach and those who rebelled against it (Calder interview 1994a; Arlow interview 1994). While Greenacre criticised the 'convoy' aspects of the training analysis (analysands were shepherded or convoyed by the analyst through the important parts of their professional careers), some saw her as exemplifying this process herself although she was also known to shy away from NY Institute politics.[24] Sometimes the inner group cemented their relations with one another through adjacent summer homes, such as a group around Greenacre in Garrison, New York (Calder interview 1994c). According to EC chairman Manny Furer (who trained at the NY Institute between 1954 and 1958), Greenacre was 'the analyst of analysts, particularly those who were troubled' (Furer interview 1996).

Ken Calder has had a long involvement with the NY Institute. He studied there during the 1950s and was appointed as a training analyst in 1963. A former president of the NY Institute (1980–82) and the APsaA (1977) and former vice-president of the IPA, he is much respected for his principled and independent positions. According to Calder, the European clique often regarded the Americans as many in the NY Institute regard Columbia even today – they don't do real analysis. While the Europeans may have been by and large more competent as analysts (they appeared more cultured, scholarly and more analytically gifted than the Americans), over the years the issue of competence became lost and conflated with the issue of whose analyst was the most renowned (Gedo pers. comm. 1995). Calder recalled that those who knew Sigmund and Anna Freud and were part of Freud's own group in Europe (such as the Eisslers and Nunberg) seemed to have a special power and magic that they could pass on. As he put it, they behaved as though there was a right way and a wrong way. The NY Institute's approach was like the Hertz rent-a-car TV advertisement where Hertz had something, and on each criterion, the other had it 'but *not exactly*'. 'You can practice psychoanalysis, "but not exactly", unless you went through the right channels.' In the eyes of the NY Institute, Calder maintained, psychoanalysis was practised and understood much better in New York than other places. However, politics was clearly involved. Some became training analysts, even though it was clear, in Calder's view, that 'they really didn't know much about psychoanalysis but they had played the right political ladder'. This was 'strictly back pocket selection'. On Calder's account, those in control would 'select their buddies and they would select the people who would invite them for dinner' (Calder interview 1994c). According to Calder, power belonged to

> senior people who have supported rather anxious younger people who have played up to them. The power passed not on the basis of competence but on the basis of, 'Will you, the junior person, believe in me the senior person? If so, I will send you a patient.' We used to say that the person with the busiest practice was the younger person who invited senior people to dinner – that opened the doors. (Calder interview 1992)

Calder observed that while power played a large role in many US institutes, 'it was outstanding at New York' (Calder interview 1994b).

An important part of the NY Institute culture, study groups provided important gatekeeping mechanisms. Certain students were tapped and invited to join important study groups. Ruth Eissler set up a particularly significant study group of about fifteen selected people who met in her office. They had bright futures since Ruth Eissler could champion their cause and report on their abilities, unlike others who had no study groups (Calder interview 1994b). Many members of Ruth Eissler's handpicked study group were successfully slated to become training analysts. Many were careful about what they said for fear of not being selected to become training analysts (Galenson interview 1994; Calder interview 1992; see American Psychoanalytic Association 1976a). There could be no doubt that Ruth Eissler was involved with convoying (Furer interview 1996). The Kris Study Group, the original NY Institute study group for advanced candidates and graduates to discuss a variety of psychoanalytic issues, was set up in 1953. Led by the NY Institute's most revered educator, Ernst Kris, together with a visitor, it was attended by around twenty analysts. When Kris died, Arlow, Brenner and David Beres led the study group (Calder interview 1994c; Atkin 1962, pp. 27–8).

In the introduction I referred to Kernberg's four models of psychoanalytic institutes – seminary, trade school, university and art academy. Within this framework, the NY Institute over these four decades was clearly devotional and seminarian in its approach. Training analyses were incomplete if only because issues such as transference idealisation of the training analyst who exercised power were regarded by the NY Institute orthodoxy as merely regressions from Oedipal hostilities (Gedo pers. comm. 1995). NY Society member Emanuel Peterfreund argued that much analytic clinical practice is 'stereotyped' in taking the patient as 'but an example of an assumed body of clinical theory'. This, he proposed, contrasted with a 'heuristic' approach that encourages 'new awarenesses and understandings to emerge about an individual patient' (Peterfreund 1985, pp. 127–8). Peterfreund's views on stereotyping reflected his training at the NY Institute (1953–59). 'I never heard one thoughtful, critical, intelligent, meaningful appraisal of psychoanalytic theory as a body of theory. It was taught like a Yeshiva, as "the book" – you're allowed to ask questions about what "the book" meant. Did it mean this or did it mean that?' (Peterfreund interview 1983). One analyst recalled complaining to his training analyst that he was treating Freud like the Bible, the training analyst replied, 'It is not *like* the Bible. It *is* the Bible.' The difference between NY Institute and other institutes, according to this analyst, was that elsewhere 'Freud is acknowledged but not revered' (New York analyst interview 1981).

A siege mentality pervaded the power group who were committed to preserving what they had. Calder described the inner group as 'a cult that believes in the magic of their belief that they have a pipeline to the truth and others don't'. In Calder's view, this implied insecurity, 'a very good likelihood that they have that religion only because they are so unsure of what they do'. However, Calder believed they were right to have been uncertain because it is in the nature of psychoanalysis to be unsure (Calder interview 1994a).

An important element of the context was the fact that graduates of the institute automatically became members of both branches, the NY Society and the intimately related, NY Institute, the educational arm (Margolis pers. comm. 1996). The NY Institute was almost entirely financially supported by the NY Society that consisted of the membership of graduates and practitioners.[25] The NY Institute was unusual among psychoanalytic institutes because in addition to ordinary institute and society expenses, considerable outlays were involved in the upkeep and staffing of a mildly decaying building, a considerable library and the invaluable Brill Archive which housed early society and institute documents. Assessments (compulsory contributions) needed to be kept higher than the two other APsaA institutes in New York City, Columbia and New York University (NYU), which have been always subsidised by the hospital and medical school. Together with lawsuits in the 1970s, these costs were to lead to the near bankruptcy of the New York Institute and Society.

Members could not ignore the contrast between their large contributions through dues and assessments that saved and financed the institute and their lack of power in the institute, a situation that made for inevitable conflict.[26]

Despite the faculty's view that, just as democracy should not prevail in an educational institution, the members should not run the institute, the leadership made no attempt to have the faculty raise funds to make itself independent of the society. The power group opposed the institution of a lay Board of Trustees who would have been able to help raise funds for the institute (Calder interview 1994b; American Psychoanalytic Association 1976a; Arlow interview 1994). During the golden years of psychoanalysis, the idea that a free-standing institute required a preferably lay Board of Trustees was not taken seriously. In general, as Arlow put it, 'On the basis of this kind of semi-religious attitude, they cut themselves off from very valuable contacts. The sense of power and self-satisfaction of the leaders was enormous' (Arlow interview 1994). The leadership wanted to retain the myth of mystical knowledge (Moraitis interview 1996a).

Otto Isakower

Otto Isakower (1899-1972) led the principally European group that dominated the NY Institute during the 1950s and for much of the 1960s. Born in Vienna, where he trained in medicine and psychiatry, Isakower trained at the Vienna Psychoanalytic Institute, becoming a member in 1925. He escaped the Nazis by moving to England from where he moved to New York in 1940. He became a full member of the NY Society in 1943 and soon became a member of the faculty. Isakower served as chairman of a number of committees including the EC, and in 1955 together with Martin Stein, devised the psychoanalytic curriculum that remains in use today.

Like many others in the inner group that ran the NY Institute Isakower published very little (just four published articles) but exerted great influence (see Wyman and Rittenberg 1994, pp. 166-7; see also Jacobs n.d., p. 19). Although Isakower exercised such power, he was shy. He could be personable but was nonetheless arrogant and caustic (Furer interview 1996). New York analyst Theodore Jacobs recalled, 'Although Otto Isakower was a small and delicate-looking man, the sharpness of his tongue, his forbidding manner, and the sarcasm of which he was capable, struck terror into the hearts of generations of students.'[27] Analysts too were frightened of him. After all, he and his cohort controlled the important training programmes and the selection of Instructors. This involved not only the selection of who became training analysts but who would teach particular courses (Arlow interview 1994). Powerful members of the institute controlled the committee involved in the assignment of candidates to particular training analysts. Politically successful Instructors usually had a good number of candidates (Calder interview 1994a). Moreover, Isakower always supported his analysands in becoming members of the NY Society (Weil interview 1994). Very penetrating and bright, he was also generally personally isolated except for a few of the Europeans in his group and his best friend, Bertram Lewin. He never drew a crowd, but the crowd was drawn to him (Calder interview 1994c).

Isakower formulated the 'Isakower phenomenon' which explored the sense of dizziness and loss of support as we fall asleep, as well as the idea of the 'analysing instrument' which involved the notion that the patient could be heard on two levels, on the dream-imagination level and simultaneously on the waking reality level. As one of Isakower's students, New York analyst Zvi Lothane, explained, the analysing instrument

> is a special communicative interaction in a regressed state and daydream consciousness in which images surfacing in the analysand evoke – and the stress is on this evocative function – counter images in the listening analyst. By judiciously communicating his own evoked images, the analyst makes a heuristic contribution to the ever unfolding state of mind of the analysand, with emergence of new images in him, all this going to stimulate the analysand further evolving memory-fantasy constellations. (Lothane pers. comm. 1997; see also Lothane 1981)

Isakower's development of the idea of the 'analysing instrument' in the clinical situation (see Wyman and Rittenberg 1994a) could be used to provide a rationale for the mostly close, suspicious Viennese group's division of the analytic world into the few in the NY Institute who had the magic and on the other those at Columbia and other APsaA institutes outside New York who were seen to be practising psychoanalysis in name only (Calder interview 1994a). Because the concept of the analysing instrument involved both analyst and analysand utilising regression in order to function and communicate together in what Isakower regarded as the specific analytic activity of making the unconscious conscious,[28] a special sort of intuition was required on the part of the analyst. The automating of the psychic functions necessary to do analysis, away from conscious awareness, enhanced analytic work. Given how nebulous this concept is, it could be easily misused to claim arbitrarily that certain designated analysts had that intuition while others did not. The concept came to be used in an esoteric way; at the NY Institute psychoanalysis became the preserve of a small number of those deemed to possess a special gift (Calder interview 1994a). Calder who is critical of Isakower's concepts was praised for the 'accuracy' of his understanding of the 'analysing instrument' by students of Isakower (Balter et al. 1980, p. 489). Such an attitude was, Jacob Arlow argued, reminiscent of Jewish mysticism known as Cabbala:

> The feeling was that there was a way of knowing the true essence of existence, which was granted only to very special people, usually by virtue of extreme piety and scholarship. There emerged alongside of it feelings of special endowment which came from possession of secret knowledge, the kind that was not to be imparted to the general populace. The authority for that secret knowledge was transmission from one generation to another tracing the authenticity of this material to Moses. So if you really want to know how to resolve certain contradictions and

obscurities that occur in the reading of the text of the Bible the ones who really know the answers are these mystics who got it straight. That is a kind of popular myth that grows up around some important leaders. (Arlow interview 1994)

This approach was epitomised in a faculty meeting of the NY Institute as late as the end of the 1980s to which Arlow was invited to speak about his views on the curriculum. A three-hour argument ensued after which an influential member of the inner group, Ed Kronold, asked Arlow, 'Do you think that psychoanalysis can really be taught?' Of course, not everyone has a talent for doing analysis, but psychoanalytic concepts should be able to be communicated in a manner other than by osmosis.

Isakower's approach was used so that an intuitive grasp provided authentication for psychoanalytic work rather than the other way around – being 'well-analysed' was the criterion for whether one grasped psychoanalysis (Arlow interview 1994). (And what better stamp of a good analysis could there be than being analysed by a member of the inner group?) Without the secret knowledge communicated through the analytic version of the laying on of hands, others could not achieve knowledge even if they were gifted. In 1995 after major changes, Arlow met again with the Curriculum Committee and succeeded in convincing them that Freud needed to be taught as part of the historical development of psychoanalytic ideas, and not completely out of context.

Isakower was a powerful teacher. His belief and sincere devotion to id psychology were very influential. Analysts such as Mort Reiser, Leon Balter and Zvi Lothane sensed that he offered something profound. Like Elvin Semrad in Boston who influenced so many through his teaching at Massachusetts General Hospital and Massachusetts Mental Health, Isakower had an aura and a cult around him and, for a time, was treated as a guru – his few words conveyed profound meaning to a number of analysts. Isakower influenced a number of quiescent institute members, but critics were not well treated. Victor Rosen, head of the Treatment Center for some years, lost votes for his criticism of 'the analysing instrument' (Calder interview 1994c).

The European group of whom Isakower was the strongest and most visible representative looked down upon American trained analysts even at the NY Institute. As Chairman of the EC, Isakower even proposed – unsuccessfully – eliminating the names of all of the members from the NY Institute brochure on the grounds that *he* would not recommend 95 per cent of them as people who were really qualified to practise psychoanalysis. Similarly, the child analyst Berta Bornstein, a member of the inner group close to Isakower, claimed that she could count the number of child analysts on the fingers of her hand (Furer interview 1996).[29] When Isakower was Chairman of the EC, Rudolph Loewenstein proposed a set of seminars for prospective training analysts to prepare them for their special functions. Loewenstein had set up the plans to carry out such a scheme but Isakower scotched it (Arlow interview 1994).

The Isakower group carried an abiding sense of romantic pessimism that psychoanalysis was a fragile fruit that needed to be preserved. It required protection from alloy or contamination through vulgarisation – and from Americanisation, which in their eyes amounted to the same thing. The schism between American and European analysts was so great that they often barely knew one another (Weil interview 1994). From the 1940s until the mid-1980s the European analysts kept their distance from most American analysts whom they regarded as uncultured. Some of the Isakower group were condescending toward the Americans whom they considered did not really understand psychoanalysis (Jacobs n.d., p. 16). Carrying on Freud's strong contempt for the US and Americans, they seemed uninfluenced by the fact that the objects of their disdain helped to defeat the Nazis and provided their refuge in the form of very comfortable Upper Eastside lifestyles.

From the inner group's perspective, psychoanalysis might die with them or their epigones but there was a chance of its surviving through a small, esoteric and unpopular group. In their view the heyday in which the Europeans seized power should be extended at all costs since the preservation of psychoanalysis itself was at stake. Why should they hand over a professional institute to those who, while popular, did not possess psychoanalytic knowledge?

Since psychoanalysis was, in the inner group's estimation, so fundamentally misunderstood by the Americans, it was only a small step to ask what means could be taken to preserve what little remained. The faith needed to be preserved against those who would usurp and destroy its essence. Such an omnipotent and omniscient approach owes more to shamanism than science. Inevitably, this resulted in the formation of a cult. Based on his experiences of analysing members and candidates at the NY Institute, Jacob Arlow found 'a widespread, shared unconscious phantasy in which psychoanalysis as a profession is regarded as an instrumentality of magical omnipotence'. He found that 'unconsciously the goal of training is not merely to acquire insight and professional skill hut to be admitted to the council of elders. Unconsciously the process of training is suffused with the process of initiation.'[30]

In addition to their contempt for *hoi poloi* at the NY Institute, the Old Guard was scarcely enamoured of the NY Institute's own Treatment Center that offered low-cost analysis by candidates in training. (Early directors included Leo Stone, Heinz Hartmann, Victor Rosen and Leo Loomie.) As purists they were upset by any possible distortions of a direct analyst–patient relationship. Therefore, they objected to patients paying the institute rather than the analyst. Isakower was concerned about even slight variations in technique such as walking the patient to the Treatment Room in the cellar where the Treatment Center was located (Calder interview 1994b). Charles Brenner reported to the site visitors that this state of affairs had unfavourable consequences for education and training bringing about a polarisation of the EC and the institute as a whole and a poor relationship with the APsaA (American Psychoanalytic Association 1976a).

The power group disdained involvement with the APsaA. They rarely attended the annual winter APsaA meetings held in New York, and still more rarely attended the annual spring meetings held in other cities. Instead, they remained in their offices. From their perspective, it would be irresponsible for any real analyst to leave his or her ten or more patients for a day – and, incidentally, the very good fees paid by these patients to those at the top of the NY Institute food chain (Calder interview 1994c).[31] Apart from not wanting to participate in the APsaA and the IPA, there was scepticism about whether psychoanalysis was even properly practised outside New York. On one occasion, Ken Calder tried to discuss some of John Gedo's (1979) findings about successes in analytic treatment in Chicago. Members of the power group questioned the point of discussing it since nobody understood analysis in Chicago (Calder interview 1994b).

But as the 1960s wore on and the European analysts grew older, things began to change. During the 1960s and 1970s from time to time some New Yorkers became active in the APsaA: Arlow, Brenner and Calder (known as 'A-B-C'), David Beres, Victor Rosen, Burness Moore and Edward Joseph held the presidency and a number of other offices in the APsaA, and some held positions within the IPA.[32] Martin Stein, an active member of the NY Institute establishment, was an exception in being Chairman of the APsaA's Board on Professional Standards, a very influential position.

However, not only was the APsaA a problem for the inner group. There was, after all, the community at large. The problem with the NY

Institute's community relations was that there were none – it was almost xenophobic. In 1962 Victor Rosen wrote ironically, 'Most analysts seem to have regarded the community as a collective myth of archaic origin which is retained in the deepest layers of the unconscious. In most instances we do not try to analyse the fantasy but feel best advised to leave it undisturbed.' In semi-jocular vein Rosen considered the idea that the community would ultimately disappear. 'One solution to the problems inherent in this relationship is to remain quietly indoors until it disappears. In this way one day we can become a series of institute outposts across the nation with no surrounding communities to disturb us with relationships' (Rosen 1962, p. 53). Analysts could devote themselves entirely to psychoanalysis without sullying its pure gold with the alloy of psychotherapy or hospital psychiatry.

Kurt Eissler's 1965 book, *Medical Orthodoxy and the Future of Psychoanalysis*, was a polemic against the APsaA psychoanalytic establishment for its adherence to medical prerequisites and its attacks upon lay analysis (see Eissler 1965). At another level, the book can be read as an attack on behalf of the European analysts upon the Americans who never really understood psychoanalysis. Had the Americans really understood psychoanalysis they would not have bothered with other modalities of treatment. In an extraordinary passage, Eissler argued:

> The psychoanalytic profession does not ... bear up well under a plurality of loyalties. If penetration into the unknown territories of the human mind by the psychoanalytic method cannot absorb the whole interest of the explorer, that in itself is a bad sign in regard to his contribution to psychoanalysis. *It is hardly likely that such an analyst has ever truly felt the delight – one must even say transport – that is concomitant with the practice of Freud's psychoanalysis*, nor has he probably ever experienced the thrill of the discovery that comes with seeing the most characteristic facets of human personality arise out of the debris of the subject's initial and restricted self-knowledge. (Eissler 1965, p. 101; emphasis added).

While technical mastery of psychoanalysis no doubt requires some immersion, Eissler's statement is couched in the language of magic, of religious experience, of a cult complete with ecstatic insiders and profane outsiders who utilise esoteric terms in an empty way since they understand nothing about them. For Eissler, Freud appears as the misunderstood and underestimated guru who incurs the envious wrath of so many analysts for his genius (ibid., p. 7).

Ironically and revealingly, many wealthy European analysts who professed loyalty left none of their estate to their institute. Isakower made a significant amount of money through his analytic practice and made a very successful investment in land near the shore but he bequeathed his wealth to the Hebrew University in Jerusalem. His closest colleague, Lillian Malcove, left nothing to the NY Institute. She left her entire collection of Russian Orthodox icons worth millions of dollars to the Toronto Museum, which named the room housing the collection after her. Only one of the senior analysts at the NY Institute, Grace Abbatte, left anything substantial – $80,000 for a fund to finance child analysis. It infuriated many analysts that those who claimed such a pure devotion to psychoanalysis left nothing at all to the NY Institute which almost faced bankruptcy owing to the costs of the library, law suits against it and water leaks in the building that finally revealed an underground stream. Leaving nothing at all to the NY Institute probably reflected the Europeans' lack of loyalty to the NY Institute and their contemptuous view of most of its mainly American members who, in their eyes, were not really doing analysis. Not surprisingly, the fact that these senior analysts did not leave bequests to the institute contributed to unfavourable perceptions of the institute by members and to lowering morale.[33]

Given the trauma and terror suffered by the Europeans during the 1930s together with their common background, it was understandable why they grouped together socially in the US. But this carried over to professional matters, leading to a climate of paranoia in the institute which affected all its members Like refugees throughout the ages, perhaps their experiences of persecution in Europe, followed by becoming refugees and living in a totally new environment predisposed them to being more defensive, to try to cover over their fears and insecurities with a strong need to achieve and to cling on to power.

'They Keep Reappointing Themselves!'

Beneath everything lay the struggle between the Old Guard who controlled and administered the institute and its Education Committee on the one hand, and on the other the dissatisfied, vocal, defiant group of institute members who accepted neither their right to power nor its vested quality. The Old Guard's power was concentrated in the EC which then appointed all the other committees actively engaged in educational work in the institute. The European power group was under considerable challenge from those among the membership for whom the ship was too tight (Calder interview 1994c). The embattled atmosphere was reflected in Ken Calder's recollection of his first faculty meeting as training analyst in 1963 when the battles were not anywhere as severe as they became.

> Almost all of that first meeting was devoted to a highly emotional fight. I had known the individual participants for many years, but I had never seen them so animated. I thought I was watching the acting out of a poorly analyzed primal scene ... Among other things I thought the scene spoke poorly for therapeutic efficacy of psychoanalysis. I discussed the meeting with some senior faculty members. They said, 'Don't be upset. It happens all the time'! Vic Rosen said, 'Relax! It's only personal.' (Calder 1991)

That fight lasted another twenty years, ultimately becoming a struggle between the majority of the faculty and the majority of members of the society (ibid.). Ultimately, as Robert Knight pointed out in his 1953 APsaA presidential Address, the fights so endemic to the psychoanalytic field were normally about who had the right to train analysts. As Irwin Solomon, a leading member of the inner group, put it, 'In each institute this is one of the core problems: Who is to be appointed training analyst and who is not. It's really one of the major sources of trouble in institutes. It's worth thinking about because it remains a difficult task, in our institute, especially.' Solomon was believed that the problems and tensions of the 1960s and 1970s were new editions of those of the 1940s (NYPS/I 1981, p. 6). The NY Institute struggle finally diminished only in the 1980s when a new, fairer and more objective method for selecting training analysts was instituted (Calder pers. comm. 1991).

The selection of faculty – those who occupied teaching positions in the institute – was made by the power group in the EC who had complete control over the appointment of teachers. Many members felt increasingly that they were second-class citizens. According to Eleanor Galenson, 'The choice of faculty was impossible to figure out. Except that if you looked at the list every year it was evident that there were some people, like Margaret Mahler, who would have seemed a likely choice of teacher wasn't. Others might be asked to teach for two or three years, as I was a child development course. I was never told why I was asked or why I wasn't going to be teaching again. I just waited. This is what they did to everyone' (Galenson interview 1994). In a large institute like the NY Institute of necessity many analysts feel left out as there are relatively fewer positions (ibid.). Society members were understandably riled that even faculty membership was controlled in an arbitrary way by the ruling clique. As the NY Institute was unique among educational institutions in being wholly supported by the general membership, it was, as Edward Joseph concluded, 'therefore entitled to a much greater voice in educational policy matters' (NYPI 1975).

From the late 1940s onward the central power position of chairman of the EC was without exception in the hands of the inner group.[34] The legal governing body of the NY Institute, the Board of Trustees was under their domination until the late 1960s when opposition began to grow. From then on chairmen of the Board of Trustees were of a different political complexion from the Old Guard. (The position went along with the presidency of the institute that was elected by the membership at large.)[35] The jurisdictional battles between the EC and the institute's Board of Trustees almost always resulted in the victory of the EC, that is, the inner group.

The EC was in charge of the curriculum, graduation and all teaching functions. The chairs and frequently members of the subcommittees of the EC – Admissions, Child Analysis, Curriculum, Research Students and Students Committee – were chosen by the EC Chairman. The subcommittees were accountable to the EC. In short, there was no point of entry without the support of the ruling clique.

From the post-war period into the 1970s appointments to training analyst status – necessary for election to the EC – needed approval from the Instructors' Executive Committee. With a membership chosen by the Chairman of the EC from among the members of the EC, this committee interviewed analysts whom it invited to apply for training analyst status.[36] Such status could not be attained by self-nomination and evaluations according to clear, public criteria including inviting presentations from those wishing to be considered and evaluated. By comparison, in 1969, nine out of twenty APsaA institutes used invited presentations for evaluation of training analyst status, and by 1982 all but two of twenty-five APsaA institutes invited such presentations (Orgel 1982, p. 423). Members of the committee that nominated training analysts privately 'tapped' analysts with the clear and pervasive sense of their being anointed in the largest and most prestigious institute in the world (New York analyst interview 1981).[37] This committee passed its recommendations back to the EC which decided the outcomes in closed session. These would then be ratified pro forma by the institute's Board of Trustees. Norman Margolis, who saw himself as being in no 'political' camp at the time, recalled:

> I was shocked (and pleased) when informed in July 1970 that I had been appointed as an Instructor (Training and Supervising Analyst) by the EC of the institute, an appointment confirmed by its Board of Trustees. I had never spoken to anyone about this as a prospect, nor had anyone ever

spoken to me. When friends and colleagues asked how did this come about, I could honestly say I didn't know. From the procedural point of view, I have the satisfaction of knowing that my appointment was based on merit. (Margolis pers. comm. 1996)

However, this statement provides testimony to how training analyst status seemed to come from 'out of the blue'. It is scarcely surprising why many saw the process as arbitrary.

The majority of the membership found exceptionally exasperating the mechanism by which the inner group succeeded repeatedly in reappointing themselves to the EC. For elections to the EC were *faits accomplis*. Twelve of its seventeen members were elected for three-year terms. However, all the nominations, two for each seat, were made by the Instructors' Executive Committee the membership of which was appointed by the outgoing EC. (The five remaining *ex officio* members, including the president, vice-president and secretary of the institute, could be consistently outvoted.) Nominations were not permitted from the floor but the membership could choose between the two nominations selected for each seat. The inner group guaranteed the re-election of outgoing members of the EC by ensuring they did not contest each other for the same seat and that the candidates who opposed them were weaker (or vice versa if they wanted a member off). However, if all else seemed to be failing, there were always the unrestrained telephone campaigns at which the ruling clique excelled. As analysands of the inner group or on their way up the hierarchy, the members of the Nominating Committee were loyal to the outgoing EC. As a result, the composition of the EC seldom changed. None the less, occasionally they selected adversaries such as Burness Moore and Milton Jucovy, perhaps as token opposition.[38]

This self-perpetuating system was challenged by a self-scrutiny committee of the NY Institute set up in 1970, which discussed the structure and function of the EC. This committee for 'The self-examination of the New York Psychoanalytic Society and Institute' was organised and chaired by liberal-minded members, Burness Moore and Edward Joseph. The committee, supported by the Board of Trustees, felt that it could not gain sufficient access to the deliberations and procedures of the institute. Plenary conferences of the membership were held during 1970 and 1971. The institute was broken into seven committees which debated important questions in a series of workshops over eighteen months. This resulted in a number of proposals including the creation of a deanship, daytime classes, earlier admission of candidates, a Research Institute and a Center for Child Analysis. The self-scrutiny committee's Final Report was presented in May 1972 (Stone 1976, pp. 5–6).

However, the leadership acted as they usually did with anyone else's recommendations – they did nothing with the recommendations of the self-scrutiny committee.[39] Ken Calder was shocked to hear inner group representatives maintain that since the NY Institute was the best institute in the world with the largest number of candidates, there was no reason to spend any time on the recommendations. They did not recognise any problems. They felt that no help was needed.[40]

Further discussions were held between Moore, Brenner, Calder and Eugene Goldberg about how to implement some of the recommendations. Significantly, their discussions about institute succession and the appointment of training analysts resulted in the establishment of the Concerned Analysts, a reform group set up to challenge the autocratic and arbitrary system whereby the EC and its Chairman operated in secrecy far removed from the faculty and the membership. The rift between the membership and the EC was nowhere clearer than in the inner group's stand that the autonomy of the faculty who taught the institute courses was under threat. Since the EC spoke for the faculty, it seemed to follow that its autonomy needed to be preserved. However, the EC and the faculty often ended up at loggerheads with each other.

Nevertheless, there was one foil to the inner group's complete domination through the EC. Not surprisingly, it became the focus for the efforts of the opposition to the inner group. This was the institute's Board of Trustees which had final legal authority for the administrative, financial and educational affairs of the institute. It consisted of the institute officers and twelve elected members). The board ratified the major EC decisions, including training analyst appointment.[41] Especially severe conflicts arose since the board did not accept the EC's right to recommend appointments to training analyst status to the board without presenting details or reasons.

During the early 1970s, the Board of Trustees successfully fought the EC when it acquired legal advice to the effect that as the final legal authority, the Board of Trustees, needed detailed information from the EC if it was to ratify recommendations for training analyst status. (American Psychoanalytic Association 1976a). Influential on the Board of Trustees, the opposition countered the inner group's lawyers with its own lawyers who searched for loopholes in the bylaws and institutional aspects. But Eleanor Galenson regretted that five of her nine years on the Board of Trustees were too caught up with such issues (Galenson interview 1994), while another long-standing board member remembered the general sense that board membership was 'an exercise in futility and a total waste of time. It was like group masturbation' (New York analyst interview 1994).

However, rigging elections was apparently not limited to the inner group. Norman Margolis described his experience in the late 1960s during his term on the Board of Directors of the NY Society which the opposition dominated. The bylaws provided for the appointment or election of the membership of the powerful Nominating Committee whose duty was to propose the slate from which officers were elected. (NYPS 1946). Margolis recalled that the then president – a senior American analyst who became a prominent member of the opposition – made a great show of democratic sentiment by proposing an election so that younger people could be included. These younger members got the overwhelming number of votes and were declared the Nominating Committee. Then what the president described as 'an unfortunate mistake' was 'discovered'. It had just been noticed that the bylaws required that members of the Nominating Committee needed to be members of five years' standing. Therefore all but one of the younger members elected were ineligible and those older members who were friends of the president but got few votes were declared elected (Margolis pers. comm. 1996). The provision, accessible to all sides, was clearly spelt out in the bylaws and has not been changed to this day. (NYPS 1946, revised October 9, 1984). However, Margolis maintained in this case that the members of the board, 'that the president and his appointed Nominating Committee knew all of this from the outset and thus manoeuvred people on to the board who would otherwise never have been elected by the general membership. In protest, all of us on the board demanded that there be a reelection with a valid slate, and if not we would resign *en masse*. The president relented and a new slate for election was presented to the membership' (Margolis pers. comm. 1996).

The intensity of the battle was also reflected in events surrounding the election of presidential candidates in the NY Institute election of spring 1970 in which the candidates were Martin Stein and Isidor Silbermann. At the March meeting of the institute, the Chairman announced that he had received a letter from Nicholas Young and a telegram from Robert Bak (prominent members of the inner group) nominating Martin Stein as president. Charles Brenner then raised a point of order: the meeting could not proceed for lack of a quorum. However, Bak's telegram and Young's letter were read and Bak reiterated his desire to nominate Stein. The legal advice sought by the inner group maintained that the meeting was duly held and that Stein had been effectively nominated even in the absence of a quorum (Paul Weiss et al. 1970; see also Stone 1976, p. 6). The 1976 site visitors were to view this episode 'as a manifestation of the currents of divisive conflict of the time' (American Psychoanalytic Association 1976a).

As psychoanalysis was losing its lustre and power across the US the struggles came to a head in the early 1970s in the context of profound dissatisfaction, supreme mistrust and lack of confidence in the activities of the leadership. The entrenched group, which determined committees and training analyst appointment, created a bottleneck which stymied the progression of potential competitors to training analyst status (Furer interview 1996). Training analysts found it easier than others to survive financially as they could have candidates in analysis. However, they did not necessarily make much money from candidates – unless they were the full-fee variety assigned to the inner group members (Calder interview 1994c).

The appointment of two training analysts – wives of prominent inner group members – was the 'firecracker' that sparked open conflict between the membership and the EC and gave rise to the ensuing battle about what became known as 'the Brenner Amendment' which I discuss below (Galenson interview 1994; Richards interview 1996). Norman Margolis claimed that the appointments 'were made on the basis of merit but naturally the appearance of nepotism and convoying was fostered, the more so in the already heated-up political atmosphere over educational matters' (Margolis pers. comm. 1996). Galenson recalled that their appointment 'made it crystal clear that criteria for becoming a training analyst were nowhere to be found because these two people would hardly match the other people that should have been eligible' (Galenson interview 1994). In particular, the non-appointment of the much respected analyst, Herb Waldhorn (who shared offices with Charles Brenner and was close to Jacob Arlow and David Beres), at the same time as the appointment of the inner group members' wives, caused upset. Competence did not seem a sufficient criterion – if Waldhorn had been married to a member of the inner group, it was felt he would have been appointed (Richards interview 1996). Even allowing that the appointments of the wives were part of a larger group of appointments (an effort to clear a bottleneck that had developed when training analysts had not been appointed for many years. Furer interview 1996), why was Waldhorn not appointed in that larger group? Waldhorn's non-appointment was a more important catalyst for unrest than the appointment of the wives (Richards interview 1996).

Appointments to training analyst status were notoriously politically motivated, products of cronyism more than ability.[42] Something seemed rotten in the state of psychoanalysis and uproar broke out. This was not surprising since, as Manny Furer put it, the analysts at the NY Institute were always a group of 'very individualistic individuals' (Furer interview 1996).

The Brenner Amendment

In addition to the group that evolved from the 1970 self-scrutiny exercise, another group of dissatisfied members discussed institute concerns over many years. It included Jacob Arlow and Charles Brenner who influenced the generation of younger members through their work. Although not politically active, Arlow was much sought as a supervisor with the result that he still had considerable influence (Richards pers. comm. 1996b). Brenner, a much-respected teacher at the NY Institute and a national figure, suggested a significant bylaw change. His 1973 proposal attempted to change the way nominations were made to the EC, permitting open nominations from the membership at a NY Institute Business Meeting in addition to nominations from the Instructors' Executive Committee. This would have allowed observation and participation from more members outside the self-perpetuating inner group and would have opened the EC. It would help to demythologise the leadership and take the aura away from the group of training analysts meeting in secret. However, that mythology was helpful in accruing referrals and prestige (Calder interview 1996).

Over the following year a number of analysts began to meet in small groups. One such group included David Kairys (who taught at the NY Institute), and others such as Galenson who taught on faculties outside the NY Institute. They were united by concerns about the extreme inhibition of the residents who remained inhibited even after graduation as they waited for training analyst status which, like Godot, never came. By the end of 1972 there was a considerable number of active members of a coalesced opposition group which had been able to bring in those younger analysts not scared enough to join. Detailed tactical discussions ensued and a group of about twenty 'Concerned Analysts' became active around the essential issue of the Brenner Amendment. (Although he was a member of the Concerned Analysts, Brenner did not attend their meetings.) The Concerned Analysts were attempting to break up and question the power structure, to open and democratise the EC, to raise questions about using more analysts in teaching and administration and to challenge the way appointments were made (New York analyst interview 1981).

However, the inner group mounted an active campaign against the rebel group. Galenson recalled that the NY Institute leaders attacked the opposition in a very nasty way, 'smears, things said about people's private lives. This was psychoanalysts supposedly acting on an intellectual level.' Another Concerned Analyst recalled, 'They made remarks about people at private parties of a scurrilous nature. The pettiness was really rather revolting' (New York analyst interview 1981). However, the opposition was well organised and sent out explanatory letters. Although the younger analysts were afraid to sign their names, many others were prepared to fight until the end. Meetings of seventy-five to one hundred analysts were held in Galenson's 96th Street apartment. The insurgents believed they had a majority (Galenson interview 1994; New York analyst interview 1994).

Discussions about the 1973 Brenner Amendment completely dominated institute politics (New York analyst interview 1994). Several institute meetings discussed the Brenner Amendment. Kurt Eissler, Nick Young, Peter Richter, Irwin and Rebecca Solomon, Norman Margolis, Martin Stein and Ed Kronold expressed vehement opposition to the proposed Amendment. Galenson recalled, 'Very, very nasty things were said in public at those meetings about the character of the people who were trying to get the Brenner Amendment through. Like they were just power-hungry or they were envious because they were not training analysts. There was really no scientific approach' (Galenson interview 1994).

A remark by Norman Margolis really infuriated many members. Margolis asserted that the institute consisted of two sections – faculty with a loyal alumni (the membership). Margolis recalled that it struck him 'as a very bad idea that the general membership should have ready access of shaping educational policies and decisions by being able to nominate members for the key EC'. For Margolis it was 'a clear issue of faculty autonomy and academic freedom as against the danger of politicizing academic policy'. Margolis remembered referring to the inherent contradictions in the NY Institute/NY Society organisational structure since everyone was both a member of the membership organisation and of an educational institution.

> Whereas membership organisations should be run democratically, educational policy and organisation should not and could not function optimally as a democracy which is prone to be buffeted by political forces. I stated my opinion that when it comes to educational policy we should

view ourselves as members, like an alumni organisation, who support their alma mater, but who have no direct influence on the shaping and execution of educational policy. These are the purview of the faculty, as they are in any university meeting. (Margolis pers. comm. 1996)

Margolis was labelled as just as elitist as the inner group members (ibid.).

However, nobody on either side agreed with Margolis's analogy (Furer interview 1996). For the membership of the institute and the society was identical. Graduates of the NY Institute were not alumni since they automatically became members of the society and, unlike alumni, then automatically members of the institute and could hold office in both. Alumni usually go to other places to work than after graduating from their alma mater. The institute was supported by the members' dues as well as tuition, which became less and less if student numbers declined. The members were the future teachers and training analysts as these were drawn from the membership, not from a field beyond the institute (Furer interview 1996; NYPS/I 1981, p. 11). Moreover, members of psychoanalytic societies were not just out of medical school. By the time they graduated from the NY Institute; they were Assistant or Associate Professors at Medical Schools with a decade of analytic training beyond their psychiatry boards. They were not ready to be treated like children at the NY Institute (New York analyst interview 1981). In this context the dichotomy between democratic sentiment versus expertise is misleading. The Brenner Amendment did not propose a take-over of the EC but the election of some representatives from the membership to act as watchdogs.

The opposition made frantic telephone calls to ensure that analysts turned up to vote for the Brenner Amendment. In the opposition's calculations the amendment would pass. However, they had not counted on five last-minute defections (Galenson interview 1994; New York analyst interview 1994). With a vote on January 16, 1973, of 166 in favour to 101 against, the proposed amendment narrowly failed to achieve the two-thirds majority required for the passage of an amendment to the bylaws. A year later it failed again with 156 in favour, 101 against (Stone 1976, p. 6). (This report was submitted for the APsaA 1976 site visitors.) Although by that time several of the opposition were elected to the governing body of the NY Institute, the Board of Trustees, the rancour did not subside. Galenson recalled the meetings of that period as awful and full of name-calling (a member of the inner group calling her a liar). Because of the closeness of the vote the inner group was concerned that the opposition would try to pass the Brenner Amendment again. Over the next two years every meeting of the Board of Directors and the Board of Trustees became an acrimonious battleground. Norman Margolis viewed the fact that the Brenner Amendment did not succeed after so many years of effort as 'a testament to our general membership's dedication to, and conviction as to what sound psychoanalytic education should be' (Margolis pers. comm. 1996). This remark should be seen in the context of the fact that the Brenner Amendment always passed the simple majority test and only failed because its passage required a two-thirds majority vote. This two-thirds majority voting system provoked much hostility and the sense of unfairness of the majority not winning a vote had a strong impact on the society. Calder recalled that those around Brenner were 'very much hurt that a simple majority did not win the votes in the Brenner Amendment' (Calder interview 1996). Although constitutions often require more than a simple majority of those voting to pass an amendment (Furer interview 1996), it is also true that this was seen as constituting just one more obstacle keeping the majority from having power in their organisation.

As a result of the close vote an Ad Hoc Committee was appointed to find a compromise solution to involve some representation of the general membership on the EC. This committee reported to the Board of Trustees who could not reach sufficient consensus to recommend an amendment to the membership (Stone 1976, p. 6). In a minority report of the Ad Hoc Committee, Lawrence Roose argued:

> I believe that this committee's discussions foundered on the mistaken belief that if the entire membership of our institute would have any real influence on the EC, the membership would neither nominate nor vote for talented candidates dedicated to the highest standards of psychoanalysis. I reject this thesis as not worthy of our membership. Certain notions seem to have achieved the status of unquestionable facts. To my mind a myth has been created: the autonomy of the faculty must be preserved. Since the EC is a spokesman for the faculty, its autonomy must also be preserved. I know of no other institution in which a committee of that institution is answerable to no one but itself. (Roose 1975)

Roose stated further, 'The main thesis of the minority report is that the EC must directly be accountable to the Board of Trustees and ultimately to the membership of the institute' (ibid.).[43] The EC used the autonomy argument to counter any reform proposals. The minority report emphasised that the EC must be directly accountable to the institute's board of Trustees and therefore ultimately to the membership of the institute (Sternshein 1971; Roose 1975). A letter from a number of opposition members stated:

We feel that legitimate concern for faculty autonomy has been converted into a position that would continue to deny meaningful input into educational matters by the general membership. We feel that the general membership desires faculty autonomy but is increasingly impatient with a committee structure, which is self-perpetuating, and to a great extent only answerable to itself. (Coleman et al. 1975)

Another board committee had already presented its conflicting recommendations to no avail. After an unsuccessful meeting on September 25, 1975, where there had been some hope of agreement, the problem was returned to the membership for a solution (Stone 1976, p. 6).

The 1976 Site Visit

The next significant milestone came with the routine and regular APsaA site visit to the NY Institute in 1976. Site visits are regularly undertaken by a committee of the APsaA to each affiliated institute in an attempt to ensure uniformity of standards, assess problems in the institute and help the institute overcome problems from an outside perspective. The site visitors, who met with both sides, found it difficult to ascertain the nature of the issues. However, they detected that there was a self-perpetuating oligarchy ruling the institute (Galenson interview 1994; American Psychoanalytic Association 1976a).

In a letter representing 'Some Concerned Members of the NY Institute' (signed by Stuart Asch and others) the opposition communicated the undesirable state of the institute to the site visitors. According to the letter, the institute was divided into two groups. Group I consisting of about thirty training analysts and non training analysts constituted about a third of the institute while Group II composed of about thirteen training analysts and other non-training analysts represented almost two thirds of the institute membership. From the mid-1960s Group I started nominating, electing and appointing its members to administrative and educational positions and not appointing Group II members. Group II resented being excluded and organised politically. Opposition spread to the general membership and played a role in supporting the Brenner Amendment and the rights of the Board of Trustees over the EC. Asch maintained that the opposition between the two groups was harmful because of the amount of time and energy wasted in political conflict and the level of factional considerations in elections.

In a prepared statement, Charles Brenner told the 1976 APsaA site visitors that the institute was dominated by a small group representing the majority of training analysts but only a small minority of the institute membership. The choice and appointment of training analysts, he maintained, relied on cronyism (American Psychoanalytic Association 1976a).

The 1976 site visitors noted the severe financial crisis of the institute that had moved from a $4,000 deficit in 1966 to a $55,000 deficit in 1976. Members could not ignore the contrast between their large contributions through dues and assessments that saved and financed the institute and their lack of power in the institute, a situation that made for inevitable conflict.[44]

The site visitors lamented the polarisation and the dissipation of energy into areas outside the educational and scientific calling of the institute which resulted in 'potentially internecine conflict'. They declared, 'As psychoanalysts, we believe that the issues discussed with such intensity may also indicate that personal, emotionally invested issues are at stake. It also seemed to the members of the Site Visit Subcommittee that there were no crucial or substantive scientific issues at stake, and that there were no fundamental differences with regard to the practice and theory of psychoanalysis.'

The site visitors held a meeting with representatives of the ruling group who responded to the opposition's claims. The ruling group maintained that they did not see themselves as a partisan political group but as institute members who through their experience and positions intimately knew the institute's educational policies and procedures. They were opposed the Brenner Amendment and to any motion which would make it possible for the membership rather than the faculty to control the educational arm of the institute. This, they believed, would undermine faculty autonomy and academic freedom. They noted that the 'Concerned Members' at no time criticised educational policies or their implementation. Moreover, the membership had some representation on the EC via the *ex officio* EC membership of the president, vice-president and secretary of the institute. The Board of Trustees approved the major decisions of the EC. Further, a number of co-signers of the Concerned Members letter were members of the EC and Board of Trustees. Some taught in the institute and several analysts associated with the Concerned Members group had recently been appointed as training analysts. Therefore, the ruling group's representatives maintained that the allegations of exclusion and lack of participation were unfounded.[45] Norman Margolis claimed he had never seen evidence of authoritarianism or cronyism from with Group I analysts. But given the manipulations on the Board of Trustees described by Margolis above, insofar as there was any substance to the charges, he claimed that 'it seemed like a clear case of the pot calling the kettle black. In fact, in my time, some of the people most accused of authoritarianism introduced a number of key changes in Educational and faculty procedures when they were chairmen of those bodies.'

Moreover, some Group I members felt, according to Margolis, that

> the Group II members who were advocating 'democratisation', e.g., by including candidates on key committees, did not understand how this would compromise and complicate these candidates' transference in their own training analysis, and thus maybe they really didn't understand transference, a keystone of psychoanalysis. (Margolis pers. comm. 1996)

However, what upset the membership was not whether or not the inner group was superior to Group II since Group I clearly included some of the most talented and committed analysts at the NY Institute. The membership felt that major issues were obscured in the ruling group's defence of the status quo – issues about where the real power lay and how it was exercised by the ruling group. The opposition's criticisms of cronyism, autocracy, domination and installing fear and conformism among candidates struck at the heart of the educational system. The insurgents had turned to the membership because they could not influence the EC through the existing channels.

However, in the opinion of Norman Margolis, the charges by Group II were not substantive.

> Whenever changes came about they would say it was only under pressure, while at the same time paradoxically maintaining that the 'powers' were unresponsive. We, who were called Group I, believed that the '76 Site Visit concurred with our views of the way educational policies should be made and carried out. The most important conclusion was that our educational programme adhered to the highest standards. (Margolis pers. comm. 1996)

The site visitors piously hoped that the conflicts would be resolved within the next decade: 'New York psychoanalysts will once more engage with one another on issues of scientific substance as a primary concern' (American Psychoanalytic Association 1976a). However, they did not indicate how this was to be achieved. They accepted the ruling group's declarations about faculty autonomy without considering why the opposition group had resorted to consulting the membership: because there was no democratic method in the institute, given the entrenched cronyism of the self-perpetuating inner group. Aside from the proposition that individual analysts analyse their own motives, the only solution proffered was the ideal separation of society and institute, something that would have made no contribution to ameliorating the NY Institute problems complained of by the opposition. The site visitors did not address the cronyism issue or the reasons behind the fact that members with a national reputation felt like outsiders at the NY Institute. In short, the site visit report was a very 'political' document that dodged substantial issues that necessitated urgent remedy.

The site visitors advanced only one issue to help comprehend the troubles – the size of the NY Institute. With a membership of three hundred and a faculty of ninety-nine in the NY Institute, there were

> many fine people who were eligible for faculty status and for training analyst appointments and probably would be appointed in other institutes. Emotional issues over being excluded are thus bound to arise. Those invested with power are bound to feel that they want to hang on to it and implement their views. (American Psychoanalytic Association 1976a)

However, this argument is not really borne out by the history of psychoanalytic institutes: small institutes can and have been fierce battlegrounds while larger institutes can function well. The site visitors' statement avoided the question of *how* training analyst positions were distributed, whether fairly or through cronyism. It did not address the poisoning of the atmosphere, by the appointment of training analysts who were not seen to be among the best qualified. As Elliot Jaques pointed out, in order to function well, organisations must promote confidence and trust and need to be organised so as not to produce systematic paranoia and mistrust (Jaques 1996).

The site visitors suggested that 'educational matters should be left to the faculty rather than to the membership. In this regard, the institute should resemble a university in which educational matters are decided by faculty rather than by trustees, former graduates or members' (American Psychoanalytic Association 1976a). However, if a university were governed the way the NY Institute was run, there would be a strong case for intervention. Moreover, other institutes, such as the Boston Psychoanalytic, had people who were not training analysts on their Education Committees to no ill effect – training analysts do not need to make all the educational decisions (Rosett interview 1981).

The site visit report described the NY Institute in devastating terms. Why did they not suggest taking some action by the APsaA to improve the situation? (As will be seen in Chapter 4, such a course was suggested in the case of the Los Angeles Psychoanalytic Institute.) Given the pervasive mythology about the NY Institute, perhaps it was unthinkable for the site visitors to low-rate the premier APsaA institute. Moreover, given the power of the NY Institute within the APsaA at the time, such a move could not have aided the careers within the APsaA of anybody involved in such a recommendation.

In this difficult situation, why did the 'Concerned Members' not break away and form their own institute as so many before them had done in the psychoanalytic field? Or resign and join Columbia or another institute? (A few did join Columbia, but most did not.) Why did they go to so much trouble to try to gain a voice? They were certainly greatly invested in the NY Institute, most having trained there and being involved in the work of the institute. Perhaps they were just as enamoured of the NY Institute reputation as their opponents were.

At all events, both sides rightly sensed that the Brenner Amendment had major symbolic significance. The move to open the EC to outsiders would be a transgressive act tantamount to breaking a spell. Still, as one Concerned Member put it, eventually the battle

> wore out by attrition. A lot of people who were in the Concerned Analysts including myself realised having taken that stand we were finished. These people do not forgive. (New York analyst interview 1981)

During a time of increasing financial stringency, there was much enthusiasm for setting up a Psychoanalytic Foundation to support the NY Institute with a lay Board of Trustees that would help with fundraising (NYPS/I 1978a). Both the Board of Directors of the NY Society and the Board of Trustees unanimously supported the proposal but in a major turnaround, the level of support dropped considerably (although there was still majority support). Through the EC, the inner group was pre-eminent in labelling the proposal as violating psychoanalytic principles, and much bitterness, acrimony and divisiveness were aroused.

Legal Issues

Major legal proceedings issued from two lawsuits brought against the institute which almost brought it to bankruptcy. The large financial threat to the NY Institute from these lawsuits brought about increased unrest from the membership who resented greatly increased taxation without effective representation.

One drawn-out case that lasted from 1979 until 1982 involved a PhD in psychology who was accepted by the EC for analytic training and was told so unofficially by a member. Allegedly out of consideration for the health of the applicant who had a history of Hodgkin's disease, the EC then changed its mind and rejected the application. It was felt that a profound depression that could be experienced during a training analysis might affect her immune system and exacerbate her illness. The institute claimed that she was rejected because of 'disqualifying psychopathology'. During the litigation her lawyer and the Human Rights Commission asked to see the minutes of meetings involving not only the applicant but those of all other research applicants to ensure that she was treated in the same way as they were. The institute refused to do so on the grounds of 'irreparable breach of confidentiality between applicants and institute', and that it would 'compromise the human rights of students and faculty in favour of the alleged rights of the rejected applicant'. The case was settled (with a payment by the NY Institute to her of $150,000 to cover her legal fees) and she was admitted. The applicant became healthy as her disease was self-limiting (NYPS/I 1980, pp. 3–4; New York analyst interview 1994; Calder interview 1994b; Calder pers. comm. 1996a; 1996b). She is now a member of the faculty, having encountered no difficulty, and is a much-respected teacher (Richards pers. comm. 1996a).

The other case was brought against the institute and her supervisors at around the same time by a candidate who was not allowed to graduate. In twelve years of training, the candidate, the wife of an analyst, claimed that her supervisors had not informed her of the severity of their reservations about her work. Ken Calder, however, claimed that three supervisors voiced some reservations with which he as the fourth concurred. Where social and professional relationships are involved, it can be difficult to be completely open and frank in making critical appraisals (Calder interview 1994b). While the plaintiff did not graduate after losing the case (the court regarded the NY Institute as the experts on psychoanalytic education who were competent to decide whom they graduated), it cost the NY Institute another $100,000 (New York analyst interview 1994).

The 1983 Site Visit

In 1983 the next APsaA site visitors heard identical complaints about the method of appointing training analysts in a generally deteriorating situation at the NY Institute. These complaints came from analysts who felt, in the site visitors' words, that 'evaluation on clinical grounds rather than what they consider a more mysterious process of reputation, would be more convincing to them as a fair and appropriate judgement'.

That reputation was central for an analyst to be brought to the attention of those making the appointments of training analysts. According to the site visitors, some therefore experienced the necessity of contriving some way

> to come to the attention of a senior colleague for the purpose of being 'tapped'. The words 'mystery' and 'mystique' frequently came up pejoratively in this connection. Some felt the current system might unwittingly advance the former outstanding candidate whose later work has quietly faltered, and penalise the former less promising candidate who has quietly grown in clinical abilities in the years after graduation. The alternative routes of self nomination or knowledge that systematic review of the appropriate pool of possible nominees is performed, might be helpful to the low morale situation, as well as possibly unearthing potential nominees currently overlooked. (American Psychoanalytic Association 1983)

Study groups were seen by some, the site visitors reported, 'as an obligatory step toward advancement in the institute hierarchy by propitiating "the powers that be". The opinion exists that certain study groups are particularly helpful stepping stones toward training analyst appointment.'

Deploring the 'extraordinary situation' at the NY Institute the site visitors wanted to address the 'full magnitude and seriousness of the problems'. They found that 'complaints of a sense of constriction of independent thinking and initiative were ubiquitous' together with a 'pressure toward obedience' and an 'atmosphere of fearfulness'. A wide spectrum of candidates and students told the site visitors of a 'monolithic atmosphere' and a 'climate of fear of the power and influence of senior analysts'. Some senior training analysts had an 'intimidating style' which was 'demoralizing' and 'crushing to initiative' and which 'handicaps free discussion of certain issues on their merits'. An 'atmosphere of intimidation' was described of a 'monolithic' organisation in which even training analysts could 'live in fear of "stepping out of line", "hitting one's head against the ceiling", "stirring things up", etc.'. The atmosphere was often reported to the site visitors as having

> to do with 'puzzle', 'mystery' and complaints that analytic anonymity and passivity are carried inappropriately into the area of education. More than one student or young analyst described the training atmosphere as 'like one big analytic hour'. Students complained to us with some frequency of coldness and remoteness of the institute, and of what they took to be failures to communicate or an unnecessary abruptness and tastelessness of certain communications. (American Psychoanalytic Association 1983)

This needs to be seen in the context of the 'widening scope' of psychoanalysis which challenged orthodox concepts and was already taking place across the US.

A survey on the morale of the NY Institute presented to the Board of Trustees in February 1983 by board member Francis Baudry had revealed 'significant malaise and discontent' among the membership. While problems in institutes in other cities were similar to those of the NY Institute since there were insufficient candidates and patients, NY Institute members were upset about particular problems at their institute. These issues were: the senior analysts who died but had left no bequests to the institute, the fact that most non-faculty but few faculty had paid a voluntary assessment, that there were thirty-five resignations since 1976 and that only one student enrolled at the NY Institute in contrast with ten at the Columbia Institute. Moreover, a two-tier system of training analysts and non-training analysts resulted in a

> widespread feeling that there are 'ins' and 'outs'. Those who are not training analysts are sometimes regarded as 'second class citizens'. Some interviewees considered the system of selection of training analysts as inequitable and spoke of possible nepotism. They mentioned specifically that the wives of two training analysts have been appointed to the faculty in recent years. (NYPS/I 1983b)

Many analysts believed that the institute was 'run by a small cohort'. The feeling that the institute atmosphere was unfriendly and too formal was widespread and that the broad talents of the large membership were not sufficiently used in teaching and committee responsibilities. Baudry concluded that the current secret system of selecting training analysts was 'deleterious'. Responding with a spontaneous round of applause, the board discussed the importance of changing the system of selecting training analysts (ibid.).

The 1983 site visitors noted the 'contentious atmosphere', in which the polarisation was so extreme that any move was seen to 'advantage' one side and 'disadvantage' another in a 'lamentable climate of political score keeping'. Those in the middle felt left out – one analyst remarked: 'I was apolitical – people didn't want me. I was of no interest to anyone.' 'Power alignments and territorial considerations' always invaded discussions on the appointment of training analysts. When a 1983 meeting of the Board of Trustees authorised the president to appoint his own study committee into training analyst appointment, issues of jurisdiction were raised and a legal memorandum was produced. The site visitors regarded the intrusion of the jurisdictional matters between the

EC and the Board of Trustees as 'symptomatic of how serious and how intrusive the politicisation of educational matters has become at the New York Institute. When issues of turf in such ways take precedence over issues of substance as the focus, the creative energies of the governing bodies of the institute are drained.' Many found it difficult to make an objective appraisal of the NY Institute's severe financial problems since such an appraisal was 'impeded by its having been caught up in the undercurrent of political conflicts. Financial difficulties can be maximized to embarrass an opponent, or minimized to defend oneself against the accusation.' Over the past few years the resignations of forty to fifty members disaffected by the process had led to further erosion of the NY Institute's finances – and of the finances of those of its members who were asked for higher dues and additional assessment. Morale was low. The site visitors noted the 'unwillingness to listen to colleagues' and felt that the detailed corrections of minutes at the beginnings of meetings in preparation for the next major confrontation indicated despair. The site visitors found drain of energies in 'painful to see'. The importance of unassailable written records indicated how deep-seated was the conviction that the other side was untrustworthy: A routine procedure would be transformed into a 'vehicle for perpetuating differences rather than resolving them'. The political climate was marked by a debater form of discussion, in which faculty members would fight with each other for every inch of ground, 'winning' arguments, but leaving colleagues feeling that though they may have been bested in argument, they may not have been truly heard'. The complaint of not feeling heard, the site visitors observed, had grown from a 'whisper' in the 1966 site visit report to a 'crescendo' from candidates to training analysts.

The site visitors were distressed by the 'unrelieved intensity and the unrelenting draining aspect' of institute life which was reported to them from all sides. They counselled separating *ad hominem* argument from core educational issues such as the appointment of training analysts. The site visitors wondered whether the style of the towering figures in the past set the style of settling disputes by the fiat of a senior analyst. With the continuing passing of the Olympian figures, would an attempt be made to resolve things in a different fashion?

The previous few years had seen small changes in the way training analysts were appointed. Nominations could come from the whole training analyst group instead of just the EC. The site visitors suggested two further steps for consideration: self-nomination and an automatic review of those who eligible for consideration.

Another element in the power equation concerned the role and power of the director of the NY Institute Treatment Center that offered low-cost analyses by candidates in training under supervision. Holding the only paid job in the institute and being the only officer routinely available to staff and graduates, the Director of the Treatment Center was in a very powerful position. The divisions within the NY Institute helped transform substantive matters about patient selection into *ad hominem* arguments about a challenge to George Gross, a reportedly formidable personality who held office as Medical Director of the Treatment Center since 1974 (New York analyst interview 1994). Personality factors were important since the Directorship of the Treatment Center had not led other incumbents to power in the NY Institute (Gedo pers. comm. 1995). Gross continued as director well after his term of office expired in 1979 because legalities were ignored (American Psychoanalytic Association 1983). From the early 1980s Gross became president of the Board of Trustees and exercised a good deal of influence over the board which became increasingly filled with non training analysts with no power base of their own (Richards interview 1992).

The site visitors stressed an important structural point. The payment of large dues by the membership 'to support a training program from which many feel excluded, naturally may arouse resentments, and may serve, as well, as a ready avenue for the expression of conflicts or grievances whose origins may lie elsewhere'. Several members had suggested that an organisational change was necessary to solve the NY Institute's problems. While the NY Institute might pursue such changes, any institute structure had defects. Good will and cooperativeness were needed. The site visitors maintained:

> It is this focus on communality of purpose which we feel has been eroded, or damaged, or lost somewhere along the line at the New York Institute. The ideal of outstanding training and clinical practice of psychoanalysis remains strongly held, but firmly drawn sides and a contentious adversarial approach to issues dims, we fear, that communality of purpose. Attempts to reorganize the institute structure along more efficient lines would themselves be so vulnerable to these intra-organizational pressures as to make such a move more likely the result, rather than the precondition, of resolution of the institute's current struggles. The visitors were impressed that what we saw in these controversies seemed not be truly fundamental ideological differences, divergent schools of psychoanalytic thought, such as have fueled internal organizational struggles in other institutes. What we saw and reviewed in the documents of the New York Institute seemed to come closer to what Freud (and some institute

members) referred to as the narcissism of minor differences, compounded by wounded feelings stemming from long series of conflicts with which members of the institute have long been familiar. (American Psychoanalytic Association 1983)

Despite its devastating descriptions of life at the NY Institute, the site visitors did not address the structural issues which were clearly crucially important. Why was there lack of good will? Was there an agglomeration of personal problems or a problem structured into the organization. Why was it not clear that the lack of good will emanated from significant structural issues? That the highly politicised exclusion of most of the highly taxed and under-represented members who were not supporters of the inner group from training analyst selection and status naturally created ill feeling and resentment? Or that efficient organisation with community of purpose and good will would only take place with the institution of significant structural change? Moreover, there was never any hint of intervention in the affairs of the NY Institute from the APsaA as there had been in other institutes such as the Los Angeles Psychoanalytic Institute which was almost closed down at the same time of the last site visit in 1976.

A 1986 article in *New York* magazine quoted NY Institute members pointing to major tensions in the NY Institute under the rule of a self-perpetuating establishment (Smith 1986, pp. 38–45). The article reported that the power group had kept the 1983 site visit report from the membership of the NY Institute. This was, according to Jay Shorr, who led the NY Institute's committee for the site visit, because it contained 'substantial errors and unsubstantiated allegations'. However, the Board of Trustees refused to accept this refusal and voted on January 26, 1984, to see the report. The refusal of Shorr and the EC to comply caused a fury. Arthur Root observed that the 1976 Report had been distributed with more alleged errors than were claimed for the 1983 report, so that was no reason to keep it secret. Meanwhile, the site visitors were upset that APsaA officials rewrote the report, softening it and admitting certain mistakes. The revised report was made available to the membership in August, 1984. Even in 1986, the NY Institute remained guarded about that report and allowed *New York* to see only the last three pages of the report (Smith 1986, pp. 38–45; American Psychoanalytic Association 1983; NYPS/I 1986c, p. 2).

In an already polarised institute, the shroud of secrecy around the machinations of the power group increased the alienation of the membership. In no other institute during my research for this book did I hear those with power referred to so frequently as 'they'. The EC remained controlled by an oligarchy with, according to one analyst, 'coteries, little protégés and people who are hangers-on' (New York analyst interview 1981). The fact that, even into the 1990s, a number of NY Institute analysts requested anonymity for this book, is an index of the depth of ingrained alienation and lack of trust. The NY Institute was the only institute where there were any such requests. The reluctance of establishment figures at the NY Institute to go on the record was noted by a journalist for *New York* magazine in 1986. They told her that public discourse would interfere with their relationships with patients. However, she found a number of other analysts (who also had patients) who were willing to speak their minds (Smith 1986, p. 42). Not one of the more than 150 other analysts I interviewed for this book ever raised such an issue with me. The only consistent refusals to be interviewed came from some who had been members of the inner group of the NY Institute.

Changes

As Manuel Furer, Chair of the EC (1983–89), maintained, a 'sea change' in the atmosphere of the NY Institute occurred in the early 1980s: 'It was recognized that we had to increase the participation of our members, both faculty and non-faculty, to open pathways for involvement and advancement that were perceived to be closed or mysteriously complex. We had to rekindle the conviction that the institute is a valuable place to which to devote one's energies. The hallmark of this effort became self-nomination.'[46]

On January 20, 1983, the Board of Trustees appointed a committee (chaired by liberal analyst Arthur Root) which investigated procedures for improving training analyst selection (NYPS/I 1983a). While set up by the Board of Trustees, Root treated it as a wider Committee of the institute, obtaining the cooperation of the Chairman of the EC, Manny Furer (NYPS/I 1983c, p. 3). The important measure recommended by this committee was that training analyst status was to be based on two central principles: self-nomination and a review of current practice and capacities in psychoanalysis (American Psychoanalytic Association 1992). Based on self-sponsorship, two written cases of current analytic work, and oral presentations on two cases to consultant training analysts, the appointments were to be made more on merit than through the cronyism that had prevailed. In the euphoric atmosphere engendered by the victory over the Board of Trustees, the EC under Manny Furer was able to introduce some important changes (Furer interview 1996). The recommended measures (NYPS/I 1986b) were adopted by the EC in May, 1986. 'This action', the NY Society and Institute's *Newsletter* commented, 'culminates many years of discussion and debate concerning elements of subjectivity and "closedness" which many members felt had marked the previous procedures for selection' (NYPS/I 1986c, p. 1).

During the mid-1980s George Gross and the Board of Trustees had aimed for the democratic appointment of Training Analysts through an open procedure with self-nomination and presentation. It was only after Gross left the scene and was no longer president that the things he sought were instituted – self-nomination and presentation for training analyst selection. The substantive procedural changes in the way both training analysts and faculty were appointed made access more open and democratic, removing the prevailing cronyism.

With the change to self-nomination for training analyst appointment together with democratisation of the institute with clear procedures, morale markedly improved, especially since the old fights dwindled with major issues accomplished (Calder interview 1992). Jacob Arlow considered that the NY Institute situation was 'tremendously improved' having 'really turned a corner'; the situation had become 'quite harmonious, free of any personal or doctrinaire quarrels' (Arlow interview 1992). Arnold Richards could claim with some reason that the NY Institute became 'more democratic and less authoritarian' than some other major psychoanalytic institutes in the New York area – Columbia, NYU, the Institute for Psychoanalytic Training and Research (IPTAR) and the William Alanson White Institute (Richards pers. comm. 1996a). There was also a major shift in administrative faculty positions toward a younger group (Richards interview 1992).

While Furer was one of a number of analysts who brought about change (Richards interview 1996), his own considerable role led Arnold Richards to label him as the 'Menachim Begin of the NY Institute' – just as only a conservative had been able to negotiate with Sadat, he was able to exercise great influence on the inner group. He had a central role in changing the undemocratic method of Training Analyst selection (Richards pers. comm. 1996a; 1996b).[47]

The Begin analogy also holds in that the changes came from within the ruling group rather than from sources outside it. The opposition had been routed. Tired of fighting and losing they went their individual ways. The leadership knew they could now win any election, which made it easier to include some people from outside the inner group (Calder interview 1996). It was a 'revolution from within' the ruling group. Moreover, the shortage of candidates and patients meant that resources needed to be pooled to work together to get more patients and candidates (Calder interview 1996). Some opposition members later came back, and younger people were integrated into running the institute (Furer interview 1996).

Arnold Richards located an important cause of the change in 'the ascending of Charles Brenner, who had influenced a group of younger members who were now in a position to assume leadership'. These included Ernie Kafka, Mike Porder and Richards. The older generation, particularly Ruth Eissler through her study groups, was waning in its influence. After the failure of the Brenner Amendment, Brenner continued to train and influence younger people, so much so that Arnold Richards could speak of a 'silent revolution' eventually taking place where Brenner 'just hung in there and outlived and outlasted the old guard – Solomon, Richter, Young, Bussel, et al.' (Richards pers. comm. 1996a; 1996b). Brenner also provided intellectual leadership becoming a mentor to some important younger analysts who were by then part of the establishment of the EC, filling committees which dealt with issues such as training analyst applications.[48]

The stage was set for such changes since about a dozen important inner group members either retired or died. These were replaced by a younger group who trained in the 1960s and 1970s and remains on the faculty.[49] Along with American psychoanalysis in general, the NY Institute had reached what Jacob Arlow termed the 'post-Apostolic period of psychoanalysis, in which no one will be able to substantiate a claim of being the confirmed representative of the fountainhead of psychoanalytic authority' (Arlow 1985, p. 5).

Perhaps most importantly, the changes resulted from the fact that psychoanalysis was in such major decline across the country both culturally and therapeutically that many started to challenge the previously accepted myths in psychoanalytic institutions (Calder interview 1996). The decline in the number of candidates and analytic cases perhaps helped to force the recognition that major changes at the NY Institute were necessary.

By the 1980s the NY Institute was being severely affected by a dearth of new candidates as well as by the declining number of analytic patients. Earning a comfortable living practising four or five times a week analysis was becoming far more difficult. There was far more competition for what analytic cases there were. For a time the NY Institute was lucky to get two or three candidates per year (Richards interview 1992; Richards pers. comm. 1996a). The fact that these candidates were increasingly non-medical meant that the lawsuit instituted by the psychologists against the APsaA to allow non-medical candidates in paradoxically helped many of APsaA institutes to maintain their candidate numbers. The many other psychoanalytic institutes in New York provided competition for candidates and many other therapists provided less costly and time-consuming therapy. The decline in third-party payments also made less frequent and cheaper therapies more attractive. Such pressures affected almost all analysts.

The declining popularity of psychoanalysis as a therapy was crucial to the new changes. According to Ken Calder, since the 1960s, even in New York analysts began to become united against 'a common enemy, the shortage of patients, which affected all levels'. Calder asserted in a 1992 interview:

> We are all sharing the anxiety, the disappointment, and the sense of anxiety about our candidates. There is a good possibility our candidates are going to be very angry. They were led into analytic training at enormous expense, their families were disturbed by it, their pocket book was disturbed by it, etc. Then they have one or two analytic patients. The more senior people are more friendly because they see that on the horizon and already they are all sharing the same problem because nobody is feeling secure about their analytic practice.

He added dryly: 'The incidence of psychopathology diminished in London because of the blitz with people getting together against a common enemy.'[50] Calder recalled that into the 1960s the greatest prestige attached to individuals practising psychoanalysis in their offices, especially training analyses. This did not mean receiving the highest income – into the 1970s, analysts could make more money conducting ordinary analyses (for which they could charge a higher fee) rather than training analyses. During the 1960s psychoanalysts earned significantly higher incomes from their practices than psychiatrists did.[51] From the 1950s into the 1970s fees ranged from around $20 to around $50 (Calder pers. comm. 1996b). However, with the decline in the number of ordinary analytic cases candidates became more welcome for financial reasons – at least analysis could bring some income. Although they might pay relatively small fees because of the five times a week frequency, it was a reliable, predictable and fascinating part of a practice. During the 1980s and 1990s, training analyst status was sought for prestige, but taking on one or two candidates guaranteed a solid income base. Analytic fees are often around $125 per session (Calder pers. comm. 1996b). With the rise of effective psychotropic drugs and short-term cognitive-behavioural therapies, psychoanalysis several times a week for a number of years faced devastating competition. This means that the prestige and rewards of becoming an analyst then a training analyst have greatly declined. For those who wish to become training analysts, there is strong competition for the few candidates available. Given that training analysts have undergone some twenty years' training (analysts are often not appointed training analysts until they are around fifty) being a training analyst was, in Calder's words, 'a short season'. They do not take on new training cases after they are seventy years old. Because of the potential for disrupting their training, candidates are loath to be analysed by older analysts who might become ill or die (Calder interview 1992). Training analyst status, so central to professional recognition, has been especially competitive since analysts who spent decades in training feel they need to be appointed early so as to take advantage of the relatively brief period when they are eligible to take on the few candidates available. In the opinion of Norman Margolis, 'the atmosphere and our procedures have changed over the years as a reflection of the natural evolution of an organization which learns as it goes along' (Margolis pers. comm. 1996). Much of this learning was, however, hard-won. Perhaps at bottom the major reason for the changes probably lies in the retirements and deaths of the Old Guard and the shift to the new group (Richards pers. comm. 1996a).

There was also the question of the NY Institute's reputation among potential candidates. In 1986 the first-year class at the NY Institute had three students compared with nine at the NYU Institute (including two who were accepted by the NY Institute but chose NYU instead). Many psychiatric residents reportedly saw the NY Institute as cold, 'fratricidal' and unwelcoming. Classes and seminars were not seen to welcome open discussion in contrast with other institutes, and teaching positions seemed unavailable to many graduates (NYPS/I 1986a, p. 5).

As ever, the spark for change came from the issue of training analyst selection. Three analysts (Arnold Richards, Michael Porder and Bob Kabcenell) were approved for appointment to training analyst status by the EC. While the EC nominated training analysts, the Board of Trustees was required to confirm them formally. On February 21, 1985, for the first time the Board of Trustees refused to confirm an appointment, Kabcenell's, while approving the other two. This created considerable agitation as to why that recommendation was turned down, and engendered a serious confrontation between the EC on the one hand and George Gross and the Board of Trustees on the other (NYPI 1985a). Substantial jurisdictional issues were involved since the board based on its legal status claimed final authority for institute affairs whereas the EC claimed *de facto* power in the normal running of institute affairs in educational matters, a structural issue which became controversial from the late 1960s on (NYPI 1985b). Because of his flamboyance, Kabcenell provided an easy target for those wishing to challenge the EC's jurisdiction whereas the other two could not be so effectively challenged. He was not inhibited, was seen to be homosexual, and was a close friend of the Europeans, including Annie Reich, Lillian Malcove and especially Robert Bak, who was, in Manny Furer's words, 'the most inner of the inners' (Calder interview 1996; NYPS/I 1991, p. 3; Furer interview 1996). The faculty then retaliated to the board by refusing to appoint another committee to nominate training analysts. Then Arnold Richards and Michael Porder, who had been selected as training analysts, stood for election to the Board of Trustees but were defeated. However, it was clear that a new younger generation recognised that the system of appointing training analysts was unfair.

The widespread dissatisfaction with the procedure precipitated an organisational crisis. This resulted in Bob Kabcenell being appointed as a training analyst the following year as well as the EC appointing a small group which supported changing the procedures for training analyst appointment. The constitution of this important committee was an important marker in the transition of power from the older generation to the next one. The Ad Hoc Committee on Implementation of the New Procedure for the Selection of Instructors consisted of younger members who became organisationally important. Chaired by Sander Abend with Jerome Ennis, Martin Willick and Joan Erle as the other members, it did not include the older generation such as Lili Bussel, Irwin Solomon, Peter Richter or Martin Stein (NYPS/I 1991, p. 2; Richards interview 1992; 1996; Furer interview 1996).

There was pressure for change. Some members kept up their struggles throughout. As president of the institute from 1980 to 1982, Ken Calder had four goals: 'To make the selection of new training analysts more democratic; to make the selection of those with the right to train more scientific; to make the meetings of the faculty more scientific and less political; and to have improved morale as a conscious goal, especially for those who have the right to train' (Calder pers. comm. 1995).

One reason for the changes may have emanated from the work of dissatisfied Group II people who, in the opinion of Norman Margolis, 'tried to weaken the educational roles of the faculty and the EC by reinterpreting the role of the institute's Board of Trustees as being the key committee in which the ultimate educational power rested'. In law the

Board of Trustees is responsible for institute affairs and is clearly, more accountable and representative of members rather than training analysts. In a 1996 letter, Margolis wrote:

> The three major changes which resulted from these difficult years were (1) the procedure of self-nomination for training analysts and a series of clinical consultations in this connection; (2) the procedure of self nomination for appointment to Assistant Course Instructor, and the clear listing of the criteria for appointment; (3) and the rescinding of the two-thirds majority needed in the EC to endorse a recommendation to training analyst or assistant course instructor, and the similar two-thirds majority required in the Board of Trustees, ratifying these appointments. I was/am very much in favor of (1) and (2) and not at all sure about (3). However, there is no doubt that these changes are both reflective of calmer times in our organization, and have significantly contributed to that calm. (Margolis pers. comm. 1996)

Part of that calm issued from a growth of trust. The problems of past decades were related to the dissatisfactions and lack of trust in the EC to lead appropriately. Since training analyst appointments and EC membership were seen by many members to be unfair, as relying on cronyism more than merit, why should they trust the EC to make good decisions? Issues about the principle of 'faculty autonomy' were beside the point where the procedures for training analyst and faculty appointments were under such a cloud.

In the late 1980s the society's Extension Division, responsible for community outreach, was resuscitated by Manuel Furer, Arnold Rothstein and Arnold Richards. This opened opportunities for teaching and involvement for the entire membership instead of the relatively few who could teach in the institute faculty as well as being aimed at attracting more candidates.[52] Arnold Richards, who took a wider view of psychoanalysis, became Chairman of the Extension Division and editor of the *Journal of the American Psychoanalytic Association*. According to Richards, 'The organization shifted from being a group that was closed and elitist and where it was never clear how you get ahead to one where it is totally specified what the rules, procedures, the avenues advancement lay.' It changed to being an organisation where hard work is rewarded. Unlike other institutes, certification with the APsaA, requiring an advanced level of clinical achievement is prerequisite for faculty membership. Richards summarised the NY Institute attitude: 'If you want to get ahead, do the work. You can't just sit back and complain of being left out if you are not willing' (Richards interview 1992). Devotion to work is an important measure of quality.

The 1992 APsaA site visit report noted 'considerable change' since the 1983 report. There was 'more harmony among the governing bodies' as well as within the membership. The new selection procedures for training analysts seemed to be working well. The outreach programmes were also successful. A successful journal, the *Journal of Clinical Psychoanalysis,* was started. Institute concerns had shifted to the paucity of cases for candidates, decreasing applications for training, the financial problems of the NY Institute and the 'larger number (60%) of women candidates and modifications in training sequence that this necessitates, and relative lack of nonmedical applicants'. Although the Treatment Center had been revamped, applications had diminished to just fifty per year, resulting in about ten patient referrals for low cost psychoanalysis with candidates.[53]

But is New York still Anointed?

What have the changes at the NY Institute meant for the culture of the NY Institute? Does a quality of anointment remain? Given the special characteristics derived from its 'greats' and its cronyism the NY Institute retains some special characteristics which make for the prevalence of a master–apprentice model for training. According to Arnold Richards, younger NY Institute analysts conduct more psychoanalyses than in most other institutes, and faculty members are required to have achieved the advanced level of certification with the APsaA (involving a number of presented and written-up cases). According to Richards, there is a sense in the NY Institute of how hard it is to learn and understand psychoanalysis with only one or two cases, that teachers and analysts are better off the more analysis they do (Richards interview 1992). NY Institute analyses are longer than at Columbia and trainees must take one more case to graduate. But how much does this emphasis on 'standards' reflect old mythology?

In the view of an analyst with experience at both Columbia and the NY Institute, the emphasis on 'standards' at the NY Institute reflects a sentiment that some people feel they have the truth and that there should be minimal standards to define psychoanalysis to distinguish it from psychotherapy. (How much does this represent the continuation of the myth of the NY Institute?) There is a conviction that a certain amount of ongoing clinical work is required to take part in clinical debates. In this analyst's view, clinical debates require ongoing clinical experience and the notion of having the truth derives from the conviction of clinically experienced analysts that certain approaches yield better clinical results. In contrast to Columbia, where Roy Schafer's position that we never get to the 'truth' as we each have our own narrative is influential, the prevalent NY Institute viewpoint focuses on reconstruction of the experiences resulting from the interplay of childhood fantasy and experience. Thus the NY Institute model is one of 'the craftsman and how to be as good a clinician as you can be'. In contrast to Columbia the NY Institute is 'more of an apprenticeship, there is less of the university about it in terms of learning at the feet of the pros. That is what New York's strength is.' The 'pros' are the cadre of older analysts, 'the real stars who have been doing analysis for years and years, the clinicians'. While Columbia may be more interesting theoretically, the NY Institute had more to offer 'in terms of really trying to learn from the pros'. This analyst maintained that Columbia analysts fantasise that NY Institute analysts sit around talking about them, saying that they are not real analysts. 'It is a paranoid fantasy. It is a need to feel embattled. In fact, people at New York don't think much about people at Columbia. They are trying to figure out, how can I do more analysis, how can I get better at it?' However, while NY Institute analysts probably spend little time thinking about Columbia, they are in no doubt that Columbia is inferior (New York analyst interview 1992b).[54]

Lisa Weinstein, an analyst with a psychology background, was a candidate at the NY Institute from 1982 and found her training 'wonderful'. The emphasis in her training was far more clinical than critical and academic, contrasting with the training of psychologists where critical thinking is primary. In her opinion, the NY Institute was very dedicated to analysis and its continuation, and the training was 'in the way they think it should be done'. She believed the feeling of anointment came from the intensity and gratification of the clinical work along with not understanding why others did not work in the same way. 'I think there is this sense of, "We are the repository of the true way of doing analysis".' The theory was still taught as the truth.

> It is like orthodox religion in that way – this is the truth. They try to encourage you to write but the whole weight of the transference is to do it the way the elders are teaching you to do it. Not just to do it but to think about it. You are in analysis while you are in training. In New York the training is very careful. The downside of it is you become technicians. If you are just trying to train people to do what you did, in two generations you are left with nothing but arid technique. (Weinstein interview 1992)

Much of the ambience relates to the idea of training excellent practitioners (see Holzman 1976). This ambience still retains an ardour reminiscent of Kurt Eissler's experiences of 'transport'. According to Sandra Cohen, Chairman of the Extension Committee and Management Committee, NY Institute members 'love' psychoanalysis (Cohen interview 1992a). With a commitment to four- or five-times-a-week psychoanalysis (as distinct from psychotherapy), their primary professional identification is as analysts. 'The overwhelming sense at New York of what is valued and who is valued are clinicians, which means close attention to detail and technique' (Cohen interview 1992b).

Strangely, the sense of closeness to clinical material has not made for humility in the face of so much unknown terrain of human experience. Although the oligarchic leadership was overthrown, the apprenticeship model assumes the expertise and authority of the master as an expert who needs to be followed and emulated.

But the focus on clinical expertise can be profoundly conservative. With reliance on 'excellent' technique in what still remains seen as 'our' science with its own investigative tool, the analytic hour, larger critical questions can easily be eschewed. Even where some radical theses are presented, such as Brenner's revisions of analytic theory, these are seen in the guise of evolutionary work from within accepted classical theory. The assumption that there is an exclusive group with private and special access to clinical truth from Freud through the New York 'Giants' to the present incumbents persists to some extent. While building on a living tradition and assessing contributions objectively leads to development, arrogance through a sense of anointment can only bring stultification.

Sandra Cohen depicted the NY Institute as having a 'tradition like the Englishman gentleman scholars'. There is, she asserted, 'an air of gentility at New York which I approve of. People say we are too formal and use each other's last names.' This is a touch of the English aristocracy in modern times. The NY Institute reminded Cohen very much of British clubs or the tutorial system of the ancient British universities. Study groups were especially important at the NY Institute professionally and intellectually. Admission to the in club was, in Cohen's opinion, the requirement that psychoanalysis be a major life priority. Enormous devotion of time and energy to the society and institute came from volunteers who demonstrated their character and abilities through hard work for long hours. Unlike those with power in the institute who were there most nights, most disaffected analysts were not prepared to put in the necessary work. According to Cohen, becoming a part of the inner group of the institute or society currently resulted from a willingness to work hard. Working together helped with referrals, provided visibility and an indication of character, especially reliability and trustworthiness. 'If you are ambitious and want to make analysis the centre of your life, that alone helps you to be picked as the anointed at New York. The people who are choosing you have invested in it. They say, this is worth all my time. I will not go and play golf' (Cohen interview 1992a). This reflects a clubbish attitude towards those who can show themselves to be worthy. However, a willingness to work does not occur in a vacuum. Those in power can retain control through informally encouraging or discouraging those who volunteer their services. Things are never so simple as a willingness to work as well-known informal ways of attracting and rejecting people in effect remain central.

The 1992 APsaA site visitors reported that since the last site visit in 1983 there had been 'considerable change'. There was an 'amelioration of severe conflict' of 'the Wars' and the institute 'seems to be functioning harmoniously' (American Psychoanalytic Association 1992). There have been more forums with different ideas under discussion. Arnold Richards asserted that in 1996 'radical new ideas are now given a platform' at the NY Institute. There has been recent debate about psychoanalytic training for social workers, psychologists and psychotherapists without a PhD. Paradoxically, the core of the resistance to training social workers with Masters degrees is the younger analysts who want to maintain a medical identity for the NY Institute. The first appointment of a psychologist as training analyst has recently been made. A committee was set up to examine the idea of a psychoanalytic foundation, something that was vociferously opposed by the inner group twenty years before. The 1990s have seen continued small numbers of applications, many from PhDs and some from medically qualified applicants. The NY Institute has instituted an active Extension Division and a Fellowship Program in hopes of attracting more applicants (by the 1990s most institutes were receiving far fewer applications) (Furer 1996; Richards pers. comm. 1996a; 1996b). Arnold Richards described the new type of candidate in the new conditions as

> first of all a woman who is married to a partner in a New York law firm. More women who also see psychiatry and psychoanalysis as a way of having a family and a practice. So it is not the same group of people who are going into psychoanalysis to become a rich Park Avenue psychoanalyst or psychiatrist. (Richards interview 1996)

Candidates and externs have broader interests and are better read than those adopting the narrow practitioner model of earlier times (ibid). In Manny Furer's view, this new situation in which psychoanalysis is under siege from within and without means that it is next to impossible to find patients and make a living means that candidates apply for intellectual and personal reasons. A dedicated candidate must see an analytic case for $25 an hour. As he put it:

> To do it means like in England at a certain period, you must accept sacrifice. The world has changed. To become an analyst now you sacrifice time and money. You come out with a debt between $70,000–140,000 and you are not going to be able to pay it back. Even if you did psychotherapy the fees are low. There's an advantage to that in that you'll get people who are more dedicated. It's gone back to that kind of thing, it's not a profitable profession. (Furer interview 1996)

The inner group approach at the NY Institute reflected the reliance on authority endemic to the history of psychoanalysis. Psychoanalysis proceeded not only from the accumulated experience and ideas of analysts and their predecessors but also by charisma and authority. Psychoanalytic schools often developed around personalities from Freud, Jung, Adler, Melanie Klein to Jacques Lacan and Heinz Kohut (Wallerstein interview 1987). Freud set the model for authoritarianism of analytic organisational affairs, as he was not tolerant of others' criticisms of his ideas (Holt 1989, p. 341). Freud even identified psychoanalysis with his own beliefs, leading those who disagreed with him, from Jung to Ferenczi, to leave the fold. The attitude that psychoanalysis was the esoteric possession of a small inner group was an extension of the extraordinary importance given to an analyst's progenitors – who analysed one's training analyst, and so on – not the assessment of the quality of an analyst's current work. This view echoed Freud's establishment of a secret Committee in 1911 to preserve psychoanalysis against its enemies – he presented its members with rings in 1913.[55] This approach led analysts to maintain the very transferences to parental figures which psychoanalysis was supposed to dissolve. Since the 1920s the training analysis has been the most important aspect of psychoanalytic education (supervision and seminars are of far less significance). Until the late 1970s it was standard practice in APsaA institutes for a training analyst to report on the progress of a training analysis to the Education Committee contaminating an already troublesome relationship still further. Perhaps nobody ever terminates analysis, but candidates, far from saying goodbye to their analysts, join them at the institute, thus cementing identifications. This process affects the manner in which analysts treat their patients, colleagues and candidates.

Instead of becoming freer, zealots manifest often unrecognised deep ambivalence about psychoanalysis. Unanalysed hostility can cement group alliances among an inner group and project the bad aspects outside on to 'them'.[56] Idealisation of one side that has it all (the idealised analyst) with a commensurate repudiation of the other (the denigrated analyst) represent two sides of the same coin that reflect unresolved identifications in which the analyst is all-important.

In Ken Calder's view, the NYPI from 1950 to 1997 could be studied with profit from the point of view of out-of-balance thinking. That study, with a parallel to the present one, would begin with the movement of analysts from Europe to the US. Those analysts faced reality dangers – Hitler, leaving homes and offices and finding homes and offices, needing to master English, and so on. While those dangers were all too real, the sense of danger at the NY Institute stemmed too much from fantasy. There was thought to be safety in cults where a minority of like-minded analysts reacted with suspicion, political battles and cult thinking – we know what we know because we know. Logic, reason and scientific inquiry were slighted. Corners were cut and officers were appointed on the grounds of safety rather than innovation and wisdom. The attitude towards analytic theory and practice was also regressive. Instead of recognising psychoanalysis as tentative conclusions, to be modified with time, logic and evidence, there was a strong attachment to dogma. The 'truth' was often the result of a fiat from an honoured leader. Doubt was considered to be the enemy, rather than a respected detail of the scientific method. So, on the one hand an exaggerated sense of danger gave birth to the pathological thinking of cults, suspicions and clichés and, on the other hand, led to distortions of the science of psychoanalysis by claiming more for it than it has earned (Calder pers. comm. 1997; Calder interview 1996). The history of the NY Institute constitutes, as Calder put it, 'a clear example of the psychopathology of a group in which repressed mechanisms of defence are substituted for healthy mechanisms of defence. The source of danger might be imaginary or real' (Calder pers. comm. 1998). Exaggerating the dangers to psychoanalysis from outside the institute, the inner group fostered an 'us' and 'them' culture. Mistrust and suspicion were powerful forces that eroded confidence and trust and got in the way of the fulfilment of the tasks of the institute.

The problem of what happens to ideas when they are institutionalised endures in a particular way at the NY Institute. Complex ideas often become simplified when applied by others, taught and applied by a larger and, on average, less talented cohort. This difficulty is compounded when a science turns into a movement and that movement changes further into being applied as a dogma. Authoritarian approaches repel many talented people who decide to go into other fields, leaving the field open to more closed-minded thinkers. Those fortunate to have been analysed by the few more liberal minded analysts were protected from this to some extent (Furer interview 1996). The field must be open for challenge from within as well as open to other fields of inquiry for development and criticism, Otherwise, dogmatic, unsophisticated thinking will persist and the potential for the development of the field will be lost.

This happened at the NY Institute where the exercise of autocratic power close psychoanalysis off from other disciplines. Moreover, since promotions depended on politics and acquiescence rather than capability and creativity, psychoanalysis was closed from capable and congenial people both within the field within and outside the NY Institute. This damaged the development of psychoanalytic inquiry. The legacy of those 'Giants' who insisted on the preservation of their proprietary science at any cost and closure towards others assisted in the massive decline of psychoanalysis in intellectual and clinical circles.

Finally, a somewhat more open and democratic institute came about. However, the problem went beyond the particular institutional arrangements. For psychoanalysis is part of a long journey in understanding human nature. Freud and certainly many of his followers including those in the inner NY Institute group, assumed that psychoanalysis was a point of arrival and did the best they could to make sure that nobody travelled beyond it (Moraitis interview 1996a). Given structural flaws in the rules of governance, for much of its history the NY Institute fell into a bad state when the 'Giants' behaved in a dictatorial fashion and further delegated day-to-day power to less talented analysts who profited from 'reflected glory'. As John Gedo observed, 'The long-term tolerance of this illegitimacy perpetuated the vicious circle of arrogating to oneself the desiderata of the profession on the basis of empty claims' (Gedo pers. comm. 1995). By convoying certain analysts through their training analysis and then into institutional power while simultaneously systematically excluding those with a more open and pluralistic approach, the NY Institute inner group oppressed generations of analysts and harmed their own cause. By so closing off innovation and dialogue they contributed to the very thing they feared – the erosion and decline of psychoanalysis in the New World.

2 THE BOSTON SPLIT

The first major split in an APsaA institute in two decades took place in 1974. Five senior training analysts walked out of the Boston Psychoanalytic Society and Institute (BPSI) to form another much smaller institute, the Psychoanalytic Institute of New England East (PINE). In 1975 this institute became the second APsaA affiliated psychoanalytic institute in the Boston area.

These events caused high emotion in Boston as well as in the APsaA which, uncharacteristically, permitted the split to occur.[1] The exploration of the complex reasons behind the Boston split will shed further light on the dynamics of psychoanalytic institutions.

BPSI psychoanalyst and psychoanalytic historian, Sanford Gifford, who chairs the APsaA's History and Archives Committee, closely observed the split (Gifford has been intimately involved with the BPSI since he became a candidate in 1946). He believed it 'doesn't lend itself to elegant structuralisation or defining issues. From the beginning it was obscure even as it was happening' (Gifford interview 1981). According to BPSI analyst and Harvard Business School emeritus professor Abraham Zaleznik, 'There was no scientific, etiological or substantive basis of the split', but 'there are rationalisations' (Zaleznik interview 1981).

I will argue that the split arose out of problems with the use of and access to power in psychoanalytic politics and in the life of the institute. In particular, this included access to training analyst status, an issue we have been crucial in the New York Psychoanalytic Institute. Such problems, in turn, point to issues about the nature of the profession of psychoanalysis itself. As the leader of the APsaA visiting committee to Boston put it, 'Training analyst status and the differentials that come from that turn out to be behind just about every problem that gets to any magnitude' (McLaughlin interview 1994a).

History of the BPSI

The BPSI has had several lives. The first Boston Psychoanalytic Society, formed by James Jackson Putnam, became a constituent society of the

IPA in 1914 but ceased to meet after Putnam's death in 1918. The Boston Psychoanalytic Society was revived in 1928 by an early member, Isador Coriat, who united three study groups that represented followers of Carl Jung, Otto Rank and Paul Schilder. This amalgam was reorganised in 1930 and was joined by a group of Americans led by Ives Hendrick. Hendrick was one of the best trained Americans of the time, having just returned from two years' training at the Berlin Psychoanalytic Institute (Gifford 1994, p. 652; Hendrick 1961a, pp. 1–2, 14–16).[2] Hendrick and the three other young psychiatrists who had studied at the Berlin and Vienna institutes set up the first 'Freud Seminar' in the winter of 1930–31. After some struggle with the senior members who opposed setting up a training programme, the seminar led to formalised training procedures (Hendrick 1961b, pp. vi, 2–4, 22–4; Michaels 1961, p. 156).

The following years saw training procedures created that were more authoritarian than the Berlin institute which served as the BPSI's model. The BPSI provided training with analyses conducted by a recognised 'training analyst', a faculty who taught seminars, and a 'control analysis' with low-fee patients. Both the new Boston Psychoanalytic Society and the Boston Psychoanalytic Institute (with the same membership as the society) were affiliated with the APsaA in 1933. During 1934–35, the Boston Psychoanalytic Institute organised a full programme of didactic courses was, and on December 31, 1935, the institute became a legal entity. A division of labour was arranged whereby the Trustees organised the business affairs of the institute while the Education Committee elected by the society handled the educational affairs. However, roles were always intertwined; many members of the Education Committee were also Trustees, the 1935 constitution even stipulating that the medically trained Education Committee members were also to be Trustees (Hendrick 1961a, pp. 49–52). In 1947, society and institute structures were combined officially as the Boston Psychoanalytic Society and Institute (S. Gifford 1978, pp. 330–6).[3]

The milieu of the Boston area is significant. Over one-tenth of American medical residents are trained in the Boston area and many analysts hold academic appointments in medical schools in the Boston area, the major university centre for the US. In addition to their positions within the BPSI, training analysts and others held important academic and institutional posts in psychiatric services, general hospitals and medical schools. Boston's pre-eminence as a centre for the training in medicine and psychiatry was established in the 1930s and this fertile psychiatric soil was an important element in the development of the Boston Psychoanalytic Institute. The historically close relationship between psychiatric hospitals and departments of psychiatry and BPSI members has been a distinctive feature of the BPSI since its inception (see Hendrick 1961a, pp. 57–62).[4] The doctors who undertook their psychiatric training in the many residency training programmes in the Boston area were exposed to these analysts. Many were thereby influenced to understand and use an analytic viewpoint, to go into analysis or to apply to the institute for training. Boston is unique in that no city compares as a university city, and the university psychiatric programmes were for many years psychoanalytic in nature (Myerson interview 1982).[5] The unusual degree of involvement of Boston analysts with hospitals has been an important part of Boston psychoanalytic culture for decades. It provides one reason for the remarkably good reputation for decades of psychoanalysis in Boston medical circles.[6] However, those who left the BPSI to form PINE believed that the achievement of such extensive community involvement was at the expense of a focus on analytic work. Whereas in New York during the 1970s the prototypical analyst would analyse ten hours a day, the work of the Boston analyst was more varied with greater involvement with the community and universities. Many Boston analysts saw their patients early and late in the day to engage in administrative or scholarly activities at the medical school in the middle of the day (Rosett interview 1981; Gifford interview 1992).[7]

According to the BPSI Constitution, the society is responsible for all functions except for the educational programmes concerned with training, teaching and graduating candidates. The Education Committee under the aegis of the Boston Psychoanalytic Institute carries these out.[8] Paul Myerson, president of the BPSI 1972–74, expressed the prevailing view of the ramifications of the BPSI structure: 'If the BPSI had been set up originally as a totally autonomous institute not beholden in any way to the society, the institute could have done what it pleased.' Most psychoanalytic institutes are like the New York Psychoanalytic Institute where the institute is separate from the society and is not overseen by it. However, the BPSI was set up in terms of the Boston Charter in which the membership prevailed and the institute was under the aegis of the membership organisation, the society. Consequently, the society could at least theoretically 'stack the Education Committee' if it needed to overpower the institute at any time. In Myerson's view,

> If you have an autonomous institute, what price do you pay in terms of its being moulded in the character of a few people who have hidebound and never changing ideas about who should teach and what psychoanalysis is all about? It's the advantages of democracy over dictatorship.

There are some advantages to dictatorship at certain times but there are some great disadvantages. The disadvantage here would have been that it would have made many disgruntled people in Boston. Which I think would have influenced the practice not only of analysis but psychotherapy in Boston and would probably have led people away from the BPSI. (Myerson interview 1982)

Thus, although the society and institute were part of a unitary institution for much of the BPSI's history, in reality the BPSI was under the direction of the institute which the Committee of Training Analysts controlled. Since the system of checks and balances made the institute constitutionally and financially answerable to the society, the institute could be challenged if the membership felt it necessary.

Many who remained in the BPSI viewed the problems that led to the split along these lines, as resulting from a struggle between democracy and autocracy, between heterodoxy and orthodoxy. However, those who left saw such divisions as the wrong cut – from their perspective, autocracy was not the major or relevant issue. However, they saw other issues as important, such as commitment to psychoanalysis as a large part of analysts' professional lives, expertise and standards, and the optimal size of an institute.

It would be simplistic to see the split as about democracy versus autonomy, where the democrats remained in the BPSI and the autocrats split off to form PINE. Still, it is important to note that the unified structure of the BPSI (along with the Los Angeles Psychoanalytic Society and Institute) occupies one end of the spectrum of the relation of society to institute. Most psychoanalytic societies and institutes are more or less separate entities but the formal relationships vary greatly within the APsaA. While the institute is responsible for analytic education (including the appointment of training analysts), the society acts is a forum for scientific presentations and debate with little power over training. The Chicago Psychoanalytic Institute, with its own large budget and lay Board of Trustees, is a distinct entity, whereas in Boston and Los Angeles the society and institute are components of the same institution. While separate from the society, the New York Psychoanalytic Institute relies on the membership of the society, which is coincident with the membership of the institute. The greater the separation of society and institute, the greater the institute's power and autonomy. Training analysts and appointed officers such as director or dean have more power in relatively autonomous institutes.

Considering the differences between how an organisation is formally supposed to run, how it appears to work, how it does work and how it should work are essential to understanding it.[9] Psychoanalytic organisations have a generic problem: society and institute aims may and often do conflict. As we have seen, the society acts as a forum of ideas and advances the aims of its members whereas the institute's aim is educational. The educational aims of the institute are often tainted by and conflated with the power requirements of the particular group or clique that controls it. This is widespread since no clear, public procedural protocols operate about the definition of psychoanalytic terms and practices, the aims of psychoanalytic education, or the nature of psychoanalytic institutions. Given such ambiguities, society members suspect the 'expertise' of the training analysts and other institute members. Power plays dominate when definitions are unmoored and ambiguity is endemic.

The training analysts who controlled the Education Committee of the institute directed the educational arm of the BPSI, the institute. That committee, consisting exclusively of training analysts, and its sub-committees directed the training of all candidates (Mann pers. comm. 1995). The training analysts' power in performing institute functions in Boston came to be increasingly resented by the membership. It angered the ordinary members that as members of the Education Committee the training analysts elected themselves on to the Students' Committee which governed candidate promotions and graduation (Gifford pers. comm. 1995d). As early as 1958, there was unrest that the society was the 'tail of the kite'. By the 1960s an unusual apathy prevailed within the society/institute which was under the *de facto* rule of an oligarchy of training analysts, this within a formal structure in which the society – and thus the members – officially owned the institute.

However, significant divisions within the training analyst group filtered down to the membership. These divisions were epitomised by the deep personal rivalries between two powerful and eminent Viennese émigré couples, close to Freud, Edward and Grete Bibring and Felix and Helene Deutsch. From the 1930s into the 1960s when a new generation of Americans took over (Modell 1994, pp. 358–9; Valenstein interview 1996; Silverman interview 1996), these two coteries dominated the Education Committee. The American analysts became identified with one camp or the other (Valenstein interview 1996). Sam Silverman, who trained at the BPSI in the late 1940s, recalled:

> When it came to how things were to be taught, the training analysts and the faculty knew it. You were listening to 'This is the wisdom, this is what is to be done, this is how you think.' They didn't say this but the people next to Freud directly or indirectly, people who were in Europe

or people who came from this country to Europe got the 'word' and were not easily challenged. I think this was true of both sides. We know what psychoanalysis is, we will teach it to you and presumably, you then carry the torch, you become the keeper of the flame. (Silverman interview 1996)

The first society president trained after World War II, James Mann, was elected in 1964. All previous presidents were long-time members who had been involved with the BPSI since the early 1930s. They included refugee European analysts close to Freud. According to James Mann, they 'were the "senior" analysts, very much admired and very much in control of both society and institute' (Mann pers. comm. 1995). The BPSI's increasing size meant relatively fewer faculty positions and cases to go around. Inevitably, this stymied careers. Given the inherent tensions of the BPSI's unified structure, the eruption of conflict was inevitable at some point.

For the BPSI and American psychoanalysis in general, the 1940s and 1950s were halcyon years, 'the years that were fat', where analysts chaired major psychiatry departments.[10] Psychoanalysis was losing its pre-eminence among American mental health professions by the late 1960s with the introduction of more effective psychotropic drugs and the development of alternative therapies, Moreover, the research and training grant pool within NIMH was drying up – the decline in grants was felt especially keenly in Boston with its academic focus.[11] Though still the 'finishing school' for a psychiatric career, psychoanalysis was becoming less popular with patients who were beginning to opt for the newly available shorter and less expensive treatments. However, the BPSI's size was increasing: the membership grew from 68 in 1953 to 144 in 1963, reaching 250 members by 1973 (Gifford 1984, p. 7). Thus, there was a larger pool of analysts to treat a smaller group of suitable patients. Analysts found it difficult to get enough analytic patients in the relatively small cities of Boston and Cambridge.[12]

This reflects a general problem of psychoanalytic institutes – how many analysts should be trained? While larger candidate numbers bring more training cases in the short term (first to those training analysts on the top of the 'food chain'), a larger membership ultimately meant smaller slices of a smaller analytic cake. Greater competition for a diminishing market meant that the APsaA's expansionist approach to attract more students became self-defeating.[13] The nature and size of the psychoanalytic market often shifts over the decade between the beginning of a candidate's analytic training and graduation.

This is just what happened for those graduating from the BPSI in the late 1960s. Understandably, analysts did not readily relinquish a profession that demanded a further ten years' study beyond their psychiatric licensing. So by the late 1960s there was no longer room for analysts in the many teaching hospitals in the Boston area including the seven associated with the Harvard Medical School, Tufts, Boston University, state hospitals and the Veterans Administration. As analysts began to turn inwards to the BPSI to find the intellectual and social satisfactions increasingly denied them outside, they became involved in what in 1973 Sanford Gifford saw to be 'a conventional power struggle in which we must fight to keep or to gain our fair share in the training functions of the institute' (Gifford 1973). As Gifford put it,

> Attempts were made to re-establish within our sheltering walls the clinics, teaching and research facilities, and the professional camaraderie we had previously enjoyed outside. A new reformist spirit arose, motivated by a variety of factors: by a yearning for professional solidarity, by economic anxieties related to our increasing size, and by a need to re-establish our identity as analysts. These needs were expressed in various proposals to broaden the scope of society activities, to reduce the traditional oligarchy of the Education Committee, and to make the position of faculty and training analyst more accessible to our membership. (Gifford 1984, p. 7)

Candidate numbers, which exceeded those in any other APsaA institute, brought significant faculty burdens of administration, committee meetings, and more office staff. In February 1970, the Education Committee appointed an Ad Hoc Committee to study the setting up of a deanship to lessen the burden. The proposal was for making the training programme more like a graduate school, humanising it by paying more attention to students (Mann pers. comm. 1995).

The Deanship

On March 10, 1971, the society agreed to fund the position of dean in what the BPSI president described as a 'spirit of unanimity' (Daniels 1971). James Mann was approached to take up that position to devote ten to fifteen hours per week for a modest salary. Mann said he agreed

> out of the feeling that this was a genuinely progressive step since it indicated that the Senior Faculty, which now included other post World War II trained analysts, recognised that there could be ways of reducing the burden and making for smoother function of the institute. I did not

recognize that this was to be done without diminishing by one iota any of the control and direction of the faculty. (Mann pers. comm. 1995)

In the words of the president, Ed Daniels, Mann's appointment as dean was 'hailed'. The appointment was on a two-year experimental basis from September 1971 with the task, according to Daniels, of 'coordinating the academic, intellectual, and scientific affairs of the society' (Daniels 1971).

Mann decided to devote most of his first year to the student body.[14] What he learned was disturbing. By October 1972 he could say: 'For most candidates, the period of studenthood (a period ranging from five to ten years) was markedly colored by fear and by a conception of the institute as some kind of mysteriously functioning organization which enhanced the sense of fear and, in some instances, bordered on paranoid considerations.'[15] Mann encountered

> a persistent fear that expressions of dissent or of searching questions were not only taboo but that there was some kind of reporting apparatus so that everything became known to the 'institute' with the dangers of setbacks in the progress of the candidate. No one seemed to know just how and by what rules the institute functioned so that the question of fairness was always raised. (Mann pers. comm. 1995)

Not surprisingly, many institute graduates were angry and resentful. They still felt like strangers after many years in the institute. They did not know how to become involved in teaching or other institute or society activities. In his report, Mann added: 'The training program infantilizes candidates and candidates make their own contribution to that. The anonymity and ambiguity of the institute procedures and judgments add to the sense of infantilization as well as to a suspicious and even paranoid one ... the institute is sorely in need of humanization.' Mann felt that this statement

> was received by some of the training analysts as severe criticism of their analytic excellence. I refused to accept all the candidates' criticisms as manifestations of their neurosis but [it was true] that we analysts in our organization do little to relieve those aspects of their difficulties that were real. The implication seemed clear that, in my opinion, the need of the 'senior' analysts was to maintain rigid control over every aspect of the institute within the senior group to the exclusion of the aspiring 'children' including graduates. (Mann pers. comm. 1995)

As Mann put it in 1972, 'It is the training analyst who proposes, prohibits, promote, and disposes. The general atmosphere of the time encourages rebellion, protest, and anti-establishment sentiment so that the desire for openness and less intrusiveness promotes strong feeling about the encrusted authoritarian establishment, the "Training Analyst Club"' (report quoted in Engle 1996, p. 32). At that point, according to Mann, some members of 'the senior group rose in protest, expressed unusual anger and bitterness toward me. A number of meetings were held for all society/institute members to discuss my report. Emotions ran high and the senior analysts demanded my resignation. I agreed believing that this would end the controversy' (Mann pers. comm. 1995).

Some saw Mann's personality as the problem. They saw him as remote, as having the wrong kind of personality for the job (Gifford pers. comm. 1995b). Valenstein, for example, maintained that 'the major organizational mistake was choosing Jim Mann to be dean' (Valenstein interview 1996). However, according to Gifford, 'even if he had been a different personality I think it still wouldn't have worked' (Gifford interview 1981). Mann riled many analysts personally, and his authoritarian behaviour alienated others further. The 1972–74 president, Paul Myerson, recalled Mann acting inappropriately by not consulting members about anything he did (Myerson interview 1982). Mann undermined the autonomy of subcommittees when a battle over turf developed between the new Coordinating Committee (that included the dean and subcommittee chairs) and the Education Committee. BPSI analyst Ralph Engle noted, 'A storm of protest arose in the Education Committee over the right of the Coordinating Committee to make decisions without its consent. At the root of the uproar was a decision to have all communications to candidates be sent from the dean, who was perceived as usurping the Education Committee's power' (Engle 1996, p. 32). That all correspondence had to bear the dean's signature was, in Arthur Valenstein's view, 'just like being back in the army, which is "By order of the Commanding Officer, Colonel so-and-so". We spent too much time in the military to stand for that sort of thing. He added insult to injury.' Mann's authoritarianism was odd, given his concern about the lack of democracy at the BPSI (Valenstein interview 1996). Although these actions by the Coordinating Committee were finally rescinded and the power and autonomy of the Education Committee restored, as Engle put it, this 'also led to divisiveness within it, as well as between the committee and the dean' (Engle 1996, p. 32).

In his hamfisted way, Mann had tried to break the *de facto* power of the Education Committee over the unitary society/institute. But who had the right to power? Should it have been the 'people', that is, the membership of the society that supported institute activities, or the faculty of training analysts who expected autonomy as authorised 'experts' in the area?

During 1973, Mann talked with many dissatisfied society members, particularly those middle-aged members who had not made it to training analyst status. This group was mobilised against the training analysts who were seen to hold on to unduly high standards and control of the institute. So great was the opposition to the mobilisation of this group that Education Committee members from all sides reached a consensus that Mann should not continue as dean.

Mann's efforts rebounded when he tried to assert his authority against that of the Education Committee, the body that appointed him. In 1973, the Education Committee approved the recommendation of an ad hoc institute committee to study the functioning of the deanship chaired by Paul Myerson.[16] They recommended that the two-year experiment of the part-time deanship be discontinued. The Education Committee had recommended the establishment of the deanship before they had 'worked through the ambiguities inherent in the introduction of an important new position into so complicated an organization as the Society/Institute'. The Ad Hoc Committee recommended 'an interruption to the office while its functions and structure were further evaluated' (Myerson 1973a). Myerson told the members that the Ad Hoc Committee's recommendation to interrupt the deanship was based on 'the considerable strain that had developed within the Education Committee' since the creation of the deanship had done 'more harm than good'. It was essential to have an evaluation period where 'new, and hopefully, more structured ground-rules' could be formulated and time allowed for the escalating polarization to subside. While this did not imply abolition of the deanship, a 'cooling off' period was required for a new committee to make recommendations (Myerson 1973b). After informing Mann of the decision not to continue his position, Myerson announced it to the society through the *President's Newsletter* on May 24, 1973.

Most members were not impressed. Gifford recalled that the decision was seen as 'an outrageous act of abusive power by the Education Committee' (Gifford interview 1982). The leading society activist during that period, Leonard Friedman, regarded the manner in which the suspension of the deanship was presented as 'immensely oligarchic and autocratic'. Friedman recalled that the Education Committee 'rather arbitrarily decided that they were going to fire the dean even though the membership in the majority supported the deanship being continued. That was the last straw in terms of the high-handedness of the Education Committee.' Friedman met with other society members to consider future action (Friedman interview 1981). Myerson recalled that 'people got very, very angry indeed' about such a *fait accompli*. The society seemed set on a collision course with the training analysts. Some members suggested that *everybody* should be a training analyst, some that nobody should be a training analyst for more than five years (Myerson interview 1982). The furore released the pre-existing tensions between society members and the Education Committee.

At the next business meeting of the BPSI on June 13, 1973, many members voiced their dismay at what they saw as the autocratic fashion in which Mann was fired. That meeting asked the Education Committee to reconsider its decision but this was to no avail. The Education Committee's action underscored society members' experiences of exclusion from institute activities (Myerson interview 1982). In his *President's Newsletter,* Myerson emphasised that, as was the case with similar tensions between society and institute in six other institutes he had site-visited,

> the heart of the matter is the *question of appointment to training analyst status*. Who is to be appointed, who makes the selection, and how? I do not mean that this is the only source of the tension, but I do believe that unless there is open and constructive discussion of this matter, the tension between the society and the institute will remain unresolved ... To put the debate in a nutshell, it is a question of 'maintaining quality control' vs. 'opportunity for development'. (Myerson 1973b; original emphasis)

Myerson suggested that three business meetings in the coming academic year be devoted to discussing this issue (ibid.).

Society Unrest and the Reformist Movement

The suspension of the deanship became the focus for protest as factions crystallised around Mann, in a curious coming together of the dissatisfied of all ages (Gifford interview 1982). In Gifford's view, the termination of the deanship signalled an implied vote of no confidence in the fruits of the deanship in the education of candidates (Gifford interview 1982). However, the economic and professional dissatisfactions, which gave rise to the deanship, had not been solved and the ramifications of the deanship were leading towards still further polarisations.

Gifford recalled meetings where Leonard Friedman acted as a 'tribune of the people'. A JD (doctor of law) as well as an MD, Friedman was, in Gifford's view, an 'arch-legalist', 'litigious and the master of parliamentary procedure'. According to Gifford, Friedman alienated many analysts because he appeared to be the fanatical leader of the anti-Education Committee faction (Gifford pers. comm. 1995a; 1995c; Gifford interview 1982). Myerson recalled Friedman as 'a very forceful person who would hold up extreme positions'. Friedman upset significant training analysts who worked very hard only to be told that they were feathering their own nests. Myerson added:

> Obviously, they're going to be very angry. They felt unappreciated. The other group felt that they weren't appreciated either – nobody had promoted them. It's more Marxist than Freudian in its origins. At least it was more due to economics or system difficulties with the haves and the have-nots and I think that always leads to a certain strain in an institution. (Myerson interview 1982)

Although Friedman had not previously been much involved in society activities, he now represented the reformist members of the society. A sizeable minority shared his specific concerns while others had specific grievances. Friedman estimated that of the two hundred and fifty members there was a nucleus of fifty to sixty reformists. Another twenty showed some sympathy, while 60–70 per cent were uncommitted. Friedman viewed the 'basic stifling force' in the BPSI as 'the way the Education Committee was chosen, and the way they chose training analysts, which seemed to me totally oligarchic and doctrinaire. Although scarcely the model of a democratic institution, the governance of the university would be a better model. I thought the Education Committee ought to be elected by a majority of the society' (Friedman interview 1981). He proposed an elected Education Committee of forty members as a minimal contribution to righting these structural problems (Friedman 1974). However, he would like to have changed the structure of the BPSI by taking the training analysis function away from the institute. This would have allowed candidates to choose any reputable member for their personal analysis. That analyst would never be contacted for a report on the candidate. The Education Committee would make its decision solely on the candidate's performance in seminars and supervised analyses (Friedman interview 1981). At the time, many younger members wanted a nonreporting training analyst policy according to which the candidate's training analyst would not take part in the deliberations of the Students' Committee nor be consulted by it about that candidate's progress.[17] Friedman knew his proposal was bound to upset 'the establishment' who urged withdrawal of a constitutional amendment he submitted to that effect.[18] According to Friedman, the leadership did not want the issue to come to a vote at such an emotional time.

Instead of pushing the amendment to a record vote, Friedman proposed that the BPSI meet as a Committee of the Whole to consider all views. A series of both small group and plenary discussions about training analyst status and related issues resulted. Friedman dropped his proposal when it became clear after some months that his position did not command sufficient support. For the amendment to pass, a two-thirds majority vote was required after discussion at two society meetings (Friedman interview 1981). Many proposals for selection and appointment of training analysts were debated. The meetings urged reform of the structure of the institute and the democratisation of the Education Committee (Myerson 1973c; Gifford interview 1982). The debates brought the confrontation between society and institute to a head as the interests of the members who felt disenfranchised clashed with those of some of the training analysts.

Over the next several months, training analyst Bob Gardner (who was to become the leader and spokesperson of the group that split) emerged as speaking for what was generally viewed as the more conservative view, hinting that he had some entirely new alternative proposals. However, according to Friedman, Gardner did not reveal his position until the training analysts split. 'Evidently, the alternative proposal was for the split, but he presented it at the time in a very ambiguous way.' In December 1973 a committee consisting of the Education Committee representatives, the reformists and the uncommitted middle, was established to discuss proposals for change and evolve solutions to the society/institute antagonisms. This process resulted in the majority eventually rejecting Friedman's radical proposal that everyone should become a training analyst. James Mann said it would lead to chaos. The Education Committee denied that democratic procedures were appropriate to a psychoanalytic institute. They saw the institute as a hierarchy of expertise: the training analysts group had special knowledge on which they based their decisions and should not be subject to the decision of others who were not privy to that knowledge. The control of important information by a minority was, in Friedman's view, anathema to democratic values (Friedman interview

1981; Myerson interview 1982). It 'violates the peer structure of our group', Friedman argued, to assign responsibility for all educational activity to the 9 per cent of the membership who were training analysts.

> The lack of objectively specified standards, the lack of objectively specified training standards, the lack of an established training procedure for those wishing to prepare for the work of doing training analyses, the attitude of secrecy about these matters – all are more appropriate to a club than to a scientific body. (Friedman 1974)

The January 1974 minutes of a small discussion group of the Committee of the Whole expressed the concerns of the time:

> There is a sense of malaise ... there is a sense that there are two classes of membership in the society, with one class being relegated to the category of second class citizens ... A small, self-perpetuating segment of the society controls the affairs of the society through the Education Committee, as virtually all significant policy decisions are subsumed under the heading of 'educational matters'. (Boston Psychoanalytic Society 1974, January 2)

Although some training analysts would make only minor concessions, Myerson remembered Gardner as being more flexible. However, the society was not impressed with a report in which Gardner tried hard to draw up rules giving more power to the society but keeping the power on institute matters within the training analysts' group. Gardner and Samuel Kaplan proposed greater separation of institute and society (Gardner and Kaplan 1974). According to Myerson: 'This was, however, only after there had been many meetings. We were meeting practically weekly and I was getting all kinds of phone calls and pressure from various groups. I managed to keep my cool very well but come weekends I'd have dreams of beating people up' (Myerson interview 1982).

The society's rejection of Gardner's report provided, in Myerson's words, 'the basis of the split'. Nothing had been resolved from the many meetings of members with the Committee of Training Analysts. Dissatisfied that the society refused to leave the educational role to the institute, Gardner and others took the matter back to the Committee of Training Analysts (Myerson interview 1982). On April 4, 1974, the Committee of Training Analysts endorsed a proposal by Rolf Arvidson, Malvina Stock and Bob Gardner to appoint its own subcommittee to explore the option of two institutes in one society. On May 23, the Committee of Training Analysts discussed the report of the subcommittee and rejected the option as unfeasible.

Then, in an extraordinary move, the establishment decided to bail itself out and leave when it found itself unable to win. On May 28, 1974, five leading training analysts announced their plans to form a new institute in a letter to the president of the BPSI. 'This institute', they wrote, 'will be small and independent and will evolve in the direction of a full-time academic organisation. A number of innovations in analytic education are contemplated. This institute is intended to be complementary rather than competitive' with the BPSI and they hoped to cooperate with and remain members of the BPSI (Arvidson et al. 1974). Five analysts were necessary to create a new institute since the APsaA stipulates that an institute cannot operate without at least five bona fide recognised training analysts. These analysts (who became known as 'the Boston Five') were Bob Gardner, Ed Daniels, Malvina Stock, Rolf Arvidson and Sam Silverman. The BPSI was apprised of the letter of intent to the APsaA to form the Psychoanalytic Institute of New England East (PINE).

The idea for a split had come about from discussions within the training analyst group (Gardner interview 1996). Gardner emerged as their representative since he was an articulate, eloquent thinker with strong ideas (Silverman interview 1996; Gardner interview 1996). Those who left had close connections with the Bibrings (Silverman interview 1996). A meeting of the Committee of the Whole on May 29 was told that having rejected the 'two institutes in one society' proposal, these five analysts were organising a new, small, autonomous institute outside of BPSI. 'As might be expected, this last communication was followed by a strong negative reaction from many of the members present', wrote Arthur Valenstein in his first *President's Newsletter* two days later. 'The atmosphere was highly charged emotionally and, as I see it, the fact that a good many of the comments were critical and castigating did not help matters either.' A psychoanalytic scholar, Valenstein made a 'plea for moderation and objectivity, the time for fault-finding and "the casting of stones" should best be past' (Valenstein 1974). This would not be heeded.

The Split

When the Boston Five announced their intention to leave to the training analysts Committee on May 28, 1974, Gardner expressed the hope that the other training analysts would join them in forming their own institute. The reasons given were the irremediable tensions and fighting in an acrimonious atmosphere together with the view that the best educational procedures occurred with a small group of dedicated analysts who devoted most of their time to thinking and working within the psychoanalytic field. Implicit in this, Myerson later suggested, was the view that those within the training analyst group who held major academic positions within psychiatry departments (such as Myerson who was Chairman of Psychiatry at Tufts) were diluting psychoanalysis in Boston. Some of those who split felt that the BPSI members diluted Freud and psychoanalysis (Schwaber interview 1992; Valenstein interview 1996). That new report was then brought to the society whose members though outraged pleaded for these analysts to stay. They dropped the more radical demands including the proposal that everybody become a training analyst.

However, society members had understandable complaints about the institute's sometimes very high-handed and autocratic administration. Myerson recalled that no matter what the quality of teaching was, there was a tendency to prevent others becoming involved in the education of candidates. According to Myerson, the institute attempted to control the nature of the society's activities, taking a dim view of the extension courses and clinics society members desired (Myerson interview 1982).

The society/institute discord was reflected in a conflict within the training analyst group. There the battle was between those wanting to continue to function within the relative autonomy of the institute and those wanting a greater degree of society participation in institute matters. Myerson recalled that about half of the training analysts decided to go with the secessionists while the other half, who thought the troubles were exaggerated, decided to stay.

Could the BPSI leadership have averted the level of polarisation that eventually resulted in the split? A senior candidate at the time, Robert Pyles, considered that the split could have been prevented had the BPSI leadership assumed a 'real leadership position' during the anti-authoritarian era of the early 1970s. The lack of such leadership left the field open to others, such as Friedman, to act as spokesman for an important part of the society. For Pyles, 'There was no way to negotiate with him in a meaningful way. There was a real breakdown' (Pyles interview 1992).

Like a couple unable amicably to agree to disagree while facing a painful divorce, there was intensity in the uncontrolled aggression. On the one hand, the institute secessionists held that psychoanalytic standards were being eroded and that the BPSI should be more focused on psychoanalysis. On the other hand, society members wanted more democracy and more for themselves. They wanted less oligarchic, authoritarian and rigid control of education, access to power, to training analyst status and referrals, the maintenance of ties with academic psychiatry and more involvement with the outside community.

The unrest came from middle-aged members; for graduates the debate was very much an economic question (Myerson interview 1982). A burgeoning membership and declining patient numbers per analyst together with a greater focus on the BPSI as a source of referrals brought increasing pressure on the generation controlling the institute to pass the baton on to the next generation by broadening access to training analyst status and institute power. At a time when analysts who were not training analysts had trouble finding two or three patients, training analysts could count on having at least two who were trainees. That obvious differential made for more envy, jealousy and rancour bringing back the focus on the training analyst as the top of the food chain (McLaughlin interview 1994a). There was a question of supply and demand. Maintaining that training analyst status was a major dividing issue as it is elsewhere Arthur Valenstein recalled that there were a limited number of training analysts in an organisation largely centred on the institute. Nor did the society provide much opportunity. A great deal of restlessness, anger and frustration emerged from society members who in Valenstein's view had 'no place to go at the institute either except to vent their spleen' (Valenstein interview 1996). He recalled:

> There was resentment of the old timers who came from Vienna and were our teachers. But that wasn't expressed by the group at large. It was hidden behind an honouring, veneration and, when they began to pass on in the 70s, idealisation of them. And the mantle fell on my generation. Then what was really owed the old timers as well as the new timers came on as an incipient storm. I think the rage and hostility belongs all the way back and not in the present. But it fell out in the present right then and there because then the idealisation in respect of their peers needn't be maintained – they were not the older generation. They were continuing in the same mode and that was no longer accepted. Then people came into positions who were also very angry. Like Jim Mann – totally tactless, confrontational and inflammatory. Enlisting some of the most inappropriate people behind him, some with dubious character, some with their own crusade like our lawyer Friedman. They used him. They got what they wanted, which was to take over and precipitate a split. (Valenstein interview 1996)

Maintenance of 'standards' resulted in restricting involvement in teaching candidates and, more importantly, stemmed the flow of new analysts into the training analyst group. At the December 1974 meeting of the APsaA, several site visitors expressed concern that many of the 'younger' members (in their forties or fifties!) felt no voice or room in the educational structure of the BPSI (American Psychoanalytic Association 1975a).

The split finally occurred when those wanting to form PINE had had enough of wrangling and dissension, enough of the endless haggling and attempts to reorganise the structure of the institute and the society (Gifford interview 1982). Gardner exemplified this understandable position when he asked, 'Can you imagine a busy practitioner having to come home to have supper and go to one crazy meeting after another – at the same time carrying out usual administrative functions, at the same time dealing with the tensions within any family'?

According to Gardner, some training analysts 'honestly thought just a little more meeting and it will be all right. Others thought, this is already beyond the pale. If this goes any further, it will be totally disruptive, let's stop it while we can. Those were perfectly legitimate differences' (Gardner interview 1992).

In any case, Gardner never thought the idea of a split was intrinsically bad – although that did not mean he was fomenting a split (Gardner interview 1992). After all, what is intrinsically wrong with analysts leaving one institute to form another? The APsaA has always been against splits. Sometimes it might make sense for the APsaA to mediate to find out whether something is easily resolvable. However, if that is unsuccessful, why not simply allow the split? From the PINE viewpoint, theirs was a perfectly rational move and the opposition to it was irrational. The New York–Columbia split in 1946 was strongly opposed yet manifestly turned out well for all concerned. It did not take candidates away from the New York Psychoanalytic Institute but established more faculty positions and a larger pool of applicants. The BPSI–PINE result was finally positive for both institutes and brought about a greater pluralism in the Boston area. It brought about more vacant faculty and organisational positions in what was a very large society/institute.

After the initiation of the split by the Boston Five, others followed within the next few months. These included three analysts who were close to each other socially and professionally – Grete Bibring and Helen Tartakoff who were highly respected older analysts as well as Arthur Valenstein who had very good ties with the older generation (Silverman interview 1996). As society president in the wake of the split during 1974–75 Valenstein attempted to maintain unity but left when the possibilities of constructive working together seemed to have been exhausted. He was strongly sympathetic to PINE making his continued presidency of the BPSI untenable. On March 31, 1975, Valenstein sent a letter of resignation as president to the membership. He wrote that his own views and policies – 'live and let live' in the context of the evolution of two autonomous institutes – were at variance with those of the other BPSI officers (Valenstein 1975). 'I resigned as president because as a matter of ethics I couldn't do otherwise', Arthur Valenstein recalled. 'I didn't trust the motives of people who wanted us to stay. There was no chance for rapprochement. There was too much water under the bridge' (Valenstein interview 1996). A neutral member, Charles Magraw – the first non-training analyst to become president – replaced Valenstein as president (Gifford pers. comm. 1995c; Gifford interview 1996). Understandably, some analysts followed or were sorely tempted to follow their friends and analysts over to PINE.

PINE devised and circulated a position statement to all BPSI candidates at the request of the APsaA and of the BPSI candidates. Within a small institute comprising 'a few candidates and a few teachers in the professional closeness and lively atmosphere of a workshop' PINE envisioned an 'adventure of ideas'. PINE would be devoted to 'shared curiosity and search' and a flexible curriculum would be attuned to individual needs. No doubt referring to what they considered one of the BPSI's failings (faculty involved with psychiatry and teaching hospitals at the expense of their institute work), PINE stated: 'Teachers in PINE will make a central commitment to the practice and study of psychoanalysis and to the activities of PINE. They will make no major commitments to other professional organisations except in respect to carefully selected projects.' Reacting to what they left, the PINE analysts proposed that the administration was to be 'low key' with as few committees and officials as possible (PINE 1974). PINE never bought a building and analysts still vie with each other not to be on committees (Gardner interview 1992). The issue of size was emphasised as a reason for creating a new institute.

> When an organization reaches a certain size and complexity, all growth cannot take place within. There must be a judicious development of new and independent growth in cooperative interplay with the original organization. Such developments are not to be confused with secession or disintegration. (PINE 1974)

Presented in this way, it was not so much a question that the BPSI had disintegrated but that it was too large. PINE was promising to cooperate with the BPSI organisation. No direct reference was made to the problems within the BPSI. While size no doubt involved greater problems (such as greater formality and administration and proportionally fewer faculty positions), deeper issues were at stake.[19]

Both those leaving and those staying had important concerns about the nature of psychoanalytic education. It has been assumed that those leaving were against democracy and openness. Although the PINE analysts stereotyped those remaining as mindless democrats unconcerned with psychoanalytic standards while those remaining mistakenly regarded the PINE analysts as conservative oligarchs, both those who left and those who stayed were all reacting in different ways to the authoritarianism that was so endemic at the BPSI. Many BPSI members were concerned about the power of training analysts while the training analysts who left were worried about the power of a large institute which they saw as so rigidly bureaucratised as to make a challenging student-centred psychoanalytic education impossible.

Gardner epitomised the interest in teaching in a small, intimate environment.[20] As an 'institute without walls', PINE contrasted with the BPSI, which occupied a building with all that this entailed. One of the five, Sam Silverman, maintained that an important part of the reason for the splitting of the Boston Five was that they believed that in contrast to the history of the BPSI where oligarchy ruled, education should be student centred rather than training analyst centred. Silverman wanted to form PINE for the purpose of 'open-ended discussion I felt was not possible at BPSI. No limits, no fears, allowing one to speak out about what one thought without expectation of recrimination or bad mouthing. Too much politics – there is always politics in an organisation but too much is another matter' (Silverman interview 1996).

PINE applied to the Board on Professional Standards of the APsaA on June 24, 1974, for provisional affiliation. For most of the remaining year, there was little discussion; many did not believe that anything would happen yet the silence from PINE over much of that period hardened the lines of bitterness (Gifford pers. comm. 1995c).

It was a three-stage battle. First, there were the protracted deliberations of the Committee of the Whole of the BPSI, in which the reformers battled the Old Guard. Second, the Boston Five wanted to leave, form an institute and be recognised, and the mainstream of the BPSI did not want to let them go. Third, the split was finalised after an APsaA committee visit to Boston and battles within the APsaA (Gifford interview 1996).

Gifford recalled the stages in his own reactions while he was an elected non-training analyst member of the Education Committee. Initially, when the Boston Five decided to leave he did not like the fact that it was so divisive. Then he felt 'good riddance and only wished that Friedman and half a dozen of his closest allies would do the same' so that the majority would be left in peace (Gifford 1974c).[21] Gifford began to see PINE as 'a possibly interesting experiment' in September when Gardner proposed dual membership. Gardner maintained that they were not so much withdrawing as offering an additional, specialised form of teaching for the very small numbers that wanted it. Gifford began to see PINE as 'different from the usual vertical split that has occurred in so many other psychoanalytic institutes and that Boston was always regarded as uniquely virtuous (and a bit snobby about it) in having escaped'. While the BPSI may have been too small for a split into halves, 'perhaps a tiny pseudopod could withdraw itself, partially separate, and still keep in open communication with the parent cell' (Gifford 1974c).

During the last months of 1974, PINE began to set up its faculty. Inviting Sanford Gifford to join the PINE faculty, Gardner wrote that PINE was an 'exciting venture' and that participation in its faculty would not preclude involvement with the BPSI. 'Most of the faculty of the new institute will serve in both institutes, and we look forward to cooperation and creative exchange between the two organizations.' Gardner maintained: 'We can build a small, first-rate psychoanalytic organization without political and hierarchical hoopla' (Gardner 1974). Gifford was glad to accept: 'The idea of a small, friendly group, with a minimum of committee-work appeals to me' (Gifford 1974c). The contrast with the BPSI could not have been stronger. Even the BPSI candidates of the period felt alienated and echoed the feelings in the New York Psychoanalytic Institute around the same time. Instead of using 'we' language, the BPSI candidates used 'them versus us' language. During a period when training analysts still reported on the progress of their analysands, candidates did not trust the privacy of their communications, creating endless paranoia (Boston Psychoanalytic Society 1974, January 7). PINE, it must be remembered, was not a society but an institute, a teaching institution with an invited or appointed faculty. (PINE's society remained the BPSI until 1989 when its own society was formed.) PINE could have started larger but wanted to remain small and intimate. PINE later discouraged some others including training analysts from joining (Gedo pers. comm. 1994). However, PINE's promise not to 'deplete the ranks or resources' of BPSI 'now or tomorrow' was not strictly fulfilled since half of the BPSI training analysts left for PINE (Engle 1996, p. 32), although their ranks were quickly replaced in the BPSI. PINE was right about its further claim: 'it is and will remain small' (PINE 1974).

The BPSI continued to fight the PINE secession. On December 8, 1974, most of the officers of the BPSI telegrammed the Board on Professional Standards urging delay of consideration of the affiliation of PINE to allow further time for the resolution of the conflict without a split. 'Approval will obliterate any possibility of reconciliation', they wrote. They feared 'irreparable' damage to the BPSI from the new institute and requested 'the help of The American to explore and resolve the differences' (BPSI 1974). This was followed up by a letter with sixty-one signatures which included those of eight training analysts and twenty members of the faculty, petitioning delay and the need for negotiation – the then president, Arthur Valenstein, was not a signatory (Magraw et al. 1974; American Psychoanalytic Association 1975a). The APsaA Board on Professional Standards accepted both the BPSI's requests, voting to defer the application for provisional status for a new Boston institute until the next meeting of the APsaA in May 1974, as well as accepting the BPSI's invitation for a subcommittee of the board to mediate (American Psychoanalytic Association 1974).

After the December meetings of the APsaA the rancour at the BPSI Education Committee reached such a high level that Gifford was tempted to heed his friend, Arthur Valenstein's advice to any sensible would-be neutral 'to head for the woods'. Further, a fertile soil for rumours was created because Gardner had said little since the application of PINE for APsaA affiliation (Gifford 1975a). Challenged about his silence, Gardner told Gifford that the time had passed for public statements, and that he had been requested by the APsaA's Board on Professional Standards to say nothing until a Visiting Committee had come to Boston (Gifford 1975b). Nevertheless, from Gifford's perspective, the silence 'only intensified the mutual antagonisms and hardened each side into more intransigent positions' (Gifford 1975a). Gifford wrote at the time:

> Personal animosities on all sides had intensified, and the grim, humorless voice of self-righteousness was heard everywhere. A close friend in private might suddenly sound like a Savonarola, or even a Torquemada, at public meetings. Enforced silence and ignorance of current policies from the new institute had made all discussion meaningless or filled with mistrust. I felt personally silenced, when I had always talked freely about my likes and dislikes to friends on both sides. (Gifford 1975b)

The option of two institutes within one society was not viable in the context of the prevalent anger and bitterness. Gifford concluded, 'There is no choice but separation, to be arranged with as much remaining friendliness and civility as we can still muster' (Gifford 1975b).[22]

The McLaughlin Committee

As we have seen, the Board on Professional Standards accepted the urgent request from the officers of the BPSI consultation and investigation by a committee of the APsaA's Board on Professional Standards at the December meetings of the APsaA. Consequently, an ad hoc committee of the Board on Professional Standards visited Boston on January 24, 1975 for two and a half days to investigate the possibility of mediation and reconciliation. The committee met with many groups, including the candidates. The BPSI then had a membership of 250 with 125 active participants, including 60 active faculty. The APsaA group was led by Pittsburgh analyst James McLaughlin, then a recent secretary of the Board on Professional Standards. McLaughlin was universally respected for his integrity, independence, thoughtfulness and perspicacity. McLaughlin considered that the increasing personal antagonism and atmosphere of mistrust made any meaningful reconciliation impossible. The committee concluded that the health of psychoanalysis in Boston would be better served if two institutes 'different yet excellent, could eventuate as against the probably corrosive consequences of an attempted forced unity'. It recommended that the Board on Professional Standards acknowledge the inevitability of the split and foster negotiations to find optimal methods of separation and explore 'what could be accomplished in reducing acrimony and fostering decent coexistence' (American Psychoanalytic Association 1975a, p. 874).

The chair of the APsaA's Board on Professional Standards, Joan Fleming, set up the McLaughlin Committee with the express intention of delaying the split and negotiating further. Fleming's approach was to create a communicative educational atmosphere in troubled institutes. However, she miscalculated in choosing James McLaughlin, Carl Adato and Larry Hall as its members, since none of them intended taking the 'inspector-general' approach so characteristic of the Committee on Institutes during that period. However, the members of that committee, who were not friends of the PINE analysts,[23] were convinced that a split was not undesirable and recommended that the APsaA allow a split. 'We came back with the sense that this division was a *fait accompli*. It was like an alienated marriage that had gone so far that a divorce was inevitable. Surely, this is a big enough city that these two organizations can prosper' (McLaughlin interview 1994a).

Fearing destructive local consequences and dreading possible precedent which would create effects nationally, the BPSI strongly disagreed with the consultative committee and instead recommended a five-year moratorium. However, the Ad Hoc Committee maintained that given the existing pain and damage 'there was clearly no solution which could remotely satisfy all concerned'. The group viewed philosophical and educational differences as minor as compared with a crisis brought about by conflict and dissension (American Psychoanalytic Association, 1975a, p. 874). One group portrayed the BPSI as too large for optimal analytic education while the other saw Boston as too small for two institutes. PINE deplored what it saw as the too broad, experimental curriculum, unwieldy size and conglomerate nature of the society and maintained that it had the advantages of smallness, minimal fiscal/administrative outlays and maximal involvement of teachers and candidates. None the less, the BPSI feared damage if some of its best teachers left and that its public image would be compromised. They were afraid that PINE would develop into a significant rival of the BPSI and not remain a small, relatively informal group.[24]

The idea that Boston was not big enough for two institutes was, in Gifford's view, 'hysteria of the silliest kind'. This was not borne out during the next decade in which both institutes prospered. The other fear was that PINE would create dozens of ill-trained training analysts. However, PINE appointed very few training analysts. The great silence created much bad feeling since the silence seemed, in Gifford's words, 'spooky and secretive'. PINE did not answer the question as to what it stood for and represented in detail, making PINE sound more like a philosophical society than a training institute (Gifford interview 1996). Gardner regretted not having been more public about what PINE stood for although he had spoken with many analysts individually about it (Gardner interview 1996). Analysts' fantasies expanded to fill the vacuum.

The APsaA put PINE under the aegis of its Committee of New Training Facilities. The CNTF explored PINE facilities and voted in favour of it after which it went before the Board on Professional Standards. The APsaA had asked PINE to wait for consideration of accreditation as an institute because, according to Gardner, 'it was creating so much storm and upsetting people so much' (Gardner interview 1981). At the May 1975 meeting of the APsaA in Los Angeles, the board gave PINE approval to proceed by a large majority (American Psychoanalytic Association

1975b, p. 875). There was great heat on both sides but most board members were indifferent. A petition was submitted that PINE would destroy the old institute, that PINE was taking the BPSI's best teachers and that the BPSI would be left in chaos. 'We didn't believe that', Gardner asserted. 'We thought they were overestimating what we meant and underestimating what they could do. At this point, I was absolutely incensed, not about the grounds of the controversy but about the notion that one should prevent the development of a new school. That seems to me a little close to book burning when it gets into that' (Gardner interview 1981). There was a fierce debate at the APsaA's Board on Professional Standards in which Gardner won the day for PINE by delivering, as John Gedo recalled, a 'positively Churchillian' rebuttal of the BPSI position. Gardner framed his argument in moral terms of 'academic freedom' (Gedo pers. comm. 1994).

The APsaA performed a pivotal role in allowing the new institute to be affiliated since PINE was the only secession permitted by the APsaA since the era of the 1940s and 1950s splits. The last split was at the Philadelphia Institute in 1956. A precedent could have been created whereby the APsaA would support discontented analysts who wanted to split rather than resolve problems. As we shall see, the APsaA opposed the split in the Los Angeles Psychoanalytic Institute, which occurred not long before PINE, and was near to closing it down. The APsaA did not countenance a later split in the Washington Institute, punishing those trying to leave and has allowed no others to this day.[25]

Why was PINE so special? Abraham Zaleznik thought that if it had not been for highly respected analysts identified with PINE – Bibring and Tartakoff – the APsaA would not have let it happen (Zaleznik interview 1981). Myerson thought the PINE analysts 'were very friendly with some of the people on The American [Psychoanalytic Association (APsaA)] big committees and I think they influenced them. Malvina Stock, Bob Gardner, Valenstein and Tartakoff had many friends in the APsaA and they had been very active there' (Myerson interview 1982). A member of the Boston Five, Rolf Arvidson, agreed with Myerson's view, suggesting that Stock, Valenstein and Gardner were on powerful committees and had powerful friends within the APsaA (Arvidson interview 1982). Gardner disagreed: 'I never had "power" in The American. Neither I nor others in PINE were powerful members of The American. Tartakoff and Bibring were semi-retired analysts' (Gardner interview 1992).

While this was true, another factor was relevant. While Gardner may not have had personal influence with the APsaA, the APsaA leadership had especially good relations with the Grete Bibring–Helen Tartakoff–Arthur Valenstein nexus, who were on the Bibring side of the Bibring–Deutsch rift. (Some believe that the rift was a causal factor in the split, while others do not.) Sanford Gifford commented:

> I think, looking back, that the Deutsch–Bibring rift played little if any part in the split. Its origins were in the early 1940s, and the battle was joined over Deutsch's populist efforts to establish a psychotherapy clinic for veterans and their war-widows, which was opposed by the Bibrings and (probably) Ives Hendrick as *not analysis*. The rift existed, like underwater shoals, only palpable when you strike a rock; most candidates completed their training without being aware of it. However, by the time of the split, Edward Bibring and Felix Deutsch had long been dead. Helene was no longer very active in Institute politics. And Grete Bibring's and Helen Tartakoff's flirtation with PINE was short-lived. (Gifford pers. comm. 1997)

Arthur Valenstein, who was analysed and supervised by Edward Bibring, was respected as a training analyst as he inherited Bibring's mantle as a teacher of theory (Valenstein interview 1996). As chair of psychiatry at Beth Israel, Grete Bibring was Valenstein's chief, and Helen Tartakoff was close to Grete Bibring (Gifford interview 1996). Many in the APsaA would not have lightly rejected an institute proposed by these very senior analysts. On the other hand, Joan Fleming – the then Chairman of the APsaA's Board on Professional Standards – and members of the Board on Professional Standards were influenced by the BPSI's campaign and strongly opposed the split. The independent McLaughlin Committee reported against the position that the APsaA wished it to adopt. It was obviously a complex scenario. Had the McLaughlin Committee recommended otherwise, the split might well not have eventuated. The APsaA was not so much in favour of the PINE option as divided. Whatever the case, a necessary condition for accreditation of the split by the APsaA was that respected analysts were identified with PINE. PINE had seized what Gardner described as a 'rare moment' (Gardner interview 1981).

The BPSI's fears were not warranted. While a number of analysts left, many remained in the BPSI. McLaughlin recalled there being 'no sense of an exodus, of burning bridges behind, and a curse on those behind. I did feel there was more anger towards the PINE group coming from BPSI because of their sense of having their excellence somehow impugned by this designated superior group somehow pulling out. But I think that happens anytime that people get up and split off' (McLaughlin interview 1994a). Members often see their institutes as families, and being left can be viewed as akin to being deserted by a spouse. Although an institute is not a family but a professional organisation, many BPSI members felt a sense of abandonment and betrayal that only began to be healed two decades after the split. Ralph Engle wrote that BPSI's view was that

> the role of The American was crucial and that PINE's friends in The American had made the split possible. BPSI felt betrayed, as The American had seemed to act so uncharacteristically. In similar situations before (and since), it had always played the mediator, working diligently to avert a split or to patch one up before things went too far. (Engle 1996, p. 32)

Apart from the fact that betrayal was a 'two-way street' – those who formed PINE felt betrayed by Jim Mann and other leaders within the BPSI (Valenstein interview 1996) – the 'friends in The American' hypothesis is not borne out by the facts of the particular situation. Since the division seemed to the members of the Committee to be a *fait accompli*, the Committee wanted to help them make it work. Fleming was furious with the three members of the Committee for their recommendation.[26] The McLaughlin Committee's decision in favour of PINE was vital since it had not carried out Fleming's instructions to attempt to conciliate and delay the split.

The McLaughlin Committee listened to different views. The quiet, modulated fashion of the Committee's interviews with many Boston analysts contrasted with McLaughlin's recent experiences with Los Angeles analysts, although the underlying passions in Boston were very strong indeed. McLaughlin thought PINE viewed itself as 'pure in the analytic position' and heard from PINE that the BPSI was getting too big and hardening its administrative arteries. In McLaughlin's opinion, 'BPSI did not want them to split but couldn't stand them any longer and the PINE people wanted out. There was not the destructive *ad hominem* attacking of one another as far as we were hearing, PINE tried to keep it at the level of, "Let's simplify administration, Let's do analysis that is less cluttered with administration"' (McLaughlin interview 1994a).

None the less, McLaughlin was made aware of the level of difficulty in progression through the BPSI to training analyst status. 'The issue of who got to be training analyst and who didn't was as powerful there as it is at every institute in the country.' Nevertheless, as McLaughlin observed, the considerable polarisation meant that, as in any other institute, the focus centred on who has the power to deal with that polarising situation, the training analysts (McLaughlin interview 1994a).

However, some BPSI members who joined PINE became disillusioned with PINE too. Several new members, including Sanford Gifford, Abraham Zaleznik and Ed Daniels, joined at the beginning but left during the first year. Others, including Grete Bibring and Helen Tartakoff, did not resign but withdrew. Gifford concluded: 'I came close to loathing the zealots on both sides' (Gifford pers. comm. 1995b).

One event especially triggered resignations and withdrawals from PINE. This involved Rolf Arvidson (a founder of PINE and one of the Boston Five), an unorthodox and innovative analyst whose approach to analytic education alienated a number of members of PINE.[27] His habit of taking candidates to the opera and the cinema was seen by some as cultic and superficial. He was viewed as polarising, arrogant and over-emphasising innovation. On one occasion, Sanford and Ingrid Gifford brought Helen Tartakoff and Grete Bibring to a meeting at Arvidson's house in February 1976 (Gifford 1976). Gifford recalled:

> Much of the meeting was taken up with Arvidson's effusive account of how he was going to meet all the new candidates and had taken them to see Bergmann's *The Magic Flute* after which they sat on the floor and talked about the psychoanalytic implications of the film. Both Grete Bibring and Helen Tartakoff were very upset by that degree of intimacy with candidates before they even started their training. They brought up some polite questions about that issue and were put down (Gifford interview 1996; see also Gifford 1976).

Those criticising him included Grete Bibring; Helen Tartakoff (who later withdrew somewhat from PINE) Abraham Zaleznik, and Ed Daniels (who later rejoined the BPSI). Arvidson had seen Gifford as a spy for the BPSI telling him that if he had come to wreck PINE he was not welcome. (Gifford 1975d). Though scarcely a mole, Gifford said he 'really welcomed his attack as a useful pretext to drop my link with PINE' (Gifford pers. comm. 1995b).[28]

However, clearly Gardner's was right in contending that Boston psychoanalysis was not harmed by the split. Ultimately, both institutes prospered.[29] The evils so dreaded by the BPSI analysts did not happen. PINE did not burgeon in numbers nor did it create a large number of bogus training analysts – PINE appointed one training analyst in ten years. The BPSI did not become a low standard, populist organisation with no real interest in analysis nor has PINE come to wrangle for domination of the Boston market. In Gifford's view, the BPSI 'probably incorporated most of the reformist points that were brought up by the reformers at the time of the split'. The BPSI was not a narrow training centre but has numerous extension courses. An organisation of people who support the BPSI, 'Friends of the Institute', have four speakers a year. Gifford commented:

> The hope is we would get more patients and it hasn't happened. Scientifically the institute is thriving; in terms of attracting candidates, it has kept up remarkably considering the difficulty of finding analytic patients. Many of the candidates want training and fully accept the idea that they will never have a full-time analytic practice. They may be lucky to have one or two analytic patients. But they really think of analytic training as the best way to get training in psychotherapy. (Gifford interview 1992)

The events of the split show how group paranoia can flourish and dominate, promoting deviance amplification so that the warring groups move further and further apart making the differences irreconcilable. However, as in so many other psychoanalytic controversies, the conflicts ultimately involve anointment – the role of and access to training analyst status. Many of the problems derived from events surrounding the deanship and their sequelae, together of course with the closely related omnipresent issues concerning access to training analyst status.

Behind the Split

Why should disagreements about educational philosophy and size have led to a split?

Almost all those who left told me that ideological factors about differing theoretical approaches were not involved (for example, interviews with Gifford, Gardner, Pyles and Hoffer, 1992). Gardner held that it was a question of the BPSI having passed its optimal size (Gardner interview 1981). Robert Pyles, current president of the APsaA, was president of the Candidates' Council who represented the BPSI candidates in training when it was created in 1972. Pyles reported the bewilderment of his fellow candidates at the time of the split. Although those BPSI candidates who went over to PINE did not do so out of ideological or theoretical differences (Pyles interview 1992), there were major differences in how an institute should be run and its involvement with the community. John Gedo asserted that 'there was a *serious* disagreement about educational philosophy and the very goals of an analytic institute'. In Gedo's opinion, 'Bob Gardner's standards for minimal competence are much higher than those of the group he left behind. The BPSI has always pursued a policy of imperial expansion. Bob was distressed by the plans to emphasise ancillary programmes 'such as extension and community programs' (Gedo pers. comm. 1994).[30]

The lines were by no means rigid. It was never simply populism versus elitism or democracy versus autocracy. Many of those who stayed did not agree with Friedman's group, nor had much sympathy with the idea that institute issues were matters of expertise. On the other side, one of the Boston Five, Rolf Arvidson, was very much a populist, regarded the leading analysts who left as most traditional, and autocratic, 'the ones who want to keep things as they were' (Arvidson interview 1982). Arvidson's reasons for leaving were quite different from those of some of the others. According to Arvidson, the other senior analysts who left

> were quite convinced that the BPSI would go down the drain, that all the radicals would take over. But they would save this group of puritans who would keep the flame burning. In the early 1970s there was a revolution going on in the BPSI – people were speaking up. The people who wanted to change had no ideas. The only thing they wanted to become was training analysts. I said, 'All this fuss just for changing some rules about how to elect training analysts – what an absurdity.' So I couldn't have stayed there with these people and I went with the group that left. What I should have done of course was to just have left, period! (Arvidson interview 1982)

The question of the degree of focus on psychoanalysis concerned standards, since, in the opinion of Gardner and his PINE colleagues, to be a skilful analyst required practising a good deal of psychoanalysis in an ongoing way. The training analysts who were to form PINE considered many of the analysts who worked in hospitals and universities should have been ineligible for training analyst status. This was because they did not devote most of their time to five-times-a-week analysis and analytic theory. Therefore, power should not be in their hands.[31] Secret views as to who was or was not a good analyst influenced responses to the new proposals for playing a greater part in the BPSI (Gardner interview 1981). Those passed over for training analyst status were dissatisfied and joined the rebel group. Many joined who did not want to be training analysts but had other axes to grind. They had not been sufficiently appreciated, had not been asked to give courses, did not like the atmosphere, or their feelings had been hurt (Myerson interview 1982).

Gardner suggested that the curious American anglophilia and anglophobia were important for understanding the split. Gardner saw

Americans as preoccupied with royalty and aristocracy, honouring and imitating royalty, aristocracy and autocracy while fighting against it. 'Independence Day is every day of the year.' However, the problem for Gardner is when that division is fantasy and when it is reality. A small number of analysts started beating the drum against autocracy, 'but it only took a few and it got louder and louder'. Since the BPSI structure gave the society a great deal of control over the institute, there were differences of opinion as to where to put the tilt. According to Gardner, 'We were very big on autonomy for the institute – that was defined by those who liked to define George III against George Washington as "autocracy". They had a vested interest in calling it "autocracy"; we had a vested interest in calling it "autonomy".' The democracy–autocracy axis provides one way of understanding the differences while another is to consider this divide as screening the real differences. But what were the real differences? In Gardner's opinion, they were 'tragic differences in viewpoint that reasonable decent people could not resolve' (Gardner interview 1992).

Indeed, these differences were not resolvable. One group wanted control of the institute in the interests of autonomy, the other in the interests of democracy. The 'democrats' believed oligarchic power, was being exercised, meaning that the gate was being kept shut to society members wanting a say in institute policy or wanting to achieve training analyst status.

The BPSI's increasing size together with its society/institute tensions provided a setting in which established power relations were bound to be challenged. To many society members there appeared no normal and legitimate process whereby the institute leadership would pass on power to the next generation. Many society members saw their analytic career paths as arbitrarily blocked by the institute leadership. The many members who worked (or had worked) in other institutions did not regard their community involvement as detrimental to the BPSI's psychoanalytic mission. For them the bureaucracy, size and numbers of meetings were the price of a fair and legitimate process of running a professional association of equals. What was ultimately at issue was that the lack of common trust that society members could achieve office or training analyst status in a fair manner involved an inevitable power struggle. Society members wanted more power for the society and its members in the institute.

Zaleznik observed that it was

> a rebellion against that kind of authority with certain economic motives, certain professional motives and advancement to becoming training

analysts. I think the training analyst issue is paramount in this whole affair and that the PINE people or those who were associated with them were perceived as not really allowing a younger group to come in and become training analysts and to assume their position. (Zaleznik interview 1981)

Zaleznik suggested one explanation, that Bob Gardner, younger than most of the others who left but highly regarded, was looked upon by the membership as a favoured son. Zaleznik maintained that it involved

> the dynamic of a leader-follower relationship that is inverted in which the favoured child is now supported and put into a very prominent position. And I suspect that in that favoured child syndrome the discontent of the people who felt that they were not being promoted to training analysts would have some connection along those lines. It is a question of the favoured son and those who then feel left out. Those who felt left out started the rebellion but instead of being countered the favourite son took off, taking the parents with him. There was a great period of tragic mourning, of grief at Boston when these people left; they were terribly unhappy and hated to have them go. Those who left were and still are viewed as among the most gifted teachers and it is the feeling of their being negated as progeny. (Zaleznik interview 1981)

This psychodrama on the theme of the favoured son may have exacerbated the anger and envy of many of the younger generation who were in fact being shut out of the institute. Why should they not have been included? The reality of the situation made Gardner a son who really was favoured. The fact that everybody agreed that Gardner was very talented did not make the form of the process any easier to accept (Zaleznik interview 1981). However, of the Boston Five who left, Daniels returned to the BPSI soon, Arvidson left the psychoanalytic field, and Stock died of cancer soon after. Valenstein left only after. It is not at all clear as to who the parents could have been. In Gifford's view, it was not the parents who left to form PINE but 'slightly older brothers and sisters'. Not a power broker temperamentally, Gardner was forced to be the leader because nobody else was. Similarly, Valenstein was no power broker (Gifford interview 1996).

Valenstein maintained that people who wanted to be training analysts who, after the split, became training analysts fuelled much of the discontent (Valenstein interview 1996). Myerson maintained that had they stayed some of the Boston Five would have opposed a number of applications for training analyst status because they did not like the way the applicants talked. 'They made nasty remarks about who was warranted to be a training analyst so that if they had remained then there still would have been the tension. They were right in leaving' (Myerson interview 1982).

The advantages of training analyst status are politically, economically, professionally and psychologically considerable. These include power, prestige, involvement in the institute, increased professional reputation, access to analysing candidates and more referrals. Training analyst status can be the mark of professional success in psychoanalysis, of being a 'genuine analyst', of no longer being excluded from the analytic parental bedroom. The status of training analysts is not simply that they are in a position to exercise political power. Training analysts are often seen to be the 'real' or genuine analysts. They are the analysts of the analysts-in-training and their status is redolent with fantasy and myth (Arlow 1969, pp. 104–20; 1970). Gatekeeping and access to training analyst status were fundamental to the Boston split.[32]

Arvidson maintained that the model that prevailed at the BPSI was of 'the training analyst who has "power". And the fantasy everybody has of course is that something very special goes on between the training analysts. The fact is the only thing that goes on between them is a lot of meetings; they don't have any different ideas' (Arvidson interview 1982).

The way that the BPSI was organisationally set up may have been a reflection of the especially democratic and collegiate traditions in the 'Athens of America'. However, within this formal structure, if the institute was in fact in control, why was this established situation challenged only in the early 1970s instead of earlier? Leonard Friedman told me that he thought that anyone who became an analyst was 'reasonably conservative at the core and to press for change is no likely event'. He saw reverberations of the 1960s when students wanted more of a role than the university governance. 'It was part of the psychological climate that made this seem a reasonable step to take at the time. I am sure it couldn't have happened ten years earlier' (Friedman interview 1981).

When analysts perceive outside problems for psychoanalysis, the threat may be transferred into problems played out within the analytic culture. An ideal, pure and unsullied analytic imago becomes invoked as a solution, which so often has contributed further to the problems of analysts. In a 1974 discussion paper to the BPSI Gifford maintained that the dissatisfaction within the BPSI related to disappointment in psychoanalysis itself becomes 'displaced onto a dissatisfaction with BPSI "structure". We are, in my opinion, barking up the wrong tree, seeking "constitutional" solutions for scientific and personal problems.' For Gifford,

> Besides seeking a sheltering mother in the stony bosom of the BPSI administration, we are also 'blaming mother', in a natural but childlike way, for everything else that has gone wrong in our professional lives. Like Harlow's monkeys, we are seeking comfort from a chicken wire mother (composed of committees and by-laws) who was never intended to provide warmth, and no wonder we are disappointed. (Gifford 1974a)

After the Deluge

PINE remained a small group pursuing their own interests just as they proposed. The result for the BPSI was that it became more democratic with a gradual move toward a better balanced society/institute relation and the Education Committee has more elected members. After the split, many teaching positions and positions of power were opened up, allowing for the appointment of quite a number of new and younger training analysts. But, contrary to fears, there has been no flood. The Students Committee remains composed entirely of training analysts so the more radical proposals have been not implemented (Gifford interview 1982). As we have seen, the peacemaker president of the BPSI (1975–78), Charles Magraw, became the first non-training analyst elected president. The BPSI maintains, as Gifford put it, a 'certain old-time maverick position' among APsaA institutes. It has always had the highest number of academics and the highest number of members who never joined the national organisation and were regarded as malcontents. With time and another generation of analysts, the inter-relation between the BPSI and PINE has become less bitter (Gifford interview 1982; Myerson interview 1982; Holzman interview 1981). PINE leaders made access to training analyst status from the PINE membership easier after a few years. The existence of two institutes has provided more teaching and power positions all told.

Even had the split not occurred, there would have been major reforms within the BPSI, altering the balance between the society and institute (Gifford interview 1992). PINE remained an institute without a society until 1991 when the Psychoanalytic Society of New England East was accepted as an APsaA affiliate.[33] After several months of negotiation, the BPSI and PINE wrote to all their members in July 1995 offering dual membership. For $100 members of one society could join the other society as nonvoting members, attending the other's programmes and meetings (BPSI/PINE 1995). This is at best a symbolic gesture – members of both societies can in any case attend the others' meetings free. Why should they pay for the privilege?

The obvious physical differences show up the attitudinal ones. The BPSI owns a three-storey building (once the residence of a Massachusetts Governor) which houses a library, lecture theatre and seminar rooms for training and research meetings. The BPSI offers significant outreach programmes mainly to mental health professionals.[34]

PINE members have been happy to keep a small institute with no building with its associated administration and costs. As distinct from most other institutes, the lust for power seems notably absent in PINE as 'power' is often thrust upon unwilling office bearers. This small organisation accepts just three or four new candidates annually. If PINE were to acquire a building or become involved in financial constraints requiring assessments from members beyond the faculty, some society/institute tensions would arise. Tensions could also arise because there were not sufficient faculty positions for graduates, but the mix of twenty-five members and twenty-five candidates currently allows enough participation by interested members.

The Psychoanalytic Culture

Another element in understanding these complex events concerns the quality of the psychoanalytic culture itself. Begun as a revolutionary and subversive approach psychoanalysis became a pervasive part of American culture (albeit in bowdlerised form) but lost a great deal of its vitality. Heinz Kohut wrote that 'enthusiasm' for psychoanalytic ideals and the intellectual enterprise was a relatively absent quality in psychoanalysts of the next generation to his own (Kohut 1974, pp. 730–1). Those who left to form PINE not only felt a lack of enthusiasm for psychoanalysis as an enterprise at the BPSI but also enthusiastically rallied around the charismatic figure and winning personality of Bob Gardner (Goldberg interview 1994). According to Chicago self psychologist Arnold Goldberg, who knew the BPSI situation, 'A great deal of the malaise of psychoanalysis is due to our waning enthusiasm brought about by a lack of idealisation of either the theory or the leaders. The turn to personal grandiosity after this failure is responsible for the incredible outbursts of narcissistic rage seen (all too frequently) amongst our colleagues.' Dismissing the blame for the BPSI troubles as related to size, ideology or organisational structure, Goldberg believed that sadly 'it is all hurt feelings and a lack of someone to really look up to' (Goldberg pers. comm. 1994).

Donald Burnham postulated that two currents, orthodoxy and eclecticism, vied with each other in psychoanalytic institutes and served as an impetus for splits. Those with eclectic leanings including those working in universities and hospitals might favour a large, diverse group while the orthodox would rather a 'smaller, more select group' and these issues persist even after the occurrence of the splits (Burnham 1978, pp. 106–7). There is a resonance of this in the Boston split in that those focusing on the wider community remained located in the BPSI while some of those favouring a greater focus on psychoanalysis left.

The analysis of the split demonstrates again the centrality of the issue of training analyst status as fuelling the fires of discontent within psychoanalytic institutions. However, what is the public assessment of 'good' analysis and 'bad'? Institutional and educational decisions so often seem to reduce down to a power struggle and make it difficult to go beyond the private club structure of psychoanalytic institutions into the public realm. However, such a structure raises deeper questions about different conceptions of psychoanalysis and its role, the role of anointment, its relation to the experiential nature of psychoanalysis, and to the lack of a psychoanalytic knowledge base that is agreed to for training as a psychoanalyst. I return to such endemic problems in the concluding chapter.

3 ON THE MAKE: THE CHICAGO PSYCHOANALYTIC INSTITUTE

> It used to be a writer's town and it's always been a fighter's town ... Whether the power is in a .38, a typewriter ribbon or a pair of six-ouncers, the place has grown great on bone-deep grudges ... 'City of big shoulders' was how the white-haired poet put it. Maybe meaning that the shoulders had to get that wide because they had so many bone-deep grudges to settle.
>
> Nelson Algren, *Chicago: City on the Make* (963, p. 62).[1]

The 'Hustler town' Nelson Algren so trenchantly depicted has much in common with the story of the Chicago Psychoanalytic Institute, the only APsaA institute in Chicago. From its beginnings, Chicago's leading psychoanalytic institute was 'on the make'. A crucial structural fault in the Chicago Institute allowed boosterism, authoritarianism and conflicts of interest to flourish. This flaw ultimately brought about the fall of its director as well as a revolution by the members to bring a greater measure of democracy and ethics to the Chicago Institute's structure.

The Chicago Institute was set up in 1932 with a lay Board of Trustees. The board was able to raise a considerable amount of money not only to run the Chicago Institute but also to boost the institute's influence and budget. Frequently, members and officers of the lay board lay on the couches of the Chicago Institute directors and executives who were legally responsible to them.

The power of the Chicago Institute director was enhanced through the ability to direct rewards (grants, position and status), using the largesse brought about by boom times for psychoanalysis. Power was further augmented by an abundance of funds raised by the wealthy and socially prominent members of the Board of Trustees in the period that psychoanalysis had so much cultural capital. The Chicago Institute had the status of a cultural asset for the Chicago intelligentsia as much as it was a therapeutic resource (Kligerman interview 1981). In a city where machine politics is second only to architecture as an art form, the directors of the Chicago Institute increasingly became consummate machine politicians. They managed the board which raised much of the budget, and manoeuvred various institute committees, sections, enterprises and members through a system of favours, privileges and punishments.

The structure of governance placed the director in two-way commerce with the Board of Trustees, at the same time as having real power and authority over institute activities. A corruptive influence became endemic when the director and staff analysed key board members who were supposed to supervise them. The director appointed board members who then acted in a supervisory capacity. The stage was set for conflict since key members of the board wanted control given that they raised most of the sizeable institute budget, and the director, who managed the institute, wanted autonomy and control vested in him. The way out for the director was to appoint board members beholden to him and to manoeuvre the board to his purposes. Many psychoanalytic institutes rely on tuition and the society for most of their upkeep but an institute that wants increasing power and influence in the outside world needs a vehicle to achieve it. The lay board provided autonomy for the institute from the society but was caught up in the politics of an expanding budget and power. Directors (and for many years 'the staff') were perceived as bosses by the membership not because of their personalities but because of the structure of governance. The director had financial power and lawful power over administrative matters without the need for the members' approval. (Members did not select the director but were only part of the selection process since the board made the choice). Thus 'authoritarianism' was set into the structure of the position of director in relation to the membership. The fact that the director was in office for so long meant that the office was often identified with the person. The fact that the director was thought of as not listening to the membership or being authoritarian was not primarily a matter of personality – governance was structurally in the director's pocket.

The system came to an abrupt end when, in 1988, George Pollock, the director since 1971, was accused of behaving unethically in taking donations from a patient, charges he vehemently denied. This denouement eventuated when the system itself was near breaking point. Favours were not as available to be called in at a time when psychoanalysis was losing its allure nation-wide with fewer patients, candidates and funds.

The history of the Chicago Institute also bears some striking similarities to that of Russia. The Chicago Institute, too, had its share of enlightened and not so enlightened despots. After the 1917 Revolution the old czars were replaced with communist ones and it was only with

Gorbachev and afterwards that democracy was realised, albeit falteringly and with many problems of its own. Similarly, the Chicago Institute had a succession of czars, which terminated only with the 1988 departure of George Pollock. Although Pollock himself introduced reforms, his reign was not generically different from those of previous incumbents. It was only with the overthrow of the system itself that real changes were effected. After the revolution after Pollock left there was much suspicion of authority. So many checks and balances were implemented that the functioning of the Chicago Institute became unwieldy.

Early History

There were two short periods of interest in psychoanalysis in Chicago in the early part of the century: in 1911–12, during which Ernest Jones presented a paper to the Chicago Neurological society, and in 1921 when a series of brochures was issued (Grinker 1965; 1995, pp. 155–95).

Chicago's earliest Freudian psychoanalyst, N. Lionel Blitzsten (1893–1952), was founder and first president of the Chicago Psychoanalytic Society. A legendary figure, Blitzsten wrote little but was much quoted by those whom he supervised, analysed and taught. After a few months of psychoanalysis in the 1920s in Berlin, probably with Franz Alexander, Blitzsten was given permission by Alexander) to take analytic patients in Chicago because Alexander thought that the Chicago population consisted mainly of Indians! (Grinker 1995, p. 175; Kavka 1984, p. 469).

Franz Alexander (1891–1964) played a seminal role in Chicago psychoanalysis. A Hungarian, Alexander was the first training student of the Berlin Psychoanalytic Institute. He held the first visiting professorship in psychoanalysis in the US in 1930 at the University of Chicago. After a year during which the psychoanalytic ideas he was presenting were received very badly, Alexander went to Boston but returned to help found the Chicago Institute in 1932 with the financial support of Alfred K. Stern as well as the Rosenwald, Rockefeller and Macy Foundations (Pollock 1978, p. 114; 1983, p. 12).

A cadre of Europeans (mainly Berliners) rather than Americans founded the Chicago Institute that was set up as a daughter institute of the Berlin Institute from which Alexander and many other analysts in Chicago came.

Alexander was director from the founding of the Chicago Institute in 1932 until the fall of 1956 when he left for California. He was a very productive writer and researcher with both a humanistic and a scientific approach using rigorous testing methods, especially on psychosomatic specificity research (Pollock 1983, pp. 15, 19). Especially interested in research, Alexander wanted to establish Chicago as a premier research institute along European university lines.[2] In addition to involving Chicago analysts in collaborative teaching and research (ibid., p. 19), Alexander was also a charismatic leader who attracted many European analysts to Chicago. Karen Horney for example was appointed as associate director at the desirable salary of $15,000 in 1932 dollars (ibid., p. 11). This exemplified Alexander's considerable abilities in raising finance, even during the Great Depression.

As the first director Alexander set a precedent by analysing a leading member of the lay board which oversaw and was legally responsible for the Chicago Institute. In 1986 George Pollock, who was accused of taking donations from a patient, referred to Alfred K. Stern's importing Alexander: 'Mr. Stern put up the money for a local psychoanalytic institute. Then he lay down on the couch to become Alexander's first patient' *(Chicago Tribune,* May 10, 1987).

Stern was later accused of subversive activities. To avoid a trial, he fled the US to live in Prague where he remained (Gedo pers. comm. 1997; Pollock 1983; Slight interview 1984).

The Independent Institute

Unlike almost all other APsaA institutes, the Chicago Institute did not emerge out of the psychoanalytic society but arose independently. Responsible for the training and qualification of analysts, the institute was set up as a totally separate entity from the society, and remains separate from it. The psychoanalytic society consisting of the graduates was of no consequence to power. From its beginnings the institute was authoritarian, oligarchic and self-perpetuating.

Alexander modelled the Chicago Institute on the Berlin Psychoanalytic Institute he left. However, the Chicago Institute's lay Board of Trustees was an innovation that provided funds and more power to the director through his having some control over naming and influencing board members. For decades Chicago Institute funding derived from its own activities and the contributions brought in principally by its Board of Trustees. Like a university the Chicago Institute was set up and legally incorporated through the state of Illinois and received its charter through the Board of Trustees. This structure contrasts with the majority of other APsaA institutes. Classically the

Board of Directors is elected from the psychoanalytic society with the proviso that they not be Training Analysts, that they not have the double function of overseers on a board at the same time as being active participants.

The Chicago Institute's Board of Trustees was composed of lay members who were not psychiatrists or psychoanalysts. The board owned the charter, had fiduciary responsibilities, selected the institute director, and had legal authority for the organisation and administration of institute affairs (Lewin and Ross 1960, p. 15). Once appointed the director dominated both institute and board. The board went along with decisions that were made by the director in consultation with the staff, a group of analysts with lifetime tenure, or from 1971 the Psychoanalytic Education Council, a group elected by the membership. The board never interfered with the functioning of the institute during Charles Kligerman's experience of four decades in the Chicago Institute (Kligerman interview 1992; *Chicago Tribune*, June 9, 1996).

Until George Pollock instituted a limit of two five year terms when he became director, there was no limit on the tenure of directors. Alexander was director for twenty-four years followed by Gerhart Piers for fifteen years. Pollock succeeded in reigning for seventeen years until he was deposed.

As in the Berlin Institute, the staff met every day for lunch, discussions and meetings (Kligerman interview 1981). Restricted to institute staff and certain guests the lunch tradition endured for decades. While it contributed to the cohesiveness within the institute group, it demonstrated the clear divisions between insiders and outsiders.

In Charles Kligerman's opinion, the Chicago Institute had a unique combination of an authoritarian leadership that had the Berlin tradition of

> experimental or research-mindedness, a greater flexibility of outlook than one would find in traditional analytic institutes, even though we were supposed to be a traditional Freudian one. Even though analysts in Chicago had disallowed Alexander's particular premise, his spirit lingers on. There's a tolerance of an experimental approach. (Kligerman interview 1981)

The Staff

Another pivotal and unusual aspect of the organisation made the Chicago Institute distinctive. Until the Pollock regime in 1971 the institute was to all intents and purposes run by an oligarchy of the director and the institute staff. The director did not have absolute power within the institute but shared it with the 'staff', a group of about twenty analysts with lifetime tenure. The membership of the fixed number of staff was only changed through replacement when a member died. Since the director and staff decided who would replace those who died, the staff was self-perpetuating. There was not even a retirement policy despite the fact that there were so many old analysts on the staff, probably because many of them were so prestigious (Kligerman interview 1981).[3] Thus the system of governance was a self-perpetuating hierarchy with clashes about who should occupy leadership positions and how power should be shared.

Alexander set up the Chicago Institute with a staff instead of a faculty appointed simply to teach particular courses. Before World War II the staff coincided with those who taught since the numbers of candidates and teachers were small. However, later when numbers markedly increased many training analysts were not on the staff. While in most institutes the position of training analyst commanded power, in the Chicago set-up of board, director and staff, training analyst status was more a side show lacking the quality of anointment of being on the staff. It did not involve the high status and power that membership of the staff conveyed (Kligerman interview 1992). As John Gedo (who trained at the Chicago Institute 1956–61) recalled, outside the director and staff 'everybody else was in outer darkness' (Gedo interview 1992). The 'us' versus 'them', 'in' versus 'out' division was clear and absolute. On the one hand, the director and staff were the oligarchic leaders of the institute (accountable to the board only in theory) while, on the other, all other analysts were together in the same boat, including the training analysts who were not members of the staff. There was no democracy or even a system of consultation. The director and staff selected the researchers, adjuncts and training analysts from the pool of graduates including training analysts who were not on the institute staff. According to Charles Kligerman, a member of the staff who was involved with psychoanalysis in Chicago since 1946, there was 'no organised faculty. There was a pool of analysts in the city who were graduates of the Chicago Institute who would be tapped if we needed them. It was a privilege' (Kligerman interview 1994).

Given the authoritarian structure, some of the inevitable alienation of the graduates of the institute was compensated for by a pay-off. In the heyday of psychoanalysis after the war until the 1970s, the system delivered the goods in terms of society members being given assignments and other crumbs from the royal table. In the heyday for psychoanalysis across the US, graduation from the Chicago Institute guaranteed referrals and a very good lifestyle.

Within this autocratic context Alexander ruled like an 'enlightened despot'. He valued the research culture and held liberal ideas in psychoanalysis. However, he had enemies among the staff. Alexander's 1956 departure from Chicago to Palo Alto was, in Roy Grinker Sr's opinion, 'at least partially due to his staff's discontent and their open revolt against his liberality' (Grinker 1995, p. 168).

Alexander's liberal and unorthodox ideas included three days a week analysis (instead of four or five times a week), his criticism of the libido theory and the use of 'role-playing' to manipulate the transference to provide a 'corrective emotional experience'.[4] The fact that Alexander fought the APsaA on such issues (along with Grinker and Sandor Rado) and tried to take the institute out of the control of the APsaA clinched the staff's antagonism, according to Roy Grinker Sr (interview 1981). Alexander's stubborn belief that children's problems were solely due to their parents meant that he felt it necessary to treat the parents and not the child – a belief that led to a neglect of child psychiatry in Chicago, holding it back there for decades.[5]

While most critical of Alexander, Blitzsten, the institute's founder, never split for two reasons, according to Jerome Kavka, an analyst and historian of the Chicago Psychoanalytic Society. First, because Blitzsten had little administrative talent and did not do well with classroom instruction, and second because the institute and society were separate, the society providing an outlet for different viewpoints (Kavka 1984, p. 475). Stuart Brent, a literary bookstore owner who knew Blitzsten well, observed him often behaving like a potentate orchestrating his followers fawning over him (see Brent 1962, Ch. 6). Blitzsten's followers were able to infiltrate the staff and ultimately brought Alexander down and remained influential into the 1960s. There were also major differences between the group around Alexander and the group around Maxwell Gitleson who became president of the APsaA and of the IPA. Gitleson was aligned with a more conservative group and, despite being a training analyst and president of the APsaA, did not join the Chicago Institute faculty under Alexander.

Heinz Kohut remembered that Alexander was 'treated badly and undeservedly'. It was not arguments that toppled Alexander but a counter-Alexander movement – 'it was like communism and revisionism, religion and heresy', as Heinz Kohut recalled (Kirsner 1982, p. 495). The major confrontation with Alexander occurred when the staff engineered a move to a more conservative curriculum. A committee consisting of Joan Fleming, Heinz Kohut and Louis Shapiro reshaped the curriculum to represent the ego psychological approach of Hartmann, Kris and Loewenstein.[6] While remnants of Alexander's approach remained, Shapiro and Fleming became increasingly influential and both became deans of education. With the ascendancy of that group the ambience changed so much that Alexander was forced by the staff to leave (Kligerman interview 1994).

The Piers Regime

The board appointed Gerhart Piers director on November 8, 1955, to be effective in the autumn of 1956. Piers was more congenial and pleasant though less brilliant than Alexander (Kligerman interview 1994), He was, in Gedo's words, 'a Viennese version of Franz Alexander', who, like Alexander Piers, exercised effective power in the institute. However, like European monarchs, Alexander and Piers never burned their hands with much administration, delegating many of the day-to-day activities to Helen Ross and Joan Fleming respectively (Gedo interview 1996a; Richmond interview 1996).

Some compromise was clearly achieved which overcame the tensions between the Alexander group and its opponents. Alexander's collaborator, Thomas French, became director of research. Joan Fleming (later a prominent APsaA official) who was analysed by Blitzsten and remained very close to him, was appointed as dean of education, a position equivalent to the chair of the Education Committee in other institutes. Piers became, in John Gedo's terms, 'a do-nothing ruler' (Gedo interview 1994) by the time that he had delegated most of his power to Fleming towards the end of his reign (Gedo interview 1996a). None the less, Gedo smelled corruption in the regime (Gedo 1997, pp. 46–9). Political games were endemic and Institute leaders disapproved of independent thinking (ibid., pp. 57–9).

Nevertheless, the Piers years brought a change in locale for the Chicago Institute, a major expansion of child therapy programmes for social workers and the establishment of a Teacher Education Program which focused on the human factors that promoted or impeded teaching. The Graduate Clinic was formally organised and institute teaching was organised around a weekend schedule to accommodate candidates coming from distant cities, including St Louis and Denver, which became new geographic facilities of the Chicago Institute.[7] Piers also altered the membership of the lay Board of Trustees by bringing in a wider range of Chicagoans (Pollock 1983, pp. 21–2).

Towards the end of his reign Piers became ill and incompetent, but since there was no internal policing mechanism, nobody would take the responsibility to tell him to wind it up (Kligerman interview 1994; Gedo interview 1994). Piers finally resigned in 1970. However, the situation provided the opportunity for changes to prevent it from happening again, and major changes were introduced. The Board of Trustees introduced five-year terms for directors in 1971.

The Pollock Regime

At the comparatively young age at forty-eight George Pollock was appointed associate director in February 1970, and then director in January 1971 (Pollock 1983, p. 22). Along with Phillip Seitz, Pollock was the youngest member of the staff and Pollock served an important role in the Piers regime when he replaced French as director of research by 1961 (Gedo interview 1994; Gedo 1997, p. 42).[8] Although the staff did not exclude younger analysts from teaching, training analyst appointments or even aspects of administration until the mid-1960s, such appointments were at the staff's pleasure bringing no rights to power. Gedo taught immediately after graduating, 'But the minute I offended Fleming, I was out!' (Gedo, pers. comm. 1997).[9]

Forceful and energetic, Pollock's strong intellect was stretched over a large number of projects. He enthusiastically took on all the aspects of the job of director, including the business side, which was of little interest to most analysts (Kligerman interview 1994). As Gedo put it, Pollock 'was willing to do everything. The expression, 'Let George do it!' applied quite literally to the Chicago Institute during those years. Everybody let George do it' (Gedo interview 1994).[10]

A 'can do' person in the right place at the right time, Pollock was a very strong and effective director who was able to impose his influence on the Chicago Institute in the name of change and expansion. Like others in the dynasty of directors, George Pollock boosted and was enthusiastic about the Chicago Institute. He emphasised how the Chicago Institute would thrive through continual fundamental change. In 1975, Roy Grinker Sr observed that Pollock had 'extensive energy, ambition, optimism and enthusiasm. There is considerable disagreement concerning his achievements but I can only praise him for opening up the institute, liberalizing the faculty, moving ahead with many new ventures, permitting and encouraging the younger men to think creatively, independently and even criticize the establishment' (Grinker 1995, pp. 155–95).

The *Chicago Psychoanalytic Literature Index* was begun, as was the *Annual of Psychoanalysis,* and the Chicago Institute Library expanded. In 1973, the State of Illinois authorised the Chicago Institute to offer the first PhD programme in psychoanalysis in the world. Extension programmes, postgraduate and teacher education, child therapy services and training programmes, and research were further expanded. In the area between the east and west coasts the institute was unrivalled, and continues to act as a centre for 'satellite' and former 'satellite' institutes such as those in Milwaukee and Cincinnati.

Like many in his generation of Chicago Institute graduates, Pollock was impatient with the structure in which the staff made all the decisions. He immediately introduced radical changes in the organisation. In a remarkable *tour de force,* Pollock persuaded the institute staff to relinquish their life appointments. He replaced the staff by a new educational decision-making body, elected by the institute membership, the Psychoanalytic Education Council (Kligerman interview 1981; 1994; Pollock 1978, p. 118). Every Chicago Institute member of the APsaA of five years' standing became routinely considered for training analyst appointment.

Pollock was able to secure these changes by seizing opportunities provided by a confluence of factors including the vacuum left by the ineffectiveness of Piers' last years as director. Moreover, significant changes in the ecology of psychoanalysis and of the membership of the Chicago Psychoanalytic Society were occurring. By the early 1970s, the generation of candidates that flooded psychoanalytic institutes across the US after World War II had reached an age to have some power in their professional associations. As we have seen in the cases of the New York and Boston Psychoanalytic Institutes, at that time federal funding was drying up for psychoanalysis. Psychoanalysis began to lose its allure as other treatment modalities for mental illness such as biological and other psychotherapies were becoming more developed and widely accepted. As a result, analysts could not so easily derive their professional, financial and intellectual rewards from the universities and hospital departments of psychiatry, and institute graduates moved their focus back to the psychoanalytic institutes for professional rewards. However, the large graduate population had nowhere to go in the Chicago Institute. By that time the aged and entrenched staff of the Chicago Institute did not involve younger analysts as teachers, training analysts or administrators.

By instituting an organised faculty and the establishment of the elected Psychoanalytic Education Council, Pollock brought about a broader institute membership and a greater degree of democracy. Nevertheless, Pollock was able to manage both council and faculty directly or through committees he appointed as director. For example, the director or his committee could stipulate which people stood for which slots – nominees had to run against specific incumbents making it hard for new members to be elected (Gedo interview 1994). Incumbents were usually reelected to the council throughout Pollock's terms. At the same time Pollock tried to give more power to the faculty (Kligerman interview 1994).

Everybody was compensated for their work at the Chicago Institute, whether it was teaching, administration, committee work or interviewing candidates. The Chicago Institute was always very well off with income derived from grants, contributions, tuition and fees.[11] The Chicago Institute budget under Pollock passed that of the APsaA. Pollock became 'the biggest entrepreneur in world-wide psychoanalysis', as Robert Wallerstein put it. 'He can juggle more things at one time than anybody else can' (Wallerstein interview 1987). Charles Kligerman recalled, 'The reputation of the institute was very large. Tremendous activities were going on and George Pollock could claim they were his. He got his own thumb in everything. He covered the whole universe in a vigorous way' (Kligerman interview 1994).

Nevertheless, in a 1981 interview Phillip Holzman (at the Chicago Institute during the 1970s) noted that 'a primary weakness in the institute' was that Pollock did not 'seem to know how to share responsibility' (Holzman interview 1981). Robert Wallerstein showed some prescience in a 1987 interview:

> People line up as George's friends and supporters and also there are people who can't get along with him and who feel that although he has brought in a lot of money, it has not been uniformly for the good. All these little subsidiaries he has set up like his Psychosocial Center and his training programs for teachers, the clinical program for child therapists – all those things may well come crashing down when George has gone. There is no institutional guarantee there.

The Machine

The Chicago Institute is consonant with the city itself. For a long time Chicago's machine politics has been similar to New York's 'Tammany Hall' – a major melting pot of powerful ethnic groups as well as tough unions and other organised associations. It is a city with a strong identity, yet it also has strong and virtually autonomous subcultures that belie this unity. Successful Chicago politics has consisted in the ability to negotiate and balance the demands of various forces and to be able to buy off opponents. The position of Chicago Mayor has always been a delicate balancing act. As a Chicago 'boss', Mayor Richard Daley Sr dispensed favours to groups that would be beholden to him.

So it was with the Chicago Institute from its inception. Like the Mayor of Chicago, the director of the Chicago Institute was undeniably 'the boss'. A vital feature of the position was political – to keep the various factions from being too dissatisfied. Until Pollock left there was always a strong and powerful political leader of the Chicago Institute who had, owing to institute structure as well as personal temperament, been dominant and oligarchic rather than democratic.

This structure provides some of the reasons behind why the Chicago Institute never split despite its many internal struggles. One of Pollock's chief lieutenants, Sol Altschul, observed that the Chicago Institute never split because of the character of Chicago.

> Because this is second city we feel more vulnerable and under attack. To use an American western metaphor, the wagons have been drawn up in a circle. Under these circumstances we need every gun we have even if we have our own rivalries so that if we split we'll have two small institutes and we'll be even weaker vis a vis New York than we are now. (Altschul interview 1981)

Charles Kligerman noted Chicago's self-consciousness as second city which 'pays a great deal of attention to certain single things' exemplified by the city's pride about the University of Chicago as its pre-eminent university and architecture as its dominant art form – and, among the intelligentsia, the Chicago Institute. Moreover, the atmosphere in the Chicago Institute 'fostered an environment in which Kohut could do his work'. He maintained that if Heinz Kohut

> reached his ideas with the level of conviction that he did in another place, they would have quickly come to a parting of ways and he would have had to form a completely deviant group that would have been outside the APsaA. Both Horney and Alexander would have been considered heretics where they were. But not here because we can tolerate divergence because of our liberal experimental approach. (Kligerman interview 1981)

Whatever the cultural reasons, there were important economic considerations for staying in a well-funded institute. The extensive assets and budget provided sufficient reason that the Chicago Institute never split. Beyond the Chicago Institute's prestige, nobody wanted to leave the money, the rented premises, the referrals, the infrastructure or the perquisites.[12]

A middle-aged Chicago analyst with a very Chicago perspective described the structure to Roy Grinker Sr in 1975:

> It seems to me the issues devolve essentially into the experiences with, and reactions to, the bi-level structure into which most social groupings inevitably tend to divide, i.e., the archaic but ubiquitous antagonism between the 'ins' and the 'outs'. From an historical perspective the general lines of move and counter move, like a chess game, do not really change much. Only the cast of characters and the specific contemporary issues, which mask the interminable power struggle, change. (Grinker 1995)

There was always an 'in group' and an 'out group'. Only the staff and later holders of certain ranks and offices were invited to lunch. Certain analysts were given a disproportionate amount of teaching, prestigious positions and training cases whereas others were not.

To be 'in' in the Chicago psychoanalytic scene meant being part of the institute, which, as we have seen was totally separate from the society which had no power. Power was vested in the institute controlled by the director whose position embodied charismatic leadership. This leadership was not so much a personal fiefdom but intrinsic to the institutional structure. Any incumbent would be inclined to act in a monarchical way. Especially under Pollock's directorship between 1971 and 1988 when the institute became large, the control exercised seemed to be of the type that social theorist Herbert Marcuse described in a wider social context where the social structure and function of the whole determine the particular parts. Marcuse described 'repressive tolerance' where the presence of democratic liberties offers superficial freedoms while denying deeper ones (Marcuse 1965, pp. 81–117). Consisting of accredited analysts the Chicago Psychoanalytic Society was a free scientific forum but was irrelevant to decisions and money. The 'talking shop' provided an outlet for criticisms and frustrations to be vented but to no avail.

As an effective manager and entrepreneur, Pollock was able to 'deliver the goods' until the late 1980s when the power and prestige of psychoanalysis declined too far to provide them any more. Groups and individuals with claims were rewarded and effectively coopted to the institute culture dominated by Pollock. The attitude of many Chicago analysts to Pollock was clearly ambivalent: while Pollock helped provide a relatively comfortable existence, he was considered by some to be somebody it was useless to oppose.

Although the complex administrative structure of the institute gave the impression of delegation of responsibility, the divisions enhanced the de facto power of the director. Although prestigious positions could be attained, the labyrinthine complexities of institute matters meant that nobody knew much outside his or her immediate area. Because the director had his finger on the pulse, only he was in a position to know everything necessary to make decisions.

Nevertheless, as Charles Kligerman observed, all this was not just peculiar to Pollock: 'This culture did not begin with Pollock nor was it specific to him. It was part of the way the institute was set up and part of the Chicago culture' (Kligerman interview 1994). The behaviour of Pollock or his predecessors rests not so much on personalities but on the role of the director and the structure of the institute. When someone has occupied a position for so long, the position and the person seem to meld together even though the person may be working within parameters set by the structure.[13] The structure of the Chicago Institute meant that the director had real authority. Although the Board of Trustees had power, the director was in charge of the actual everyday running of the Chicago Institute. The director was the channel for two-way communication between the board and the institute, headed the Psychoanalytic Education Council, and had large appointive powers.

The Chicago Institute was transformed from an Austro-Hungarian structure under Alexander into what Gedo recognised as 'an American patronage system'. Gedo recalled that Pollock 'had money, political power, local patronage, and patronage jobs in the APsaA'. Moreover, because of his positions in the American Psychiatric Association and the APsaA (he became APsaA president in 1974), Pollock was able to use his influence nationally. Locally, he had political power and influence with well-off board members. Provided his authority was not threatened, Pollock could give rewards but also jobs to people who could handle them. Gedo recalled, 'We each learned in our own way how to remain friendly with George Pollock' (Gedo interview 1994).

For a long period Pollock's two main and trusted supporters were involved in running the organisation under Pollock's direction as associate dean and dean of education (Moraitis interview 1992). Chicago analyst Meyer Gunther observed that

> It is big city patronage politics. Strangely enough, this began under Alexander as almost as a limited democracy of the nobility and the aristocracy. And it deteriorated progressively in my opinion despite a

major broadening of the institute when Alexander left and the Blitzsten supporters came in. (Gunther interview 1992)

In 1988 Meyer Gunther studied committee appointments made at the Chicago Institute between 1975 and 1987 during George Pollock's directorship. He found the presence of motives were more complex than finding 'the best person for the job'. Especially in the 'Big Three' most powerful committees which held sway over education and training – the Training Analyst Committee, the Selection and Matriculation Committee and the Progression Committee – Gunther found that a small number of analysts were represented quite disproportionately in committee membership. In the top twelve committees of the institute over the time studied, 20 per cent of the time was served by just three analysts and the next 20 per cent by another five, meaning that eight analysts served 40 per cent of the time on committees during George Pollock's tenure. Gunther concluded:

> All the core program committees seem to have involved the work of the same dozen or so analysts who, often in the role of chairperson, ran their committees for most of the thirteen year period. The inference I would draw from this would be *the major motive* was one of stability, continuity of function and safety of function – all very predictable ... This arrangement would guarantee getting the work done in a satisfactory way according to some presumably desirable, predetermined standards of what was considered to be effective functioning. Once the pattern was established, I suspect the dictum, 'Don't fix it if it isn't broken', probably was the rationalization for perpetuating these central figures in their dominating roles at the institute. (Gunther 1988b)

Gunther added that there was no clear-cut evidence about what criteria were used to decide these appointments. He continued:

> However, one can suspect that there was operating in the background the universally present dynamics of any self-perpetuating power elite who were convinced not only of their capacity to be effective and ability to demonstrate it, but convinced that their predictive effectiveness was evidence of their exclusive possession of these special talents. But, in reality, these people were all experienced analysts who could be depended on to carry out the operation of their committees in a reliable, conscientious, effective and ultimately 'mainstream' manner. Whatever their differing ideological complexions might be, they clearly shared one thing in common. *They were all good team players.* They were not oddballs, major idiosyncratic thinkers; they certainly were not 'loyal troublemakers' nor Lone Rangers. (ibid.)

In addition to the membership of committees, the allocation of teaching was also skewed in favour of a relatively small number of instructors teaching most of the courses (ibid.). In 1984 Moraitis noted that four or five people had seemingly permanent official status deciding 'who gets in, who gets out, what is being taught, how it's taught' (Moraitis interview 1984). Gunther speculated:

> The aim of this structure – a well-organized, predictable smoothly functioning educational 'production line' – might well have been enthroned by Pollock at the expense of the enriching, but less predictable effects of creativity, diversity, independence of thought and hence the inevitability of less efficient functioning. (Gunther 1988b)

The ideal of rational, predictable functioning in a mainstream manner is not collegial but managerial (see Kernberg 1986, pp. 799–834). Gunther believed that in order to have a different kind of institute, 'we'd better learn from our past experience and design a structure that supports and reflects our new aims. Specifically, we'd better learn how to function with a more collegial-democratic structure' (Gunther 1988b).

The Psychoanalytic Education Council consisted of the director and seventeen other members who were, mostly, re-elected consistently and on an indefinite basis. Moraitis recalled that the nominations were made by George Pollock and very seldom would a new member be elected to the Council. 'I was never quite sure how this actually occurred, but there were no formalities maintained in the process of voting and counting the votes. Of course, this was not a democratic organisation'.

Moraitis recalled that most of the Psychoanalytic Education Council meetings he attended were spent with Pollock making reports, often about issues that had very little to do with the institute. Nevertheless, once in a while, an issue would come up which, according to Moraitis,

> would be very quickly squashed and attention redirected. If there was any conflict, George would think of nominating or appointing a committee to explore the issue. By the time the committee reported it was too late to do anything. In the 1970s, a committee was appointed to re-evaluate the curriculum and the whole training program. That committee came up with some very interesting suggestions about how to proceed, among which was the appointment of preceptors to follow the candidates' growth and to co-ordinate the educational development of each individual. The committee report was submitted in the 1970s and was and then tabled, and did not finally come up until *twelve* years later. Somebody at the meeting said that the United States mail is really much slower than one would have thought. It's really a sign of how things were dealt with and how quietly and subtly people were ignored, put

aside, not really given attention to and proper audience. Ironically, when the issue was brought to his attention finally, a new committee was appointed to bring up to date the results of the old one. This was done quickly and I was a member of that second committee. Then the issue was tabled once more because it 'was not timely to act on'. When I first joined the committee, along with another analyst, I started asking some questions which people didn't use to ask. We were considered enormously brave for being able to simply inquire rather than simply avoid asking questions. (Moraitis pers. comm. 1990a)

On the 24th floor of the Chicago Institute and in the Conference Room, luncheon was served for the selected few who were close to the administration. The lunch had a long tradition from when Alexander specifically reserved it for the staff of the Chicago Institute. Council members were invited, although the majority of them would not attend lunch. Moraitis commented: 'Eating there was considered a distinction, as an indication of being a member of the inner group which was taken very seriously by some of the people who were close to Pollock' (Moraitis pers. comm. 1990a).

Another part of the system of rewards concerned training analyst status and the assignment of candidates to training analysts. Because the power structure of the Chicago Institute was located in the board, the director and the staff or council rather than being vested in an Education Committee which was running the Chicago Institute, training analyst status assumed secondary importance in Chicago. Since training analyst status, unlike in most institutes, carried little power, it was not too difficult to achieve training analyst status in Chicago. Not long after Pollock's reign came to an end most training analysts were not analysing any candidates while the others generally were each analysing one or two candidates. In 1990 there were fifty-eight active (and thirty-one inactive) teaching and training analysts in the institute in a faculty of eighty-six.[14] Moraitis commented that this was 'an amazingly high number of training analysts for any institute, and this was because George Pollock granted that title very generously unless there was something very definitely wrong with the individual and clear evidence why he should not get the title. Of course, the title did not mean that the training analyst would be asked to do very much or assume any responsibility. So it was simply an honorary degree which helped the analyst's self esteem, his self image and the image maybe on a national level, but locally it had very little meaning' (Moraitis pers. comm. 1990a).[15]

Since there was no cost for handing out the rewards of training analyst status, this approach provided clear advantages for the leadership.

Reward made the recipients happy as well as hungry for the opportunity to employ their status within the system.

By itself their newly awarded status conferred no power, only entrance into the pool of training analysts who could be assigned candidates by the leadership. The allocation of candidates and positions (increasingly scarce relative to demand) was in the gift of the director or a committee under his control. Training analysts were cemented into the system since those deciding who among the training analysts actually received training cases were powerful.

Arnold Goldberg was the major opponent of Pollock throughout, but he had no power in the council. Any effective action against Pollock would have needed to come from his lieutenants, which was never a real possibility (Gedo interview 1994).

A powerful figure in the APsaA and internationally, Heinz Kohut was also a charismatic figure in Chicago. He had always been a good source of referrals and his classes at the institute were very popular with candidates. George Pollock praised him for his encouragement of younger people in his obituary in to Kohut (Pollock 1982, pp. 284–5). Kohut helped Pollock as he had others in the institute, and Pollock did not cast Kohut out when he developed his new ideas: 'We supported Heinz's research because it was worthy of support, not necessarily because it was something which we agreed with in all details' (Pollock 1982, p. 283). Kohut received considerable contributions towards his research in self psychology from Pollock. However, another interpretation might be that it functioned at least partly a political accommodation where Pollock tried to ensure that Kohut would not rock the boat too much at the institute (Moraitis pers. comm. 1990b). The Chicago Institute did not support Kohut when he was developing his ideas but during a much later period.

Pollock reacted strongly to possible opposition. When Kohut mooted the idea of revising the curriculum and including an informal postgraduate course in self psychology within the institute, Pollock reacted forcefully, since the suggestion could be construed as an institute within an institute which would have challenged Pollock's control. After an intensive telephone campaign against them, Kohut and fellow self psychologist, Arnold Goldberg, were not re-elected to the Council in 1978 (Kligerman interview 1994; Gedo interview 1994; Kohut to Lotte Köhler, June 1978, in Cocks 1994, pp. 368–71).[16] As Goldberg told me in 1981, 'Every time we try to do any kind of study with selection, with progression, with curriculum, etc. they get very frightened, they get very angry and they put the kibosh on. You've just got to leave them alone' (Goldberg interview 1981). Analysts who were not compliant were excluded. One analyst, George Klumpner, was removed from committees and dumped when he stood again for the council after he asked to see the institute budget (Gedo interview 1992; 1994; Gedo 1997, p. 111). According to John Gedo, Pollock thus 'demonstrated that if you took certain liberties, he had the power to clip your wings. Therefore people ceased to challenge him. It no longer looked like a Central European system – it looked like an American university on the surface' (Gedo interview 1994). (Pollock changed the title of 'director' to 'president' to bring it more in line with universities.) Arnold Goldberg told me in 1981, 'Don't think for a moment that it's anything but a trade school. It's like automechanics' (Goldberg interview 1981).

The research culture shifted considerably from being centred in the institute when Alexander was the major intellectual leader and director. In the Pollock era the director was by no means a major intellectual presence and the institute became a shell. Much of the intellectual work took place outside the formal organisation of the institute, such as by John Gedo, Merton Gill and the self psychologists who became effectively split off (Moraitis pers. comm. 1990b). The group of self psychologists which included Kohut, Goldberg, the Tolpins, Michael Basch and Ernest Wolf was, in Arnold Goldberg's view, emotionally and intellectually clearly split off (Goldberg interview 1981).

The institute had moved from charisma to a Chicago form of bureaucracy (Moraitis interview 1984). The combination of boosterism and hustling mixed with conflicts of interest prevailed. It fitted Nelson Algren's description of Chicago 'living 'like a drunken El-rider who cannot remember where he got on nor at what station he wants to get off. The sound of wheels moving below satisfies him that he is making great progress' (Algren 1963, p. 86).

The board appointed Pollock to a second five-year term from 1976, and then again (overriding the two-term limit) in 1980 for an additional five-year term from 1981. Yet again, Pollock was selected for an additional three-year term (effective July 1, 1986) on December 13, 1985, through a search committee formed by Lou Shapiro and Nathan Schlesinger. Again, this was beyond the constitution (Goldberg pers. comm. 1997).

The Board of Trustees

Since the ultimate fiduciary and organisational power of the institute was vested in a lay Board of Trustees of around forty members that owned the charter the role of the board is a vital element in the story.

Consisting of a variety of people, many wealthy and socially prominent, they were able to raise money for many institute functions.[17]

Members of the board were often in analysis with Chicago Institute leaders, especially the director. Since the director selected the members of the lay Board of Trustees – a number of the director's patients were members – and the Board of Trustees picked the director (Gedo interview 1994; Moraitis pers. comm. 1991; Moraitis interview 1992; Goldberg interview 1992). While most of the board members were barely involved, its small Executive Committee was more central. Most members of this committee were close to Pollock, or had been or were in analysis with him. This made the supervisory aspect of the Executive Committee a difficult and possibly conflicted one, resulting in Pollock having a virtually free hand (Moraitis pers. comm. 1990a). As Goldberg put it, Pollock 'played them like a fiddle' (Goldberg interview 1992). Gedo saw the board as 'an instrument in the hands of the director. If there should be a clash with the faculty, it's a weapon in his hands' (Gedo interview 1992). Yet Pollock's ability to prevail included, as Charles Kligerman put it, many 'tangles' with the board.[18]

With an annual institute budget of almost two million dollars under Pollock, much emphasis needed to be on soliciting money by the lay board who had little or no knowledge of psychoanalysis.[19] Board members never had a passion for core educational issues of interest to the analysts but emphasised the orientation toward community service, public relations, and spreading influence (Moraitis pers. comm. 1991; Gunther interview 1992). As Moraitis observed, the notion that it was desirable to accept money from patients was so widespread among faculty members and administrators that an ethic was established at the Chicago Institute that 'it is all right to accept large sums of money from patients if they are given for the promotion of psychoanalysis. As a result of that ethic, the Chicago Institute became the richest institute in the country. Overall, it was accepted as a sort of modus operandi, it was within the boundaries of analytic behaviour.' The consequences of what Moraitis termed 'a commercialisation of psychoanalysis' was the reinforcement of a structure that took the emphasis away from intellectual pursuits towards fund raising, promotion campaigns, handling the media, and budget considerations. The price was too high (Moraitis pers. comm. 1991).

Waiting for the Fall

However, two related sets of circumstances entered the picture. By the mid-1980s, as in other parts of the country, psychoanalysis in Chicago was going into steep decline with rapidly diminishing numbers of candidates and referrals. Pollock conceded that the future for psychoanalysis was bleak (Gedo interview 1994). As Moraitis commented, 'A diffuse pessimism was spread all over the Chicago Institute about its future and the future of the profession in Chicago' (Moraitis pers. comm. 1990b). With a shrinking institute and most of the sinecures already allotted to those who had held the positions for many years, the number of rewards left to hand out shrivelled. Since nobody was disqualified, this left a large number of institute members with no rewards and nothing much to do. The faculty–student ratio was very unbalanced with the number of applications down and a large faculty of eighty, including sixty training analysts.[20] The number of training analysts had doubled since Pollock became director (Gunther interview 1992). The patronage system, based on the assumption that it would keep expanding, stopped working when it became overextended. Finally, with no more room for people coming up from below, the more restricted patronage bred further resentment and less allegiance to Pollock (Gedo interview 1992). Kligerman recalled Pollock becoming 'less and less popular', getting 'more estranged from people who he might have depended on' (Kligerman interview 1994). Resentment grew geometrically as the gravy train had even less gravy to dispense to anyone (Gunther interview 1992). Even the staff lunches were cancelled for lack of funds (Moraitis interview 1992).

The other circumstance related directly to Pollock as he withdrew much of his energy, time and attention from the Chicago Institute. A major heart attack and heart surgery took him away from the Chicago Institute for some time. Pollock's involvement with the affairs of the American Psychiatric Association (treasurer 1980–86 and president 1987–88) increasingly took time away from institute matters (Moraitis pers. comm. 1990a). Moraitis recalled that Pollock 'felt he was in a very small pond and he was too big a fish to stay in it. I know that he was very unhappy settling for the directorship of the Chicago Institute.' He announced that he had entered into negotiations with Northwestern University where he was a professor to become Research Director in psychiatry and made it known that he was looking for more lucrative and powerful jobs elsewhere (Moraitis pers. comm. 1990b).

With Pollock's attention and interest were obviously on other things, Moraitis remembered that the institute felt a sense of abandonment and alienation by a director who was viewed as irreplaceable. Moraitis considered this to be part of an 'idealised image', idealised in that Pollock 'was considered as the one and only who could unite the institute and could maintain its cohesiveness and structure' (Moraitis pers. comm. 1990a). Pollock's pessimism and withdrawal, Moraitis believed, brought about 'a sense of vacuum or void in leadership. The leader was departing. There was no plan for succession' (ibid.).

Pollock was clearly aware of the problems and dangers of long-term appointments to the directorship when he introduced amendments to the regulations instituting a limit of two five year terms in 1971. He was asked then if ten years was enough. Charles Kligerman recalled Pollock's reply: if he couldn't get what he wanted accomplished in ten years he did not deserve it. 'But as time went on he began to have second thoughts about that', Kligerman noted (Kligerman interview 1992). These regulations were suspended so that Pollock could be appointed for a third term from 1981. Kligerman, a member of the search committee for the director at that time, recalled that 'we couldn't find anybody who we thought could be a suitable director'. The search committee decided against inviting Arnold Goldberg to be director and saw no other alternative than giving Pollock a third term, Kligerman recalled. Later Kligerman said that giving Pollock a third term 'was a huge mistake'. The committee recommended that the search should begin earlier next time so that there would be time to develop a new leader. 'Nobody demurred very much' from the decision to reappoint Pollock (Kligerman interview 1994). There was really no contest with Pollock. The board on which Pollock had immense influence changed the bylaws. Nobody would have challenged Pollock for the position of director given Pollock's power and the sense of Pollock as irreplaceable (Moraitis pers. comm. 1997).

The Chicago Institute colluded with Pollock by reappointing him. In a 1992 interview Charles Kligerman maintained, 'The sad thing is that although it was an unhealthy arrangement, it did give the institute a certain prestige that it has lost since then. Its power and prestige has declined in the city. This was one of the powerful institutes in the world' (Kligerman interview 1992).

Part of the problem was the extent to which Pollock seemed to identify himself with the institute implying that his interests and the institute's interests necessarily coincided. The position he occupied and the effectiveness with which he exercised his power nurtured such an illusion. Yet, the apparent split between his own good and that of the institute ended his career at the institute and blemished his reputation within psychoanalysis.

The Fall

In March 1988 it was discovered that the estranged son of an expatient was suing George Pollock for exploiting the patient and gaining financial advantage from her, thus violating psychiatric and psychoanalytic ethics. The son held that Pollock had profited from his mother's will at his expense. The details of the suit began to appear in the press in May.[21] Details began to be revealed of the legal contest over the $5 million estate of Anne Lederer, a wealthy widow, who was a board member and Pollock's patient. Anne Lederer had died in 1984 at the age of seventy-eight and the trial was set for September 22, 1988. She had inherited a sizeable amount of money from her father who was with Sears Roebuck and Co., and her husband had been a prosperous Chicago ear, nose and throat specialist. In the Cook County Probate Court, Lederer's only child, Francis, accused Pollock of exploiting for selfish gain the fourteen-year psychiatric relationship with Lederer. Pollock was accused of exercising 'undue influence' over his mother from when she began treatment with Pollock in 1969 until she died. She was treated for depression five times a week and Pollock continued to prescribe medication until 1983, according to court records.

Anne Lederer left $200,000 to her son and several thousand dollars to two grandchildren. But she left most of her estate of around $5 million to the Anne P. Lederer Research Institute founded by her in 1980 to promote psychiatric research. Francis Lederer alleged that the establishment of the institute was mainly meant to financially benefit Pollock since Pollock was supposed to serve as the director of this institute at a substantial salary. Pre-trial proceedings revealed that the trust that had been set up for Pollock yielded him and his family $80,000 a year together with other money for his depression research (Warren et al. 1988).

In sworn pre-trial testimony witnesses stated that Anne Lederer treated Pollock as a replacement for her husband who died in 1973. Pollock was said to have advised her about much of her life, including eating, domicile and which attorneys should revise her will, as well as giving her gifts and flowers and phoning her most days.

Pollock's attorneys maintained that Anne Lederer was just following a family tradition when she left most of her estate to charity. Their expert witness, a psychiatrist at Rush-Presbyterian-St Luke's Medical Center, claimed that Anne Lederer was not under undue influence. Through his attorneys, Pollock claimed the charges were a distorted, twisted exercise in fiction (Warren et al. 1988).

As an expert on mourning, George Pollock had a special interest and expertise in treating elderly patients (McDaniel 1979). Pollock had not treated Anne Lederer analytically but rather by making the institute her home. She spent a good deal of time working in the library to which she had donated a sizeable amount of money. She was treated as part of the family at the Chicago Institute and clearly profited from it. Lederer's fund was well-known for its support of many institute activities. One of Pollock's supporters discovered the suit through his son, a Chicago attorney, who noticed the suit against Pollock about the will in the *Law Bulletin*. He asked his son to follow the legal manoeuvres and told selected colleagues about the scandal. Gedo commented that this demonstrated that the system was at breaking point since someone who benefited so much from the system was 'ready to pounce on Pollock if he laid himself open in any way. In a sense, it was a coincidence that what broke it was this scandal. If it hadn't been this, something else would soon have come up.' Some APsaA leaders took private delight in these developments. 'Everybody was just waiting for the man to fall', Gedo recalled (interview 1992).

In March 1988 analysts who knew approached a Board of Trustees official and suggested asking Pollock to stay on the sidelines until the issue was resolved. The trustee went to Toronto where Pollock was attending a conference of the American Psychiatric Association, and solicited his agreement to the plan.

Pollock told individual faculty members that his personal business was none of theirs, and that he had done nothing wrong. When the council confronted Pollock about the issue of the trusts, emotion ran high. When Pollock turned up with his lawyer, the council realised that they were dealing with a legal issue and not a collegial discussion.

In his opening statement to the council Pollock reportedly argued that his actions were not at variance with what Freud did at different times in his life. In no way could he be held responsible for unethical conduct given the fact that the founder of psychoanalysis had acted similarly. He wondered whether the accusations represented the countertransference of some faculty members. Moraitis remembered raising the possibility that

> given the reaction of the faculty and the objections to that, that maybe he would like to return the money or make some gesture in that respect and settle the issue that way. I got so emotional during the meeting that I walked out of it because I felt I couldn't control myself and was very upset about it. And then I came back. Obviously, the faculty was not satisfied with George's responses and from then on the process began of

trying to persuade George to step down from his position. (Moraitis interview 1992)

Soon after the confrontation Moraitis and Pollock attended an event where they signed copies of a book they co-edited. Moraitis recalled that Pollock would not speak to or look at him: 'The lines had been drawn, the war had been declared. It has been the same ever since.'

Moraitis recalled a very long and arduous process of trying to decide how to proceed. The council met frequently, always in executive session where no records were kept. At some point there was a vote of the faculty at large to request Pollock to step down which was transmitted to Pollock by a delegation from the faculty (Moraitis interview 1992).

Kligerman suggested to the group that Pollock should be asked to resign because of loss of confidence in him. During the process the faculty was not immediately informed of all the thinking and negotiations by the council which handled the situation semi-secretly, allegedly because of the threat of lawsuit from Pollock (Moraitis interview 1992; Richmond interview 1996).

As a friend, Charles Kligerman suggested privately to Pollock that he step aside on leave of absence from his position that was to terminate in fifteen months. Pollock refused on the grounds that since he had done nothing wrong, this was tantamount to an admission of guilt. Pollock did not accept Kligerman's justification that if there were a question about a chairman of a corporation, there was nothing wrong with taking a leave of absence without prejudice while the issues were resolved (Kligerman interview 1992). None the less, according to Gilda Buchbinder, head of the Board of Trustees, Pollock decided to take leave 'to prepare for the trial of the lawsuit and to address matters raised by news releases about that case'. Henry Seidenberg, vice president of the Chicago Institute, Buchbinder said, would assume Pollock's presidential duties during his absence (Hale 1988). Pollock had previously designated Seidenberg as dean of education to be acting director when he was away (Moraitis pers. comm. 1990a). Seidenberg was made acting director in May 1988.

The court proceedings ended with the declaration of a mistrial followed by an undisclosed settlement (Perkiss 1988; *Law Bulletin*, November 14, 1988).

The council was instrumental in dealing with the crisis and took the management of the institute upon itself. Since the council was still viewed as the seat of Pollock's power while the faculty was less blessed by Pollock, the faculty needed to be consulted. While a struggle ensued about succession and reorganisation, there was, Moraitis recalled, 'a remarkable consensus' about the situation surrounding Pollock (Moraitis pers. comm. 1990a).

During this period some members argued that instead of forcing Pollock to resign, he should have been suspended, and that a dialogue should have been established about why all this had happened, what the affair represented in the institute's structure and whether it represented a basic defect in the Chicago Institute. Faculty member Arnold Tobin remembered:

> Only two or three people spoke up and said, how was the group at fault, how did we fail him as well as he fail us? I must say there was a total uninterest in that kind of discussion. It didn't take place. It isn't going to take place and there is very little interest – for a group of people that are interested in psychology we have a remarkable lack of interest in group psychology and how we relate as individuals to the group. (Tobin interview 1992)

The faculty, including Pollock's most trusted supporters, unanimously passed a motion of no confidence. The vote asked Pollock to take a leave of absence. After three five-year terms and the half of a new three year term, When Pollock took leave of absence, he was at once hired at Northwestern University.

The Chicago Psychoanalytic Society, with democrats George Klumpner as 1987–88 president and George Moraitis as its 1988–89 president, decided to instigate its own investigation. The society saw it as part of its role since articles appeared in the press about the institute (Moraitis interview 1992). The society finally decided not to pursue its investigations in Chicago and to refer the issues to the APsaA which, after long deliberations, decided to do nothing about the matter (Moraitis pers. comm. 1998).

Many board members were very sympathetic to Pollock. As Pollock's ex-analysands, a number retained close ties with him. Moraitis recalled, 'They didn't want to let him go – they felt he was betrayed and railroaded and that he should fight back. So there was a strong opposition to his leaving and a strong opposition to the faculty's behaviour. There were some very powerful feelings operating from both sides' (Moraitis interview 1992).

When the council voted fifty-nine to nil to ask Pollock to resign from the institute Barrie Richmond recalled that 'there was not one person in that room who did not feel in some way indebted to George' (Richmond interview 1996). Although Pollock had been helpful and treated some analysts well, he had lost his power to call in favours.

While Pollock was never expelled from the group, 'he is a man without a country as far as we are concerned', Kligerman contended (Kligerman interview 1992).

However, Pollock clearly felt wronged by the institute, consistently maintaining that his innocence on all accounts. It is understandable why he distanced himself from the Chicago Institute since they were so critical of his actions. The issues should not be reduced to personalities as the whole train of events needs to be seen in the context that the position of director until Pollock was structured as that of a powerful and dominant boss with an undesirable level of personal authority.

The Reorganisation

A strong reaction set in after Pollock left. When the council considered how to proceed, the necessity for reorganisation became evident. Moraitis recalled several stormy revolutionary meetings 'characterised by very sharp attacks against those who maintained positions for a long time under George's umbrella. These were the chairmen of committees who had maintained their jobs for a very long time and teachers of courses who had been teaching them for decades' (Moraitis pers. comm. 1990a).

The energy of the Chicago Institute was therefore devoted to its reorganisation along ultra-democratic lines. None of the accoutrements of the Pollock regime was spared as 'power to the people' became the order over the following years. There was not only *glasnost* but also *perestroika*. An association of equal colleagues replaced the hierarchy. Checks and balances were introduced to ensure that nobody could stack committees or take unfair advantage. An elected Committee on Committees instead of the director decided the chairs and membership of committees (Moraitis pers. comm. 1990a). That was the downside. In Gedo's view this was 'the finest single example of "democracy run riot", a democracy where personal popularity is what is important'. It became 'a fantastically cumbersome system' (Gedo interview 1992). The new regulations listed the functions of directors but not their powers. The structure became increasingly complicated militating against work being done effectively.

However, the 1991 APsaA site visitors were full of praise for the Committee on Committees they thought to be 'the finest example of the changes brought about by the Reorganization'. They regarded the tensions as part of an evolving process and admired the way the Psychoanalytic Education Council worked. They observed a meeting in which they asserted: 'The good-natured, warm tone of the meeting did not restrain the straight direct manner in which the councilors talk to each other and express their points of view. What a change this must be!' The committee congratulated the institute 'on the achievement this represents for the Reorganization – to replace an over-centralized, top-heavy monarchical system and move to a democratic system with balance of powers in so short a time is remarkable' (American Psychoanalytic Association 1991, pp. 16–17).

The revolution involved a major transfer of power over to the faculty, although the Board of Trustees remained. Nevertheless, associations with Pollock tainted members of the board. The board became less important since psychoanalysis was no longer popular and did not command as much fund-raising potential. Income from the annual institute fund-raising benefit and from contributions from the board was in decline. In dollar terms, income from grants and contributions was one third of what is was a decade before, not even allowing for considerable inflation over that period.[22] However, as Gedo noted, the members 'did not want to cut themselves off from the Board of Trustees partly because of the fantasy of social cachet, and partly because they did not realize how little money the Board of Trustees actually contributed. It gave them a sense of security' (Gedo interview 1992). This took place in the climate of the general decline of the profession.[23]

Pollock was killed in effigy many times over in an atmosphere in which justice being seen to be done became at least as important as its being done. As the Pollock regime was about power and not ideas, the revolution reacted to what many felt were abuses of power without changing the climate of ideas. In a 1992 interview, Michael Basch maintained, 'They are still fighting the institute after Pollock left. They are still fighting the last war. They are dealing with everyone as if each director were going to be like George Pollock' (Basch interview 1992).

Since Pollock did not resign but took leave of absence in 1988, his term needed to be completed before a new director was appointed. Once the Committee on Committees was instituted, energies became focused on the process of selecting a new director whose term was to begin after Pollock's term officially expired in June 1989. A somewhat acrimonious political campaign, unheard of in the institute, was waged while tensions between board and faculty ensued where the board rejected the faculty's right to select the director (Moraitis pers. comm. 1990a; Moraitis interview 1992; Kligerman interview 1992; Gunther interview 1992).

Finally, a compromise was reached and Arnold Goldberg, Pollock's longest standing opponent and a self psychologist, was elected for a three year term in October 1989. He was generally regarded as a fair and competent administrator (Basch interview 1992; Gill interview 1992; Goldberg interview 1992). Because of the cumbersome new structures, Goldberg often found it difficult to get tasks done. Goldberg recalled:

> When I took over as director, we had a deficit that would have closed the organisation. We would have had to literally have closed in four years. I was left with a potential deficit of $300,000 a year. I did many things which I felt saved the organisation from that fate. My feeling was that I bent over backwards to be democratic. But I also had the feeling that certain things had to be done, one, that did not lend themselves to referendum, and, two, that were not relevant to 'shall we all vote on whether I can rent this office and give a decorating allowance to the person?', something we have never done before. (Goldberg interview 1992)

Considerable tensions developed between the director and the membership, some of which related to personality (many did not like his harsh and direct manner, others found him dictatorial) and some related to structural issues (Gill interview 1992).

Tom Pappadis followed Goldberg as director. In the opinion of Moraitis the Pappadis administration (1992–98) emphasised two things: 'constant consensus, and the need to maintain a balanced budget and good physical surroundings' (Moraitis interview 1996b). Pappadis successfully managed the move of the institute from a mildly dilapidated building to a more expensive, salubrious, upmarket one. The board became still less important and the institute survived because of tuition, contributions and dues (Pappadis interview 1994). There was concern on the board about the past practice of having board members as patients of faculty, especially of the director (Bartling and Hall 1993, p. 13). During this period, the Chicago Institute introduced a Master's degree programme in psychoanalysis together with the University of Chicago.

Elected in 1998, the current director is Jerry Winer, an open-minded analyst and full professor of psychiatry at the University of Illinois. Winer has serious educational and intellectual interests as well as administrative expertise. The author of sixty articles and reviews, he has edited the Chicago *Annual of Psychoanalysis* over the past seven years, is a member of a number of APsaA committees and is chair of the International Psychoanalytic Association's Ethics Committee. Winer recognises that psychoanalysis in Chicago was 'in a time of eclipse' that mandated 'fresh approaches' to return to a place of 'prestige, leadership, and influence in this city and beyond'. He proposes furthering relationships with universities in joint projects, pursue funding from new spheres, broaden the range and audience of the research seminars, and increase the visibility of the institute in Chicago (Winer 1998). Winer is the first Chicago Institute director to be a full-time academic (Winer pers. comm. 1998).

What were the fruits of the Reorganisation? While the Chicago Institute moved to a less divisive, far more congenial democratic atmosphere, the number of candidates remained small and intellectual activity did not increase with more democracy (Moraitis pers. comm. 1990a; interview 1996a). As Arnold Goldberg put it:

> To say that democracy is the best flower for creativity, we know this is not the case. The best we know is argument is the best ground for new ideas to come about. Struggling, argument, fighting over issues. What has happened with this institute with democracy is that they reread it as egalitarianism. Egalitarianism means that we don't disagree, we have to be nice guys. That's the tragedy. (Goldberg interview 1996)

Apart from John Gedo's work and the continued developments among the self psychologists, there has been little intellectual activity.

The self psychologists have thrived with better practices than others have but they have been effectively split off from the institute for two decades. The 1997 annual conference of self psychology held in Chicago was sold out with 700 registrants (Ritter 1997).

Organisationally, the pyramidal structure of the Chicago Institute was replaced by a system where nobody has any control, where everybody complains about being powerless. After Pollock, members were not ready for another figure who did not consult and wielded power strongly. The aftermath of the Pollock regime degenerated into what Moraitis termed a 'circle of impotence' with a 'vicious cycle' where the power to effect changes is stymied by an unwieldy committee structure involving excessive oversight (Moraitis pers. comm. 1997).

The institute needs downsizing as the organisation is, as Gedo put it, 'absurdly overblown for the number of candidates we can expect. It's a banana republic, full of generals without troops. So we have to shrink, we have to concentrate on psychoanalytic matters, scholarly matters, give up these imperialistic ambitions' (Gedo interview 1992). In 1994 there were fifty-seven candidates and ninety faculty (Pappadis interview 1994). Candidates came mainly from the wider pool of social workers and psychologists who were accepted into APsaA institutes after the psychologists' lawsuit, but even so in 1996 there were three new candidates and no class was held (Goldberg interview 1996). Training analyst status has remained an empty space since there are so few candidates. However, the faculty has been increased, as have the assessments on faculty members. John Gedo likened this income producing device as akin to the old European regimes selling patents of nobility. The spirit had not changed despite the revolution (Gedo pers. comm. 1997). In Gedo's view, insofar as the Pappadis administration showed the awareness that something needed to change, it tried to turn the clock back to the days of imperial glory, and tried to accomplish this by the usual administrative machinations. Currently, this means increasing enrolments by making the Chicago Institute more 'user-friendly', with the implication that most would be accepted and few requirements would be enforced. Unfortunately, the institute was not able to run a new class for 1999–2000 because of lack of enrolments. According to Gedo, the present tensions are between the minority who want to upgrade the intellectual level and the apparachiks who ensure that this will not happen (Gedo, pers. comm. 1997). As Arnold Goldberg told his contemporaries, 'we lived through the rise and decline of the science. The only thing that will save us is the recrudescence of intellectual thought' (Goldberg interview 1992). None the less, there is more tolerance; as folksinger Judy Collins might have put it in her concert benefit for the Chicago Psychoanalytic Society, everybody listens to 'Both sides now' (Knight 1995).

4 FEAR AND LOATHING IN LOS ANGELES

> The very thing that brought me and so many others to LA after the war was the climate. Not only the weather, but also the emotional and intellectual climate. We quickly became the most important society outside the East Coast because this was an attractive place. It's also not an accident that this is tinsel town – the movie capital, the excitement capital. With the glories of the climate comes the excitement of the beautiful, thrilling people, people who make great analytic patients. There was always great rivalry for patients. The point is that this is a place of exciting people and with it comes great ambition, visibility, exhibitionism, cultism, factionalism, exciting ideas – and eccentric ideas.
> Leo Rangell, in Wilson (1993a, p. 17)

I

For Leo Rangell, who arrived in Los Angeles in 1946 the year that the Los Angeles Psychoanalytic Society and Institute (LAPSI) was founded, Los Angeles deserves more intense research than other places (Wilson 1993a, p. 15). 'Southern California has always been more exciting and more disturbing than any other place I know. Perhaps the two go together. Ordinarily, a disturbed excitement should make for a very creative place. But places that are creative can become deserts when things go wrong. And things have gone wrong with us' (ibid.). Things went so wrong in Rangell's opinion, because of the unique *dramatis personae* in Los Angeles (Rangell interview 1992).

LAPSI had a disturbed history from its beginnings. In 1950 just four years after it was founded, the institute split, and subsequently again became badly polarised during the 1950s and 1960s. Under the guise of theoretical differences major political struggles developed between Freudians and followers of the 'English School' of Melanie Klein, as well as between LAPSI and the APsaA during the 1960s and 1970s. This fascinating and colourful history is marked by what one protagonist, Bernard Brandchaft, identified as 'two interwoven patterns: the development of ideas and the trajectory of scientific evolution, and the use of ideas for political, personal power purposes' (Brandchaft interview 1992).

The story of LAPSI is peculiarly perplexing and mysterious. I found an especially evident 'Rashomon' quality in Los Angeles – psychoanalysts would give utterly divergent yet often enough internally consistent accounts of events. Added to this was very intense emotion about what had happened often decades before.

Those seeking to understand the Los Angeles situation have rarely looked at the whole picture. Often the 'Freud–Klein troubles' of the 1960s and 1970s are not seen in terms of the preceding history. One protagonist, Leo Rangell made this point very well:

> People started when they came in – as though there was nothing before that. 'The history of Los Angeles was when I arrived in Los Angeles'. Someone came from the Menninger Clinic in 1956 – 'that's when the Los Angeles business started'. The fact that there was a split five years before that, grew on a soil five years before that, is irrelevant. (Rangell interview 1992)

This chapter examines how many seemingly independent political events in LAPSI's political history can only be properly understood in the context of earlier events.

Early History and the 1950 Split

Established in 1935 under the aegis of the Chicago and Topeka Institutes, the Los Angeles Psychoanalytic Study Group, was the first West Coast psychoanalytic organisation. For the ensuing decade the principal problem was the question of lay analysis given that a number of European émigré psychoanalysts working in Los Angeles either were not physicians or their European medical qualifications were not recognised in California. The APsaA's 1938 rule prohibiting membership of lay analysts in its societies made for a particularly difficult situation for these analysts. The significant number of important lay analysts in California (some were its leaders) were outraged at the rule change and defied it by continuing to admit lay analysts. Karl Menninger and Robert Knight from the Topeka Institute publicly exposed the Los Angeles Study Group for permitting lay analysis in 1939. Then, insisting that San Francisco could better enforce the ban in California than could Topeka, they encouraged ten Californian medical analysts to form the first West Coast society in 1942, the San Francisco Psychoanalytic Society. The

APsaA agreed, and Topeka was released from its responsibility for California – and its lay analysts (Friedman 1990, pp. 228–9).

While half of the Charter Members of the San Francisco Psychoanalytic Society came from San Francisco, Ernst Simmel from Los Angeles was elected as the first President. In 1934, A. A. Brill asked Simmel to come to Los Angeles to 'put it on the psychoanalytic map'. Simmel was co-founder of the Berlin Institute for Psychoanalysis and established the first psychoanalytic clinic in Berlin, *Schloss Tegel* (Shershow 1986, p. 5). Room was left to establish a separate Los Angeles society which would be able to deal with the lay analysis issue as it saw fit (Kandelin 1966; Windholz, in American Psychoanalytic Association 1975c, pp. 36–7).[1] During the 1940s and into the early 1950s more than twenty-five psychoanalysts 'emigrated' from Topeka after being trained at the Menninger Clinic and the associated Topeka Institute for Psychoanalysis.[2]

LAPSI had major conflicts from the time of its founding by Ernst Simmel, Ralph (Romi) Greenson and others in 1946 – Greenson had just become the first graduate of a psychoanalytic institute on the West Coast (Greenson 1962, p. 14). Together with Greenson the Viennese and German analysts dominated the institute. A violent ostensibly theoretical dispute resulted in many of the other analysts splitting off in 1950 to found a diverse group that was to become The Society for Psychoanalytic Medicine of Southern California. Franz Alexander, director of the Chicago Psychoanalytic Institute, influenced many of the analysts there. The new group represented a more liberal counterpoint to the prevailing orthodoxy in LAPSI which, on the other hand, was unorthodox in including almost all the European lay analysts. By naming itself 'The Society for Psychoanalytic Medicine of Southern California', the new institute signalled its difference and distance from LAPSI which harboured lay analysts.[3]

A 'power vacuum' was left by the early death of Otto Fenichel shortly before LAPSI was officially founded and the death of Ernst Simmel the following year (Shershow 1986, p. 9).The LAPSI atmosphere was then, according to Leo Rangell, 'rife for something to happen'. In this era, the APsaA allowed splits – the New York–Columbia, Baltimore–Washington and Philadelphia splits just preceded the 1950 Los Angeles split (Rangell 1993).

Ideological and personal reasons led to the 1950 split. Franz Alexander's ideas greatly influenced a number of analysts, particularly Alexander and French's 1946 volume, *Psychoanalytic Therapy: Principles and Application* (Alexander and French 1946; Greenson, in American

Psychoanalytic Association 1975c, p. 26). Alexander and French's book introduced considerable modifications in psychoanalytic therapy techniques: flexible techniques involving changing tack to fit the needs of the moment, and the 'corrective emotional experience' which involved the therapist compensating for what the patient lacked in childhood. There was a major struggle between those who saw these ideas as attacking the very essence of psychoanalysis and those who vehemently denied this. However, the new group, some of whom had trained at the Chicago Institute, adopted a different approach. They felt they could have lived with the ideological differences were it not for what they perceived to be the other group's authoritarian and doctrinaire attitudes which they felt made scientific inquiry impossible (Gabe, in American Psychoanalytic Association 1975c, pp. 49–50). One leading analyst, May Romm, considered that there was a significant division between the American trained physicians and the European, mainly lay analysts. The Americans, she felt, 'were treated as interlopers and completely ignored ... It became obvious that those of us who were trained in the USA were considered by those who were trained in Europe as being of inferior quality and beneath their notice' (Gabe, in American Psychoanalytic Association 1975c, pp. 49–50).[4] One side consisted of 'orthodox' European analysts, including lay analysts whose patron saints were Sigmund and Anna Freud. On the other side were 'modern' or 'contemporary' medically qualified American analysts whose patron saint was Alexander who experimented with three times a week psychoanalysis and group therapy (Mandel 1996a, pp. 6–7).

While accepting Freud's cardinal concepts (Romm quoted in Eisenstein 1975, p. 7), the membership of the new group was theoretically diverse. However, according to Judd Marmor, a member of this group, most 'shared strong convictions about the issues of academic freedom and the importance of a medical background in psychoanalysis' (Marmor 1975).

From its inception, training practitioners was far more important for LAPSI than understanding and researching psychoanalytic theory (Tidd 1962, p. 8). The major differences between the classical group and the new group influenced by Alexander were over training issues, questions so often found at the heart of disputes within psychoanalytic institutes. The new group was viewed as minimising the distinctions between psychoanalysis and psychotherapy,[5] and was accused of 'sloppy' teaching by the classical group (Lewy 1963, p. 9). Those influenced by Alexander were in favour of fewer hours per week for a training analysis.

Romm's Technique Seminar 'brought it to a head', Greenson recalled. He recollected her saying

> outlandish things to the candidates, such as, 'Don't have an hour end unpleasantly. Why should it end unpleasantly? I always like to say a nice thing at the end of an hour'. Or give the patient a friendly pat. We had heard indirectly she sometimes kissed one or another of her patients at the end of the hour. And I would say to my candidates who I was supposedly analysing, 'Look, if she ever says that again, you tell her you don't think that's psychoanalysis!' (Greenson 1962, p. 19)

Greenson remembered everything being decided by a close vote and that 'every society meeting was charged with such fervour and such hostility. We were always so afraid of doing anything that would hurt our stand. We were so bitter, vitriolic'. Taking candidates became crucial because 'building up a dynasty for yourself' was dependent on it. 'We had terrible battles, it became untenable. It was just impossible to work; we were upset all the time and our candidates were upset all the time' (ibid., p. 20).

Leonard Rosengarten, who was active in the Los Angeles Institute from 1950, summed up the differing perceptions: 'The old group saw the new group as heretical and a threat to classical analytic training. The new group viewed the old group as intolerant, stultifying and as a threat to academic freedom.'[6] The increasing polarisation had virtually led to administrative and institutional paralysis (Marmor 1975; Tidd 1962, pp. 3–4), and LAPSI was headed for a split.

The Education Committee, consisting of the training analysts, was almost evenly divided between the old group and the new group.[7] Both sides agreed to split, and a bargain was struck so that a new group could be affiliated with the APsaA. Both groups would agree to the appointment of an extra training analyst on their side so that the new group could have a fourth training analyst to fulfil the APsaA's minimum requirement of four training analysts for forming a new institute. Carel van der Heide was appointed for the original group while Norman Levy was appointed for the new group. The formal split was announced on February 16, 1950, and the Southern California Institute was admitted to the APsaA on April 30 (Greenson 1962, p. 20; Eisenstein 1975, p. 5; Rosengarten 1986, pp. 17–18). Since the Southern California Institute was admitted as a constituent society of the APsaA, the APsaA could not have viewed the new group as having given up the basic tenets of psychoanalysis (Eisenstein 1975, p. 3).

With three notable exceptions, candidates demonstrated the power of their emotional attachments to their training analysts by joining the institute their training analyst joined. Rangell was one of three candidates of Martin Grotjahn's who did not follow him into the Southern California Institute. 'But', Greenson later laughingly remarked, 'none of ours ever went to theirs. I don't know whether that was such a bargain. There were some I think I would have liked to give them' (Greenson 1962, pp. 21–2).

II

1950–64

When Leo Rangell arrived in Los Angeles in 1946, he felt that psychoanalysis seemed ideal. Psychoanalysis was then, according to Rangell, 'as golden as the Southern California sun'. The treatment of the war neuroses together with the arrival of the European analysts who had fled Hitler advanced psychoanalysis, attracting much professional and popular interest. While LAPSI had become almost paralysed in the late 1940s, the period following the split became for some a 'golden age' for psychoanalysis. Both societies expanded and graduates quickly developed full analytic practices (Wilson 1993b, p. 20; Shershow 1986, p. 9). Mel Mandel who began training at LAPSI in 1952, recalled that the animosity between the societies 'was as thick as a heavy fog' (Jeffrey 1996, p. 26). Still, within LAPSI the 1950s provided some 'periods of quiescence' (Leavitt interview 1992).[8]

By the early 1960s, the 'golden age' was over. The LAPSI Education Committee was again divided into entrenched blocs which prevented the appointment of new training analysts. This time the polarisation was between supporters of Ralph Greenson and of Leo Rangell. According to Ivan McGuire, a member of the Education Committee during much of this period and who, along with Carel van der Heide, had developed the LAPSI curriculum, that committee was 'tight and in-bred and ingrown' (Rodman 1982, p. 4; Bail 1991a). Heiman van Dam who, as a representative of the Committee of Child Analysis, reluctantly attended Education Committee meetings over this period, described the meetings as 'unbelievably disturbing. The passions, the concerns and the personal attacks of the members of the Education Committee on each other were unbelievable.' What van Dam remembered as the 'terrible amount of fighting' between members grouped around Greenson and those around Rangell was related to a number of factors.

Some of it was personality, some of it had to do with technical problems – some were more orthodox, others were more experimental. The outcome was that they would attack each other, sometimes through their candidates – 'Look what this candidate of yours said in my seminar!' Rather than working together, they worked against each other (van Dam interview 1992).

These intense interfactional struggles had reached their zenith by 1964. As one of the younger analysts allowed to attend meetings, Norman Atkins remembered being shocked when he saw 'the disintegration of our Education Committee in 1964–65. It was irrational, emotional, violent. They stood on chairs screaming at each other' (Atkins interview 1992).[9]

1964 also saw an APsaA site visit to LAPSI. While praising the level of teaching, the site visitors voiced great concern about the severe problems in Los Angeles that remained – 'the destructive relationship which existed among members of the institute'. The site visitors noted:

> The complaints seemed to transcend the commonplace bickering often encountered and thus should be considered most seriously by all concerned with psychoanalytic education in Los Angeles. The tensions and anxieties revealed to us were at a high pitch and did not bode well for the future. The descriptive terms encountered by the site visitors included 'autocratic', 'paranoid', 'vindictive', 'dominated by fear', 'self-seeking', 'self-centered', etc. (Bail 1991b, p. 16)[10]

The site visitors referred to 'malicious gossiping about each other by older analysts at social gatherings. This malicious backbiting is done in the presence of lay people as well as young analysts.' This exerted a deleterious effect on the image of the profession, particularly on 'young' psychoanalysts and students. The report continued:

> This image must also be adversely affected when 'young' psychoanalysts do not write papers since they do not dare read a lecture before the society. To do so would be to invite harsh, destructive, devastating criticism according to our informants. (ibid., p. 17)

Active in the institute between 1950 and 1977, Leonard Rosengarten concurred with the site visitors' estimate: 'There was something unprofessional and unanalytic about the period – about the analysts' personal conduct – because they were so angry with each other. They were indiscreet.' However, despite their criticisms, the site visitors did not want any major changes instituted. One of the site visitors even suggested to Rosengarten that a few of the younger people who were complaining that they were not able to teach could be 'given a sop' by being appointed to the faculty (Rosengarten interview 1992).

Some of the Site Committee's misgivings had been expressed earlier by others who lamented the lack of encouragement of younger members to give papers, or even discuss them at meetings. The 'give and take' so characteristic of the pioneering pre-war days was now absent (Tidd 1962, pp. 6–7). For Ivan McGuire, psychoanalysis had become 'more like a religious cult than a scientific body'. He described the widespread feeling of 'repression and lack of freedom' in LAPSI:

> Candidates often complained they were afraid to say anything at all. They had to please their analyst, especially if they got to the point of having supervised cases. They would begin to talk about one supervisor saying one thing, another supervisor something else. Especially if they talked about deviations from orthodox views, they would sometimes get into trouble with their training analyst. That made training almost a travesty – the candidate wanted to finish training, felt he was asked to be spontaneous and speak freely knowing that he would be punished for it or at least it would be dangerous. The atmosphere was like that at meetings and everywhere else. (McGuire interview 1992; see also Rodman 1982, p. 15)

McGuire recollected that if candidates expressed views that did not coincide with their training analyst, they would be 'rebuked for it, censured. They would get the idea that they should not entertain such ideas and should write the cases up in an acceptable way' (McGuire interview 1992). During this period, training analysts were required to report to the Education Committee on the progress of the training analysis – LAPSI became the first nonreporting institute in the APsaA in 1967 (Ourieff interview 1992).

Otto Kernberg's observations about the 'devastating effect on the "quality of life"' of a pervasive paranoid atmosphere in institutes applied here. This atmosphere is connected with the fact that candidates feel severely inhibited from openly expressing their views when their training analysts are present at the same meetings (Kernberg 1986, pp. 803–4). Kernberg further described institutes marked by a

> narrow intellectual frame determined by the locally prevalent views within the broad theoretical spectrum of psychoanalysis, intellectual toadyism or kow-towing to venerable fathers of the local group, petty 'cross-sterilization', and discouragement of original thinking. (ibid., p. 806)

Such descriptions were applicable to LAPSI from the 1950s at least into the 1960s. Further reasons for LAPSI's problems resulted from the time around the 1950 split. The small number of analysts in the early 1940s and the subsequent deaths of the most important of these, Fenichel and Simmel, made for difficulties. This was especially true since they needed to train the large post-war influx of candidates. Just before the split, there were sixty-seven candidates (Eisenstein 1975, p. 4) and eight training analysts.[11] LAPSI was, in Greenson's words, 'flooded with candidates' (Greenson 1962, p. 19). Moreover, as Atkins observed, because a number of training analysts were appointed by each group simply as a means to bolster itself, when the split occurred 'neither group was left with adequate enough experienced training analysts which is really where a lot of troubles started'. In the 1950 split both groups appointed insufficiently experienced training analysts to form an Education Committee to have an institute that could be part of the APsaA. Thus, the Education Committee problems pointed out by the 1964 site visitors may have had their roots in the political appointments of the late 1940s and early 1950s. Atkins argued that this 'provided the organisational soil for the emergence of self-proclaimed super-analysts'. If LAPSI had remained as one group incorporating the best of both sides, the position of 'superanalysts' who ruled in both institutes (Greenson and Rangell in LAPSI, and May Romm and Judd Marmor in the Southern California Institute) might not have emerged (Atkins interview 1992).

So the loss of leaders (particularly of Fenichel who had been able to contain dissent) together with the fact that already scarce resources were cut in two by the split, produced deleterious effects on LAPSI (van Dam interview 1992). Moreover, as Bernard Brandchaft maintained, there was continuity in the group dynamics that began with the first split:

> These arguments were centred around passionate declarations of the superiority of the concepts being used. Each one represented himself to be the better psychoanalyst, and in all of the disputes one or both of the parties were always branded not as having adversarial positions on the basis of differing observations and therefore concepts, but as introducing into psychoanalysis developments that were damaging to the science of psychoanalysis itself. (Brandchaft interview 1992)

The passionate declarations of the 1950s and 1960s centred on personalities, the divisions between the two real leaders of LAPSI, Greenson and Rangell. The Education Committee was divided about equally between adherents of each leader, and promotions to training analyst status were stymied for a decade because each side would block the other's candidates. Besides, the problems were apparently not just within the Education Committee but between the Education Committee and the membership. The 1964 site visitors had heard complaints from administrative officers and members 'that there is no communication between the executive branch and the membership at large' (Bail 1991b, p. 17).

Impropriety in the conduct of training further disturbed the institute ambience. Symptomatic was the case of a long-standing member of the Education Committee who had deteriorated, demanding prescriptions from his candidates for Nembutals, sedatives and narcotics. Norman Atkins recalled,

> He threatened to write adverse reports on those who wouldn't cooperate. He would reward those who did cooperate in different ways by sending patients, sharing costs. One candidate was appalled because he knew all the intimate lives of all the other candidates – it came up in the analysis. There were complaints about this to the Education Committee. They did nothing, and the one student who really stood up was kicked out of the institute. (Atkins interview 1992)[12]

This period in the history of LAPSI is a particularly important basis for understanding much of the framework within which the 'Freud–Klein troubles' occurred during the later 1960s into the 1970s. If the matter is viewed historically, the springboard for the dissatisfactions with the mainstream theories did not lie with whatever faults the theories may have had. Rather, a displacement took place whereby the wrongdoings of the training analysts were transferred, as Leo Rangell argued, onto the faults of the theories. The theory was blamed instead of the corrupt situation (Rangell interview 1992; Rangell 1982, pp. 29–56).

Ralph Greenson and Leo Rangell

After the 1950 split, both Leo Rangell and Ralph Greenson were unequalled as international psychoanalytic figures in Los Angeles. However, Greenson was LAPSI's most controversial figure.

Author of a classic clinical textbook, *The Technique and Practice of Psychoanalysis* (1967) and over sixty papers and articles, Greenson was unusual in moving outside the ambit of his analytic colleagues to give many public lectures.[13] His psychoanalytic interests were wide-ranging. He was most concerned that analysts with different theoretical approaches seemed to talk at each other (Wilson 1993b, p. 21). He was famous – now even infamous – as being Marilyn Monroe's analyst. Upon graduating as an analyst, Greenson quickly became a major influence in the Los Angeles psychoanalytic scene. He soon became an important figure nationally and later internationally and was active in psychoanalysis until his death in 1979.

Born in Brooklyn in 1910 as Romeo Samuel Greenschpoon, Greenson was one of a set of fraternal twins (his twin was infelicitously named Juliet). From childhood on Juliet excelled at music and became a famous concert pianist – Romi both admired and resented her achievement. According to research by Donald Spoto, 'Her applause, recognition, public acclaim and admiration created an acute sibling rivalry and weighed heavily on him' (Spoto 1993, p. 467). This may have accounted for Greenson's undoubted zest for showmanship, his eagerness for applause and his Hollywood involvements (Spoto 1993, p. 471). Unable to excel at the violin, Greenson followed his father's route into medicine. He undertook pre-med work at Columbia University and, completed his medical degree in Bern, Switzerland as quotas were placed on Jewish students in New York in that era. He interned in Los Angeles at Cedars of Lebanon and then travelled to Vienna where he trained with the psychiatrist William Stekel for nine months. Upon returning to Los Angeles, he quickly found that Stekel's technique did not work well with patients and commenced analytic training with Otto Fenichel, graduating as an analyst in 1942 (Wilson 1993b, pp. 19–20; Spoto 1993).

After graduating, Greenson joined the Army Air Corps and was stationed at Yuma, Arizona. There he became interested in war neuroses and used sodium pentathol for interviews. Transferred to Fort Logan, Colorado, he continued his work at a hospital for the rehabilitation of those suffering from war neuroses – this was where he first met Rangell (Wilson 1993b, p. 20). Leo Rosten based his novel *Captain Newman M.D.* (1961) on Captain Greenson. Indeed, Greenson received 12.5 per cent royalties from the film version which starred Gregory Peck (Spoto 1993, p. 470).[14]

In 1947, Ernst Simmel appointed Greenson as a training analyst (Greenson 1962, p. 18). After the split, Greenson became president of the Los Angeles Psychoanalytic Society (1951–53) and Dean of Education (1957–61). He was Clinical Professor of Psychiatry at the UCLA Medical School. Whatever his official positions he wielded a good deal of power and influence within LAPSI. Greenson was nationally and internationally well known not only for his numerous psychoanalytic writings but also for his real flair for lecturing and teaching. His institute seminars were especially highly regarded at LAPSI. Hilda Rollman-Branch felt that although Greenson was 'a character' and 'narcissistic', his tactlessness could be forgiven because of 'his enthusiasm and inspiration. He was without a doubt the best teacher of psychoanalysis any of us have ever had' (Rollman-Branch, pers. comm. 1992). None the less, some still saw him as shallow (Spoto 1993, pp. 471-2).

Greenson greatly enjoyed public speaking. Rosengarten remembered his giving 'a wonderful impression to the public. He was a wonderful speaker, spontaneous. He could listen to any paper, get up and comment on it. He was a little outlandish at times but very capable. He was able to attract people and he could get twenty analysts' practices filled with patients' (Rosengarten interview 1992). As psychoanalysis is based on private practice, a good source of referrals can be very influential. As James Grotstein pointed out, Greenson was 'very powerful not only because of his eloquence but also because he controlled referrals. He was an enormous referral source so a lot of people were dependent on him. He sorted the cards' (Grotstein interview 1992). Several older lay analysts were especially beholden to him for referrals and the protection they needed as lay analysts.

Greenson was a passionate man with strongly held views. Three analysts each reported to me that after a disagreement Greenson did not speak to them for years (interviews with Brandchaft, Ourieff and Rosengarten, 1992). He was given to irrational fits of anger (Spoto 1993, p. 587). Elisabeth Young-Bruehl, Anna Freud's biographer, aptly described Greenson as 'a hard-living man of passionate enthusiasm and even flamboyance, a man for whom psychoanalysis was ... a way of life' (Young-Bruehl 1988, p. 371).

Supervised by Milton Wexler, Greenson shared offices with him for some years, and was greatly affected by Wexler's ideas about the importance of closeness between analyst and patient (see Wexler 1951, p. 166; 1965, pp. 279-86; Greenson and Wexler 1969, pp. 359-86). Greenson moved nearer to Wexler's point of view about psychopathology, that it has more to do with developmental failure than conflict and had to be remedied with actual experience. Wexler gradually extended this view from schizophrenia to cover all psychopathology. Despite his textbook, Greenson considered himself as challenging classical psychoanalysis (Atkins interview 1992). He was hurt to be considered an agent of established classical analysis (Brandchaft interview 1992).

However, Greenson was closely connected to Anna Freud and her group in London. His Foundation for Research in Psychoanalysis in

Beverly Hills provided an important source of funds for Anna Freud's work in London as well as for Albert Solnit's New Haven group around the journal, *The Psychoanalytic Study of the Child*. The fund financed Anna Freud's purchase of Freud's London home and half of the Hampstead Clinic's 1968 budget shortfall of $60,000 (Young-Bruehl 1988, pp. 379–80; Atkins interview 1992). The chief wealthy donor for this Foundation was one of Greenson's patients, Lita Annenberg Hazen (Young-Bruehl 1988, p. 371).

However, Greenson wielded his power within LAPSI unwisely. Had he acted in a more cohesive way within LAPSI and backed this up with the money from the Foundation, perhaps there would not have been the general dissatisfactions that allowed the opportunity for the Kleinian and object relations influences to develop. Unfortunately, the Kleinian approach was not so successful because of its intrinsic worth but due to the needs created, as Atkins put it, by the 'wreckage' at LAPSI (Atkins interview 1992).

As a contributor to psychoanalysis, Greenson was open to new ideas from many sources,[15] but was not loath to claim them as his own. He even wrote about his own 'unconscious plagiarism' of other psychoanalytic thinkers (Greenson 1969, p. 341). As a passionate, powerful, charismatic and forthright man with high visibility, he was the subject of many attributions including charges that he was under the domination of others such as Anna Freud or the New York leadership of the APsaA. While he had highly placed friends, Greenson's hubris rendered him in a sense incapable of being dominated by anybody else or by anybody else's ideas unless they became incorporated as his own.

Leo Rangell, born in 1913, was twice President of the IPA (1971–75), twice president of the APsaA (1961, 1966) and three times president of the Los Angeles Psychoanalytic Society (1956–58, 1964–5). He is now honorary president of the IPA. He is the author of more than 350 articles and several books (Rangell interview 1992; Wilson 1993a, p. 15). He was a neurologist before beginning psychoanalytic training at the New York Psychoanalytic Institute. He completed his psychoanalytic training at the Los Angeles Psychoanalytic Institute after arriving in Los Angeles in 1946. During World War II, Rangell and Greenson were both stationed in Denver teaching psychodynamics to flight surgeons and treating traumatic neuroses of returned prisoners of war with sodium pentathol (Wilson 1993a, p. 16). Rangell and Fenichel met for a few days when Fenichel – who had been Greenson's analyst (Greenson 1962, p. 2) – visited Greenson in Denver, but Fenichel and Rangell never became close personally.[16]

Los Angeles psychoanalytic politics inspired Rangell's formulation in 1973 of 'The Syndrome of the Compromise of Integrity' (Rangell 1982, p. 41) with its emphasis upon the importance of the incorruptibility of the analyst (Rangell 1974, p. 11).[17] Rangell argued that while neuroses resulted from compromises between the ego and the id, the syndrome of the compromise of integrity was the result of the successful assault of the ego's narcissistic wishes on superego standards. As Rangell expressed it, 'Within each individual there's a three or four way conflict going on in which either he compromises his id and develops a paralysed arm, or he compromises his superego and becomes a sociopath acting out, a character assassin of other people, or a crook with money or sex' (Rangell interview 1992). Referring to psychoanalytic life in general – and Los Angeles in particular – he asserted that psychoanalytic integrity was sacrificed when internal conflicts of interest were

> resolved in favor of narcissism at the expense of principles. These occur in small and larger committees, in the large society, in one geographical area as much as another, and at all levels of responsibility. Character assassination by a small number is made possible on a wide scale, if not by the crime of silence, by the sin of omission on the part of many. Impaired morale and ill-will, scientific deterioration and even corruptibility are accompaniments too frequent to be ignored. (Rangell 1974 , p. 10)

Rangell held that such situations went beyond the manifest theoretical content of the disagreements and pointed towards underlying problems.[18]

While some theoretical affinity existed between Rangell and Greenson, behind the scenes there were major personality differences, rivalry and mutual criticisms. The sibling rivalry that was an especially important personal area for Romeo Greenson probably affected his feelings of rivalry with Leo Rangell. They were close contemporaries. They worked together during the War and were both actively involved with the same institute. Initially at least they were both of the same analytic persuasion. Both wrote prolifically and were the major Los Angeles figures recognised both nationally and internationally. The rivalry intensified as Rangell became more famous and achieved greater prestige as APsaA president while Greenson achieved neither national nor international official positions. He was scathing about Rangell's achievement of the IPA presidency (Rangell 1974, p. 11).

Rangell believed it imperative for analysts to focus on rational debate and discussion, on a charisma of ideas and not persons. (Rangell 1988a, p. 60). As Rangell put it, 'Charisma is to be scrutinized, not followed. The effect that it produces in those it influences is regressive, not enhancing. The bond between the leader and the emotionally led is based on an unconscious identification' (Rangell 1988c). According to James Grotstein, 'Rangell was the only one of the senior analysts who went anti-Kleinian and remained a gentleman.' However, Greenson behaved differently. 'Greenson was a stand-up comic who could insult the audience, make them feel terrible, he was formidable, there was a nasty twinge to him' (Grotstein interview 1992).

Greenson was the charismatic leader of a group under his control while Rangell declined such a status (see Rangell 1988a, pp. 55–6). Rangell's personal sensitiveness was insignificant beside Greenson's hubris. Rangell struggled against Greenson's excesses so tragically exemplified in Greenson's involvement with his patient, Marilyn Monroe.

The approach Greenson recommended in his 1967 textbook could not have been further removed from his treatment of Marilyn Monroe between 1960 and her death in 1962. In his well-researched biography of Marilyn Monroe, Donald Spoto charged that Greenson 'betrayed every ethic and responsibility to his family, his profession and to Marilyn Monroe' and blamed Greenson for his 'egregious mishandling of his most famous patient'. There was, according to Spoto, a 'proprietary and grotesque control of patient by therapist' (Spoto 1993, pp. 497–8).[19]

Spoto asserted that Greenson was obsessed and grossly over-involved with Monroe, and may even have been negligent in relation to her death (Spoto 1993, pp. 649–50).[20] However, even if there is some factual foundation, this judgement is probably still too harsh. Greenson's approach can be seen in terms of the experimental approaches of the time that were demonstrated to be misconceived only later. Since Greenson did not view Monroe as an analytic case, other approaches and parameters could be seen as legitimate and potentially valuable. The 'cutting edge' ideas of a generation ago may have appeared to vindicate Greenson's approach to treatment of such a difficult borderline patient.[21] Besides, Greenson told his colleagues that he decided to offer his family as a substitute for the family Monroe never had because she would have killed herself sooner if he had committed her to a mental hospital (Rankin 1992).

However, as LAPSI's most powerful and favoured psychoanalytic leader for such an extensive period, Greenson's conduct had significant consequences for the contemporary and subsequent history of the organisation. However, Greenson's approach to Monroe did not take place in a vacuum. His close relationship with Wexler, Hollywood's then premier 'shrink to the stars', and the influence of Wexler's ideas upon him was important not only for his approach to treatment but shaped an important chapter in LAPSI's history.[22]

The Wexler Affair

The most significant political event in LAPSI after the 1950 split occurred in 1964, two years after Monroe's death, and directly involved both Wexler and Greenson. Rangell's integrity was challenged in circumstances that led to his permanent withdrawal from LAPSI affairs.

Rangell acceded to the Nominating Committee's request to assume his third time presidency of the Los Angeles Psychoanalytic Society during 1964–65. During Rangell's presidency one of Wexler's patients complained to the society that Wexler had physically attacked her. According to the complainant, she and her analyst, Wexler, got into a fight and he had slapped her. Then, as Norman Atkins recalled, Greenson, who shared offices with Wexler, 'ran into the office when he heard the screaming and wrestled Wexler to the ground and pulled them apart' (Atkins interview 1992).

As president of the society Rangell believed he was duty-bound to deal with the complaint. (The patient had complained previously but a preceding president had swept it under the carpet). Because he did not want the personal responsibility for undertaking an investigation, Rangell wanted any decision about procedure to be made not by him but by the executive as a whole. Rangell had the patient tell her story to every executive officer who included Maurice Walsh, Norman Atkins, and the then vice-president, Maimon Leavitt. According to Rangell:

> They decided unanimously that the patient's complaints needed to be taken care of because while she was probably borderline – maybe worse – the incidents that she described were so believable and vivid that it had to be dealt with. Not only the physical behaviour, the hit, but behaviour which led her to have certain expectations from Wexler which fitted in with some of the theoretical ideas that he had about great closeness between patient and analyst which were acted out in the Monroe case with Greenson. (Rangell interview 1992)

Greenson confirmed before members of the Executive Committee (at that time the Ethics Committee was the Society Executive Committee) that there had indeed been a hit, that the patient was not delusional about that (Rangell interview 1992). After preliminary meetings to determine whether there should be an investigation or not, the Executive Committee unanimously voted for an investigation of the incident to take place. However, Wexler was very upset when he found out that Rangell seemed to have been investigating him without his being apprised (van Dam interview 1992, Mandel interview 1994). At that point,

> Wexler and Greenson came before the society and circulated letters saying that Rangell was out to destroy them. They initiated a recall petition for the whole board and Rangell in particular for malfeasance. (Atkins interview 1992)

Wexler had been a lawyer in New York before training as a clinical psychologist and analyst (Friedman 1990, pp. 229–30). Wexler instigated the appointment of a committee to investigate whether the process had been fair. Rangell chose two members, Heiman van Dam and Charles Sarlin, while Wexler chose Gerald Aronson and Rudolf Eckstein. The society selected Mel Mandel who had been involved with LAPSI since 1951 as the chair as he belonged to neither side. According to Mandel, the Rangell-appointed members of the committee were stronger fighters than those appointed by Wexler (Mandel interview 1994). Partly because of the composition, the investigating committee did not find that Rangell had acted wrongly. Yet neither did they find in his favour. A rule was established that no psychoanalyst would in future be investigated by the Los Angeles Society without being informed (van Dam interview 1992; Mandel interview 1994).

With a few exceptions the society rallied behind Greenson and, Atkins recalled, Rangell felt 'very depressed and unappreciated' (Atkins interview 1992). According to Leavitt, many members felt the ethics charge to be political, that it was 'handled very badly and was a reflection of the animosity there' (Leavitt interview 1992). Whether the ethics matter was politically motivated or not, it was bound to be seen or used as such in the politically charged situation. But Rangell did not believe that it was political:

> Greenson hated the committee that talked to him because he blamed me as the president for fomenting this and almost for initiating it. I didn't even know this patient, she came to us. It was ugly, painful, also bitter. I came back to do an extra job which I didn't need. I was doing it in an upright way almost to an nth, nth degree, and instead the large group of the rank and file was suspicious because they were under Greenson's and Wexler's influence. I then served my second Presidency of the American.

Within a year I was nominated as President of the IPA. I was a tremendous focus of envy and displacement of transference. (Rangell interview 1992)[23]

The charge was that Rangell and his committee had operated in ways that it should not have done. Mandel felt that those on Rangell's side were much better prepared and knowledgeable about how to protect him than those on Wexler's side. Mandel recalled,

> that it was decided that the Ethics Committee should not have proceeded the way it did but that didn't constitute some terrible damage in and of itself, that it ought not to conduct things in the future that way. It didn't constitute a capital crime. They were in effect slapped on the wrist for what they did but also vindicated. They weren't proved to be in violation with some ethical code of their own. Wexler didn't feel at all vindicated and left the group but brought that on his own head by not having people who better understood what he had to have presented on his side the way Leo's people did. So we produced a unanimous report that didn't entirely vindicate Leo but did essentially say that Wexler's behaviour with his patient was understandably a cause for some kind of investigation. (Mandel interview 1994)

The investigation was, however, testimony to how poorly the institute was functioning (van Dam interview 1992). Norman Atkins thought that the investigation 'so scarred the membership and the students' that nobody was in good shape to handle later events in a rational and constructive way:

> There was an enormous regressive effect on the whole group and everyone behaved like disturbed children from a very disturbed family from then on. I don't think we have recovered from that yet. The family secret was this whole impeachment experience about the revered father and the tyrannical father whom everybody loved and hated at the same time. They were afraid of him. The conflict over that hate and love and seeing the father so attacked I think was such an embarrassment, was such a regressive experience. I am sure it entered into everyone's analyses. (Atkins interview 1992)

The investigation through the Ethics Committee may not have been tactful on Rangell's part since there was suspicion that Wexler would not be fairly treated by a committee dominated by Rangell and his supporters who were not seen to be neutral (Atkins interview 1992; Mandel interview 1994). Justice needed to be seen to be done (Mandel interview 1994). Yet during that period there was no lawful alternative to the way that Rangell was proceeding and Rangell was in a cleft stick.

Atkins insisted to Rangell that they had to fight, that he must not resign. Atkins summed up some of the consequences to LAPSI:

> Rangell was vindicated but he was forever scarred. He never took part constructively in the workings of the institute again. Greenson felt vindicated and became rather tyrannical. Wexler was permanently wounded and withdrew from the society which was a tremendous loss to us. (Atkins interview 1992)

The investigating committee agreed that Rangell had acted within the letter of the law, but this law was subsequently changed in the new bylaws.[24] However, the moral question shifted to a procedural one and everyone forgot the original charge. There was more than a legitimate *prima facie* complaint of a patient that it would have been unethical to ignore, especially if Wexler's ideas and cases histories were taken into account. In one case, Wexler reported physical battles between a woman patient and himself.[25] Rangell kept distant from it and involved others in the inquiry. Was Rangell's major mistake was not to have informed Wexler about the inquiry as soon as practicable after the complaint? As Mandel put it,

> If he didn't want to leave the impression he was after Wexler, he would have had to change the system. In today's climate, you would expect a committee to be appointed that would be seen to be impartial but in the climate then it would not have been expected. (Mandel interview 1994)

However, the structure of LAPSI – and of most psychoanalytic institutes – was such that it is hard to distance politics from ethics. The Rangell–Greenson conflicts made this appear like just another political battle with official positions being exploited for political gain. Yet the original question was to do with the actual behaviour of Wexler and Greenson (and perhaps the context of this behaviour within Wexler's theoretical framework). It was symptomatic of the state of LAPSI that the basic charge was not considered. It moved right out of the drama when it should have stayed at centre stage. However, it did raise the question of how ethical issues should be handled. It could be argued that in the conflictual atmosphere in LAPSI at the time, that, as it were, a 'mistrial' really needed to be decreed since justice neither could be done nor be seen to be done. As a closed institution, LAPSI faced attendant difficulties in differentiating judge, jury, defence and prosecution. Even if those in authority behaved totally ethically, Greenson and Wexler could quite understandably feel uncomfortable about their enemies judging them fairly. Perhaps it is in the guild nature of psychoanalytic societies that they should not hear ethics charges against individual members who on an important level they are there to protect. Such charges ought perhaps to be heard by a duly constituted outside quasi-judicial body.[26] The smell of corruption remained in LAPSI after the Wexler affair. This no doubt contributed to greater mistrust of those in power as well as further fuelling negative attitudes towards the psychoanalytic mainstream because these were the ideas of those in power.

The morale of the Los Angeles Psychoanalytic Society and its individual members suffered greatly through this affair. Not only did Wexler withdraw from LAPSI (he obviously did not feel exculpated) but Rangell's withdrawal from LAPSI dated from this time. Rangell had not been unpopular – after all, he had been invited to be President and duly elected. But as Atkins put it, after these events, 'he was a dead man' Atkins interview 1992. Rangell did not become embroiled in the events surrounding the Freud–Klein disputes during the 1970s. Rangell said he resigned from LAPSI during the 1970s because he was 'intensely opposed to the turn of events, not only to the content but the tone and motivation ... Because of the events of those years the training of an entire generation suffered' (Wilson 1993a, p. 18).

The LAPSI Climate

Perhaps the most important trigger for interest in other theoretical and clinical psychoanalytic perspectives in the 1960s was the climate of the institute. As Heiman van Dam explained:

> The terrible atmosphere transmitted itself into the training programme. At best, training analyses are not very good – not all training analysts are equally suitable and not all candidates are equally suitable. The result is that there are quite a number of candidates where the outcome of the personal analysis is not what one would hope for. The LA Institute was weak. I have heard of people being graduated by the old Education Committee who said, 'They will never do us any harm, why don't we graduate him?' 'We should have gotten rid of him a long time ago, but let's graduate him.' After they graduated, a number of candidates discovered that they were not very good either with themselves or with their patients. So they became dissatisfied with the classical method, quite rightly so. As a result of the tensions in the Education Committee, I imagine in Los Angeles we had more failures in training and training analysis than elsewhere. So Los Angeles became ripe for something else. (van Dam interview 1992)

With understandable exaggeration, van Dam considered that Los Angeles became

> somewhat of a garbage can of psychoanalysis. Some people have come here who were decouched elsewhere. They come to Los Angeles and become a training analyst overnight. There has never been anybody in Los Angeles who has lost his status as a training analyst. (ibid.)[27]

Those for whom analysis had not worked turned to other approaches such as the Kleinian or Fairbairnian approaches (van Dam interview 1994). Rangell argued that when analysts have experienced their analysis as inadequate, instead of blaming their analyst or the climate under which the analysis was conducted, they blame the theory under which the analysis and training were conducted. Obviously, this is a complex issue for there may be something profoundly wrong with that theory, and it is often hard to separate the theory from the person of the analyst (Rangell 1982, p. 35).[28]

An old analytic saw has it that 'the first analysis is for the institute, the second is for yourself'. The training analyst plays a real role in the candidate's institute life and can act as a 'convoy' to safely guide and protect the candidate through his or her professional training at the institute (Arlow 1972, p. 559) – or the training analyst can play a real role in opposing that progress. In either case, the candidate is beholden to the training analyst. Since the analyst plays a real role in the candidate's life, the analytic process is not as free (and therefore not as helpful) as ordinary analyses. As Rangell pointed out:

> The 'analytic family' is more than a semantic cliché. The analyst, supervisors, teachers, peers, and other analysts constitute a dynamic social structure which corresponds in an almost one-to-one manner with the hierarchic structure of the original family. Herein lie a special challenge and the unique problem of the training analysis. Almost as in child analysis where the actual family surrounding the patient interferes with a transference displacement to the analyst, in this case the patient lives within an ongoing derivative family which can serve as a strong potential drain away from the threatening developing transference. (Rangell 1982, p. 47)

The problems as to how (or whether) an adequate analysis is possible in such circumstances need to be recognised rather than acted out. Especially during the period under discussion, candidates were very much in the power of their training analysts since their analysts reported on the progress of the analysis to the Education Committee. It was normally felt necessary to please their analyst which meant that important issues might never be analysed. The combination of the problems of the training analysis – especially where there is reporting and corruption – with the problems of the institute laid the ground for further analytic unrest in Los Angeles.

The unrest was exacerbated in 1964 by the results of a study undertaken by the Committee on Psychoanalytic Practice which showed how little psychoanalysis was actually being done by LAPSI members. In addition to showing the disaffection members felt for the organisation, the study showed that relatively few analysts were conducting full analyses four or five times a week (Rosengarten interview 1992; Bail 1991a; Mandel interview 1992; Leavitt 1986, pp. 26–7).

With the dearth of analytic patients, some were taking cases that are more marginal for analysis which Leonard Rosengarten, who cochaired the committee, felt should not have been taken on as analytic cases. Some analysts were dissatisfied that the institute had not trained them to treat psychotics and that therefore they had an inadequate education.

Much of the dissatisfaction, once again, related to the question of the appointment of training analysts. Training analyst status was attractive if only because a small number of training analysts each had a good analytic practice which included a significant number of candidates (Rosengarten interview 1992). However, the progression to training analyst status was being thwarted by the Education Committee. There was a significant push to open the institute, especially to make training analyst status reachable in a normal career path.

In the context of the lack of analytic cases and the small chance of achieving training analyst status, the attraction of the alternative perspectives of Klein and object relations was evident, since they could help analysts work with a broader cohort of patients than the classical neurotics they had been trained to treat. Klein, for example, focused on primitive, paranoid and psychotic processes, and Fairbairn concentrated on schizoid processes. All of these issues contributed to the dissatisfaction that led to the Reorganisation of the Institute and Society in 1967 and the simultaneous appointment of sixteen training analysts. Meantime a pivotal development was looming.

The Reorganisation: 1964–67

Alongside the beginnings of the Kleinian development, during 1963 and 1964 various proposals to reform LAPSI had been made by the Dean, Lawrence Friedman, and other training analysts. All were shelved.

Because it seemed impossible to bring about changes, Friedman resigned as dean in 1965 (Leavitt 1986, p. 27).

In 1964, at an early summer party at Maimon Leavitt's house a group of younger analysts in their forties decided to do something about the difficulties and try to change the organisation (Leavitt interview 1992; Mandel interview 1992). Arthur Ourieff recalled his part in it:

> When Leavitt and I were picked out to be training analysts, I didn't like it or the closed environment. It was not to do with politics or ideology – I didn't like the idea of being selected. One night at a dinner party, I was talking with Mike [Maimon] Leavitt over a drink and I said, 'We've got to do something about this hierarchy'. Mel Mandel came into the bar where we were standing and we all agreed that we would form a committee to see what we could do to help the training analysts and that's what started the Reorganization. It had nothing to do with ideology, it had to do with the fact that we were in our forties and we wanted to get on with it. And I was reacting to being one of the chosen. (Ourieff interview 1992)

The group of four, which continued meeting at Leavitt's house, was extended to include Brandchaft, Rosengarten, Hilda Rollman-Branch and some others. Not wanting to be seen as a rump group, in the autumn of 1964 they asked that the group become an official committee of LAPSI. Chaired by Maimon Leavitt, the Joint Committee on Mutual Problems of the Society and Institute was appointed soon after. Leonard Rosengarten and Arthur Ourieff chaired a subcommittee to investigate the training school while Leavitt chaired a subcommittee to investigate the society (Leavitt interview 1992; Leavitt 1986, p. 27; Mandel interview 1992; Rosengarten interview 1992). Two attorneys helped to draft the new bylaws: John Piggott, the head of the largest legal firm in Los Angeles, Gibson, Dunn & Crutcher, worked on the society, and Marvin Freeman, who was later to become a judge, worked on the institute (Rosengarten interview 1992). Marvin Freeman commented in 1974 on the situation at the time:

> I was first told that the way in which one became a training analyst was to be approved by previous training analysts and that it was a one hundred percent self-perpetuating concept. I was told that what we were doing was considered by some as revolutionary; that is, we were changing the system from the handing-on of the court concept for self-perpetuation to something new and certainly much more democratic. I was very pleased to be part of a group like that because that is very appealing, obviously, to most people in this free country. (Bail 1991b, p. 96)

With the investigatory committees in place, Leavitt remembered, the years 1965–67 were spent talking about reorganising LAPSI more democratically. According to Leavitt,

> Some of the older people who were in control felt we were making it too loose, too democratic, removing authority and control. Some felt despairing and some actively supported it. There was surprisingly little real opposition. (Leavitt interview 1992)

Heiman van Dam opposed the Reorganisation:

> I felt that the mess within the Education Committee was bad but that they wouldn't cure anything just by opening it all up – I predicted they would create a mess among a much larger group of people and essentially that is what they did. I resigned from LAPSI. (van Dam interview 1992)

Greenson accepted the Reorganisation but Rangell accepted it less well.[29]

The groundswell for change among the membership had succeeded. At the beginning of 1967 the institute (which was responsible for training and run by the Education Committee consisting of Training Analysts) directed by Jack Vatz and the society (the collegial and scientific arm of LAPSI run by the members) which was presided over by Maimon Leavitt adopted the new bylaws whereby the formerly separate institute and society were brought together as a single entity. The new bylaws were adopted by the society, as Leavitt recalled, 'by a favourable vote of 90%, unheard of in our organisations about anything, even adjournments at midnight. It was this consensus that convinced the Education Committee to relinquish its control and accede to the plan, as well as the merits of the plan itself' (Leavitt 1986, p. 28). As Mandel put it,

> We democratised it and took the power out of the hands of a small Education Committee and put it into the hands of the membership. The old guard had no power – they were unhappy with it but they had to live with it. (Mandel interview 1992)

In one of the many reports back to members that helped maintain their involvement, Leavitt replied to those who thought that the atmosphere, not the organisation, needed changing:

> But organisational changes can be effective if they themselves foster a climate of change and improvement, if they reduce some of the hierarchical sources of conflict, if they force a reassessment of individuals of

their roles, if they reflect the wish of the membership and help define the areas of conflict. (quoted in Leavitt 1986, p. 28)

The new bylaws brought the institute, which used to have its own Board of Trustees, under the aegis of the Board of Directors of the society, making the institute responsible to the society (Rosengarten interview 1992). In Leavitt's words, the bylaws

> were an attempt to reorganise the training school and preserve its autonomy, and yet establish an organic relationship with the society members as a whole ... It was an attempt to improve the administrative structure and simplify the complexity (even though it still maintained a fairly complex organisation), to improve the sense of participation by the members, improve the efficiency and capacity to function of the Education Committee, now known as the Coordinating Council, to give the faculty a greater voice in the operation of the training school, thereby lessening the dominating and conflictual control by the training analysts, and generally to create a certain degree of participatory democracy, along with an autonomous training school. (Leavitt 1986, pp. 28–9)

The new Coordinating Council that replaced the old institute Education Committee had limited terms of office for senior positions so that people would not become entrenched in positions of power. The Council consisted of the director and the assistant director plus the chairs of six committees – Admissions, Candidates Evaluation Committee, Special Projects, Curriculum, Faculty and Child Analysis Committees (Bail 1991b, p. 19). The Coordinating Council whose structure remains the same today consists of thirty-six members, each committee consisting of six members. It was not entrenched and static since younger members were involved and offices were often rotated around the membership (Rosengarten interview 1992).

At that time the number of training analysts was increased by sixteen simultaneous appointments, and the process of becoming a training analyst became relatively automatic after a graduate had performed adequately for a stipulated time on the teaching faculty, been a member for five years, and had become a member of the APsaA. (Rosengarten interview 1992). Since appointment to training analyst status had relied so heavily on politics rather than merit, paranoia was bound to ensue. This was not a question of abolishing the position of training analyst as such but of according everyone the title. Since LAPSI's problems for decades were not only to do with the appointments or non-appointments of training analysts for political reasons as well as the clearly sensed corruption and inadequacy in analyses, the question of how merit was to be established was side-stepped in making training analyst status automatic.

At the time, Ourieff was happy about the appointment of the new training analysts. Those appointed then included Mel Mandel, who was very influenced by object relations, as well as Kleinians Bail, Brandchaft and Grotstein. During the period of the Reorganisation, Ourieff recalled that object relations work 'was in the background. It was healthy, object relations was my natural way of working'. He felt that he had been naive to have not been concerned about the growing strength of the object relations group (Ourieff interview 1992).

The bylaws established a 'rule of three' which meant that a training analyst could only analyse three candidates at a time (see Bail 1991b, p. 20). According to Rosengarten, who like Ourieff was one of the devisers of the bylaws, this rule was framed 'because we wanted a distribution of candidates to many analysts' (Rosengarten interview 1992). That rule was often circumvented or honoured in the breach. The site visitors reported the case of a candidate, currently in analysis, who was told by his analyst that he had to wait for another candidate to terminate before his analysis could officially begin (Bail 1991b, p. 20; Kleinman interview 1992). There were reportedly instances where, in order to circumvent the rule, an analyst would tell the institute that the candidate had terminated when he or she had not – thus allowing the analyst to take on another candidate.[30] The 'rule of three' was not aimed against any particular theoretical group (such as the Kleinians who had little power in the institute in 1967) but was enacted to redress the prior oligarchic problems.[31]

What upset the APsaA, according to Rosengarten, was not so much the Kleinian development, nor the quality of teaching but LAPSI's simultaneous appointment of sixteen training analysts in 1967 (Rosengarten interview 1992). This made fifty-five training analysts in all of whom twenty conducted supervisions and training analyses (Bail 1991b, p. 58). Why was there such a large number of appointments? As Mandel argued, 'Since there were no training analysts appointed for a long time, all of us who qualified had to be appointed and The American had to go along with this. They didn't like it from the beginning.' In the 1970s the APsaA 'blamed the democratisation for our difficulties as well as the appointment of the training analysts. They thought and may still think that institutes should be absolutely independent and not at all subject to any oversight by the societies. All of them are the opposite to Boston and us' (Rosengarten interview 1992).

Rosengarten contended that while the Reorganisation received a good deal of criticism to do with the appointment of all the training analysts and an alleged drop in quality in teaching,

> Today, all the institutes throughout America are trying to go to this plan that we had in developing the Coordinating Council, having these several committees and all the faculty serving on these various committees and shifting around, rotating, changing the jobs and bringing new people in (Rosengarten interview 1992).

Mandel asserted, 'The Reorganization of 1965–67 was designed to contend with problems of the 1950s, and I think it succeeded' (Mandel 1986, p. 43). However, while some important defects were remedied, many of those problems continued to play themselves out in what was to continue to be the very complex history of LAPSI. With the institute and society brought together more analysts were able to participate in teaching process, more training analysts were appointed and the institute was no longer controlled by an oligarchy. Leavitt wondered whether the changes might have been more effective

> if it had been possible to operate under them without the pressures and turmoil consequent upon the simultaneous development of strong groupings of different theoretical orientation which took on political importance, and which in its own way, continued some of the prior conflictual situations in a new arena. The changes in the organisation brought about by the Reorganization were an effort to open up the organization and intellectual life to fresh and divergent viewpoints, and this very change then allowed the developing Kleinian theoretical and political grouping an opportunity for expression and participation that under the previous organisation would probably not have been possible. Under the previous arrangements, it is open to question whether might have taken on the strength that they did, or, if they had, would they have led to as much conflict? (Leavitt 1986, pp. 29–30)

III

The Development of the Kleinian Influence

The Kleinian interest, which seemed to set the agenda for LAPSI in the 1970s, began much earlier. From the late 1950s the major development in theoretical and clinical interest in Los Angeles was the burgeoning appeal of the two British object relations schools of W. R. D. Fairbairn, and then far more importantly, Melanie Klein.

Fairbairn's approach and its later development by D. W. Winnicott and Harry Guntrip together formed one of the two British object relations schools which has been a major preoccupation of the 'independent group' within the British Psychoanalytic Institute. This school has focused on providing a complete 'psychological' account of personality structure. Rather than postulating innate biological drives Fairbairn assumes that the child at birth was an energised pristine unitary ego which primarily seeks relationship. For Fairbairn, pleasure lies in the fulfilment of relationship and not the other way around. Personality depended on relationships with significant others, particularly in the first years. Special interest was devoted to the events of the first six months of life in which the most basic splits in the ego into a plurality of egos and internal objects in dynamic relationship too (see Guntrip 1961, p. 356). Schizoid factors in the personality were the most deeply rooted, and very often, the psychopathological processes that begin afterwards serve as defences against them. In the 1940s Fairbairn, a Scottish psychoanalyst, propounded his new theory of object relations and argued against the pleasure principle as primary. Instead, pleasure was always a signpost to the object (Fairbairn 1952). Its influence outside the United Kingdom has been primarily through individuals. Only recently has there been much general interest from the psychoanalytic community in the US (see Grotstein and Rinsley 1998; Sutherland 1989).

In contrast, Melanie Klein's object relations school has inspired a major international psychoanalytic movement. Klein's work focused on very early experience and the importance of the early roots of the Oedipus complex. She introduced play material as a way of understanding the child's unconscious fantasy and recognised that analysis of the transference in child patients was as potent an instrument for understanding children's conflicts as it was in adults. She emphasised that the child brings two basic and conflicting drives into the world, love and hate, life and death. According to Klein, the way the baby tries to deal with this conflict is in the first instance by expelling the death drive into the outer world and later by attempting to integrate the two drives and tolerating the conflict in a lifelong struggle. Klein explored the role of the mother's breast and the nipple as the child's first reality and developed insight into primitive defences which are important to an understanding of the functioning of the inner world, particularly splitting, denial, introjective and projective identification. As opposed to Freud who thought that psychosis was entirely cut off from both normality and neurosis, Klein believed that psychotic mechanisms are present in everybody. She treated the interpretation of infantile transference, including the negative transference, as central to psychoanalytic work.[32]

With the exception of some Los Angeles analysts, Melanie Klein's approach has until recently found few American supporters. To be labelled a 'Kleinian' in the US has been, to quote a leading American psychoanalyst, 'an epithet rather than a description' (Cooper 1990, p. 187). However, nearly half the membership of the IPA are Kleinians – the Kleinian approach is an accepted stream of teaching in British, Spanish, Swiss, French, Italian and Finnish psychoanalytic institutes, and predominates in most Latin American institutes affiliated with the IPA.

According to Los Angeles analyst Morton Shane, some Americans objected to Klein's perspective because her postulate of the death instinct was seen to be atavistic. Her ideas about early development were seen as questionable because she attributed cognitive capacities to the infant which neuropsychobiological research deemed impossible. Moreover, her mode of interpretation seemed to circumvent defence analysis (Shane 1986, p. 34). Klein has been often dismissed in the US as id psychology. Robert Wallerstein recalled that no article of Klein's was assigned during his analytic training in Topeka – 'She was regarded as a crazy woman.' Except for LAPSI, APsaA institutes do not currently teach Kleinian theory.[33] However, many Kleinian ideas have been absorbed into American psychoanalysis by way of Kernberg's ideas, through child analysis, and through the use of her concepts of projective identification, splitting and envy usually without their origin being acknowledged (Mason interview 1992).

In 1956, Bernard Brandchaft sparked the first interest in Klein in Los Angeles among recent LAPSI graduates. Brandchaft became interested in Klein while he was treating a schizophrenic patient under the unsuccessful supervision of a classical analyst, Frances Deri. Since there was nobody in Los Angeles attempting to treat psychotic patients psychoanalytically, Brandchaft wondered whether there was anybody somewhere else who was currently treating psychotic patients so that he could get help with the patient (Brandchaft interview 1992).

The first graduates' study group, composed of Bernard Brandchaft, Hilda Rollman-Branch, Gerald Aronson, Harvey Lewis and Melvin Mandel, was established. Brandchaft saw the group's purpose as increasing understanding of clinical phenomena and familiarising its members with a wider theoretical background. This reflected 'a common and widespread feeling; that there was more to psychoanalysis than we had as yet been able to experience' (Wilson 1983, p. 4; Aronson interview 1992). After Brandchaft graduated in 1956, there were sporadic meetings before the group was properly organised in 1958. Brandchaft recalled:

> We began a detailed study each week of ideas that were not being taught sufficiently at the Los Angeles Psychoanalytic Institute and attempted as well to widen our study efforts into auxiliary disciplines like embryology and ethnology. Harvey Lewis was interested in the relation between the development of teeth and the development of the personality. The interest in teeth got us interested in the phenomena that were then being described by Melanie Klein about the phase. First Abraham and then Klein who had been analysed by Abraham had written papers that were then fifteen to twenty years old but they hadn't really percolated that much into the US. We began studying these papers about oral sadism and how the development of teeth could influence the development of sadism, and in the process, we got interested in Melanie Klein. (Brandchaft interview 1992)

A number of papers were either planned or delivered (ibid.).[34] As part of a 1959 panel moderated by Melvin Mandel and on behalf of that study group, Brandchaft made the first Kleinian theoretical presentation to an American psychoanalytic society to LAPSI (Mandel interview 1992; Brandchaft interview 1992). According to Brandchaft, 'The first reactions to this paper were not hostile, they were curious.' He experienced some responses as aloof, with many analysts feeling he needed to develop more clinical information to test it out (Brandchaft interview 1992). Brandchaft remembered no extreme reaction to a Kleinian perspective at the time. In his opinion, this reaction arose only later after repeated seminars and particularly after some visits by British Kleinians (ibid.). However, Mandel's recollection was quite different: Greenson and Rangell had been 'fighting to get to the platform and Greenson saying, "I can't wait to take on Kleinian psychoanalysis". It frightened us.' The group never presented the second scheduled panel with Gerald Aronson and another member of the study group. The group members 'weren't about to put our heads on the chopping block as happened the first time' (Mandel interview 1992; see also Malin 1991, p. 57). Rosengarten remembered the group being treated 'rather poorly'. Some, not including Greenson, believed that it was wrong to present Kleinian material before the society at all (Rosengarten interview 1992).

Klein's ideas were not being taught at LAPSI. Bernard Bail recalled the only part of his training concerning Klein was a paper by Edward Glover which attacked her (Bail interview 1981; Bail 1991a). Bail recollected being instrumental in forming a study group when he graduated from LAPSI in 1958. That group comprised Norman Atkins,

Robert Stoller, William Horowitz and Marvin Berenson. This group, he asserted, was reformed into another group two years later (Bail 1991a). This group, which Arthur Malin also claimed to have initiated, contained Bernard Bail, Marvin Berenson and James Grotstein (Malin 1991, p. 57; Grotstein interview 1981; Bail 1991a).

Ivan McGuire, who was classically trained in Detroit with Richard Sterba, was a significant influence in the study of object relations during the 1950s and 1960s. McGuire was very interested in object relations and provided different ways of understanding patients. Greatly impressed by Fairbairn's early papers in the *International Journal of Psychoanalysis* in the early 1940s McGuire began to talk about it in seminars and supervision in the early 1950s. McGuire remembered many responding as though he was blaspheming. McGuire was probably the first to teach Fairbairn but a few years went by before there was any significant interest in Fairbairn followed by interest in object relations (McGuire interview 1992). As McGuire generally supervised most of the young people undergoing training, he was the seminal supervisor for a whole generation (Mandel interview 1992).[35] One of his analysands, Arthur Ourieff, observed, 'Of the people who went into analysis with him, Casady, Aronson and I remained fairly attuned to the Freudian group whereas those who went into supervision with him were much more influenced by his thinking. He was the intellectual ferment, the one who was urging people on and encouraging them' (Ourieff interview 1992). As a Freud scholar, McGuire influenced many LAPSI members to read Winnicott, Fairbairn and Klein as well. McGuire was later to turn against both Klein and Bion – Kleinian analyst Carolyn Hays, for example, told me that in supervision he had 'tried to talk me into abandoning anything to do with Klein' (McGuire interview 1992; Grotstein interview 1981, Mandel interview 1992; Bail 1991a, Malin 1991, p. 58; Ourieff interview 1992; Hays interview 1992).

With the growing interest in Klein, there was interest in hearing the British Kleinians. On the recommendation of the first Kleinian analyst to come to the US, Gwen Evans, a leading British Kleinian, Herbert Rosenfeld, came to visit Los Angeles in 1962. Bernard Brandchaft gathered a group to sponsor Rosenfeld which consisted of Carolyn Hays, Bernard Bail, Arthur Malin, Marvin Berenson, and James Grotstein, together with Brandchaft. The first meeting with Rosenfeld, held at the home of John Lindon,[36] was so full that some of the audience had to stand on the patio (Brandchaft interview 1992; Hays interview 1992).

McGuire, whom Brandchaft had invited to that meeting, was unfavourably impressed with Rosenfeld.[37] McGuire regarded Rosenfeld as 'pretty autocratic. He made pronouncements like Moses receiving the tablets on the Mount. He had that character of stating something as the real, ultimate truth, stating as a fact what could not have been more than a speculation' (McGuire interview 1992). The manner in which people flocked around Rosenfeld at that lecture, treating him as a prophet enraged McGuire, as he was trying to counteract ideology at LAPSI (Atkins interview 1992). No follower of groups, McGuire was alone (Bail pers. comm. 1990). From that point McGuire's influence as a dissident in Los Angeles began to subside (Brandchaft interview 1992).

Rosenfeld returned to Los Angeles twice. After the first meeting at Lindon's house, the interest was so great that the meetings were transferred to the Beverly Wilshire Hotel attracting around sixty students from 1962–67. Brandchaft invited Rosenfeld, Hanna Segal and Wilfred Bion to speak at these meetings and to supervise. (Brandchaft interview 1992). Opposition began to develop to the meetings not only because they were held outside the institute and therefore allegedly divisive but also because of their content (Brandchaft interview 1992; Leavitt interview 1992).

Brandchaft visited London for four to six weeks every year between 1962 and 1967 (when he spent seven months there) to find out more about psychoanalysis outside Los Angeles and the US On his first and subsequent visits, Brandchaft interviewed a number of analysts there including Winnicott, Paula Heiman, Hanna Segal and Masud Khan (Brandchaft interview 1992).

Frustrated by their training many LAPSI members, especially the younger ones, began to develop an interest in Melanie Klein and British object relations work. The 1964 Site Visiting Committee was struck by the presence of a group of young graduates who were studying the work of Melanie Klein. The committee's reaction was a harbinger of future troubles: 'Though they protested vigorously they were not becoming "Kleinians", it seemed a moot point to us', the committee declared. 'It seemed to us they are talented young men being allowed to withdraw from the stream of Freudian creativity' (Bail 1991b, p. 17). Note the assumption behind the term, 'withdraw' here. It is a moot point whether they were leaving Freud by investigating Klein.

Why was Klein taken up so much in Los Angeles while Fairbairn was not? McGuire felt this was because of the British Kleinians who came out, especially Rosenfeld.

> It was like a magnet – somehow they jumped on that idea and almost overnight became true believers, they suspended their judgement. Those that did became very ardent and enthusiastic about it. They spoke as

though they had received some revelation. They were such exponents of Klein – I thought a lot of it was rather bizarre, almost a travesty, a caricature of anything that might resemble scientific, even logical thinking. All sorts of things were attributed to infants' desires which were imaginary. To use them in a therapeutic way seemed farfetched, sometimes inhuman, too. (McGuire interview 1992)

By 1965 the Kleinians had gained considerable sway at LAPSI, and had become in McGuire's view, 'like a crusade'. Many of those not involved felt 'disaffected, disenfranchised, like a jackass preying in the wilderness'. There seemed no way to contain the Kleinian surge. He was put off by the 'religious' quality of the adherents: 'The repressive atmosphere of the real orthodox and a crusade – the revealed truth of the Kleinians – was not conducive to any exchange of ideas. It deteriorated into recriminations, accusations, and indictments and became a struggle between God and the Devil, between the devil and Daniel Webster.' McGuire lost the close connection with the institute that he had for the preceding fifteen years (McGuire interview 1992).[38] In addition to the introduction of new ideas, something else was happening that needed considered, sceptical and careful study.

The Rosenfeld visits with their development of followers occurred in an institute dominated by a group which was opposed to a significant Kleinian influence there. One who wielded a great deal of *de facto* power, Ralph Greenson, was particularly inimical to the Kleinian influence, although he had used certain Kleinian concepts himself. Those dissatisfied with mainstream ideas felt effectively forced to go outside LAPSI to pursue alternative perspectives.

The Kleinian group was very active in bringing the British Kleinians, holding seminars, conducting supervisory sessions and addressing meetings. As Mel Mandel put it,

> The beginnings of broad-scale training appeared. Since this activity was organised privately, that is outside the official programmesmess of our institute, the outcome was that a privately sponsored organisation was brought into being. It had all the ambition of a formal training body, but could not hope to accredit graduates at the American unless it could somehow make use of an accredited institute, ours was the most natural and logical training school to cultivate for that purpose. (Mandel 1986, p. 43)

This was a harbinger of further trouble. On the one hand, it is clear why the Kleinians wanted their own training in the face of so much opposition in LAPSI. On the other hand, it is understandable why many

LAPSI members were concerned about the extent of the Kleinian influence. However, given the APsaA's monopolistic position in psychoanalysis at the time, it is evident why the Kleinians wanted influence in LAPSI – LAPSI provided a way into IPA membership. (At that time anyone in the US who wished to become an IPA member needed to train through an affiliated institute of the APsaA. In Los Angeles, that meant either LAPSI or the Southern Californian Psychoanalytic Institute.) Given the opposition to them, it is also clear why they had their own meetings and seminars, developing a new and self-contained analytic group within LAPSI. Had it been known that the APsaA did not in fact have the franchise for psychoanalysis in the US, the Kleinians could simply have left LAPSI and formed their own institute (see Wallerstein 1998a; 1998b). Different approaches are not generally allowed to coexist easily within psychoanalytic institutions – the British Psychoanalytic Institute with its three official streams is unusual and the result of an extensive history of intense and painful politicking. While LAPSI was most oligarchic and with two cliques continuously battling for power, those in power were unlikely willingly to move over to allow yet another group in.

As the leader of the Kleinians in Los Angeles in the 1960s, Bernard Brandchaft was of seminal importance in the Kleinian development. Had he not lived in Los Angeles, the extensive interest in Klein would in all likelihood not have occurred (Mason interview 1992). As Ourieff put it, Brandchaft took over from McGuire as the 'intellectual leader' of those analysts interested in object relations (Ourieff interview 1992).

Wilfred Bion visited Los Angeles in spring 1967 to lecture, and in January 1968, left London, having accepted Brandchaft's invitation to live and work in Los Angeles (Wilson 1986, p. 6, Mason interview 1992; Bail 1991a). A major independent and original thinker in his own right, Bion was strongly influenced by Klein. He was analysed by Klein and credited many of his findings and ideas as restatements and modifications of her work (Mason 1981, p. 10; Mason pers. comm. 1994). Bion largely agreed to come to Los Angeles so as to have more time to write. Moreover, he thought he would be able to spend considerable time conducting psychoanalyses without being hampered by the inevitable committee work or administrative responsibilities he would have had in the British Psychoanalytic Society had he remained in London (Bail 1991a; Wilson 1983, p. 6; Mason pers. comm. 1994; Mason, in Mandel 1996a, pp. 20–1). Over seventy years old when he arrived in Los Angeles, Bion never became a member of LAPSI and avoided a direct part in the political situation in Los Angeles. He felt that many of attributions made about him in Los Angeles were, as he put it, 'wide of the mark'. In Los Angeles Bion feared being inappropriately 'thrust into the role of being a sort of messiah or deity' and did not want to be involved in disputes as to whether or not he was Kleinian or crazy (Bion 1992, pp. 376-7). Although he was often revered, Bion did not seek a following. Bernard Bail found him 'always a modest man to the point of self-deprecation' (Bail pers. comm. 1990). In 1979 Bion said that he had planned to stay 'for a short space of time, I thought perhaps five years' (Bion 1992, p. 376) but remained in Los Angeles until a few months before his death in 1980.[39]

Very soon after Bion arrived, Kleinian analyst, Albert Mason came to Los Angeles from London. Mason had been originally invited by Brandchaft with the support of the Bails and Grotstein (Brandchaft interview 1992; Bail 1991a; Mason interview 1992), and had been encouraged by Bion to go to Los Angeles.[40] Although Mason was born in the US, his family migrated to London when he was a young child. He later trained in medicine in London and subsequently in the Kleinian stream at the British Institute for Psychoanalysis.[41] When he joined LAPSI, he was the only Kleinian there with a Kleinian training. As a leading proponent of Klein, Mason's considerable lecturing, teaching and clinical skills were doubtless both envied and admired (Leavitt interview 1992). Mason aroused interest and influenced quite a number of Los Angeles analysts through his analytic work and supervisions.[42] In the early 1970s Mason had at least five analysts in analysis, at least twenty on and off in supervision, and conducted seminars of analysts. The fact that Mason wanted to be at the centre of activities at LAPSI created further antagonism. Mason's arrival more than Bion's posed a challenge to the Kleinian leadership at the time. Although Bion was an *éminence grise*, he had retired from politics, while Mason, twenty years younger, was ripe for the fray. There was a demand for analysis and supervision that Bion and Mason could not meet. They attempted to find Kleinians who would come from London because it looked as though, as Mason put it, 'a bridgehead had been formed. That was why there was such a hostile counter-reaction' (Mason interview 1992; Mason pers. comm. 1994; Leavitt interview 1992; Brandchaft interview 1992). Prominent British Kleinians – Herbert Rosenfeld, Hanna Segal, Hans Thorner, Betty Joseph and Donald Meltzer – were invited by the small but enthusiastic LAPSI Kleinian group, principally by Brandchaft, Bail and his then wife, Carolyn Hays, and Albert Mason.

Bernard Bail, a training analyst who was one of the sixteen appointed training analysts at the time of the 1967 Reorganisation, became a central figure in the institute disputes. He was deeply influenced by Bion. Bail had received a Purple Heart as a bomber pilot in Europe during World War II. After the war he trained in medicine and undertook psychoanalytic training at LAPSI, graduating in 1958, and taught at LAPSI for the next fifteen years ('Biographical sketch', Bail 1991b).[43] Both Bail and his then wife, Carolyn Hays, supported the visits of the British Kleinians to Los Angeles, organising lectures, supervisions and guarantees of costs (Bail interview 1981; Bail 1991a). Bail continued was a leading figure in the Kleinian development and became the focal point of the disputes when he threatened a lawsuit after the institute suspended him from teaching in 1974. Together with Mason and others, Bail gathered together the material to protest to the IPA about discrimination against the Kleinians in LAPSI.

One member of the group, James Grotstein, was initially sceptical about Klein and Bion and sided with his analyst, Ivan McGuire, who opposed the Kleinians. Grotstein changed his mind when, after the termination of analysis with McGuire, He entered supervision and then analysis with Bion and supervision with Mason (Grotstein interview 1981; Grotstein pers. comm. 1992). Like Bail, Grotstein was appointed a training analyst in 1967 Reorganisation. He was influential through his teaching residents at the UCLA medical school.

Though a friend of Bion, Bernard Brandchaft became increasingly distant from the Kleinians whom he had led during the 1960s. Brandchaft believed that he had underestimated the extent to which those in positions of authority would feel threatened. He had thought that they would be interested in attempting to expand their understanding. 'I was also very upset about the response to the reaction and began to separate myself from the group of Kleinians even while agreeing with some of the basic principles she had put forward' (Brandchaft interview 1981). Brandchaft subsequently became interested in self psychology and led a number of analysts out of the Kleinian group.[44]

While those in power were scarcely lacking in hubris, neither were the Kleinians. Brandchaft saw provocations from both sides, including himself. 'The Kleinians were making public criticisms of the work of everybody else.' A widely reported statement by Donald Meltzer, a visiting British Kleinian, was representative. He is said to have equated Kleinian analysis with contemporary psychoanalysis and classical analysis as belonging to the early part of the century. Brandchaft commented:

> It was not only that, it was the attitude of haute superiority that was being expressed and reflected in a thousand different ways. The other side was the utter defensive contempt of Kleinian practice that found its

target in caricatures of what Kleinians were about. It was on both sides and it was interactive. There was still no interference in the teaching of the institute. I was voted 'teacher of the year' four years in a row 1975-78. At an earlier time, I had been penalised by being turned down to join the faculty for a couple of years by the personal opposition of a member of the training committee on the grounds that I was a Kleinian. As the Kleinian movement began to develop more esteem, the opposition to it became harder and harder as well and the climate within the institute began to deteriorate. (Brandchaft interview 1992)

James Grotstein believed that the three leading Kleinians in the Los Angeles Institute, himself included, had been partly to blame for what happened. They were 'unreasonably obnoxious, certain, omnipotent: "We have the truth". I know I felt that. The trouble is I think we all did ourselves in. We were right but we were wrong'. Grotstein felt that with the exception of Albert Mason, the visiting British Kleinians made him 'feel like a naughty colonial' (Grotstein interview 1992). In Grotstein's view,

> Klein really was not well merchandised. Although Herbert Rosenfeld's lectures and supervisions were enormously successful, his manner was unfortunate. Donald Meltzer made a blundering statement to one of the candidates when he came out here in 1972 and said, 'One has to make up one's mind whether one wants 1937 analysis or 1972 analysis'. Overnight somebody who was in a preceptorship with me dropped out and we haven't spoken to each other since Meltzer said that. So we American Kleinians hope that the English don't come over. (Grotstein interview 1981; Grotstein pers. comm. 1992)

A wide section of Los Angeles analysts viewed the Kleinians as arrogant and inflammatory.

But were the British Kleinians any different from the American Kleinians? Hostility was no stranger to the British Kleinians. During the 1940s, they were engaged in major confrontations with the Freudians, particularly Anna Freud and her followers, over ideology and power to train. Were the American Kleinians still 'more royal than the king'? They seemed to be more stereotyped, austere and inflexible. Mandel maintained that many of the Kleinians practising in Los Angeles 'may have been practising in such forms that they were even more orthodox than the Kleinians in Britain. In addition, their style of practice aroused tremendous problems for those in the training institute here.'

In Mandel's view, the Kleinians had not demonstrated their results sufficiently to many members of LAPSI. The known results appeared meagre. If the Kleinians' results were questionable, Mandel maintained, then the Kleinian technique might have no validity. Their view of Klein came by way of 'the results or the techniques claimed by the local Kleinians. Their argument wasn't with Klein internationally but the local Kleinians' (Mandel interview 1981).

Morton Shane, a conservative analyst at that time, was struck by the militancy of the Kleinians. The Kleinians felt theirs to be a new, stronger and more powerful framework 'which stirred up resentment in those who felt the Freudian framework was powerful and shouldn't be challenged'. Shane was impressed with the sensitivity with which Bion and Segal worked with the transference.

> But it was the contentiousness that got everybody's back up and it got to be on both sides. My experience was that we could talk to each other and issues explored. If someone is in analysis in the Kleinian mode, there is a tendency not to hear, and dismiss and the other way around. The analysis seemed to be the key. (Shane interview 1992)

While the Los Angeles Kleinians were no doubt scapegoated, the Kleinians also reacted very provocatively and became more strident as the polarisation continued. The polarisation resulted in a decreasing middle ground – the leaders of the institute were seen by many (the Kleinians included) as enemies of the Kleinians whom the leadership purportedly viewed as a threat to psychoanalysis. It would be mistaken, however, to see the Kleinians as of one hue. Brandchaft, for example, was generally well-regarded at LAPSI. He was personally friendly with a number of classical Freudians who, in Bernard Bail's recollection, 'looked upon his interest in Klein as Brandchaft's peculiarity' (Bail pers. comm. 1990). Another Kleinian was regarded as very militant, and was seen by many to consider mainstream people's practice to be not analytic. Understandably, this militancy on the part of a small number of Kleinian analysts and some candidates upset many non-Kleinians who felt strongly under attack. Many did not distinguish among the Kleinians and generalised the behaviour of some Kleinians to all of them.

Mandel recalled the effects the polarisation between Kleinians and mainstream Freudians had on the teaching during the early 1970s:

> This nucleus of Kleinians was very aggressively recruiting people. And when it came to teaching in the institute, the fights began not only among the faculty but among the candidates. Teaching became impossible. Half a seminar would be loaded with Kleinian-oriented candidates and the other half with otherwise-oriented candidates and you'd try and teach a seminar and spending all your time either pushing forth your own position between these two forces or trying to be a referee

between the fights that were breaking out between them. Education came
to a standstill. The last course I taught was so impossible that I never
went back to teach a didactic course for a long time. That was no
atmosphere to teach, it was like ghetto warfare. (Mandel interview 1981)

However, others felt that the atmosphere was not as bad as Mandel
described. Lee Shershow, a candidate between 1971 and 1975,
remembered the classes as 'tense at times but not that bad' and believed
that 'the "ghetto warfare" of classes may have applied a little earlier'
(Shershow interview 1992).[45] Why this experienced difference? Perhaps
the level of what was regarded as being 'unteachable' varied. Perhaps
since the Kleinian-oriented analysts and candidates were the underdog,
they may have viewed the situation more charitably, particularly in
view of the fact that the charge that LAPSI had become unworkable
was also levelled by the APsaA. Nevertheless, given the unrest, tensions
and disputes everywhere else in LAPSI at the time, classes could not
have been particularly congenial.

Some of the problems related to what Arthur Ourieff, director of the
institute (1973-76), thought were 'the negative aspect of the
Reorganisation'. LAPSI 'opened the choice of training analysis to the
market place' which almost became an extension of the UCLA residency
training programmes. For, according to Ourieff, James Grotstein (a 'very
charismatic, very brilliant and very impressive person') became the
most popular analytic teacher and together with Malin developed a
coterie at UCLA that was 'very contagious'. The UCLA residents would
then come to LAPSI, go into a Kleinian, Fairbairnian or Bionian analysis
and attend seminars. 'It became horribly chaotic.' During that period,
Brandchaft was beginning to separate himself from the Kleinians.
Ourieff recalled that with the arrival of Mason and Bion LAPSI 'had a
Red Army and White Army without any resolution' – the majority 'were
still on the more conservative side. But the vocal and rebellious ones
were on the other side. The teaching and the seminars just became
impossible.'

Aiming at excellence at LAPSI, Ourieff despaired that first year
candidates became 'so radicalised by their analyses that there was no
proper critical thinking going on' (Ourieff interview 1992). With
candidates polarised into camps, the ambience was characterised more
by opposing religions than by deviant theories, a situation to which
the site visitors could not fail to have reacted. Not knowing how to
direct training in such a morass, Ourieff became 'almost frenzied'.
Students were not

taking these new ideas and trying to understand them as an evolutionary approach, but as going to the Mount like Moses did and hearing the Ten Commandments. I found some people so fanatical that I had no way of knowing how to cope with this, as the person in the responsible chair who has to make the decisions about what to teach and not teach, what to allow in first year. (Ourieff interview 1992)

Why Klein received so much attention was not as the result of carefully considered work but arose to fill the vacuum that was left by the extent of the previous problems in LAPSI. Ten years later the vacuum would have been filled – and was – by self psychology. Rather than help LAPSI's problems, APsaA intervention would exacerbate them.

The 1973 Site Visit

1973 was a fateful and tumultuous year for LAPSI and heralded three still more turbulent years. That year's APsaA site visit marked the beginning of the APsaA's involvement in what was until then largely a local matter.

The Reorganisation ameliorated LAPSI's problems but had not solved them. The ideological struggles were rapidly increasing. In February 1973 the APsaA's regular Site Visit Committee investigated the Los Angeles situation and was severely critical of everything they saw. That committee included some powerful APsaA members.[46] The committee reported in October 1973, finding that the Los Angeles Institute's method of appointing training analysts 'does not conform in spirit or custom to the standards and objectives shared by the other analytic institutes of the American Psychoanalytic Association' (Bail 1991b, p. 31).

The 1973 Committee noted that the bad atmosphere in the Los Angeles Psychoanalytic Institute was not only because of the current struggles between classical analysts, Fairbairnians and Kleinians.

> [T]he earlier strident conflicts among the contestants of the 1964 era [the last site visit] are still alive. The distrust among members of the more Freudian orientation permitted, and perhaps even fostered, the growth of the other groups. The misuses of training analyses and the harsh interactions among institute members seem to have existed prior to the introduction of the English schools of analysis into the Los Angeles Institute. (Bail 1991b, p. 40)

The committee questioned

why there has been such a long tradition, unaltered by the 1967 reorganization, of misuse of the analytic situation, of destructive competition among analysts resulting in the ultimate withdrawal by many of them, of difficulties with authority, of a harshness and an inability for objective discussions, and of a recurring lack of commitment to analysis. May not these be manifestations of shared shortcomings in the personal analyses? (ibid., p. 43)

The later 'ideological' problems between classical Freudians and Kleinians should be seen as superimposed upon the earlier struggles between Freudians. Since the earlier struggles had caused quite outside the theoretical arena. Blaming the Kleinians for LAPSI's problems was simplistic and misleading. Issues surrounding the democratic reorganisation of the institute resulted from earlier struggles and the oligarchic nature of the institute. The Site Visit Committee chairman Justin Krent reportedly put it aptly when talking about whether the APsaA simply wanted to get rid of the Kleinians or other undesirable groups:

If anyone thinks he can get rid of any group and the problems of the Los Angeles Institute would be solved – *he is crazy*. The central problem of this institute is the corruption and the immorality that exists and has existed all these years, even before the Reorganization. (Bail 1991b, pp. 74–5)

The director of the institute from 1971 to 1973, Maimon Leavitt, did not consider LAPSI to have had great problems over that period. He ensured that there was a fairly large Kleinian representation from LAPSI in the site visit interviews so that the site visitors would get an overall picture. However, Leavitt concluded that the site visitors were not really there to find an overall picture. That visit, Leavitt asserted, 'was more destructive than helpful. They came out on a witch-hunt' (Leavitt interview 1992). The APsaA did not like the Kleinians gaining entry into Southern California and, Leavitt maintained, the Reorganisation was considered to be disruptive of the usually accepted authority structures. Taking power from training analysts and spreading it widely was a radical change at the time, as was the move to broaden and open up training analyst selection processes. In particular, Leavitt saw Justin Krent as 'very damaging', 'unsympathetic to what was going on' and looking for trouble (Leavitt interview 1992).[47] Leavitt believed the site visit intensified LAPSI's troubles. Krent and Homer Curtis, two of the committee's strongest members, were conservative and, Leavitt thought, considered the activities at LAPSI to be anathema. Instead of addressing the ongoing conflict (which those in power in LAPSI at the time felt could have been capable of resolution within LAPSI itself), the site visitors condemned the institute as being incompetent and threatened action against it (Leavitt interview 1992).[48]

The committee was appalled by what they saw to be the low calibre of the institute, the intensity of the internecine fighting, the confusion of the candidates and what they conceived to be the undue influence of the Kleinians over them, as well as by what they regarded as the deleterious results of the method of appointing training analysts. The institute was seen to be near paralysis. The committee felt that 'the most difficult problem facing the institute' was 'that the coexistence of the English schools with traditional analysis has confused the candidates and detracted from their training'. They also believed that LAPSI ought to find a means of selecting training analysts 'consistent with the aims and practices of other institutes' and that the institute ought to consider assigning analysts and supervisors to candidates instead of allowing candidates to choose them (Bail 1991b, p. 44). Quite plausibly, Grotstein sensed that 'what really bugged the APsaA was that our reorganization allowed any graduate member to become a training analyst after five years – without any especial qualification' (Grotstein pers. comm. 1992).

The site visitors found that the candidates were confused, did not have a proper grasp of any school of thought, and did not find the juxtaposition of theoretical orientations enriching. They observed one class session where there were co-instructors of different orientations and felt that this 'was neither a useful classroom exercise nor a scientific discussion but rather a forum for a politicised attack of one instructor upon the other' (Bail 1991b, p. 28). The site visitors also noted that while 'it seemed impossible to do analytic teaching' a few years previously, 'this is no longer the case, but as a result many experienced, well-qualified analysts withdrew from teaching' (ibid., p. 36).

The site visitors' report lambasted almost every aspect of LAPSI. The administration had been hindered by the democratic reorganisation; routine administrative work was not accomplished (ibid., p. 22); 'the Coordinating Council does little in the way of evaluation or originating policy'; the framers of the bylaws had been 'so desirous of preventing abuse of power' that the Council 'was stripped of the authority it needed for effective functioning'; the Council did not perform the tasks of an Education Committee within the APsaA standards (ibid., p. 23). The site visitors disliked the way the Candidates' Evaluation Committee functioned since the committee depended on the reports of a supervisor who had been picked by the candidate (ibid., p. 24). The Admissions Committee accepted candidates 'without attempts at selectivity and discrimination generally found in other institutes' (ibid., p. 25). As for the curriculum, candidates 'did not appear to be at the same level of training as their peers in other institutes. They seemed confused about many of the basic concepts of analysis, about the historical development of Freudian analysis, and were deficient in the more current areas of analytic thought.' This could be accounted for, they thought, by the fact that 'modern developments of classical analysis appear to have been inadequately taught or have not been given sufficient emphasis'. The candidates did not know important works by such authors as Anna Freud, Hartmann, Kris and Loewenstein – 'the single course on Ego Psychology is an elective'. The visitors saw the candidates' confusion by the way that Kleinian-leaning instructors would compare the early Freud with Klein 'as though Freud's later writings never existed' and they 'considered destructive the practice of having Freudian and Kleinian analysts co-instruct a course'. They asserted that the curriculum did not accord with its stated aim of teaching classical psychoanalysis nor did it accord with the APsaA guidelines which mandated that the curriculum be designed so that students 'gain an understanding of the fundamentals of psychoanalysis as developed by Freud and his co-workers' (ibid., p. 26).

The committee was most concerned about the effects of the Kleinians at LAPSI who had re-analysed some of the faculty and a significant number of faculty families. The Kleinians influenced many of the applicants, and their involvement with residency programmess helped interest residents in the direction of Kleinian analysis. The site visitors appeared to believe a highly inflated estimate that 'up to seventy-five per cent of the candidates are pro-Kleinian' (ibid., p. 27).

LAPSI's stance on the appointment of training analysts was of special concern to the site visitors. The Reorganisation made that status open to anybody who had graduated five years earlier, had adequately performed as a teacher and was a member of the APsaA. The committee considered that the institute needed to intervene actively far more than this in assessing such factors as ability, interest, time devoted to analytic practice as well as 'the ability to understand the processes of psychic growth derived from an understanding of the maturation of ego and superego'. They added that most of the Coordinating Council members, across theoretical orientations, thought the process in place to be satisfactory. The committee believed that with all its pitfalls, the institute should select training analysts – the Coordinating Council was shelving their responsibility and leaving it up to the candidates. 'Because of the necessity for selecting their own training analysts, the candidates are in effect determining who shall train and who shall not.' The committee considered that LAPSI did 'not conform in spirit or in custom to the standards and objectives shared by the other analytic institutes of the American Psychoanalytic Association' (ibid., pp. 29–31).

The committee assailed the candidates' 'free choice policy' for supervisors and analysts (ibid., p. 34) as well as their courses and instructors (ibid., p. 35). The site visitors cited analysts not active in administration who

> are disheartened by what they consider to be a lack of intellectual standards within the group and by the impossibility of holding analytic discussions of any significance without incurring personal attacks. The more traditional group are described both by themselves and by others as pessimistic, helpless vis-a-vis the English schools, demoralized, wearied by the long history of fighting, and bewildered by those in leadership positions who maintain that the diverse views are beneficial to the group. (ibid., p. 41)

The fact that 'the more traditional group' could be 'bewildered' by the leaders of LAPSI who felt that teaching 'more diverse theories' was intellectually beneficial indicated major educational problems. The site visitors maintained that in general, education had deteriorated since 1964 and 'the general atmosphere of the institute is not one conducive to classical analytic training' (ibid.).

The committee reached three major conclusions and recommendations. First, they regarded the most difficult problem to be 'the juxtaposition of different theoretical orientations' because it 'confused the candidates and detracted from their training'. Second, they recommended the implementation of 'a more appropriate means of selecting training analysts'. Third, they suggested that the institute 'consider the assignment of analysts and supervisors' instead of this occurring through the free choice of the candidates' (ibid., p. 44). The use by the committee of terms such as 'confused', 'detracted' and 'appropriate means of selecting training analysts' indicate an orthodox, closed training model akin to the NYPI during that period.

Of course, LAPSI reacted negatively. The committee challenged the goals of the Reorganisation, especially around the fundamental issue of the appointment, role and function of training analysts. They wanted to reinstitute the authority of the institute as opposed to the society, remove the influence of the candidates on their education, and reinstitute evaluations for training analyst status, including the idea of re-evaluating all training analysts. Further, the committee wanted to reassert the dominance of mainstream ego psychology and virtually to eliminate the Kleinian influence.

Quite understandably, Maimon Leavitt called the site visit report 'devastating'. The site visitors had 'accepted every complaint as indicative of widespread disaffection' (Leavitt 1986, p. 30). At a faculty meeting, Leavitt is minuted as having 'felt that the site visitors were quite biased in what they discovered and that we need to ask the site visitors what is rumor, what is reporting and what is observation in their findings' (Bail 1991b, p. 151). But Leavitt noted a positive aspect: 'Even though I personally feel that the committee's distaste for our philosophy and policy implementation distorted their view of the quality of our education, nevertheless the report served the useful purpose of forcing us to a sober reconsideration of our situation' (Leavitt 1986, p. 30).

The site visit report was tantamount to a declaration of war by the APsaA on LAPSI – and the Kleinians. Three years later, the APsaA even sent a committee assigned the task of shutting LAPSI down. The struggles were inevitable given LAPSI's attack in the Reorganisation on some of the fundamental ways that the APsaA viewed the nature of training and training institution and the appointment, role and function of training analysts. That there were influential Kleinian training analysts in place and Kleinian teachers made the situation still more explosive.

The director, Arthur Ourieff, saw himself

> on the firing line, and it was my job to save the institute. I did not want our institute to become a Kleinian institute. I was very happy to have individuals work that way – I did not want it or anything to be predominant. When I talk about traditional American analysis – I still talk about it – it's the hundred years of Freudian knowledge that I think every analyst should have a basic education in. Just like doctors have to have a basic education in physics and chemistry – not that they ever use it, but they should know it. And then you branch out from there. (Ourieff interview 1992)

Ourieff considered neither himself nor other 'conservative' Los Angeles analysts as 'Traditional American Psychoanalysts'. He was even open to an arrangement whereby there were different teaching streams as in the British Institute of Psychoanalysis. Ourieff was willing to have a Kleinian section from first year provided that the education would be intermingled at a later date. When Ourieff discussed the double track idea with the APsaA, they looked at me as though I was crazy. That was just not acceptable in any way, shape or form. I did that publicly as well as privately. I talked with [powerful APsaA officers] Stanley Goodman, Weinshel and Joan Fleming about that – it was just not acceptable as one of the solutions to the absolute chaos. It hurt me so – I saw these young people spending a fortune not getting anything. (Ourieff interview 1992)

Since there was 'no way' the APsaA would accept the double-track idea and no way to convince the Kleinians 'that the American wouldn't accept that', Ourieff was in a cleft stick as director.

In December 1973, officials of the Los Angeles Institute met with a committee of the APsaA to discuss the report. While the APsaA's committee consisted of different people from those who had been on the investigating committee, it nonetheless backed up the Site Visit Committee's report. Any doubts as to whether the site visitors represented APsaA policy were removed. At that meeting the APsaA's reaffirmed that 'Kleinians' were to be eliminated from the faculty of the Los Angeles Institute and the combined committee of LAPSI and APsaA representatives decided to call themselves 'Traditional American Psychoanalysts' (TAP) to distinguish themselves from Kleinians (Bail 1991b, pp. 60–3; 172–7).

At the faculty meeting of January 9, 1974, Ourieff reported on meetings in New York with the Chairman of the APsaA's Board on Professional Standards and other senior officials of the APsaA as well as the Site Visit Committee. The APsaA officials suggested that LAPSI candidates

> should be notified that some of their supervisory work might potentially be unacceptable to the Membership Committee of the American and the at they would have to provide information to the Membership Committee of their ability to carry on successfully a psychoanalysis in the traditional fashion. They felt that in the future, in order to meet the minimal standards, our approach to training should be a more traditional one; and that therefore they would not recommend that future analysis or supervision be carried out in which the focus would be not that of traditional analysis. (Bail 1991b, p. 60)

Ourieff then reported on a series of interim measures recommended by the Coordinating Council and LAPSI's internal Site Review Committee (consisting of the Coordinating Council plus three other LAPSI officers). On the suggestion of 'the people in New York', this committee recommended a moratorium on any changes so as to allow 'time to debate and come to grips with our problems'. The standby measures recommended in the meantime so that the institute would continue to function were the assigning of supervisors to candidates, a review of case selection and a freeze on new training analyses. The director and assistant director stated that the Site Review Committee and the Coordinating Council felt that all training and supervising analysts should be re-evaluated in terms of the APsaA's requirements (Bail 1991b, p. 62). This would of course remove Kleinians from training, and finally as training analysts. The minutes of that institute meeting quoted Ourieff as stating:

> It is clear that the American feels that our training should be traditional analysis and that therefore, incompetent traditional analysts as well as people with a 'Kleinian' and a Fairbairnian orientation should not be empowered to undertake future training analysis or supervision. (Bail 1991b, p. 63).

APsaA officials later denied having told Ourieff what he reported.

At a society meeting six days later Ourieff further reported on his meetings in New York and confirmed that the APsaA demanded firm changes in the institute if it was to remain within the APsaA. The minutes of this faculty meeting stated this about the APsaA's attitude:

> Their firm point was that the training model criterion is a classical analysis (American, traditional, Freudian were the terms used), and analysis done in a 'Kleinian' or object-relations model does not qualify. (ibid., p. 68)

The APsaA officials were concerned that LAPSI had cut the power of training analysts and maintained that changes in the selection of training analysts had led to the troubles. Ourieff asserted that a number of low calibre training analysts, who were appointed through the new procedures, became involved with the administration of the institute. Ourieff regarded the statement about 'incompetent analysts' and Kleinians as inflammatory, but the APsaA directive was 'absolutely clear'. The APsaA officials were too astute to tell LAPSI directly to get rid of the Kleinians. Instead, they declared that LAPSI could not stay within the APsaA if it had both incompetent (not carefully selected) training analysts – and Kleinians (Ourieff interview 1992).

The APsaA officials added that the APsaA would not guarantee to accept cases supervised for membership of the APsaA that were not 'within the model of the mind understood as the appropriate model by the American' (Bail 1991b, p. 69). The Kleinians were to be penalised on account of their beliefs, ideas that were shared by a large number of members of the IPA. Arthur Ourieff maintained that 'it was absolutely implied that we had to get rid of the Kleinians' and that the situation was Ourieff's problem, not theirs. At a meeting with Stanley Goodman and Edward Weinshel from the APsaA, Ourieff was told that if LAPSI was to remain within the APsaA, LAPSI had to do something about its infectious and destructive problems. The APsaA officials refused to help him (Ourieff interview 1992).

Morton Shane, a LAPSI analyst with close connections with the APsaA at the time, regarded the APsaA as having 'chickened out'. The APsaA's insistence that only Freudians could be accredited and that LAPSI should not allow Kleinians into the institute was illegal, and there was also Bail's threatened lawsuit alleging discrimination by LAPSI on the grounds that he was a Kleinian (which I return to below). Shane maintained that the APsaA leaders must have talked to a lawyer when they denied having told LAPSI to get rid of the Kleinians. In Shane's opinion, the APsaA would have backed down had LAPSI stood up to them (Shane interview 1992).

However, Ourieff did not feel he was strong enough to challenge the APsaA fully (Ourieff interview 1992). While it was politically naive not to have obtained the APsaA's policy in writing and since the APsaA officials were not honest about what had been said, Ourieff was placed in an impossible position (Rosengarten interview 1992). Caught between his loyalty to LAPSI and his embarrassment before the APsaA, as director of an institute he was frightened about the APsaA. Although a Kleinian, Grotstein believed Ourieff did the best he could: 'I think he is a gentleman and a very fine analyst. He teaches well. I can say nothing negative about him' (Grotstein interview 1992).

Six weeks before an APsaA site visit to the Southern California Psychoanalytic Institute in 1974, the Dean of Education, Sam Eisenstein received what he termed 'a strange request' from the APsaA: 'Will you identify which of your (a) faculty, (b) teachers, (c) supervising, and (d) analysing instructors are not oriented to classical analysis?' Eisenstein commented, 'This was the first of repeated requests of that nature. Our statement that there are probably a few analysts on our faculty who do not practice classical analysis, but that none was a member of the Education Committee, was listened to with incredulity.' Later, during the site visit the chairman of the Southern California Psychoanalytic Institute was blatantly told, 'You are not being honest with us. Come on, who are the Kleinians?' Then, Eisenstein noted, names of the members of the Education Committee were mentioned and 'we were asked to specify what kind of analysis they were practicing' (Bail 1991b, pp. 226–7). LAPSI analyst Ed Kleinman recalled that Eisenstein replied to the APsaA:

> 'We have no list of Kleinians, no list of Freudians – we have a list of analysts. If you want a list of analysts, I will give it to you.' That is an admirable stand. I don't think our people fought for anything but their own well-being and they continued to do that. (Kleinman interview 1992)

The APsaA officials had disowned the leadership of LAPSI and were demanding of LAPSI that they get rid of the Kleinians, that Kleinians should not be allowed to teach, train or supervise, Because Ourieff never got anything in writing, as Albert Mason put it, 'They hung him out to dry. Apart from the threat of a lawsuit, it would have reflected on the American badly internationally' (Mason interview 1992).

In his secretary's report to the Board on Professional Standards in 1976, Edward Weinshel said:

> Unfortunately, rumors were circulated by both groups to the effect that the American Psychoanalytic Association considered the basic problem in the Los Angeles Institute to be the controversy in regard to Freudian and Kleinian points of view; this was not correct. Of much more concern was the unrelenting hostility and distrust among various groups and individuals whatever their theoretical orientation. There was no discernible basis for the presence of so much bad feeling. The primary obstacle to effective institute leadership and psychoanalytic training was the atmosphere of divisiveness, readiness for quarreling and non-cooperation that so often prevailed. (American Psychoanalytic Association 1976b, pp. 3–4)

This representation of the APsaA position can be challenged on several grounds. First, while the description of the level of quarrelling and divisiveness in LAPSI is accurate (the APsaA's own role in further fomenting it is not mentioned!), the APsaA was scarcely indifferent to the theoretical orientation of the courses to be taught within the institute. The APsaA view never varied. They strongly recommended that the basic teaching should be classically Freudian, 'traditional American psychoanalysis'. Second, by claiming that it was untrue that the APsaA regarded the basic problems at LAPSI to be the controversy between Freudians and Kleinians, Weinshel called into question Ourieff's and LAPSI deputy director Rollman-Branch's reports on their meetings with himself and other APsaA leaders in which the LAPSI leaders claimed that they were instructed to 'get rid of the Kleinians'. However, it is far more likely that the APsaA realised they could not get away with such statements publicly, especially with the threat of a lawsuit from Bail which would claim discrimination on the grounds of theoretical orientation.[49] Third, the APsaA was not so much concerned with fights in the society as with those in the institute, most particularly with the Kleinians' training analyst status which gave the Kleinians some power in the institute over training and standards.[50] Fourth, approaches by the APsaA to the Southern California Psychoanalytic Institute demanding a list of Kleinians in their institute belied the statement that the APsaA was concerned only with the animosities within LAPSI and unconcerned about the theoretical orientations of the protagonists.

Weinshel's statement showed up why Ourieff's position as director of LAPSI was untenable. While publicly denying discrimination on theoretical grounds and placing the responsibility on local personality issues, none the less 'privately' the APsaA told the LAPSI leaders that they had to 'get rid of the Kleinians' from the institute if they wanted to remain within the APsaA and that Kleinian training was not acceptable for membership in the APsaA. Faced with the choice of either admitting discrimination or blaming Ourieff, APsaA officials denied their private directives and made Ourieff a scapegoat.

The Greenson–Mason Debate

By the time of 1973 APsaA site visit, the LAPSI's polarisation had come to reflect the polarisation in London between the Anna Freudians and the Kleinians. Although there were few straight Anna Freudians in Los Angeles, she was none the less influential. The official negative reaction to Klein was, according to Grotstein, related to three issues: first, to Anna Freud's influence over a number of Los Angeles child analysts; second, Kleinians were seen as a threat because of their popularity – Albert Mason was particularly popular; and thirdly, according to James Grotstein, 'it had to do with the obsession of one man – Greenson. I think if Greenson had died earlier, the problem would not have been so inflammatory.' Greenson led the anti-Kleinian movement at the beginning until it took hold and became an independent force. Grotstein recalled that at a dinner party Greenson told him that 'he had promised Anna Freud that he would destroy the Kleinian movement in the US and I believe he meant it. He acted in all sincerity and he acted as if he had that as a mission.' According to Grotstein, Greenson helped 'to unify the fear of the Kleinians, that they would take away patients, they were going to break down the institute and colonise and take it over' (Grotstein interview 1992). None the less, Greenson was so close to Anna Freud that his close friend, Leo Rosten said that Anna Freud 'put him in charge of her armies here' (Farber and Green 1993, p. 91).

But the bitterness in the Los Angeles Institute mushroomed following the events of the evening of September 20, 1973, when Ralph Greenson presented the paper, 'Transference: Freud or Klein', to the Los Angeles Psychoanalytic Society that he had presented at the IPA Paris Congress in July 1973.[51] This paper was the result of Greenson's investigations into Kleinianism. He attended private seminars and sought case supervision from visiting British Kleinians. According to Brandchaft, Greenson's interest in Klein derived from the personal friendship between Greenson and Brandchaft (Brandchaft interview 1992). Greenson wrote, 'I told my Kleinian colleagues that I was coming to learn how Kleinians work and was not interested in becoming a Kleinian' (Greenson 1974, p. 522). Greenson and Wexler investigated Kleinian approaches using case material. Around 1968, they regularly participated together in a research group presenting their work with some prominent members of LAPSI who included Alfred Goldberg, Gerald Aronson and Bernard Brandchaft. The discussion, Brandchaft believed, could have been critical but 'would have been a credit to any scientific community'. Brandchaft met with Greenson privately for discussion where Greenson carefully listened to Brandchaft's session notes. Brandchaft remembered that Bernard Bail volunteered to present some of his clinical material to the research group and was invited to do so. Brandchaft maintained that it was this material together with some material from some sessions that Greenson had with Herbert Rosenfeld in London that formed the basis of Greenson's view of the way Kleinians worked clinically (Brandchaft interview 1992).

However, Mason considered that Greenson had been caricaturing the Kleinians before the time of the study group (Mason interview 1992). If that is the case, the issue of whose material he regarded as Kleinian was not so relevant.

Greenson's paper dealt with the differences between Freudian and Kleinian approaches to transference, and expressed Greenson's 'negative experience with the Kleinians' (Greenson 1973). Greenson felt that discussions between Kleinians and Freudians gave the impression of 'people speaking two different languages at each other with one ignorant of the other and both firmly prejudiced against the other'. He had 'become impressed and puzzled by the growing number of adherents to Kleinian psychoanalysis' (ibid.; see also Greenson 1974, p. 521).

Greenson's paper explored whether the hints of rapprochement between Klein and Freud were significant or trivial, and speculated about what made the Kleinian school attractive. Greenson chose the subject of transference, elaborating four aspects so as to 'expose differences between Freudian and Kleinian points of view' (Greenson 1973; see also Greenson 1974, p. 522). In his reply to Greenson's paper at the IPA conference Herbert Rosenfeld maintained that Greenson misrepresented the Kleinian position, making it 'very difficult to consider his paper as a basis of scientific discussion of differences in analytic theory and practice'. Rosenfeld held that Greenson's statements about Kleinian approaches were taken out of context and that some of Greenson's remarks 'are quite meaningless to me and which I cannot relate to my own work or that of my colleagues' (Rosenfeld 1974, p. 49).

Greenson was greatly upset and offended by the discussion papers that followed by Brandchaft and Mason – the fact that it happened to be Greenson's birthday made matters still worse. Brandchaft maintained that Greenson 'constructs a picture of a Kleinian analyst generally taking the most extreme views and examples of bad analysis and implies that this near caricature is typical and universal' (Greenson 1973).

However, it was Mason's remarkably hostile presentation that really upset Greenson. Mason agreed with Herbert Rosenfeld's comments as a discussant of Greenson's presentation at the IPA Congress. Mason declared that Greenson had entirely misconstrued Kleinian clinical work and dealt with controversies that had been intensely discussed in the 1920s to which Greenson did not refer. The work for the paper, Mason continued,

> has been supported by a grant and it has the collaboration of five other authors as well as Greenson. Despite all these contributions and Greenson's contention that he is familiar with Klein's work, there is reference to only two of Mrs. Klein's works. In contrast, Greenson himself rates three references, more than the founder of child analysis and author of seven books. All Mrs Klein's answers to Greenson's points that she made [in books] are ignored or unread. (Greenson 1973)[52]

Mason claimed that many of Greenson's ideas had originated in Anna Freud's criticisms of Melanie Klein discussed in Melanie Klein's contribution to a 1927 'Symposium on child analysis' (Klein 1927, pp. 139–69) and wondered why Greenson's arguments so closely paralleled those of Anna Freud. Mason then cited a paper of Greenson's in which Greenson admitted to 'unconsciously plagiarizing' ideas from Freud, Ferenczi and others (Greenson 1969, pp. 333–57). Perhaps Greenson was again unconsciously plagiarising Anna Freud. On the other hand,

> To be ungenerous would be to assume that he is consciously dragging up old and largely resolved conflicts because he just wants to have a fight, and enjoys an atmosphere of hostility and suspicion between the Klein and Freudian groups. (Greenson 1973)

According to Mason, many issues had been 'dragged up after having been put to rest' many years before because Greenson wanted to fight. Recently, Greenson

> attacked the classical Freudians, the orthodox Freudians, the neo-Freudians, the New York school, the Fairbairnians, Alexanderians, recently the forty-five minutes an hour analysts, and I believe those who live in Beverly Hills and drive Cadillacs. (ibid.)

Mason felt that Greenson was assigning himself 'the role of protector of the faith, a kind of Attorney General of psychoanalysis. Now it's the Kleinians who are the heretics.' Mason did not think Greenson was so much defending Freud as 'attacking straw men he sets up for his own reasons'.

After the discussants' presentations, Greenson replied that instead of discussing differences, 'I found myself insulted, berated, mocked, humiliated by the discussants' (ibid.). However, Greenson was mistakenly putting Mason and Brandchaft together. Mason's was the stinging attack while Brandchaft's argument was intellectual in character. Greenson claimed he had cited 'ample evidence' from cases of Hanna Segal and Klein herself but, according to Greenson, neither of the discussants had said that they did not agree with what was said or that they would not treat patients that way.

> All that was done was to mock me, attack me, and for what? Because, yes, I am a defender of psychoanalysis. I attack many of my Freudian colleagues who are orthodox, who don't treat the transference, who ignore it, who wait too long. I attack the forty-five minute back-to-back revolving door treatment analysts, yes I do. I also attack those that want Cadillacs and not good results, yes I do, and I am not ashamed of it. But I did not come to fight. How dare you use the kind of language toward me that you did! That's *chutzpah*, plain *chutzpah*. Yes, I don't think I deserve it. This paper – wrong though it might be or weak though it might be – deserved at least some degree of respect. I don't think I got it from either one of the discussants. I am very willing to discuss this paper

with any of you, all of you, but not in this atmosphere. I'm sorry. Good night. (ibid.)

The chairman, Ed Kleinman, then closed the meeting by asking the audience to 'join Greenson for coffee and cake in celebration of his birthday'. Kleinman described the meeting to me as 'horrific' – after the meeting people were dazed because of the personal attack on Greenson. Kleinman was invited back to Greenson's home after the meeting where 'everybody was in shock. So that compounded the Kleinian bad reception.' In Kleinman's opinion, the meeting 'was a dramatisation, it was the nidus built up to that. I think it made things miserable. After that, I think it was even worse, the lines were very angrily drawn' (Kleinman interview 1992). Bail recalled that the fact that it was Greenson's birthday had 'aroused a great deal of sentiment in the audience and by the time the evening was finished it was an absolute disaster. I'm sure from that moment on Greenson vowed that he would do whatever he could to destroy the "Kleinian movement" as they began to call it in Los Angeles and I think he worked tirelessly at attempting to discredit, to make fun of, to belittle, to get rid of the Kleinians here' (Bail interview 1981). Two decades later Mason felt that the thing Greenson

> hated the most was that he did not believe in the existence of projective identification despite the fact that he wrote a paper in which he admits to having unconsciously plagiarised several others including Freud. I pointed out that unconscious plagiarism is being in a state of projective identification. He then says I accuse him of plagiarism! I think he confuses conscious with unconscious – of course, he broke so many boundaries in his life and work that it is not surprising to me that he did not differentiate between conscious and unconscious frequently. (Mason pers. comm. 1994)

How much the events of that evening contributed to later problems or were symptomatic of them is arguable. The meeting was one of a continuing series of vehement confrontations that had characterised the history of LAPSI (Mandel interview 1992), an evening which dramatised already existing intensities of feeling (Ourieff interview 1992). The debate certainly fuelled animosities and exemplifies how far the atmosphere in LAPSI had deteriorated by that time – and it was to deteriorate still further. From Greenson's paper it is clear that whatever his previous attitudes towards Klein, his current ones were almost entirely negative and may have catalysed some of the following events and reactions to them. Of course, it would be mistaken to attribute the problems to one man, especially since, as we shall now see, the APsaA's involvement was so important.

Bernard Bail's Removal from Teaching

Candidates from both sides were drawn into the ideological and political disputes as the polarisation continued. Some Kleinian candidates became so embroiled that they never recovered, Brandchaft recalled, while others in strict 'classical' analysis were 'regaled in their analytic sessions with arguments about the superiority of the classical view and why Kleinians weren't doing analysis at all'. Tinged with hysteria, the atmosphere was rife with rumours masquerading as facts (Brandchaft interview 1992).

Each side caricatured the other. The Kleinians lumped all their opposition into one ego psychological-Anna Freudian camp. They did not note the differences among their opponents nor did they even get the nature of the opposition right – they thought their opponents simply lackeys of the New York ego psychological APsaA establishment.

The LAPSI leadership – Leavitt, Ourieff and Rollman-Branch – were pluralistic and open to object relations approaches. Strongly influenced by Harry Stack Sullivan and Lionel Blitzten during his training in Chicago, the director, Arthur Ourieff, regarded object relations as his 'natural way of working' (Ourieff interview 1992). The assistant director, Hilda Rollman-Branch, was very interested in Klein's work, having integrated some Kleinian ideas into her approach. One Los Angeles ego psychologist disseminated his view around the APsaA that Rollman-Branch was a Kleinian (Rollman-Branch pers. comm. 1992). Mainstream analysts in LAPSI resented being considered by the Kleinians as Anna Freudians; instead, they saw themselves as 'Freudians or classical analysts or mainstream analysts' (Shane pers. comm. 1992).

However, those opposing the Kleinian development did not generally make distinctions between most of the Kleinians, labelling them as one univocal, aggressive clique. Brandchaft was close to some of the LAPSI leaders, and Mason, Grotstein and Bail were very different in their views and actions.

There were constant deviance amplifications: the institute leadership was concerned that the Kleinians would take over the institute whereas the Kleinians did not see why mainstream American psychoanalysis should continue to be the basis of training and felt that they were treated as heretics and were being unfairly oppressed.

It was in this climate in February 1974 that the Curriculum Committee of the institute met to select the next semester's offerings and instructors. At their meeting, the committee decided to remove a 'Kleinian' instructor, Bernard Bail, from teaching his continuous case seminar. Bail had taught a continuous case every spring for several years and had already been assigned the case for that year. Bail learned that the director, Arthur Ourieff, was not going to let him teach a course

> on the grounds that I was a Kleinian and it was disruptive to the education of the students. In the meantime, the American and its committee were talking with the officials of our institute – Ourieff, Leavitt, Rollman-Branch and Fine – and attempting to come to some kind of plan as to how to oust us since we were then scapegoated into being the responsible people for the trouble in the institute. Their first move was to pick on me and say that I was not allowed to teach. (Bail interview 1981)

Bail maintained that there were no grounds for his dismissal because he had 'superlative' reviews as a teacher (ibid.), although others expressed different views on this issue (Ourieff interview 1992; Brandchaft interview 1992). Bail had taught many courses over twelve years and conducted many supervisions (Bail interview 1981). Lee Shershow attended Bail's dream seminar in 1971 as a first year candidate, found it 'excellent', and considered that Bail had been generally regarded as a good teacher (Shershow interview 1992). Albert Mason recalled Bail getting good recommendations as a teacher – his dream course was 'highly commended'. According to Mason, Bail was discontinued because he was a Kleinian (Mason interview 1992).

For many years, Ourieff was chair of the Curriculum Committee that assigned the teaching. 'I insisted that Bail be assigned. I made sure that he came up in his regular rotation to teach a clinical seminar.' Ourieff maintained he was not be bothered by Bail's threatened suit. However, since he was a training analyst 'he had as much right to teach as anybody else. And he taught regularly all through those years on rotation.'

Ourieff felt that because of their zeal, he could find no way to arbitrate with the Kleinians:

> They were intent on taking over the institute. I think they were quite open about that. They wanted a Kleinian institute here in Los Angeles, and they thought they had the power and ability to do it. At a certain stage, I think they probably did because they had a lot of candidates. (Ourieff interview 1992)

The decision to remove Bail was a close vote of four to three on the Curriculum Committee. It was carried fortuitously since one of the members was a substitute for one of the regular committee members who was not able to be present, and the substitute was not aware of the complexity of the situation (Brandchaft interview 1981). Those present at the meeting were the then committee chairman, Norman Atkins, together with other committee members, Drs Fine, Foxman, Patterson and Tedesco. Also in attendance were the director, Arthur Ourieff, and four institute members including Ralph Greenson (Bail 1991b, p. 77). Norman Atkins recalled that Greenson had pressured prominent members of the committee and was

> insistent that Bail be kicked out of the course and even that Bail be disenfranchised as a training analyst eventually. But the first step was to kick him out of the course. At that time I was very much a civil libertarian, it absolutely offended me. It was a matter of principle – whether you liked Bail or not, whether you agreed with his teachings which were leaning toward Klein or not, you just don't kick somebody out because you don't agree, especially after the seminar has been started, the curriculum is going. It's not that it's going to happen next year – it's next week's seminar. I thought it was wrong. Tremendous pressure was put on me to remove him from the faculty and from the seminars, and I just refused to do that. (Atkins interview 1992)

That pressure came from Greenson and his associates who, Atkins was convinced, 'have never forgiven me for my obstinacy' (ibid.). Hilda Rollman-Branch informed me that

> in a *confidential* meeting, it was discussed not to have Bail teach another clinical course because when he taught that seminar he had told candidates not trained by him that what they did was not analysis, and this kind of discouraging attitude did not seem desirable. At any rate, this decision had been leaked to Bail by somebody who probably at that time had one foot in each camp, and it certainly has not helped anyone. Without any kind of remonstration or request for an interview with the Faculty Committee or discussion with the Coordinating Council, Bail with the support of Mason went ahead to institute a lawsuit. (Rollman-Branch pers. comm. 1992)

Brandchaft took exception to the immediate threat of suit. Brandchaft agreed that 'there probably was discrimination against him. If a different instructor had the same criticisms, he undoubtedly would have been treated differently ... They acted against him at this time surely from an oppositional position to him.' However, Brandchaft claims that Bail did not consult the other Kleinians about a joint effort, alternative tactics to remedy the injustice or to explore other possibilities of redressing the injustice that might have kept it localised. 'One gets the impression not only of a hysterical element entering into it but a need to use this further to amalgamate a theoretical position into an idealistic cause' (Brandchaft interview 1992).

While some were upset by Bail's response of threatening a writ, others felt that perhaps the only way that Bail had to protect his own rights and interests was the threat of a lawsuit – one senior Los Angeles analyst told me that 'the threat of great discomfort' was the only way the APsaA could be moved. The Kleinian contingent supported Bail and worked passionately together on this issue, chipping in money and arranging an attorney (Grotstein pers. comm. 1992). Bail clearly had an excellent case of discrimination had it gone to court.

Bail recalled, 'The people most vociferous in terms of the lawsuit were the London Kleinians. H. Segal especially wanted me to drop the suit and got Betty Joseph to talk to me in the same vein. Segal apparently did not care whether I would jeopardize my standing, even my livelihood' (Bail pers. comm. 1990). Brandchaft confirmed that he personally knew the London Kleinians to be unhappy about the threat of suit: 'The initial reaction among the leadership of the Kleinians in Great Britain was that they were appalled that that could happen and that they could in any way be associated with it.' In London 'there had been bitter controversies, discrimination, redress of the discrimination, then discrimination again – that went on for years in London but nobody would have considered going to the courts to not only consider it but being assessed punitive damages'. Brandchaft regarded Bail's threatened suit as 'an extreme and unprecedented measure'. He believed that it was difficult to get the measure of the consequences for a psychoanalytic group of the threat at the time:

> There was no way in which one could give reassurance against that threat being carried out, of their being ruined for life, of their being assessed punitive damages that would have permanent consequences in their life, even those that were not really involved with the controversy. (Brandchaft interview 1992)

Whether or not these consequences were realistic (there were no details of what damages would be demanded), there can be little question that analysts were concerned about the consequences of a suit for their personal and professional livelihood.

However, there was another more important difference than the personalities involved. The LAPSI leadership was acting under what they considered to be the clear direction of the APsaA to get rid of the

Kleinians from the institute. The APsaA did not back the institute up on this matter more because of the threat of the lawsuit than the notion that it was simply a local political issue.

Mandel recalled the events at institute and society meetings after Bail's threat of the lawsuit: 'Ourieff came to the institute in order to seek indemnification for legal costs if their decisions led us ultimately into a trial by Bail. And the institute authorised this indemnification. But they had to go to the society for the indemnification.' At LAPSI, the society controls the institute's budget – the institute is not separately funded. The institute referred to the views of Los Angeles Superior Court Judge Marvin Freeman, who drafted the 1967 Bylaws of the institute when he was an attorney. They claimed that Judge Freeman did not think substantial damages would result if Bail's suit actually came to trial. However, Judge Freeman, who was neutral in the dispute, denied that he had said that and agreed to address the society on the whole Kleinian issue (Bail 1991b, p. 91).

In his address to the society in June 1974, Judge Freeman made it clear that there were very good grounds for a suit (ibid., pp. 96–116). LAPSI needed to clarify in writing its purposes and whom it excluded:

> The issue you have today is an unclear issue, of the interrelationship between Kleinianism and pure Freudianism and between competence and incompetence. I only suggest that you get to a clear issue. You are doing yourself, the movement, the science, and the field, a disservice if you don't do that. (ibid., p. 104)

LAPSI had to make up its mind as to how to define what a 'Kleinian' was and then how far it regarded itself as a private 'country club' which had the right of arbitrary selection of its members and how far it was a quasi-public scientific body. That was a difficult question since the mission and structure of LAPSI fell somewhere between a private club and a hospital in that it was privately organised but provided health services (ibid., p. 103). As LAPSI was not a private club, LAPSI had to detail its standards as a university or college does (ibid., p. 100). The situation was further complicated by the relationship between the Los Angeles Institute and the APsaA. If it were claimed that the Los Angeles Institute leadership was merely trying to carry out the requirements of the APsaA to which it was affiliated, the question as to the explicit nature of the contract between the Los Angeles Institute and the APsaA was paramount. If Bail persisted with the lawsuit, Freeman believed that he would have no choice but to sue the APsaA as well. Still, the first issue to be addressed was what was deemed acceptable and unacceptable within the Los Angeles Institute. Judge Freeman invoked an analogy:

> If I were the owner of a McDonald franchise, the parent organization would have to spell out in advance how thick my hamburgers have to be before they withdraw my franchise because they don't like my hamburgers. You have a franchise, and I think that it has to be spelled out what your qualifications are, but that depends on your relationship with the American. It seems to me that the American can't come in and say we just left you a franchise. Where did they tell you in advance what you are supposed to do? (ibid., p. 101)

Judge Freeman emphasised that explicit criteria needed to be spelled out because the law was opposed to arbitrary action. Judge Freeman told the society:

> If you have somebody come before the committee, and he presents his credentials, he now wants to be a teacher, and the answer is no if he is identified with Kleinianism, it's going to be like excluding somebody who is a tiny bit Negro. You may have another reason, but the civil rights commission is going to say you didn't because he was a Negro. (ibid., pp. 106–7)

In any case, the IPA, from which the APsaA itself receives its charter, has a large Kleinian membership and Klein is seen as a follower of Freud, not as a deviation like Jung. Klein may or may or may not be acceptable to some analysts, but her work is certainly within the psychoanalytic framework of the IPA.

The indemnification of the institute was discussed at a society meeting. Mandel recalled:

> Although they were not Kleinian, a lot of the society members were not members of the faculty and weren't all het up about the dispute. They refused to indemnify the leadership at which point the leadership had to severely limit its aggressive behaviour against the Kleinians. That is what got it back to a stalemated position. I thought to myself, 'Thank God we put an organisation together where the society as a whole could veto that.' The last thing I wanted to see was to authorise people to have the authority to do things that would lead to suit. (Mandel interview 1992)

Bail was therefore permitted to continue his seminars but promotions and the accreditation of training analysts came to a standstill. Faculty meetings challenged the rights of Kleinians to teach in the institute while maintaining their rights to participate in the society (Mandel 1986, p. 45).

As a member of the faculty committee overseeing the promotion of all faculty members, Mandel became a force for the creation of a moratorium on the appointment of training analysts. In his view, it was not possible for a Kleinian to obtain a fair hearing for promotion (Mandel interview 1981).

> I fought and won a moratorium against Faculty promotions because Mort Shane was trying to get somebody promoted who was not Kleinian and would not promote a Kleinian. It was I who said, 'I don't care for Kleinian philosophy but people are going to be treated fairly here. If you won't promote somebody just because he is a Kleinian, I am going to fight against your promoting anybody'. (Mandel interview 1992)

For Mandel, not only was it unfair but it 'would subject us to ridicule' if it came to court. 'So I did push through that committee a moratorium. Until this issue was resolved, nobody else would be promoted to training analyst' (Mandel interview 1981).

Wanting to go ahead with the re-evaluation of training analysts, in December 1975 the leadership sent a mail ballot to faculty members about whether there should be a reevaluation where each training analyst would sign a pledge as that he or she would not sue the institute in the event that they would not be reappointed. A legal opinion was tendered that such a pledge 'would weigh heavily as evidence of an improper and legally unsound requirement' and that it would 'only encourage litigation'. The motion was defeated (Bail 1991b, pp. 181–5).

Unaware of LAPSI's 1974 moratorium the APsaA instituted its own moratorium in LAPSI against appointing new training analysts or accepting candidates. According to Mandel, the APsaA helped bring about a crisis and fairness was maintained. The threat of Bail's attorney meant 'that people were dealt with fairness which otherwise might not have happened. I think they would have run roughshod over the Kleinian group' (Mandel interview 1992).

However, the situation in LAPSI had considerably worsened. Mandel lamented:

> As 1975 was ending it was clear that almost three years of negotiating had come to a standstill. All our efforts to develop acceptable machinery which would get the institute moving had produced no solution, and the attempt to ram through a forced solution was stymied by legal threats. We were adrift without sail, motor or rudder. (Mandel 1986, p. 46)

For Mandel, the logic behind the idea that Kleinians should not teach or train from the local standpoint was

> that our classes were too disrupted, that instructors and candidates were fighting and we could not get on with education. From the point of view of the politics, The American was concerned that we were not teaching Traditional American Psychoanalysis. That is what was being brought to the platform of LAPSI and increasing the likelihood that we were going to come to some kind of horrendous end. From 1974–75 the organisation made numerous attempts to find ways – reevaluation requiring a two-thirds vote for training analysts to be recertified. I think it was transparently clear that the idea was that certain difficult people would not be appointed training analysts. Maybe Brandchaft might have been appointed a training analyst but certainly the more difficult, recalcitrant, pugnacious people would not. We came very close to designating the beginnings of such a committee. But at the last minute the effort fell apart; they just couldn't muster enough votes to develop a two-thirds majority. So these things were faltering very badly. (Mandel interview 1992)

The problems seemed intractable: Leonard Rosengarten believed that 'the problem couldn't be solved because of a few impossible, difficult people'. But he also felt that 'The American was not satisfied. They wanted the Kleinians out – it is as simple as that. They can deny it. They can lie about it.' It was impossible to correct the problem with certain Kleinians 'fighting and with the American saying they are out' (Rosengarten interview 1992).

Between 1973 and late 1975, officers of the board on Professional Standards (which oversaw the institutes) met with representatives of the Los Angeles Psychoanalytic Institute at the semi-annual meetings of the APsaA. In a statement to the APsaA's Board on Professional Standards on December 17, 1975, the Chairman of its Committee on Institutes, Leon Ferber, stated:

> We have documentation of the extraordinary efforts made in Los Angeles in attempting to carry out the recommendations contained in the site visit report. It should be acknowledged that certain changes have been effected in the educational program. However, the basic problems remain unresolved. As the Los Angeles Institute's officers tried to carry out the recommendations of the Committee on Institutes, there was continued divisiveness which prevented success in instituting the desired reforms. The... threat of a lawsuit made things even more difficult. (Bail 1991b, p. 213)

Ferber added that because of this situation, the APsaA's Committee on Institutes was considering further means to deal with the situation in Los Angeles (ibid.).

The Susanna Isaacs Case

This situation and atmosphere was epitomised by the case of Susanna Isaacs, a British Kleinian child analyst who came to live in Los Angeles in 1974 and applied for membership of LAPSI. She was invited by Albert Mason because there was a 'big need' at the time for a Kleinian child analyst, and she was very keen to come (Mason interview 1992). Her application for membership of LAPSI was approved by the Membership Committee but after a telephone campaign against her, she was subsequently turned down in a membership ballot in January 1975.

In 1973 Isaacs was appointed a training analyst in the British Institute for Psychoanalysis where she had trained as a child analyst in the Kleinian stream. Isaacs was highly qualified. She had an MD from the University of Chicago and was a Fellow of the Royal College of Physicians and a Fellow of the Royal College of Psychiatrists. She succeeded Donald Winnicott in his position as Physician-in-Charge of the Department of Child Psychiatry at London's Paddington Green Children's Hospital where she had worked for the eleven years before her move to Los Angeles.

After she had been recommended for membership by the Membership Committee of LAPSI, there had then been a routine membership ballot. However, because of a technicality, another ballot was arranged and the original ballots sealed away in the LAPSI safe. Normally a recommendation by the Membership Committee would be automatically ratified by the membership. As Albert Mason put it, 'If the Membership Committee recommends somebody, the members just sign because they don't know who the people are in any case. In the case of somebody coming from abroad, they take it on trust that the Membership committee have investigated them' (Mason interview 1992). However, in an unprecedented move in such circumstances, the membership did not approve her application by the requisite majority after the second ballot, and her application was rejected on January 31, 1975 (Bail 1991b, p. 246).

Why was she turned down? She had an unblemished reputation and the membership did not know her. This happened because she was a Kleinian; a telephone campaign against her between the ballots brought this to members' attention. At a society meeting one of the older members, David Brunswick, said that Susanna Isaacs had a name that was very close to that of a well-known British Kleinian, Susan Isaacs: 'I learned that she is, in fact, a Kleinian, and therefore I know how I will vote' (ibid., p. 237). At a subsequent meeting, Bernard Brandchaft described the rejection as a humiliation for Isaacs without precedent. Brandchaft was minuted as saying, 'It is sad for her and for ourselves. Our society was founded by foreign analysts and often nourished by them. The action came in an inflamed climate, without the membership being provided with information on Isaacs as an individual' (ibid., p. 236). Rosengarten considered that it was wrong that Isaacs was denied membership of LAPSI 'not because I necessarily agreed with her but because I thought she had a right to membership' (Rosengarten interview 1992).

Another reason given for the rejection involved a letter by Isaacs to the IPA before she had been considered for membership of LAPSI. Arthur Ourieff made the statement about the exclusion of 'incompetents, Kleinians and object relations analysts' soon after her arrival in Los Angeles. Concerned in this circumstance about what might happen to her application, she wrote to the President of the IPA as well as to the APsaA seeking their assurance that freedom of psychoanalytic thought would not be infringed and that her professional position would not be jeopardised. Hilda Rollman-Branch considered that Isaacs

> made herself unpopular with us when we found out that she had written a letter complaining about our society to the International, while at the same time applying to become a member of our society. I don't think one should judge from the outside what goes on in a society, but she was somewhat premature in this action. (Rollman-Branch pers. comm. 1992)

None the less, given the extraordinary atmosphere, official statements by Ourieff and the APsaA's attitude, it is evident why Isaacs had legitimate grounds for concern that she would be discriminated against solely on the grounds that she was a Kleinian. It is not clear that she was so much complaining about the society as attempting to protect her professional interests by seeking to ensure that she would not be subject to discrimination by LAPSI. Isaacs later complained to the IPA about not having been accepted as a member of LAPSI. Her rejection was raised by Mason at the 1975 IPA Congress as part of his concerns about discrimination in LAPSI. A consultative committee to consider these matters was set up by the IPA.

Isaacs remained in Los Angeles practising psychoanalysis for a number of years and then returned to the UK. She was made a member by LAPSI some years after she left the US (Mason interview 1992).

The 'Élite 16'

After the institute leaders' thwarted attempts to be indemnified and the defeat of their plans to reevaluate training analysts, the more mainstream analysts were seemingly defeated. However, they decided on another option which was to be their undoing. In January 1976, the leadership and its associates wrote a letter to the APsaA requesting permission to organise a new provisional institute in Los Angeles. On January 28, Morton Shane and Lawrence Friedman told their classes at LAPSI that there was to be a split. Sixteen analysts from LAPSI wanted to set up their own institute in the name of 'traditional American psychoanalysis'. Described by Shane as an 'élite group' among the training faculty, they included the director of the institute, Arthur Ourieff, the assistant director, Hilda Rollman-Branch, the chairman of the Admissions Committee, Maimon Leavitt together with other officials of the institute-society, and Ralph Greenson. This group wished to obtain a charter from the APsaA and secede from LAPSI. A member of this group, Gerald Aronson, recalled that what came to be known as the 'élite 16' was formed at a weekend meeting in the Psychoanalytic Building at 1800 Fairbairn Avenue in Los Angeles.[53] Aronson attended that meeting together with Alfred Goldberg, Lewis Fielding, Arthur Ourieff, Ralph Greenson, Maimon Leavitt and Rudolph Eckstein. Leavitt recalled the 'things were getting so difficult that a few people thought they had to do something about it'. There was an impulsive and desperate feeling at the meeting that both sides in the battle were wasting their energy and that those present should start a new institute (Leavitt interview 1992). According to Aronson, having decided that the rifts were not bridgeable and, that 'a purer, better, finer Freudian institute should rise from the ashes', the meeting sent a letter to the APsaA applying to form a new institute (Aronson interview 1992; Rollman-Branch pers. comm. 1992).

Deserted by the APsaA and under siege from the Kleinians, it is understandable why the institute leadership felt they had to leave. They were between a rock and a hard place. The climate was chaotic, intensified by fear, anxiety, the threatened lawsuit as well as the Kleinian threat, both real and imagined. The climate, together with the pressure on Ourieff and Rollman-Branch to take action, moved Ourieff and Rollman-

Branch to decide that the only solution 'was to give them the institute, let The American handle them' (Ourieff interview 1992).

As a veteran of the 1950 split, Ralph Greenson had experienced how awful and counterproductive the atmosphere in a warring institute could be. Greenson recalled how terrible the 1940s were: 'It became untenable. It was just impossible to work and we were upset all the time and our candidates were upset all the time' (Greenson 1962, p. 20). Speaking at the Oral History Workshop of the APsaA eight months earlier in May 1975, Greenson even foreshadowed the 'élite 16' move. Greenson emphasised there how imperative the 1950 split had been for LAPSI's survival. 'We needed distance to cool the intensity of our clashing views.' Given the 'deep-seated and intense differences' in 1975, Greenson made a proposal: 'I believe we should distance ourselves by having some kind of division in order to get away from hypocrisy and subversion' (Greenson, in American Psychoanalytic Association 1975c, pp. 27–8).

Certainly, there were striking parallels between the state of the institute in 1950 and in 1975. Mandel's discussion of the atmosphere in the early 1970s showed how far the schisms had gone:

> It was virtually impossible to teach because each camp operated out of a theoretical and clinical base essentially incompatible with the other's. No theoretical or clinical supposition could be made to begin a line of reasoning without an a priori attack. Imagine a biological society divided between firm believers in creation and evolution theory. One could no more expect intelligent discussion between that pairing than between Kleinians and classicists. (Mandel 1986, p. 43)

Nevertheless, there was a major difference from the 1950 split. The earlier split had been negotiated between the conflicting parties. That split was consensual; the current one was a unilateral walk-out amounting to a *fait accompli*. There was not the general agreement that there had been twenty-five years before that a split was both necessary and desirable and no mutual arrangements had been made.

Since both the director and assistant director of the Los Angeles Psychoanalytic Institute had signed the letter, the reaction to the move of the 'élite 16' was exceptionally sharp. As Mandel pointed out, 'You don't write a letter to form a new institute while you're still the power in the old one' (Mandel interview 1981). It was the opinion of the attorney who acted for the Kleinians that the officers had 'a continuing duty to carry out the purposes of the organization they serve. The relationship between officers and members of an organization is that of a fiduciary.' The attorney maintained that it was immoral, unethical and illegal for a director of a company to abandon that company and that the officers should resign forthwith (Bail 1991b, pp. 189–91; Bail 1991a). Moreover, since two-thirds of the institute (many of them non-Kleinians) had been left out of the élite group, the reaction was particularly strong. As Mason put it, 'If they had been included, the reaction would not have been half as sharp' (Mason interview 1990).

Leonard Rosengarten recalled being in the conference room of the Fairbairn Avenue building where he practised and hearing about the move by the 'élite 16' when Greenson entered the room.

> I immediately asked him what it was all about. He told me because of the problems in the teaching and so on that they felt they had to have to their own institute where they would not have interference from Kleinians, and that they were going to form a separate group. I asked him if they were going to invite others. He said, well, maybe later. They wanted to take over the name, the building and what have you. I said to him immediately, 'Romi, I have two things to say to you – one it's unprincipled and two it's unconscionable.' Apparently, I hit him very hard with it and he got up and walked into the office which is next to the conference room. He called the American Psychoanalytic and said, 'Take my name off that list, I am out of that.' (Rosengarten interview 1992)

Greenson later said of his decision to withdraw, 'I decided that I started in the LA Society and I'll die in the LA Society' (Greenson, quoted in Shershow 1993, p. 21). By then the disquiet among the members of the élite group had become more general. After the meeting which had formed the group, Leavitt remembered having had a very sleepless night: 'I was thinking of the people left out, of what led me to believe that I had any privileged knowledge. Consequently, I started calling, and I learned then that others had been calling around, and the next day or so we rescinded the letter'. Having reconsidered, Greenson telephoned others in the group about it the next day. All the events took place over a matter of days (Leavitt interview 1992).[54]

Ourieff regarded the move as a 'fatal mistake' – he suffered for it as his career in the APsaA was ruined (Ourieff interview 1992). As an ill-considered act of impulsive and hasty desperation, it was handled ineptly. There was no formal announcement to candidates and many who were not included in the group were upset, although, Leavitt recalled, there was 'no thought of keeping people in or out' (Leavitt interview 1992). Shane thought it had been wise to back down. 'We would have lost the building, the tradition, and have had to go our own way in terms of financing with a lot of administrative hassle' (Shane pers. comm. 1992). For Mandel, the 'élite 16' affair

> was part of the internal turmoil and the inability of our group to resolve its own internal difficulty, the flames of which were being fed by the American who were saying, 'Your first job is to get the Kleinian thing under control and you will do that by reevaluating your training analysts.' (Mandel interview 1992)

At a faculty meeting on February 4, 1976, an announcement was made that the letter had been withdrawn. A no confidence motion was then passed by a majority of those present requesting the resignation of the director and assistant director. It was seen as inappropriate if not illegal for officers of the institute to act against that institute (Bail 1991b, p. 192). However, the bylaws of the institute did not require that in such circumstances, the leadership had to resign, and they did not. The society was left hanging in a state of suspense.

The Committee on the Unification of the Institute and the APsaA's Ad Hoc Committee

After the 'élite 16' fiasco Mel Mandel thought that the moment might have arrived when somebody within LAPSI could take some effective action: 'I perceived that like good psychoanalytic work, the patient has got to get down to the bottom of the barrel: if the institute would come to a point where it would be on the edge of falling apart, that it might be possible for somebody to come in and begin a process of recreation' (Mandel interview 1981). Mandel wanted to develop a proposal 'to form a bridge between the two sides and to form a committee which would be acceptable to both sides'. As a past president of the society Mandel approached Leonard Rosengarten who was known for having helped change Greenson's mind over the 'élite 16' affair and was a past director of the institute. Mandel met with Rosengarten, Neal Peterson and Leonard Gilman who called a meeting of LAPSI. The proposed committee would investigate LAPSI's problems and deliver a report on what might be done to retain a unified institute. Mandel insisted on stipulating that the proposal needed to be acceptable to two-thirds of the membership in order to give the committee power and authority. Rosengarten had another stipulation, that everybody had to 'agree to meet and discuss things as ladies and gentlemen' (Mandel interview 1981; Rosengarten interview 1992).

A meeting of the membership passed Mandel's proposal by one vote (Mandel interview 1981) and a Committee on the Unification of the Institute (CUI) was formed. Rosengarten emphasised, 'We didn't want the institute to stop functioning.' The institute continued its work with Arthur Ourieff as director and co-operated well with the CUI's functions (Rosengarten interview 1992). Mandel and Rosengarten selected members whom they felt that could be reasoned with, who were acceptable to both sides and who could communicate with people on both sides.[55]

Quite independently of Mandel's and Rosengarten's initiatives, the APsaA became directly involved in the problems of LAPSI. In January 1976 the Chairman of the APsaA's Board on Professional Standards, Edward Weinshel, received the 'élite 16's' letter proposing a new Los Angeles Institute. He was also sent letters from LAPSI candidates and the candidates' national body, the Council for the Advancement of Psychoanalytic Education (CAPE), which voiced concern about their training being 'interfered with, delayed, obstructed, and in some instances seriously jeopardised by unusual dissension in their institute' *(CAPE News* 1976, pp. 4–5; Bail 1991b, p. 203).

Perceiving LAPSI's paralysed state, Weinshel appointed an Ad Hoc Committee, chaired by Joan Fleming,[56] whose commission was to shut down the institute (McLaughlin interview 1994b) and to protect the candidates while new arrangements were being formulated.

However, Fleming's intention was quite different. She wanted to save LAPSI and help improve the situation there, to ask for a moratorium on battling and, by taking an educational stance, attempt to understand the processes and behaviour of the group (McLaughlin interview 1994b; Mandel interview 1981). Her principal interest was in experiential learning in the psychoanalytic educative process. She believed that the entire analytic education process should aim at 'making self-analytic functions readily available equipment for working as an analyst' (Fleming and Benedek 1987, p. 20). Fleming was to put these ideas into practice in her work with LAPSI.

The CUI arranged to meet Fleming's Ad Hoc Committee when it arrived in Los Angeles and asked how high on their priority list was the reevaluation of the Los Angeles training analysts. Up to this point, the APsaA had said it was their first priority. This meant that the Kleinians would have been excluded from the training process since they were far from being the required 'traditional American analysts'. Mandel recalled that before the night was out Fleming said that the re-evaluation of the Los Angeles training analysts was not the first priority. 'When we walked out of that meeting, we had our first glimmer of hope that we might succeed if we could remove that from the top of the list of priorities' (Mandel interview 1981). From that statement Rosengarten and Mandel recognised that they 'had bought time' to resolve the LAPSI difficulties internally. While the committee was initially unwelcome, LAPSI began then to cooperate with the APsaA committee rather than treat it with scepticism (McLaughlin interview 1994b). As Mandel asserted, they

> had not been incorrect since the Ad Hoc Committee had a charge to dissolve our institute. The whole focus was again the political problem about training analysts – who is going to control the training and who is going to be the authorised trainers. (Mandel interview 1992)[57]

The CUI then issued invitations to a meeting to all members of the faculty. Mandel rehearsed the CUI to sit, listen, and not become involved, to 'learn how to listen'. This may seem a strange thing to have to tell analysts. As Mandel observed, 'It's remarkable how they know to do that in practice, but once you get out of your office you don't have to do that. You can just get in there, fight, and do anything. You don't have to listen any more'. In the 1960s and 1970s visitors from the East Coast had good reason for thinking the Los Angeles Society was not civilised since the meetings were so riotous that, in Mandel's words, 'It had gotten to be the Wild West' (Mandel interview 1981). One committee member was James McLaughlin who was the Pittsburgh analyst who chaired the Ad Hoc Committee investigating the Boston Psychoanalytic Institute (see Chapter 2). As he put it,

> there was not sufficient ordinary social decorum in allowing the rules of how to get along with people to be retained. Very good people were driven beyond their capacities any longer to think and behave logically, dispassionately because they had been driven far beyond their limits, even for California. (McLaughlin interview 1994b)

McLaughlin emphasised the vast difference in discussions when the grounds were changed to focusing on trying to understand and not getting into ad hominem attacks. Once it was clear that the Ad Hoc Committee was not sitting in judgement, its role as collegial outside consultants quickly helped to develop changes.[58] Leonard Rosengarten experienced the committee as 'very helpful and supportive'. It 'lent a good ear to our complaints. They listened to us like good analysts' (Rosengarten interview 1992). Lee Shershow remembered meeting Fleming: 'I was expecting to see these monsters and I see these smart, reasonable people. I really liked Fleming' (Shershow interview 1992). The

CUI worked for eight months soliciting recommendations and ideas and liaising with the Ad Hoc Committee (Rosengarten interview 1992). The Final Report of the Ad Hoc Committee described its approach:

> In spite of having been urged by various factions of both board and institute that we 'step in and take over', we tried to establish a working alliance with all who were willing to be involved. We were exposed to the chronic political fighting which we reflected back to them for their evaluation and consideration. We refused the assignment of adversary. We did not, however, refuse the role of analytic educators utilizing the processes of consultation and demonstration to facilitate our joint appraisal of their educational policies and organizational procedures. (American Psychoanalytic Association 1977, p. 499)

The process culminated in a workshop weekend organised by Joan Fleming at her institute in Denver in April 1976 attended by fourteen LAPSI faculty members and seven candidates. James McLaughlin regarded this as a 'master-stroke', because it took people who fought in their own bailiwick into a different situation where the educative processes she had instituted in Denver were put into action (McLaughlin interview 1994b). According to the Ad Hoc Committee, self-evaluative processes were stimulated and enhanced in the workshop that included faculty and students. 'Significantly', it concluded, 'the *candidates* found it easier to make the initial constructive shift from politics to education and to grasp and utilize the potential of this group evaluative approach' (American Psychoanalytic Association 1977, p. 499; original emphasis). The committee reported that what it clearly saw at Denver 'was not only a continuation of politicizing and fighting which has existed for many years but also a tendency to externalize responsibility and ambivalently depend upon an authoritarian attitude in their leadership'. The committee was discouraged by the fighting it took to be 'part of the Los Angeles ego ideal and tradition' and felt that LAPSI 'in its present state was not capable of conducting an adequate psychoanalytic educational program' (American Psychoanalytic Association 1976b, p. 5). Nevertheless, the workshop provided a means by which many of the fights could be discussed by outsiders who, like good psychoanalysts, could astutely hear projection.

What was being projected? Mandel recalled the insight: 'We're projecting from despair about the way we are working, and with a despair about the effectiveness of what we're doing.' The process in which one's own problems are projected onto somebody else might be happening in the group as a whole. Mandel felt that to be 'a most significant insight. Not that we didn't have such insights about our patients but we never had the insights about ourselves ... It caught my ear very sharply and I could see it. So I began to catch on to what might be taking place at an unconscious level in the whole group' (Mandel interview 1981). James McLaughlin recalled much talk at Denver 'about the sense of helplessness and immobilisation that had befallen people who could no longer find any way to get together and have any discourse and any civility and any effort to solve the problem' (McLaughlin interview 1994b).

The CUI met again with most of the analysts it had met with before and reported to the institute in May 1976. According to Mandel, the report emphasised how people had forgotten 'how to speak to each other as gentlemen and ladies. There's a certain civilised way that one must adhere to or you begin to really find yourself free to project the worst of yourself on to somebody else.' Adopted by 70 per cent of the LAPSI faculty, the CUI report described how the destructive existing climate of LAPSI which was 'not conducive to psychoanalytic education', had demoralised the institute. The committee noted 'an erosion of a constructive group identity' where 'paralysis led to paralysis followed by revolution rather than development of constructive solutions through educational processes'. The involvement of candidates 'in the bitter struggles of the faculty is destructive to their education'. The report then recorded some agreements and understandings limiting the development of schools and organisations. There was to be only one psychoanalytic institute and shadow institutes or tracks are 'intolerable to the integral functioning of the institute'. In psychoanalytic education, 'The institute will provide a thorough and rigorous study of Freud's writings as our primary and fundamental objective, and will also provide to students the teaching of diverse theoretical contributions and points of view and their clinical applications.' Furthermore, this statement should be 'respected in spirit and letter; that compliance with or violation against this agreement will be heavily weighted in the evaluation of a member's functioning as faculty' (quoted in American Psychoanalytic Association 1976b, p. 6).

The report was then delivered to the May meeting of the APsaA and both groups within the institute convinced Mandel (who was in neither camp) to become director to continue the healing process. Educational considerations began to replace ideological considerations as the primary ones. However, as Mandel observed, psychoanalytic institutes are training bodies, not educational bodies.

The biggest argument is over who are you going to train, in what technique and who is going to be your follower. In other words, it's your eternity that you're looking toward, your 'offspring', and that is where the biggest problems get created. (Mandel interview 1981)

By introducing the voice of reason and constructive engagement into explosive circumstances, Mandel and Rosengarten saved LAPSI from the brink. Mandel remained active in LAPSI while Rosengarten retired again from institute affairs in 1977 after the CUI had concluded and the APsaA's had accepted the Ad Hoc Committee's report and LAPSI was no longer on probation. As Grotstein aptly observed, 'If the institute fell apart, it was Greenson's fault more than anybody's. If it held together, it was Mel Mandel's' (Grotstein interview 1992).[59] Mandel felt that the institute had learned from the experiences: 'The institute has come through so much that we understand clearly the pitfalls of any other way of operation' (Mandel interview 1992).

In May 1976, the Ad Hoc Committee recommended to the Board on Professional Standards that

> a definitive decision about the Los Angeles Psychoanalytic Institute be deferred to December 1976; that no splits occur, that a moratorium on admission and graduation be implemented until the educational process is on a sounder basis; that a commitment be made to a sequential educational system concerned with the timing and mode of introducing alternative analytic viewpoints into that system; and that the Los Angeles Institute utilize a close consultative relationship with the American to develop an educational philosophy and to study its own group processes, its educational goals and practices. Should satisfactory progress not be evident by the time of this meeting, the board would move to put the institute on Provisional Status. (American Psychoanalytic Association 1977, p. 500)

The Ad Hoc Committee report described the consequences in these words:

> Should the above recommendations fail to result in a demonstrable improvement in the psychoanalytic educational atmosphere in Los Angeles by the time of the December 1976 meeting of the board, it would be our further recommendation that the Los Angeles Institute be offered the opportunity to request provisional status; failing this, it would be our recommendation that formal disaccreditation proceedings be instituted. (American Psychoanalytic Association 1976b, p. 6)

The Ad Hoc Committee report expressed its strong hope that disaccreditation would be avoided and noted that the changes in the situation had already occurred in the context of the possibility of disaccreditation (American Psychoanalytic Association 1977, p. 501). However, as the May 1976 Minutes of the Board on Professional Standards report put it, the Ad Hoc Committee considered that LAPSI's 'current administrative structure and destructive analytic atmosphere were not conducive to productive learning and teaching'. The committee 'expected that they would be recommending that the American would need to encourage the Los Angeles group to request provisional status. However, in response to favourable reactions at Los Angeles since the Denver meeting, this recommendation has changed.' Fleming received positive reports from the Los Angeles candidates as well as a report from the CUI (American Psychoanalytic Association 1976b, p. 5). LAPSI had been very close to being shut down.

The Ad Hoc Committee recommended that 'the Board deal at the national level with the Freud–Klein controversy in the perspective of scientific theory and its appropriate place in any comprehensive curriculum, so that no controversial view will be shut off from discussion' (American Psychoanalytic Association 1977, p. 502). Public clarity about the situation and the publishing of detailed standards were the issues Judge Freeman had regarded as central. The fact that the APsaA had told Ourieff to 'Get rid of the Kleinians', yet did not put this in writing and could thus deny it said it publicly, added greatly to the of LAPSI's unviable position. The Ad Hoc Committee did not address the Freud–Klein controversy directly except within the context of the importance of general self-evaluative approaches the Los Angeles Institute needed to adopt. Since the emphasis was educational, the general approach was not directly combative towards the Kleinians. However, the committee had recommended that 'a commitment be maintained to a sequential educational process that avoids premature inclusion of alternative conceptual viewpoints in the curriculum' (American Psychoanalytic Association 1976b, p. 6). This meant that the Kleinian standpoint would not be taught until the later years of psychoanalytic training. The committee believed that the 'ultimate resolution of the question of selection and appointment of training analysts may represent a landmark that will determine and demonstrate the effectiveness of the Committee's approach' (American Psychoanalytic Association 1977, p. 500). By December 1976, the moratorium on admissions and graduation at LAPSI was rescinded.

The APsaA was primarily concerned with the training rather than the scientific side. It was not trying to get rid of the Kleinians from the society but from the institute. The Board on Professional Standards and its Committee on Institutes are concerned with institutes and not societies. The paramount role of the board is an index of the priority that the APsaA gives to training, 'quality control', certification and qualification over scientific debate and research. The training analyst issue referred to by the Ad Hoc Committee underscores the centrality of the issue in analytic 'ideological' controversies. After all, theoretical and technical differences need not necessarily lead to political conflict. Where there is political conflict over 'ideological' differences, it is worth finding out what else is happening.

Whatever the reasons for the difficult conflicts, the polarisation continued into a self-perpetuating negative feedback which needed to be arrested. The paranoia – suspicion and mistrust – increased, as did personal enmities. Mandel recalled:

> It was said many times that perhaps the difficulties have to do more with the way people feel about each other than about the ideas. Jim McLaughlin of the Ad Hoc Committee made a comment one time that I've never forgotten. He said back home where he came from in Pittsburgh people were apt to say, 'John is a miserable son of a bitch, I wouldn't want to have him as a friend, but he may not be a bad analyst. There are some people I can see he is going to be a good analyst for.' He said that in Los Angeles what he kept hearing was, 'So-and-so, a nice guy. He really is not bad if you know him socially but I wouldn't send a patient to him under any circumstances. He's a terrible analyst.' It seemed here as though it ended up being a complaint about how everybody was functioning as an analyst rather than an acknowledgement that they didn't like somebody personally. (Mandel interview 1981)

Moreover, the ideological and political struggles may have masked something else. As Mandel put it:

> I think everybody was having some internal difficulty with that sense of despair of his or her work and analysis in general. That was the key to it for me. Rather than finding it possible to publicly acknowledge how at times they were feeling failures as psychoanalysts, they were clinging to each other for safety and projecting their failure and despair onto the other group. (ibid.)

Leavitt expressed the general feeling that the Ad Hoc Committee 'had by and large an ameliorative effect. They focused on educational values, less on the politics. Mandel did a yeoman's job' and, unlike the 1973 site visit, the Ad Hoc Committee's work was 'a real effort'. However, unlike Mandel, Leavitt did not feel that the Ad Hoc Committee saved the situation: 'If left alone the same thing would have come about. It was already starting to run its course – the passions were starting to die down' (Leavitt interview 1992). However, the role of the APsaA cannot be ignored. The 1973 site visit, its consequences and the APsaA's later interventions fomented greater division and a more destructive atmosphere, causing more strife in LAPSI than might otherwise have occurred. Both sides inflamed the other to what Shane considered 'ridiculous heights of certitude. LAPSI learned from the experience. I think, however, what LAPSI didn't learn is that they should have been much stronger vis a vis the American and not taken their direction so passively' (Shane 1992). Of course, the problem was that the APsaA could have shut down LAPSI, as Fleming was mandated to do, but which she did not implement. As is clear from the Boston situation, she was against splits but she was also clearly in favour of resolving disputes.

Shershow summarised the outcomes:

After numerous meetings between the Ad Hoc Committee, CUI, LAPSI leadership, and the leading Kleinians, LAPSI pulled back from the abyss of splits and disaccreditation. The procedure of automatically certifying senior faculty as training analysts was replaced by the present system of case presentation and evaluation. In addition, LAPSI revised its educational programmes to give candidates greater input on institute committees. By 1980, at the next site visit by The American, the educational atmosphere was much improved and everyone felt greatly relieved. (Shershow 1993, p. 22)

The CUI and the Ad Hoc Committee were aided by the fact that some of the major polarisers had withdrawn from the fray. Some withdrew because they were wounded by the 'élite 16' affair, and the Kleinians were now well disposed towards an amicable solution (McLaughlin interview 1994b). After 1976, cliques within LAPSI became inevitable but they were contained. The Kleinians did not see much chance of advancement in LAPSI and most looked elsewhere to establish themselves (Mason in Mandel 1996a, p. 24). There was a change among the Kleinians – Bernard Brandchaft developed an interest in Kohut's ideas and became the leader of the self psychologists on the West Coast, and others dropped out of the furore. Only a very small group of Kleinians remained. The Kleinians experienced a decline in the number of their candidates for an understandable reason – candidates were concerned that a Kleinian analysis would not make progress easy within

LAPSI or the APsaA (Mason interview 1990). The Kleinian faculty was commensurably reduced to 'a few die-hard ones' after the rest fled (Mason interview 1992), to what Leavitt described as 'a Custer's last stand group' (Leavitt interview 1992). The troubles were resolved partly because so many Kleinians became interested in Kohut (Ourieff interview 1992) – although in that political climate perhaps any passing ship would have done. Grotstein said he had been 'so traumatised by the "time of the troubles", in which I endured severe strain with friends and colleagues, that I withdrew from teaching at the institute for many years' (Grotstein pers. comm. 1992). Grotstein believed,

> The Kleinians became the outcasts and the self psychologists filled the vacuum. The guilt by the Freudian institute for the Kleinians became the legacy for the self psychologists who benefited from the guilt. This is one of the reasons they became so popular. (Grotstein interview 1992)

When Brandchaft turned to self psychology in 1976, he brought a number of very influential followers with him.[60] Moreover, Ourieff observed, around that time Grotstein, who had been very popular at UCLA, suddenly 'fell out of favour with UCLA residents'. Interest in self psychology picked up. 'Then almost like a bubble the Kleinian movement burst and almost overnight the antagonism disappeared' (Ourieff interview 1992). With the Kleinians having all but disappeared, victory in the institute belonged in effect to the educational conceptions of the liberal-minded Freudians such as Ourieff although, as individuals they lost influence in both LAPSI and the APsaA.

During the 1980s Brandchaft and the other self psychologists taught at LAPSI and, according to Mandel, differences in the seminars were equitably discussed. Their differences of opinion and approach were 'more tolerable than the differences that the Kleinian movement created' (Mandel interview 1981). A far more liberal and tolerant administration in LAPSI than there had been before existed in LAPSI in the context that the Freud–Klein dispute made it easier for heterodoxy to be accommodated. Moreover, Klein was always far more anathema than Kohut to American analysts, and the Kohutians were less strident. With diminishing Kleinian and mainstream influences, things changed so that, as Mandel maintained, 'in political terms: what we came upon in 1976 was a large left and a large right and a very small centre and what we have today is a small left and a small right and a very large centre' (Mandel interview 1981).

LAPSI continued its policies of tolerating and teaching eclectically. The extension programmes was revived but many of the members became involved in other more specialised institutes, especially the Kleinian oriented Psychoanalytic Center of California (PCC) and the Institute for Contemporary Psychoanalysis (ICP). LAPSI had lost its pre-eminent position. Quite understandably, Mandel blamed LAPSI's 'lethargic performance' on 'the prolonged exhaustion that resulted from the Kleinian struggles of the 1960s and 70s' (Mandel 1991, p. 26).

Current conditions allow individual psychoanalytic organisations within the US to be directly affiliated with the IPA. But this appeared not to be the case in the 1970s when everybody thought that the APsaA was the only American psychoanalytic organisation allowed direct affiliation with the IPA. Mandel wondered whether the 'horrible events' in LAPSI could have been avoided if the Kleinians could have formed their own institute in Los Angeles at the time (Mandel 1991, p. 27).[61]

Appeal to the IPA

In March 1975, eleven Los Angeles analysts petitioned the IPA for changes in its constitution and bylaws. They alleged discrimination on the grounds of theoretical orientation – that as well as incompetent analysts, those who were not 'Traditional American Analysts' (those with Kleinian, Fairbairnians or object relations orientations) would not be allowed to teach, supervise or undertake future training analyses. The signatories included Alexander, Bion, Bail, Brandchaft, Grotstein, Isaacs and Mason (Bail 1991b, pp. 135–7A). The petition was discussed at the business meeting of the IPA in July 1975 in London and the resolution was lost by one vote. Since it was a hand vote, it was virtually impossible to count accurately (Mason interview 1992).

An investigating committee was set up chaired by the Secretary of the IPA, Daniel Widlöcher (Paris) with Hanna Segal (London) and Samuel Ritvo (New Haven) as members. The committee reported in July 1977 that discrimination against the Kleinians had occurred but it did not identify the APsaA as doing the discrimination. The committee described it primarily as a local dispute with reactions and counter-reactions that needed to be viewed in the context of the many battles that had taken place since before the founding of LAPSI. The committee referred to 'confusions' and 'misunderstandings' that had eventuated in the period following the 1973 site visit report which was interpreted in disparate ways. Remarks made at subsequent local meetings intensified the controversy and amplified suspicion. The committee was sympathetic to complaints from the Kleinians, such as Bail being asked to suspend his seminar and candidates being advised not to take on

Kleinian analysis or supervision so as not to jeopardise their chances of membership of the APsaA. It concluded that the APsaA 'did not recommend any discrimination in terms of theoretical orientation, but did request a combined revision of the responsibilities of each person in the institute and the setting up of a basic training with a strictly Freudian orientation'. It added that the necessarily general and vague character of the 1973 recommendations gave rise to varying interpretations at the local level.

The committee noted three types of reaction to the introduction of Kleinian approaches to an institute that focused on 'Traditional American Psychoanalysis': first, that it was regrettable; second that it was progressive; and third that the very coexistence of diverse theoretical orientations interfered with proper training. The committee asserted that it was clear that the actions and opinions of each individual were influenced by these three currents:

> One can say that this confusion did give substance to the claim that there was an attempt to discriminate against some theoretical orientations, particularly the Kleinian. So the fact that two 'Kleinian' analysts were told to withdraw their courses lends itself to that interpretation. If it is true, as seems likely, that the candidates were wrongly advised that their application for membership of the American may be jeopardised if they had Kleinian analysis or supervision, we can see there another instance of such a misunderstanding. (Bail 1991b, Appendix)

The committee concluded that it was 'regrettable that the various interpretations have had as a consequence actions which could only be seen as discriminatory and could not help but exacerbate the situation and gave rise to counteractions which were also regrettable'.

The report side-stepped pinning the blame on the APsaA and formulated four proposals: that theoretical differences were part of the IPA; that such differences should be permitted as 'a source of enrichment and not of disorganization'; that while not developing in a synchronised manner around the world, 'it represents a task common to all'; and that if groups involved with training recognised their identity instead of their differences, 'a coherent eclectic training policy is realizable' (Bail 1991b, Appendix).

In a letter to the committee in August 1977, Bail and Mason took issue with the report: 'The Report does not undertake to deal with the voluminous record of complaints and instances of discrimination which were thoroughly and painstakingly documented' (in an earlier version of Bail 1991b). Expressing their disquiet, they argued – with not a little hyperbole – that 'the report appears to offer comfort and justification to those who initiated the program of oppression and discrimination'. They took the committee to task for its 'apparent desire to avoid dealing with the problem' and believed the committee was putting the victims of discrimination on the same level as the perpetrators (Bail 1991b, Appendix).

Bail felt betrayed because Hanna Segal submitted no dissenting report (Bail interview 1981). Hanna Segal informed me that she accepted the IPA investigating committee's report because the report established 'the basic principle that any discrimination against Kleinian analysts was not acceptable to the IPA'. Establishing that principle was important to her rather than revenge or castigation of 'culprits'. She did not consider this a great betrayal (Segal pers. comm. 1993).

Grotstein considered that Segal – not one to shrink from a fight – rightly decided that 'she could help us more through ultimate pacification'. Grotstein thought that the opposition to the Kleinians 'wanted peace rather than make it more incendiary'. He thought that quite appropriately they wanted a 'détente' because 'everybody was embarrassed about it' (Grotstein interview 1992). By this stage, there were important changes and divisions among the Los Angeles Kleinians. Brandchaft had left the Kleinian camp and regretted having been a signatory to the 1975 petition to the IPA. The committee may have also been aware that various measures were being instituted in Los Angeles anyway, and did not want to exacerbate the situation.

Mandel thought that the IPA Committee, like the APsaA, was appalled at the violence of the dispute in Los Angeles and also by Bail's threat of the lawsuit. Mandel felt that the politics in the IPA strongly favoured an evasion of criticism of the APsaA because the APsaA was so powerful in the IPA. Since some of the shadow of the accusations about the Los Angeles situation fell on the shoulders of the APsaA, the appeal had little hope. (Mandel interview 1992).

The investigating committee's conclusion that there was discrimination but that it was due to local factors 'could have been stronger'. In Mason's opinion,

> They could have laid the blame at the feet of The American instead of locally because it clearly wasn't just local. It wasn't a great success; it wasn't a failure either. It did draw the world's attention to the problem and many societies and presidents wrote in saying how unbelievable it was that a reputable school of analysis was being discriminated against. (Mason interview 1992)

More a political document than an objective investigation the report exonerated many of the actors (including the APsaA). However, it highlighted the principle that discrimination against Kleinians was not allowable and the importance of clarification of the APsaA's position on this issue was implied. However, the view that discriminatory situations arose from confusions and misunderstandings, reactions and counter-reactions omitted the significant role of the APsaA. The 1973 site visit report was not at all vague and open to interpretation, as the Investigating Committee claimed. The consequences of that visit were quite clear: training analysts were to be re-evaluated. Early training years needed to be centred on mainstream American psychoanalysis and Kleinian courses and instructors were to be removed. Because of Bail's threatened lawsuit and international reaction, the APsaA leadership denied saying that they wanted to get rid of the Kleinians and blamed the situation exclusively on local factors. While local factors undoubtedly played a part, it is simplistic to reduce these to 'confusions' and 'misunderstandings'. In exculpating the APsaA the committee's reading of the situation owed far more to politics than to an objective reading of the situation. However, the APsaA was sent a powerful political message that differences were an intrinsic part of psychoanalytic developments, that an eclectic curriculum was quite possible given requisite attitudes, and that, as a matter of principle, Kleinians were not to be discriminated against in the future.

IV

Other Institutes

In the 1980s, a few Kleinian-oriented analysts were instrumental in forming the Psychoanalytic Department at the California Graduate Institute because they felt that their future in LAPSI or the Southern California Institute was dim. This group resulted in the formation of a new Los Angeles Kleinian-oriented institute that became directly affiliated to the IPA, the Psychoanalytic Center of California (PCC) (Mason interview 1993). Together with two other institutes in the US, the PCC was affiliated to the IPA at its Rome Congress in 1989 (Moritz 1990).

Another of the institutes affiliated with the IPA was also in Los Angeles: the Los Angeles Institute and Society for Psychoanalytic Studies which was founded in 1968 and has about seventy members and thirty candidates, mostly clinical psychologists (Jeffrey 1996, p. 27).

One of the largest institutes affiliated to the APsaA, the Southern California Society and Institute is the other major APsaA-affiliated psychoanalytic institute in Los Angeles. Its heterodox beginnings in 1950 provided the climate for the flexibility and openness that still characterise it. It now also has a reputation for good training. Major dissension at SCPI erupted in the 1980s in what some called 'the training analysts' war'. Some saw the cause involving the older generation not relinquishing their reins to allow the next generation to exercise power, while others viewed the problems as arising from theoretical disagreements between traditionalists and self psychologists (Jeffrey 1996, p. 27).

This war resulted in a number of analysts leaving SCPI to form, together with a smaller number from LAPSI, the Institute of Contemporary Psychoanalysis (ICP) in December 1990 with forty-four members. It was built on the premise that no external body would exert educational control and that it would remain unaffiliated (Jeffrey 1996, pp. 27–8; J. Hadda 1991, p. 26). Its founders 'have stressed their continuing commitment to their local institutes and to the American' (Hadda 1991, p. 26). However, both commitments are honoured far more in the breach. While members may not have resigned their membership of LAPSI or SCPI, the bulk of their energy is devoted to the new institute. Founders included prominent members of both institutes. It is to remain unaffiliated with either the APsaA or the IPA. According to one of the founders, Morton Shane, who has had a distinguished career in both LAPSI and the APsaA, this would avoid 'imposing artificial restraints including the hierarchy of training analysts and purification' (Shane interview 1992). Not only has the ICP no affiliation with outside organisations but it is organised in as open a way as possible without the structures involved with certification and the appointment of training analysts (Shane interview 1992). The ICP instituted LAPSI's original proposal in the 1967 Reorganisation (but later given up in battles with the APsaA) that training analyst status should be virtually automatic after five years graduation. According to Shane, 'My involvement in forming ICP was partly to reinstitute that innovation' (Shane pers. comm. 1992). Self psychology is an important influence in the ICP. Robert Stolorow, a self psychologist who has many differences with the Chicago self psychologists (Stolorow et al. 1987), is probably the major leader in ICP while Brandchaft, Morton Shane and Estelle Shane are very active. In 1999 the ICP had 100 members from Los Angeles and 100 candidates.

The Aftermath

On the recommendation of the Ad Hoc Committee's final report, the APsaA's Committee on Institutes appointed an Advisory Committee to

LAPSI in January 1977 to further the development of a more organised approach to evaluating applicants and the establishment of more meaningful criteria for graduation. This committee worked so effectively with LAPSI to address the concerns of the Fleming Report that in May 1978, at LAPSI's request the status of the committee was changed from an 'Advisory Committee' to a 'Consultative Committee' (American Psychoanalytic Association 1980, pp. 8–9).

The 1980 APsaA site visitors to LAPSI were as pleased as the 1964 and 1973 were disturbed. The problems described by the 1973 site visitors seemed no longer to apply although the stability of the 'very significant changes' in the training programme needed evaluation over an extended period (ibid., pp. 22–3).[62] The site visitors were satisfied that the core programme in the early years of training was now classical Freudian and that different theoretical models were introduced only in later years. Courses on various aspects of 'ego psychology' were being taught. The Freud–Klein controversy had been replaced by broader and more complex theoretical issues surrounding such thinkers as Kohut, Kernberg, Fairbairn, Winnicott and Bion. As opposed to the 1973 situation, the site visitors found, 'The candidates are practicing psychoanalysis' (ibid., pp. 14, 16, 22).[63] The 1987 site visit was also complimentary about LAPSI's achievements. They praised 'a faculty of many able analysts who seem dedicated and concerned despite theoretical differences', a curriculum that covered the essentials in a psychoanalytic curriculum', 'a rich tradition of analytic excellence and intellectual ferment', and excellent facilities and 'a highly competent administrative staff which functions smoothly' (American Psychoanalytic Association 1987, p. 4). However, there was concern among both candidates and faculty about a 'lost generation' of analysts who were missing from LAPSI affairs. This lost generation was younger than the few very senior analysts who rotated around the official positions. The site visitors were 'puzzled' that while the leadership was aware of the problem, they seemed incapable of doing anything about it. The site visitors recommended offering encouragement and opportunities for faculty to get involved in LAPSI beyond their teaching. The site visitors concurred with the leadership that 'faculty attitudes' were the most problematic concerns (ibid., pp. 6–10, 33).[64] Given the recent history, such problems reflect the 'delicate balance' established by Mandel and his colleagues in order to manage some of the latent conflicts both within LAPSI and between LAPSI and the APsaA, particularly around certification issues.[65]

In a situation of relative calm and openness, the founding of the ICP jolted LAPSI (Leavitt interview 1992). It still constitutes a different threat to the integrity of LAPSI from previous rivalries. The attrition of many members' time and energy to the ICP threatens to deprive LAPSI of an active and vital membership. According to Lee Shershow, one-third of the LAPSI faculty has joined ICP – one of the attractions has been that everybody in ICP can be a training analyst (Shershow interview 1992). Scarce resources are then spread around a number of institutes, providing a major threat to the original institutes that need a certain number of people to carry out basic administrative and teaching functions.

The APsaA 1994 site visitors were impressed with the quality of LAPSI's candidates who 'compare very favorably to those in institutes across the country' (American Psychoanalytic Association 1994, p. 11). They were also struck by LAPSI's 'unique intellectual openness with its extensive Ego Psychology set of courses and its course presentations of Klein and self psychology' (ibid., pp. 6–7). While there was concern that not enough mainstream, classical psychoanalysis was being taught, the site visitors reported on the inclusion of a Kleinian course in the core curriculum which they said, 'functions quite well' in extending candidates' grasp of psychoanalysis.[66] However, they also mentioned 'the troublesome discovery of irresponsible conduct of administrative duties' in 1992, which plunged LAPSI into debt (ibid., p. 3).

Especially from the late 1980s, there was a move away from LAPSI and the Southern California Institute in terms of passion and energy to the more 'specialist' and autonomous institutes, particularly the PCC and the ICP. With the cord broken between the APsaA and the IPA and the direct affiliation of institutes a general loosening has occurred. The ICP went further in standing alone without any affiliation. Having lost much of its power and prestige the APsaA is no longer especially attractive given the number of alternative psychoanalytic organisations. With diminishing patient numbers in the APsaA-affiliated institutes and the general decline in prestige and interest in psychoanalysis as a therapy, especially for medically trained psychoanalysts, the idea of affiliation is decreasingly attractive.

The 1994 site visitors regarded one effect of the impact of the ICP on LAPSI as having been 'to invigorate efforts at LAPSI toward an identity as analysts with excellent traditional standards of treatment' (American Psychoanalytic Association 1994, p. 16). In a 'niche market' the ICP may be propelling LAPSI to differentiate itself from what the ICP stands for by offering a more 'conservative' approach. LAPSI's extramural consultant, Susan Cohen, noted LAPSI's distinctive 'psychoanalytic niche' as reflected in curriculum design, an emphasis on classical theory, and openness to other viewpoints. 'It is important that LAPSI "own" and publicly communicate this identity. Simultaneously, the members of the organisation need to strive toward greater acceptance of diversity of opinion' (Cohen 1994, p. 5).

Given LAPSI's 'somewhat turbulent history' (a split, a near split, and the threat of a *de facto* split involving the ICP), the site visitors complimented LAPSI on its efforts to coexist with other institutes and 'not yield to the emotional pull of devotees of one or another restrictive school of thought'. Pleased that LAPSI's identity was becoming clearer through the maintenance of high quality classical training, the site visitors maintained that the ICP had not as had been feared drained the applicant pool.[67] The site visitors gathered that the ICP came about through a combination of different reasoned viewpoints together with 'highly emotion-laden dynamics that are complex, personal and problematic'.[68]

Although the major problems ended in the 1970s, LAPSI continued to suffer their consequences. Even much later, the form of battles with their tinges of nastiness is the legacy of LAPSI's history (see Cohen 1994, pp. 3–4). Poor morale beset LAPSI in recent years. The 1987 site visitors referred to 'sense of apathy' while the 1994 visitors reported a 'morale' problem. An external consultant to LAPSI, Susan Cohen, reported a 'lack of widespread enthusiasm ... My impression is that there could be more energy, excitement, and involvement in the organization. However, LAPSI is functioning relatively well, and the problem is certainly not of "critical" proportions' (American Psychoanalytic Association 1987, p. 4; 1994, pp. 12–13; Cohen 1994, p. 2). Although LAPSI had financial troubles, the major problem was that the Kohutians and Kleinians were the enthusiastic psychoanalysts. They put their energy into other institutes, leaving those in the middle who are 'somehow not filled with enthusiasm'. Apart from the ICP which had many social workers as candidates, other institutes attracted small numbers (Mason interview 1992). Moreover, the lack of 'faculty development', the 'lost generation' and the centring of power in a few hands all referred to by the 1987 site visitors meant that many members felt alienated from LAPSI. By 1994, younger members were being brought on to the faculty and committees and with time the senior generation was exerting decreasing informal influence (Cohen 1994, p. 7; American Psychoanalytic Association 1994, p. 3).

With a 1994 membership of 120, problems remained about the small number of candidates and worsened given the more attractive training schedules of other institutes. This was very much the case with the ICP where the training time and the ability to become involved in analytic training is far shorter than at LAPSI. A director of education at LAPSI, Richard Fox, studied the careers of the fifteen most recent graduates and found it took an average of 10.2 years to graduate, six years being the shortest and fifteen years being the longest. This was in line, Fox asserted, with the APsaA's Committee on Psychoanalytic Education's finding that candidates from institutes that had a time-frame for training spent two years less than where there was no such time-frame – seven versus nine years (Fox 1991, p. 23). Moreover, there is an exacerbating problem: according to Fox, 'The single, most important reason for delayed graduations is the delay in developing suitable analytic cases to meet graduation requirements' (Fox 1991, p. 24).

In 1993, each LAPSI training analyst averaged just over one candidate in psychoanalysis.[69] While training analyst status confers more prestige – and consequently, perhaps, more referrals and self-referrals for therapeutic psychoanalysis – the economic advantages of training analyst status have declined with the shrinking psychoanalytic market, especially in the APsaA institutes. None the less, LAPSI maintained an attractive building in West Los Angeles, housing an auditorium, a well appointed library and archive. The society concentrates on the psychoanalytic clinic, research, community outreach and continuing education, the institute continues its focus on training. Currently LAPSI has around 150 members and 50 candidates from diverse backgrounds.

The cumulative effects of generations of inadequacy and trouble in LAPSI's educational system have resulted in a lack of intellectual leadership within LAPSI, and the enthusiasm being located outside LAPSI. As John Gedo put it, 'If the leadership of an institute recurrently turns to civil war, that can only mean that professionally there is nothing better these people are able to do. Now that their extremists of right and left have split off, LAPSI is moribund' (Gedo pers. comm. 1997). Without any current major figures with a primary tie to LAPSI, LAPSI's intellectual position within American psychoanalysis is not significant. Robert Stoller's tragic, early death in 1991 deprived LAPSI and American psychoanalysis of a very creative, independent and prolific writer and researcher into the nature of psychoanalytic inquiry and into the nature of sexuality. The Shanes and Brandchaft are now mainly involved with ICP, while Mason and Grotstein are primarily attached to PCC. Although he lives in Los Angeles, Rangell is not involved with LAPSI. On the scientific level, LAPSI can boast no figure of national or international standing.

In 1995 LAPSI joined with three other IPA affiliated psychoanalytic institutes in Los Angeles to form the new Federation of Independent Psychoanalytic Societies (FIPAS), that aims at furthering professional development, continuing education and communication among psychoanalysts in Southern California. There is emphasis on cooperating on common goals in the face of the enemies of psychoanalysis, eschewing narcissistic preoccupations with new terminology and innovative schools which have only led to increased fragmentation (Mandel 1996b).

LAPSI was important in the beginnings of democratisation in the APsaA. Not only have there since been changes and upheavals in institutes such as New York and Chicago but major changes have been occurring in the APsaA itself. LAPSI and BPSI where, as we have seen, the society controls the institute are exceptions in the APsaA in which the institute is a separate entity in all other cases. As Mandel put it, a few institutes 'are afraid ordinary members will interfere in the way the institute would function'. At LAPSI the institute's only role is to train psychoanalysts; it is not concerned with professional progress. The structure puts a restraint of training analyst core and entry to institute and training analyst status must be approved by the Board of Directors which is elected by the membership of the whole society. LAPSI's 1998 web site emphasised 'an openness to new ideas, as much as our grounding in classical Freudian thought, that is LAPSI's distinctive tradition. Our educational philosophy is based on the belief that we each come to think and function as psychoanalysts in our own unique way.'

V

Why did it Happen?

Many of LAPSI's problems can be seen as stemming from generic problems of psychoanalytic institutes and the field. Power struggles are inevitable in internally focused institutions which are akin to private clubs with no public reference. There is little clear articulation of a wide variety of interpretations of the institute's mission, what constitutes the field of psychoanalysis, and so on. There is no clear way of resolving these issues, certainly not at a local or even national level. Virtually no holds are barred in psychoanalytic battles over the right to train and qualify analysts. As with most disputes in psychoanalytic institutes the issue of access to training analyst status loomed large. As Rosengarten put it:

> All battles have always hinged around one thing: who is the Training Analyst, how do you get to be the Training Analyst and how do you get on the faculty and how do you get recognised? This is true in every institute in America. (Rosengarten interview 1992)

Training analyst status confers not only greater status and prestige but also more analytic patients and money. The APsaA and the mainstream Freudians wanted to maintain control, restrict and even re-evaluate the training analysts so that they could remove the Kleinians who were not seen to be 'Traditional American Analysts' and therefore subversive to the established order. The Kleinians had many interested analytic trainees with few training analysts to take on these candidates. Mason observed that the issues surrounding training analyst status were important here 'because your candidates almost invariably follow your orientation, so if you keep the number of Kleinian training analysts down, you keep the number of Kleinian candidates down' (Mason interview 1990).

However, every institute is unhappy in its own particular way. The APsaA rightly sensed that LAPSI was 'out of line', that the Reorganisation had brought a new approach to analytic training which was a precursor to many much later changes in APsaA-affiliated institutes. In addition, quite heterodox ideas were not only being proposed in the scientific meetings of the society but were an important part of the curriculum. Still more importantly, candidates could have Kleinian analysts and training analysts and supervisors. Given the arrangements about virtually automatic assumption of training analyst status after five years, together with the candidates selecting their own analysts and supervisors, the orthodoxy of the APsaA mainstream was under threat in the second largest city in the country.

All these elements played their part both within LAPSI and in the APsaA's involvement with LAPSI. The APsaA had the right to become involved in terms of its constitution and bylaws, and those of LAPSI as an affiliated institute. However, the question was one of *realpolitik*. LAPSI's leadership may have succumbed too easily to APsaA directives. More 'brinkmanship' and a more unified approach by LAPSI may have been possible. Throughout, the APsaA greatly exacerbated LAPSI's problems. After the demise of the 'élite 16' and the formation of the CUI, Fleming's Ad Hoc Committee contributed greatly to the amelioration. The Ad Hoc Committee did not play the role assigned to it by the

APsaA's Board on Professional Standards to close LAPSI down but instead played an educative role that brought analysts together.

Of course, as the pre-eminent role of institutes is to train candidates, training issues are central and scientific fragmentation often starts with training. As Rangell put it:

> A candidate is indoctrinated from the first year to his tenth year. The Kleinian group in LA were all analyzed by Kleinian analysts in LA. A child is imprinted with a brand of psychoanalysis. I think that analysts share the same behavior as the rest of the culture. I think that the desire to avoid responsibility resides in the hearts of analysts as much as it does in their patients. I think there's an unconscious collusion in that respect. Analysts have merged into the successful stratum of society and are striving to live in the same way as our patients live. Patients who can afford to come to us – at least when we are older and more 'successful' – are generally better off than we are. (cited in Rodman and Wilson 1988, p. 17)

Rangell's 'Transference to Theory' explored the shifting alliances of psychoanalytic groups in Los Angeles where the intermeshing of theory and group neurotic acting out produced sequences of theoretical ascendancy. As a number of the sixteen training analysts appointed in 1967 were no longer classical Freudians, the students they analysed became object relations or Kleinian analysts who then changed when their training analysts became self psychologists. Rangell said that the paper 'explains how the transferences or the displacement of affect went from the analyst to the theory and the succession from one theory to another' (Rangell interview 1992). Ordinary psychoanalytic transferences in the context of training influence loyalty and disloyalty to one's training analyst, to analytic siblings, to analytic leaders, to the institute itself and to the APsaA.

The Klein group had no power in the APsaA and was quite unacceptable in the American context whereas the mainstream Freudians exercised considerable power. When the aggressiveness of all sides was set in the context of the seemingly irresolvable political animosities of the previous twenty-five years within LAPSI, a *Waiting for Godot* scenario arose where salvation came to be seen as needing to come from outside. This happened with the introduction of Kleinians thought to LAPSI. As Mandel asserted:

> The sense of aggressiveness was clear not only in the political and social manoeuvring but in the enthusiasm of the analysing and writing papers and discussing. It became clear to many people that they had found a

new cause, a new sense of aliveness that otherwise might have fallen, that to have been a lifelong Freudian at that moment was getting no place because the whole series of ideas was bereft of a certain vitality by that time, and I think Kohut has done the same thing. (Mandel interview 1992)

The critical function of Kohut was important in the APsaA at large. By the end of the 1960s, there were moves towards increasing questioning of orthodoxy, towards criticising the predominance of Hartmannian ego psychology in the APsaA. Did the reverberations of the 1960s student movement have some influence in Los Angeles? As we have seen, the reverberations filtered through to the psychoanalytic movement in Boston a little later and involved some questioning of established authority. While such a hypothesis makes some sense, I came across no evidence for it. I was struck that in all my research about the Los Angeles psychoanalytic situation in the 1960s and early 1970s, the Vietnam War and the student movement (or even the Watts riots) were never mentioned, and that the civil rights movement was rarely mentioned. That Daniel Ellsberg's psychiatrist, Lewis Fielding, whose office was broken into in the 'Pentagon papers' saga, was a member of LAPSI seemed to have little impact. So concentrated was the internal focus on the seemingly overwhelming LAPSI problems that there was no room for the entry of the outside world. Even Rangell's thesis about the compromise of integrity did not arise from the surrounding social events of Watergate (although he wrote a book about it (Rangell 1980)) but originated with what had been happening in LAPSI. Further, both the Kleinian development and the Reorganisation had begun in earnest before the student movement and the Vietnam War became high on the American agenda. This is similar to a bigger split, the New York–Columbia split, that was being fomented during World War II, there was virtually no discussion about the context of the War at the time or in later symposia about it (although there were activities aiding the war effort by members of the Association for Psychoanalytic Medicine (Daniels 1971–72, 11 (1), p. 14; 11 (2), p. 29). This is also reminiscent of the New York Institute's pre-war animosity about the arrival of more European analysts just who posed a threat to their power (Bernard 1990).

Leavitt believed that LAPSI's later predicaments could be traced back to the 1967 Reorganisation. While the Reorganisation was beneficial, it allowed troubles to surface further. Moreover, unlike some other institutes, LAPSI has not had highly respected, charismatic leaders since

Rangell and Greenson. 'It is easy to be openly critical of someone because they don't carry that kind of weight' (Leavitt interview 1992). Most LAPSI members were very dedicated and hard-working. According to Rosengarten,

> As individuals, they were fine. You put them in a group and the group psychology takes over. You get a form of madness hits them. The conscience of the group is different from the conscience of individuals. If they can get a bit of support, they can get belligerent. (Rosengarten interview 1992)

Rosengarten maintained that economics contributed to the schism: when everything goes well economically, there is not too much dissension. However, during a recession where practice is not so good they begin finding fault and want an answer (Rosengarten interview 1992). The development of the Kleinian influence during the 1960s occurred during some economic hard times for analysts. It is not invariable: the 1950 split occurred at a time that was not a depression. However, there can be no doubt that economic hard times concentrate the psychoanalytic mind.

By the 1960s biological psychiatry and a plethora of new psychotherapies were challenging the hegemony of psychoanalysis within psychiatry. In the 1970s a more pluralist, questioning atmosphere was on the agenda in APsaA institutes. The development and appeal of the Kohutian movement became increasingly symptomatic of this process. Local history and structure set the stage for Los Angeles becoming an early locus for this climate. The manner in which that structure excluded so many from access to power was the setting which potentiated divergent and dissident views.

Cultural issues about Los Angeles help to frame some of the context within which the events in LAPSI took place in the rear-view mirror (Banham 1973, p. 24). Freedom and mobility are important in Los Angeles; as architecture historian Reyner Banham points out, freedom of movement is 'prime symbolic attribute of the Angel city' (Banham 1973, p. 36).

I often heard the complaint of Los Angeles analysts about East Coast analysts that they do not consider Los Angeles to be part of the US (for example, Rosengarten interview 1992; Mandel interview 1992). Los Angeles is almost as far away from the APsaA's East Coast headquarters as possible. Only the San Diego Psychoanalytic Institute is further. According to Mandel, 'Los Angeles being furthest away was also in a position where the most different thinking could take hold. Los Angeles has the least identification with New York as the fount of power and knowledge and New York looks upon Los Angeles as the most peculiar of all of its societies' (Mandel interview 1981). Both Los Angeles institutes have been perceived by the APsaA as 'anti the American'. There has always been far more heterodoxy in Los Angeles than other places. The 'conservatives' in Los Angeles would often be considered liberal in other institutes. The physical and psychic atmosphere of Los Angeles has bred a far more relaxed though no less passionate approaches to work. Southern Californian perceptions of East Coast attitudes scarcely encourage interest in remaining within APsaA-affiliated institutes where nothing seems to be offered, and rules and regulations offer many disadvantages.

Earthquakes, floods, fires and riots aside, the Los Angeles lifestyle, the professional contacts with celebrities and other very affluent people, and bigger fees, have been the envy of many on the East Coast (Rosengarten interview 1992). The climate affords far more outdoor activities, and the analysts there are not subject to the strictures of Eastern winters that encourage reading, writing and similar indoor activities. The ubiquity of cheap labour has meant that professionals employ maids and gardeners to service their families, spacious houses and grounds. Psychoanalysts mainly live and work in Beverly Hills and points west – about 200 psychotherapists operate in 'Couch Canyon' located on Bedford Drive. Their professional and social contacts are almost exclusively with other affluent, white Westsiders and, like so many Angelenos, they are from someplace else, and are ambivalent about Southern California.

In addition to conceptual, structural and socio-political factors, many personality factors are central and cannot be ignored. Actors such as Greenson, Rangell, Brandchaft, Ourieff and Mandel each had unique and significant roles in the drama. The history shows both the frailties of some of the all too human actors and the strengths, resilience, integrity and dynamism of others. Throughout all the dealings, there were struggles for power over important and trivial issues, good and bad theories, integrity and impropriety. Aggression and hubris was often countered with mixtures of decency, astuteness, persistence, naivety, and thoughtful and ethical action. The excitement of and the resistance to new ideas were determined far more often by the politics than by their intrinsic worth. The passion, rawness and liveliness, the excitements and sadnesses, of LAPSI all reflect the City of the Angels itself. Like Los Angeles, the history of LAPSI is far from typical, yet this seeming uniqueness may be an illusion. The rear-view mirror might reveal some of what may be in store for the non-unitary psychoanalytic institutions further east. As Mandel put it:

> I think of all the institutes in the United States we're probably more open now than anybody else only because we've already gone through our time of troubles. The others are yet to go through it in some form or another. It may not be Kleinian, it may be Kohutian for many of them, but they've got to go through some crisis and upheaval, a change in administration, a change in philosophy of leadership. (Mandel interview 1992)

The 'Rashomon' phenomenon – those seemingly incompatible stories so prominent in my discussions with Los Angeles analysts – became aspects of a greater whole, an undeniably complex web of events, persons, structures, theories and history which come together as a process in the real world. After years of research, I found that it became easier to understand the inevitably different and varying perspectives when they were situated within the ongoing and developing totality. In most cases, I became convinced that many of the seemingly incompatible views were just different aspects of the same whole. The city of Los Angeles itself is ill-defined in appearance, has a number of ecologies, no easily recognisable centre and appears to lack the more comfortable kind of unity that 'normal' cities have. Reyner Banham's view of Los Angeles applies also to LAPSI: a diversity of ecologies, mobility, excitement and openness with comparatively little regard given to traditional approaches. The history of LAPSI is not just a psychoanalytic narrative; it is very much an LA story.

CONCLUSION: THE TROUBLE WITH PSYCHOANALYTIC INSTITUTES

Conflicts, problems and even scandals have damaged these psychoanalytic institutes. However, as we have seen, many of the conflicts ultimately found some form of resolution. The NY Institute has become far more open, democratic and pluralist. In Boston the BPSI managed constructive relationships with its breakaway institute and both have prospered. The Chicago Institute became much more democratic and open. In Los Angeles LAPSI and the APsaA came to live with theoretical differences which for a time, locked them in seemingly irreconcilable conflict The APsaA has itself become considerably liberalised and open to questioning received assumptions. In the face of urgent pressures both from the outside world and from within the institutes, many analysts persisted and ultimately achieved considerable reforms. However, in my view, these changes were achieved despite intrinsic problems that remain at the heart of psychoanalysis and its institutions. The detailed histories of the institutes differ in many ways: the region, personalities, institutional structure, local flavour, and other factors make for the considerable variety that I have explored in each instance. In this concluding chapter, I want to explore some fundamental themes around which I believe all these histories revolve. I consider that many of the phenomena that I have detailed in these institutional narratives (such as clubbishness, internal focus, anointment and fratricidal behaviour in psychoanalytic cultures) can be best understood in terms of some of the ideas I will now develop.

We have seen that issues concerning the right to train are crucial determinants in psychoanalytic controversies. An excellent heuristic device for understanding trouble in psychoanalytic institutes could be: 'Search for the training analyst problem!' But why training? In many other disciplines, it is easier to find more public and objective data to settle issues. However, psychoanalysis is different, partly because of the kinds of deep philosophical and religious questions raised by the psychoanalytic search and metaphor. Answers to questions about the nature of the self, the mind, emotions, relationships, and human nature are not quantifiable, or easily classified and standardised. They are often experiential, subjective, uniquely individual, interpersonal and philosophical. The nature of this complex field is suffused with uncertainty and ambiguity.

As we have seen, psychoanalysis is far more than a field of academic exploration; it is a movement and therapeutic endeavour. These aspects feed back to the intellectual discipline. Psychoanalysts make claims to therapeutic knowledge and their institutions qualify practitioners. But what is the basis of these qualifications? Given the nature of the discipline and the level of knowledge within it, I suggest that the claim to knowledge implied by qualification is far greater than the real level of knowledge. Instead of facing this central issue, analysts often substantiate the knowledge implied by qualification in terms of anointment. Writ large in the history of the New York Psychoanalytic Institute, anointment is present in all the others as significant factors in their development. I believe that despite the reforms that have taken place, the underlying problems have not changed.

A major aspect of the problem, as I observed in the Introduction, is that a basically humanistic discipline has conceived and touted itself as a positivist science while organising itself institutionally as a religion. This fundamental misunderstanding has had serious conceptual and institutional ramifications that have impaired the development of the field. Analysts often approach psychoanalysis with an inappropriate paradigm, 'as if' it were a science on the model of the natural sciences, or a religion. But as a number of psychoanalytic theorists have argued – among them, Christopher Bollas and Joyce McDougall – psychoanalysis is not a science, and its findings are not scientific in any recognised sense of the word. We might speculate that the part played by analysts in fostering their discipline's present-day decline may well reflect a systemic misconception of their own discipline, and the resultant, widespread creation of what Bollas and Sundelson termed a 'false expertise' (see Introduction; Bollas and Sundelson 1995, p. 136). It becomes problematic when analysts approach psychoanalysis with an inappropriate paradigm, 'as if' it were a science or religion.

I

Psychoanalytic training is unusual in that it does not usually take place in universities – as is the case with psychology and psychiatry – but in its own institutions which are supposed to serve not only training but research, professional and economic functions. Because Freud was not enamoured of the university, psychoanalysis was for the most part domiciled in autonomous, free-standing institutes and societies. Psychoanalysts kept away from involvement with universities or other public institutions, preferring to lord over psychoanalysis themselves. In this respect psychoanalysis bears a structural resemblance to a political movement or a religion, a parallel Freud encouraged.

Since Freud identified psychoanalysis with his own beliefs, those who disagreed with him, from Jung to Ferenczi, were often forced to leave the fold. Beginning with Freud, psychoanalysts insisted on calling their field 'our science'; they kept themselves isolated with strict boundaries as to whom they would allow in. As Freud pointed out in *The Interpretation of Dreams*, he had always divided people into his hated enemies and his brothers. He wrote that his 'emotional life has always insisted that I should have an intimate friend and a hated enemy' (Freud 1900, p. 483). This foreshadowed later attitudes in psychoanalysis. One of Freud's analysands, Roy Grinker Sr, pointed out:

> Faith in the 'great man' is the impetus for the beginning of a 'movement'. It is also responsible for exclusion of nonbelievers, as Freud's Vienna group forced him to do to some members of the Swiss psychoanalytic society, over Bleuler's protests, and which caused that great psychiatrist to withdraw his support of the psychoanalytic movement. It is responsible for Freud's writing to Ferenczi not to be troubled with other theories for, 'We possess the truth'. It is questionable whether any other young science even as an early movement was as cultist, as self-contained, and as mystically oriented. (Grinker 1965, p. 114)

Freud made adherence to his principles especially important, with the consequence that psychoanalytic education became over the years akin to a process of anointment. In ways reminiscent of the injunction cited in Exodus – 'Then shalt thou take the anointing oil, and pour it upon his [Aaron's] head' (Exodus 29: 7) – this subjective process, like a modern-day rite of consecration, has allowed those analysts deemed good enough to be the 'real' psychoanalysts to anoint in turn their own candidates and trainees. It is no surprise, then, that the persistence of this self-perpetuating method for the transmission of knowledge has played a significant role in most institutes since the very dawn of psychoanalysis.

Anointment was well in place, in fact, already in 1911, when Freud appointed a secret organisation, the so-called 'Committee', to safeguard psychoanalysis against its enemies. In 1913 Freud gave its members rings. He was seized by Ernest Jones's idea of a 'secret council composed of the best and most trustworthy among our men to take care of the further development of psychoanalysis and defend the cause against personalities and accidents when I am no more' (Jones 1953–57, Vol. 2, p. 153).[1] Freud's role in the setting up of orthodoxy within the psychoanalytic movement is quite ambivalent; he both resisted rigid adherence to ideas, constantly revising his own ideas throughout his life, while he also fostered orthodoxy in his attitudes to the rise of the movement and his treatment of those who disagreed with him.

From early on, psychoanalysts conceived of their field as an inner sanctum of sorts, to which admission has always been highly selective and where the 'science' of psychoanalysis could be fashioned and preserved in near-splendid isolation. Even in the heyday of psychoanalysis in the US, in the 1950s and 1960s, when half the people chairing university departments of psychiatry were analysts, the institutes of which they were members called the tune. The authoritarian, sometimes cultish, approach that closed off the outside world did not reduce the appeal to the many psychiatrists and patients who were banging loudly on analytic doors. Unwilling at the time to have their analytic gold diluted with the psychotherapeutic copper of psychologists, social workers and the like, psychoanalysts remained content to develop what they called 'our science' behind the walls of their own institutes.

But psychoanalysis is not an established science. It is not a unified body of information from which derives a unified practice that can be readily and empirically tested. In point of fact, and by almost any account, psychoanalysis is an experiential, subjective, personal and interpersonal exploration for which there are no validating objective criteria. If anything, psychoanalysis is about unknowing, about the unconscious which is not known, about the uniqueness of individual discovery. In a way, this contradicts the very possibility of qualification from a psychoanalytic institute, since 'qualification' implies transmission and mastery of a body of knowledge consensually acknowledged as such. In the absence of such a consensus, then, psychoanalytic education has come to depend on the justification of its truth claims through authoritarian approaches reminiscent, as I've suggested, of some organised religions rather than through the kind of open, critical inquiry which, at least in theory, can take place in universities. Rigid, authoritarian, and closed to new ideas, the mainstream of psychoanalysis – itself often fiercely divided along the lines of the narcissism of minor differences – has generally regarded the world as heathens who disagree with 'our science' because they cannot or will not understand.

Historically, then, it has been a hallmark of much psychoanalytic education for mystification to transform illegitimate power into irrational authority. Secrecy and lack of detailed public evidence have long fostered opportunistic practices of anointment.

II

The history of the psychoanalytic profession is rife with schisms, as Joyce McDougall aptly illustrates in an article entitled 'Beyond Psychoanalytic Sects', from her book, *The Many Faces of Eros* (McDougall 1995). Moreover, in line with my contentions concerning the doctrinaire training practices of institutes, McDougall has said:

> I think our greatest perversion is to believe we hold the key to the truth ... Any analytic school who thinks this way has turned its doctrine into a religion ... when we make our particular psychoanalytic theories into the tenets of a faith, then we're restricting our whole capacity for thinking and developing ... But what is our insecurity? Perhaps it's partly determined by the transmission of a psychoanalytic education which is largely based on transference: the attachment to one's analyst, as well as to supervisors and teachers, is permeated with strong transference affects. This may result in the idealisation of thinkers and theories as well as leading to the opposite – the wish to denigrate them. But I guess this is part and parcel of the history of psychoanalysis and something we must strive to understand. (McDougall, in Molino 1997, p. 91)

The profession's penchant for idealisation originates, unequivocally, with its very founding, as psychoanalysis has always been synonymous with the figure of Freud – who identified himself with psychoanalysis and psychoanalysis with him (Freud 1914, p. 7). In a feedback system of sorts, whereby Freud's own sense of being destined for greatness was enhanced by the quasi-mystical power that is inevitably conferred on those of courageous vision and unflagging determination, he exercised a commanding appeal over those around him. And while the scope of his explorations and insights have yielded one of the most far-reaching and systematic understandings of the human condition ever propounded, it is Freud's role as a codifier that has driven psychoanalytic training and psychoanalysis as a movement. His own patriarchal and charismatic example – in a field where no single paradigm of achieved knowledge has ever generated assent – has served as a model throughout much of the history of psychoanalytic training. Suffice it to think of the power and influence exerted by the figure of Jacques Lacan in recent decades, or of the contentiousness that still animates, after nearly fifty years, relations between Kleinians and Freudians in Britain. As McDougall suggests, however, the model of idealisation/denigration is a pervasive and, indeed, a structural one. It is by no means limited to the loftier and more influential stages of psychoanalytic politics world-wide, but finds a correlate in the day-to-day life and management of even the smallest and most inconspicuous of institutes or training centres. Training issues are everywhere and routinely resolved by fiat. Passionate power struggles, on the model of those between Freud and Jung, or between Anna Freud and Melanie Klein, or between Lacan and the IPA, have been ubiquitous, and can elicit a zeal that rivals forms of the most uncompromising fundamentalisms. In political and scientific disputes, analysts often default to the skills and language they were taught in their training for treating patients – and pathologise their opponents.

Today, where training is concerned, most psychoanalytic disputes involve mythological 'standards' based more on passed down versions of the truth than on the examination of evidence. Psychoanalytic concepts are not univocally defined, and in consequence of this are the source of often raucous debate. Even members of the same schools are often deeply divided about their approaches. What is the nature of the body of knowledge to be transmitted in the training? Given that there are no agreed-upon definitions and approaches, no agreed-upon 'unit of measurement' in psychoanalysis or agreed way of measuring it, its status as a developed science is questionable. As Christopher Bollas and David Sundelson suggest in their book, *The New Informants:* 'It will take a long, long time indeed for psychoanalysis to come to anything like a convincing definition of itself.' At the same time, however, there is, as Bollas and Sundelson assert, the creation of a 'false expertise' among psychoanalysts.

> By assembling colleagues who agree with them and with whom perhaps, they can write books on a clinical topic, psychoanalysts can create the illusion that true science has taken place. But technical papers, conference appearances, and statistics about patients presumably suffering from a given syndrome are the trappings of expertise, not the substance. (Bollas and Sundelson 1995, pp. 136–7)

III

Many socio-economic and historical explanations have been offered for this behaviour. But I want to propose another that I believe goes to the heart of the matter. My suggestion applies to psychoanalytic institutions but has general ramifications on the institutionalisation of ideas in professions that demand qualifications from an unreal knowledge-base. (This does not mean that it is not warranted but that the knowledge-base is not as warranted as it is claimed to be.)

A qualification certifies that someone has been trained to be fit or competent to perform a given task. In the psychoanalytic profession, a graduate of a psychoanalytic training programmeme is certified as competent to perform therapeutic psychoanalyses. This implies that the graduate is competent in the application of a learned body of knowledge. The concept of qualification depends on the idea of a legitimate body of knowledge that is transmitted through training conferring expertise and competence. In psychoanalysis this is the work of Freud and his followers in theory and technique, and much of what is taught is regarded as established truth. Freud did not see psychoanalysis as a profession, that is, as an organised group of qualified practitioners. Today, however, psychoanalysis is a profession, often with quite rigid, formalised requirements. Graduation requires a good deal of tenacity, sacrifice, commitment and perspicacity. Psychoanalysis as a profession involves clients who trust in some esoteric knowledge of the practitioners. There is a presumption of knowledge and skill in qualification, and clients consult on the basis of the presumed competence conferred by professional training. Institutes of psychoanalysis act as gatekeepers for the profession and attempt to ensure 'quality control'.

A clue to the problems in psychoanalysis comes from asking a further question – why do disputes surround training issues? This reason stems from a *contradiction between the nature of the psychoanalytic field and that of the training of practitioners*. This is the case whether psychoanalysis is a science or an art. If it is an art, then what is it doing in a seminary or trade school with an ersatz body of knowledge to be stamped as having been inculcated in a qualification? If it is a science, then where are the public evidential support, protocols, units of measurement and criteria that are demanded by science? And where is the agreed-upon body of knowledge to be applied for training in the practice? In any case, if it is a science, it is a young one with at best few established truths. If it is an art, then the differences between individual analysts and patients cannot be standardised, quantified or readily measured.

Since there is scant agreement about anything in detail, how can analytic 'standards' be other than a myth? Outside of anointment, what can be the meaning of a 'qualification' in psychoanalysis? Where qualification is not based on an agreed body of knowledge, disintegration products abound, leaving the way open for the rule of power plays, anointment, cultism, personality, psychopathology and politics. Power plus mystification gives rise to irrational authority in the form of anointment. There is a *folie à deux* here. Mystification serves the immediate emotional needs of everyone in the system for an answer, for a putative certainty that can establish a qualification as real. It thus inspires some collusion on the part of candidates. In this situation qualification derives from an authority in training dependent on a claim to knowledge that is unwarranted and is thus suffused with mystification. I believe that the way that this atmosphere of anointment has persisted in psychoanalysis has been through the medium of the training analysis and the appointment of those who have the right to train. These issues have always lain at the heart of all analytic disputes.

Before the 1920s psychoanalytic training as such did not exist. Analytic societies were scientific clubs with no accredited schools or curricula. The approach to teaching was student-centred, flexible and individualised. In fact analytic training originally took one to one and a half years (Balint 1948, p. 167). Freud's recommendation for a personal analysis included analyses that might have lasted only a few weeks. Freud himself, in fact, did not insist on personal analysis as a prerequisite to practice.

The mandate in the 1920s for a personal analysis as part of analytic training should thus be seen within a context in which the analysis was potentially short and relatively non-intrusive. It was didactic, more in the nature of a sampling of analysis. None the less, there were strong and principled arguments against mandating even this exercise on the basis that personal analysis should be left up to the candidate and should not be connected with an Institute (see Bernfeld 1962). Along these lines, we might consider how a personal analysis was not a requirement in the New York Psychoanalytic Society until 1937 when, in reaction to an influx of unanalysed training analysts from Europe, it only then became a fixture of training.

Generally speaking, it is important to remember that the relatively small numbers of faculty and students involved with early training meant that everyone knew or knew of one another. Institutes were separate and part of a loose federation of analytic institutes which got together mainly for scientific congresses. These informal structures starkly contrast with the later enormous institutionalisation of psychoanalysis. They gave way to very formal psychoanalytic organisations with complex rules and regulations for training in accredited institutes. For example, with its regulations, site visits and accreditation of individual institutes the International Psychoanalytic Association is the only international professional organisation that sets standards for individual countries and members. The American Psychoanalytic Association is a component member of the IPA but has special status in organising its own training standards. It is a national certifying organisation that, at least in theory, controls and regulates its individual component institutes and their training through its myriad formal committees and regulations.

With Hitler came the changes to the ecology of psychoanalysis throughout the world and the epicentre moved to the US. With this move and the rise in the fortunes of the psychoanalytic movement came increasing institutionalisation. As psychoanalytic historian Sanford Gifford observed:

> Our so-called American character also brought to the analytic movement our inveterate passion for Robert's Rules of Order, for writing and rewriting constitutions and by-laws, and for generating committees within committees within committees. Although we have created a vast psychoanalytic empire, we may well ask whether there is some relation between our enormous consumption of energy in organizational activities and our rather exiguous theoretical output. Our foremost American analysts have produced a substantial literature of commentary on classic texts, elegant exegeses and magnificent clinical applications, but for theoretical innovations we have always been dependent on the work of émigré analysts. (Erikson, Rapaport, Mahler, Kohut, Kernberg) (Gifford 1995, p. 113)

While anointment clearly played an important role in the early days, there was little else about training that was set in stone at that time. Freud was alive and served as referent, model and mentor; just as importantly, he was also known to change and revise his ideas constantly, in a search for truths that precluded premature ossifications of theory. Moreover, analyses were short, and there was, as yet, no fixed body of knowledge that was passed down as absolute truth. For all of its flaws, the early life of psychoanalytic societies was not as mystified and oppressive to its students and members. It encouraged – indeed, presupposed – a shared commitment to the energetic development of the field, a field of inquiry which went well beyond the therapy.

It is, of course, important not to romanticise the early days. From its inception, the position of the training analyst in Vienna was always a very powerful one. The programme of study was informal and individualised with training analysis common to all candidates. It was left almost entirely to the judgement of the training analyst to determine whether a candidate had successfully completed the analysis and could be accepted into the Institute; an unfavourable report could seal the fate of a candidate. Margaret Mahler suffered this fate, for example, as her anointment at the hands of Helene Deutsch was delayed for a number of years (Stepansky 1988, pp. 64–5).

We can say, then, that historical factors have always conditioned the particular way in which analytic training would be carried out. Short, preparatory, mandatory analyses originally intended to give the trainee a taste of analysis lengthened into a situation where years and years of analysis assumed primary significance. As analyses became longer, 'deeper', and more formalised, a procedure which was to provide would-be analysts with a taste of the process and clarify personal blind spots became a supertherapy aimed at altering the character structure of the candidate. As psychoanalysis became more institutionalised and professionalised, it was then presumed that problems in the classical approaches would be remedied by introducing into the analytic relationship a greater degree of formality and distance.

IV

In what Lewin and Ross (who surveyed American psychoanalytic education in 1960) referred to as a classic example of 'syncretism' (that is, a situation involving 'the use of conflicting and irreconcilable assumptions'), psychoanalytic educators have become increasingly aware that there is a problem in training both for a profession and a science (Wallerstein 1972, p. 595). According to Lewin and Ross, psychoanalytic education and psychoanalytic procedure exist in two worlds:

> The two models 'psychoanalytic patient' and 'student' complement, alternate with, and oppose each other. A psychoanalytic treatment is *sui generis*. The education introduces a parameter for the therapeutic procedure, and the analytic procedure an even larger one for the education. The institutes are unavoidably trying to exert two effects on the student: to 'educate' him and to 'cure' or 'change' him. Hence the student as a phenomenon fits into two conceptual frameworks: he is the pedagogic unit or object of teaching and the therapeutic unit or object of psychoanalytic procedure. (Lewin and Ross 1960, pp. 46–7)

To complicate matters further, however, both these frameworks normally involve the single looming figure of the training analyst. In a 1927 paper to the Innsbruck Congress of the IPA, Helene Deutsch herself noted how the training analyst is often in a conflicting role because of the double task implied in the role. Already in 1927 then, the two functions – that of therapist and that of teacher – were often seen to contradict each other (Deutsch 1983, p. 60).

Moreover, as Siegfried Bernfeld argued, 'the training analyst is not, as Freudian method demands, a mere transference figure. He is instead a part of the patient's reality, a powerful and even decisive factor in it.' Bernfeld maintained that 'by policy and circumstance, the institutionalized training analysis thus bears the features of a non-Freudian technique' (Bernfeld 1962, p. 476). While there have been reforms in the rules surrounding the training analysis, Anna Freud could say in 1983 that the problem of training had not changed much in the previous forty-five years. She said that her 'colleagues who first advocated the introduction of the training analysis at the Marienbad Congress – if they had known of all the dangers, of the positive and negative transferences, and splits, and hates, etc. – would probably never have advocated it! They would have said, "Let them be as they are!"' (Freud 1983, p. 259). As Bernfeld observed,

> We possess no way by which we can rationally rank the membership into Good, Very Good and The Best analysts. Yet strangely, that is exactly what has taken place. The membership of all our groups is divided into members who are good enough for the simple paying patient and into really good ones who take care of our future membership. (Bernfeld 1962, p. 48)

However, the selection of the 'really good ones', today as in the past, does not necessarily relate to their analytic abilities. As the histories detailed in this book show, I have concluded that ideological splits and conflicts in psychoanalytic institutes were and often remain rooted in the issues of appointment and anointment that surround the figure of the training analyst.

V

The informal training of the early generation of analysts can be linked with the enormous creativity that characterised that small original group.[2] The later formalised, bureaucratic training correlates with far less creativity, a result that is scarcely an endorsement of the 'improvements' in training and reflects, in my estimation, the inimical effects of the growth of psychoanalysis as a movement on its development as a discipline. In fact, while many analysts continue to define psychoanalysis as a science, it still relies for its evidence on the 'laboratory' of the analytic hour – an essentially private exercise which bases its supposedly scientific claims almost exclusively on analysts' later accounts of cases in the form of broad, overarching and basically indisputable assertions. This is clearly not commensurate with a scientific approach. 'Scientific' articles in psychoanalysis generally look to confirm, and not to refute, clinical hypotheses (see Peterfreund 1983; 1985, pp. 127–43; Colby and Stoller 1988). Because analysts often know little about each other's work, ideas stem more from speculation than from a warehouse of communal experience and knowledge.

The problem here has partly related to a fundamental misunderstanding that confuses psychoanalysis with the model of the natural sciences. The symptomatology-aetiology-pathology conceptual model, with all its sequelae, is widespread in contemporary psychoanalysis. Indeed, many psychoanalytic institutes instantiate this model in their training, assuming a body of knowledge which is, however – because of its very nature – far from codified, and is resistant to rigid systematisation.

In psychoanalysis there is little, if anything, that is agreed upon by all schools or even within schools. Notions such as 'transference', 'countertransference', 'the unconscious' or 'analytic process' mean quite different things to different schools, and a confusion of tongues invariably develops.[3] It is as though everybody agreed that it is seven hundred miles from New York to Chicago but nobody agreed what a mile was. Or, one can imagine a scenario in which people from a number of different countries have agreed that a piece of merchandise is worth two bits of money, but nobody has specified which currency or denominations of money were used. If we say that everybody agrees that the unconscious and transference are important concepts and then we think, for example, of the Freudian, Kohutian, Kleinian, Lacanian or Jungian currencies and of the enormous differences within these currencies, we have an identical situation.

When people have their own definitions of concepts and use them in their own way, communication results in a tower of Babel. Because the same words have quite different meanings, it is both misleading and misguided to say that there is agreement about basic concepts just because analysts mouth the same words, or to maintain that there is an established common ground. If people can't agree about basic definitions, how can they communicate about anything more complex? Moreover, it is no secret that analysts apply concepts differently and idiosyncratically. Even where analysts approach their patients stereotypically, of necessity every psychoanalysis is unique. This datum may well bespeak the nature of psychoanalysis as art – it is, however, certainly no measure of a 'scientific' technique. I am not saying that agreement about basic definitions is a sufficient condition for the development of the field, but it is a necessary one. Once analysts manage to speak the same language or to conceptualise their differences with some clarity, then the development of appropriate new ideas becomes possible.

It is no surprise, then, that in the absence of an agreed-upon language training standards and expectations are also increasingly localised, and subject to the convictions and/or whims of the anointed. Cliques predominate and issues of power become paramount in defining whose 'standards' and what knowledge or curricula will prevail. Like a religious movement that progresses through the laying on of hands from generation to generation, psychoanalytic power is often legitimated through the processes of anointment described above. Again, this is exacerbated by the insular and pyramidal structure of analytic institutes. It is in this way, as Otto Kernberg maintained, that psychoanalytic education became transmuted over the years into a process that came to reflect uncannily both the seminary and the trade school models (Kernberg 1986). In fact, much analytic education (from the Latin *educere*, to elicit or bring forth) is if anything an exercise in 'miseducation,' since by and large the guild nowadays does not so much draw forth the unique talents of students (and inspire them, in turn, to 'educate' their patients) as systematically move them towards conformity with their own teachers and analysts. Consider, again, Joyce McDougall's thoughts on the matter:

> The experience of personal analysis and case supervision, as well as the close teacher–pupil relationship that characterises the transmission of psychoanalytic knowledge, are all marked by strong positive and negative transference affects. These, if not recognised, may readily be used in near-perverse ways. They certainly contribute to the violence that usually accompanies our theoretical and clinical divergences. The sanctification of concepts and the worship (or denigration) of their authors appear to me to be sequels to unresolved transference ties. Adherents then become 'disciples' who no longer question their theoretical models or continue with their own creative research. The unquestioning dedication of such disciples to their analytic schools of though may dissuade them from truly hearing their patients and thus prevent them from searching for further insight when their patients do not fit their theories. In certain respects, these disciples appear to have incorporated their leader's theoretical stance without any true introjection of, and identification to, the psychoanalytic goal: a constant search for the truth – one's own and that of one's analysands. (McDougall 1995, p. 234)

VI

Even though there are great divergences about the nature of psychoanalytic knowledge and theory, there is considerable agreement about who the good analysts are. How can this be so? Edgar Levenson has argued that psychoanalysts of every persuasion use the same algorithm in their praxis, framing what the patient says, putting it in some kind of order, and elucidating that order in terms of the patient–therapist relationship. Good psychoanalysts of all schools share an ability to elucidate more data by shining a broad beam that further illuminates the patient's particular world. The wisdom and experience attained through using this algorithm is transmitted to candidates in both supervision and analysis with varying results (Levenson 1983, pp. 8, 55).

To be a good psychoanalyst requires, I believe – in addition to an unequivocal ethical commitment and stance and some psychoanalytic experience and wisdom – three qualities. One is a high-level capability in cognitive processing and abstraction that Elliott Jaques has described. This involves an ability to move between the general and particular, and to process in a parallel manner both hypotheses and 'facts' that counter and challenge one's own views (Jaques 1996, p. 22). A second quality involves a particular form of personal intelligence. This refers to a kind of therapeutic intelligence, an ability to think psychologically about oneself and others, a singular capacity for empathy and understanding that results from a highly developed sense of, and respect for, self and of others (see Gardner 1993, pp. 237–76). Finally, the use or creation of a good psychoanalytic theory is important.

Clearly, analysts differ in their abilities to meet all three of these criteria. A very few can claim the first two in addition to the use and creation of major theoretical advances. While Freud might come under this category, there would be less agreement (but still some) about other contributors such as Heinz Kohut, Sandor Ferenczi, Melanie Klein, Wilfred Bion, Donald Winnicott and Jacques Lacan. My personal belief is that someone is generally acknowledged as a competent analyst when the first two qualities, of cognitive and personal intelligence, are sufficiently developed or noteworthy as to override any theoretical shortcomings. Paradoxically, I also believe that the advances registered or claimed by psychoanalysis as a 'science' rest on a kind of illusion generated by the individual clinical achievements of analysts who, because of cognitive and personal gifts, are able to practice artfully, that is, to work successfully with patients.

Psychoanalytic therapy is inherently difficult. The task is an exploration of the mind that involves, on the part of both patient and analyst, considerable ability for abstraction, questioning of deeply-held assumptions, the free play of ideas in an open-ended partnership over a number of years. Since there is no major corpus of established knowledge that the analyst can realistically apply as a template, the inherent creative capabilities of patient and analyst must be enjoined. Analysts need the ability, as Heinz Kohut once told me, to recognise their vantage points, to play with ideas, to be relativistic (Kirsner 1982, pp. 488–9). If these capabilities do not reach the level of the requirements of the analytic task, dogmatic templates often fill the vacuum. An important aspect of the fall of psychoanalysis lies in the institutionalisation of psychoanalytic ideas, involving the application of ideas by a larger number of less capable analysts who used codified stereotypes to fill the hole left by the uncertainties of creative exploration in a new and difficult field. (see Jaques 1996; Jaques and Cason 1994).[4]

Significant consequences can be derived from this issue about the nature and reality of analytic competence. The issue of 'false expertise' has come to the fore with the growing number of accounts of failed analyses. Accounts such as Jeffrey Masson's *Final Analysis* and Adam Gopnik's account in the *New Yorker* in 1998 point to major problems in this domain (Masson 1990; Gopnik 1998). Where antidepressants (in particular, the newer antidepressants such as Prozac) have worked where years, sometimes decades, of psychoanalysis have not, the efficacy of psychoanalysis as such is increasingly called into question (see, for example, O'Sullivan 1998). Qualifications that rely on a taken-for-granted, accessible body of knowledge as, for example, in medicine, where a general practitioner can have cultures done and can access material about which antibiotic is good for which disease. The problem is that psychoanalysis is not of that kind. As I have argued, there is no established body of knowledge, no textbook that can explain how to treat this particular patient and much relies on the individual analyst's artful capability since there is no publicly accessible data-base. Since many analysts may not possess such qualities of artfulness and capability and psychoanalysis is such a private matter between analyst and patient, many analyses are bound to fail. I believe that part of the problem of the decline of psychoanalysis comes from the fact of so many failed analyses. The problem of qualification that is unwarranted yet expected means that when the news of some of the more egregious failures becomes public knowledge, it damages the profession as a whole. The lack of success in many psychoanalytic cases is well-known among psychoanalysts. Sometimes this is attributed to the patient's pathology, sometimes to the inadequacy of the analyst. The ubiquitous divisions of psychoanalysts into 'good' and 'bad' analysts, between the 'real' analysts and the others with different training, or professional backgrounds, training or theoretical orientations acknowledges (even though at a remove) just how far this issue of competence is acknowledged as a vital one by analysts themselves. If, through no fault of their own. a proportion of analysts do not fulfil the criteria for sufficient competence, then their practice will fail to meet expectations of a 'qualified', 'expert' analyst. In my view, the impact of this structural issue has contributed to the decline of psychoanalysis as a treatment and as a methodology, especially since the development of widespread alternative treatments. It is not likely that such problems can be properly addressed by institutes in their present forms if only because freestanding institutes often maintain the closed inner focus of coteries that have run such institutes from their inception. Although this is a sensitive issue, it should not be ignored.

VII

For psychoanalysis to take a different route in the future, matters of training will have to be addressed, and alternatives proposed to the prevailing situation. Many have attempted to counter the harmful effects of the training analysis to no avail.

One radical possibility could be in the direction of abolishing the mandatory training analysis altogether and testing the results rather than the process of achieving them. The 'proof of the pudding' would lie in the assessment alone, in how well trainees conducted analyses with their patients; public protocols would prevail instead of anointment of certain people with avowedly esoteric gifts. This would leave the analysis free to produce the best results uncontaminated by political and institutional issues.

However, a less contentious approach could keep most of the advantages of the radical option while jettisoning its major disadvantage, that it does not explicitly allow for the experience of analysis that is so central to analytic work being an indispensable part of the training process. This proposal is that the candidate's analysis should be entirely separated from the institute and the rest of the training programme so as to cut the link of patronage between the analysis and the patient and between the training analyst and the institute. to preclude anointment and privileged succession. In my view, the position of training analyst should be dropped, which would remove a structural flaw that maintains power based on hierarchy, patronage and anointment. Candidates should be in analysis with an analyst of their choosing (who had completed their training five or more years earlier), who has no part of the assessment process. Therefore the analysis would be separated from the institute with no reports on the progress of the analysis. On the model of universities, assessment at institutes could then be carried out solely in terms of what the candidate produced in terms of seminar papers and presentations, and clinically through supervised cases.

It is probably too late for psychoanalytic institutions to become part of universities – that train has long left the station. But a university culture within institutes may be possible if such an approach can come to reflect the will of their members. This would steer institutes away from the transmission of a relatively unquestioned body of knowledge towards more open and sceptical questioning and research. It is generally acknowledged, along these lines, that the chance for institutes to be allied with universities has generally passed. With few exceptions (Columbia, for one), by not becoming part of academia or at least adopting the university's culture of critical inquiry, an historical opportunity was irretrievably lost. But, in line with Kernberg's suggestions, the idea of developing within psychoanalytic institutes a culture and environment reflective of the university and art academy milieu is a desirable, if not a vital, one.

I believe that the basic fault in psychoanalytic institutes is qualification on the basis of an unwarranted claim to knowledge. One way out is a radical deinstitutionalisation of psychoanalysis more in line with the kind of philosophical Delphic exploration into human nature that constitutes psychoanalysis. Psychoanalysis is a searching method of self-exploration and the most potent means we have for psychological change and understanding. Concomitantly, more open scepticism about psychoanalytic ideas needs to be accepted where the chips will fall where they may. Open-minded interdisciplinary research (philosophy, neuroscience, literature, sociology, genetics, biology, and so on) needs to be carried out, including much more definition of psychoanalysis so that analysts are using the same words to mean the same things. Even the concept of what is psychoanalytic needs to be broadened and at the same time more clearly specified. Psychoanalysis should not be seen as its trappings (number of times a week on the couch by an accredited member of the International Psychoanalytic Association). Psychoanalysis is a field of inquiry and is owned by no one any more than physics is. The truth is that spiralling costs and changes in insurance are pricing classical psychoanalysis out of the market and the intellectual attraction of psychoanalysis is no longer pivotal in so many areas. Perhaps this condition where psychoanalytic approaches have once more achieved underdog status will allow the space for the imperialism that has so characterised the psychoanalytic movement to be replaced.

The problems of anointment necessitate a major deinstitutionalisation of training. Arguably, it is questionable whether qualification as an analyst even needs to be bestowed by an institute. The issue of who authorises an analyst has occupied quite a number of analytic thinkers and practitioners, not the least of whom was Lacan; and the idea that analysts ultimately authorise themselves (and cannot really be authorised by anyone else) seems quite appropriate to the nature of the field, at least in its present state. That present state is nicely summed up in the founding statement of a recently established training centre in London, itself the product of yet another in an endless line of schisms:

> Psychoanalysis can be understood as a cultural term of reference underpinning a multiplicity of disciplines. Indeed it has become one of the dominant forms of psychological intelligibility, insisting as a topic of centrality in the theorising of the ways we are together within contemporary culture. Nevertheless, it is merely a chapter in the history of folk psychology. In other words, since the beginning of time people in suffering have turned to others for means of solace, always already informed by some form of symbolic exchange. Psychoanalysis purposefully defies clear definition as it is resistant to any attempt at unification, so that any reconfiguration will occur through the acknowledgement that it is not one, is not up for ownership or enclosure, nor can it appropriately be appropriated. (Oakley and Oakley 1998)

There needs to be in psychoanalysis a reorientation towards research which must be interdisciplinary and critical, much more in line with the model first envisioned by Freud. Freud's exemplary statement – 'Nothing ought to keep us from directing our observations to our own selves or from applying our thought to criticism of itself' (Freud 1927b, p. 34) – would act as a searing critique of many of the world's psychoanalytic institutes, whose rites of qualification have stood in the way of the field's development. To my mind, the basic problems of training are both structural and conceptual, and require urgent attention if psychoanalysis is to regain its lost credibility as both a cultural discourse and a therapy. In the meantime, however, the gap between the small base of verifiable knowledge and the high level of 'pretend' knowledge fostered by training and practice has grown to such a worrisome extent that the very question of what constitutes 'knowledge' is less and less posed nowadays.

Insofar as psychoanalysis is a method of sceptical inquiry into the unknown aspects of the human mind, it is more akin to philosophy and literature than to medicine or the natural sciences. The very nature of its inquiry, moreover, would seem to presuppose that psychoanalysis be organised in ways that might depart from the hierarchical and rigid institutional superstructures that govern, say, medical associations. The major problems with codifying and institutionalising psychoanalysis, and sealing it off from both internal and external criticism, came about through decades of valuing the movement over the method. One of Freud's major mistakes, in this sense, derived from his preoccupation that a growing focus on the therapy of psychoanalysis would destroy its chances for recognition as a science. This concern led to his consolidation of the movement, an attitude which in the long run compromised the very development and ambitions of his 'science' while fostering an imperialism antithetical to psychoanalysis' supposed method of unfettered inquiry. Moreover, the unfree and, allow me to say, narcissistic institutions bred by the psychoanalytic movement have proven regressive in more than one way. In fact, some of the negative reactions to psychoanalysis on the part of today's 'Freud-bashers' have much to do with the exaggerated and quasi-omnipotent claims that have been made on behalf of the therapeutic efficacy of psychoanalysis. Psychoanalysis as a panacea is fantasy, not reality. But it has long been oversold, at least in the US, as a cure-all for a remarkably broad range of human sufferings and emotional disorders. This exaltation, born of an illusory and deceptive self-celebration, has not only contributed to the tarnished reputation of psychoanalysis; it also betrays the discipline's sadly limited capacity for genuine introspection and critical self-assessment in a challenging and rapidly changing world.

Freud's ideas became a pivotal part of the twentieth-century *Zeitgeist*. Even the strongest of the Freud-bashers has to reckon with, if not to adopt outright, many psychoanalytic concepts that have transformed our view of ourselves and our relationships. Such reasons are enough to suggest that psychoanalysis is in no danger of disappearing from our cultural horizon any time soon. The risk will increase, however, the more psychoanalysis remains identified with the psychoanalytic profession as now constituted. Already the steep decline of institutionalised psychoanalysis is all but assured. Like would-be seminarians before the prospects of a priesthood that makes less and less practical and existential sense, fewer and fewer candidates are attracted to psychoanalysis, which itself attracts fewer and fewer patients. Still, people in suffering will continue to turn to others for means of solace, as our species has since the beginning of time. And no matter what drugs and other forms of treatment become standard, we will continue to need 'talking cures' to deal with the ways we are and want to be; with our dreams, fantasies, ambitions and perversions; with the ways we treat other people, and wish to be treated by others. We will continue to be plagued and impassioned by the timeless concerns of love, history, ethics and desire. To this end, and throughout their history, psychoanalysts have long espoused what Freud, Kohut, Klein, and a host of other masters have proposed as solutions to the problems of human existence. The time may now be upon psychoanalysis to revive, instead, the once-defining spirit of open, sceptical questioning of all concepts and teachings, including those most dear to the profession. It is time, perhaps, for psychoanalysis to be reminded of the wisdom of an Eastern maxim: 'We seek not to imitate the masters, rather we seek what they sought.' For as Christopher Bollas has tellingly admonished: 'Psychoanalysis just has to survive "the psychoanalytic movement". If it survives psychoanalysts and their schools, then it will grow and develop. But this remains to be seen' (Bollas, in Molino 1997, p. 50).

NOTES

Introduction

1. Managed Care is a health insurance arrangement whereby patients insure their medical needs with Health Maintenance Organisations (HMOs) which decide on what treatment is appropriate with their own accredited practitioners.
2. See Kaplan 1997, pp. 26–33, p. 28; Talan 1995; Scott 1997; Edelson 1988; Gedo 1991; Hale 1995; Holt 1992; Holzman 1985. There has been a steady annual decline of 1 per cent in psychoanalytic cases treated by members of the American Psychoanalytic Association since 1976 (Brauer 1998, p. 24). By 1976, analytic practice had already markedly declined from the 1960s.

    Edward Shorter represented many psychiatrists when he recently concluded,

    > As evidence began to accumulate on the biological genesis of psychitric illness, psychiatry began to regain the scientific footing it had lost at the beginning of the analytic craze. The brain was indeed the substrate of the mind. By the 1990s a majority of psychiatrists considered psychoanalysis scientifically bankrupt. (Shorter 1997, p. 146)

3. As Freud wrote to Jung on December 5, 1912, 'Let each of us pay more attention to his own than to his neighbor's neurosis' (Freud 1974, p. 529).
4. Nathan Hale has documented the rise and decline of psychoanalysis in the US in two invaluable volumes (Hale 1971a; 1995). Important general studies of psychoanalysis within the APsaA are Lewin and Ross 1960, and Goodman 1977. Fine 1979, offers a survey of psychoanalysis in the US and world-wide, as does Kurtzweil 1995.
5. The field has been so undermined that Kernberg recently outlined thirty methods used by institutes to destroy the creativity of psychoanalytic candidates (Kernberg 1996).
6. The curriculum consisting of lectures, seminars and case presentations, concentrates on theory including Freud's writings, clinical applications and technique. Supervised analytic work consists of three cases seen four or five times a week which demonstrate the development of the patient's transference neurosis, genetic factors and principal conflicts (American Psychoanalytic Association 1984, pp. 5–7).
7. Kernberg noted the role of emotion in why the religious model is applicable to psychoanalytic education. This was because of the 'sense

of conviction about the truth of psychoanalytic theory, particularly about the unconscious. The sense of conviction is usually traced to an emotional experience connected with the discovery of the unconscious in oneself, and the experience of psychological change following this discovery.' Kernberg added that this 'deeply transforming emotional experience' occurred in an intense relation to another person, the training analyst, who is 'idealized and experienced as a spiritual guide'. According to Kernberg, the genealogical retracing of psychoanalytic training back to their training analyst's analyst, to an original disciple and finally to Freud reflected 'an extraordinary emotional investment in the original founder and his beliefs, quite similar to religious practice' (1986, p. 810).

8. Freud thought that a medical background could even be harmful to prospective analysts and even discouraged would-be analysts from studying medicine (Jones 1953, Vol. 3, p. 293). Clarence Oberndorf recorded a meeting with Freud which exemplified Freud's views on the subject:

> After a few friendly words of initial greeting, Freud's first question to me was, 'And tell me, what do you really have against lay analysis?' in a tone of annoyance and impatience. I tried to explain to him that the laws of New York State forbade it, that the members in America thought a knowledge of the physical manifestations of organic illness necessary so that the physician might compare them with those due to psychological disturbance, that especially in America quacks and impostors, extremely ignorant of the elements of psychoanalysis, presumed to hold themselves out as analysts. Freud waved aside my replies with an abrupt 'I know all that', turned, and walked very slowly towards the house. (Oberndorf 1953, p. 182)

Freud maintained these views to the end of his life. In a letter dated July 5, 1938, written in English to someone who had written him asking if there was any truth in the rumour circulating in the US that he had given up his views on lay analysis.

> I cannot imagine how that silly rumor of my having changed my view about the problem of Lay Analysis may have originated. The fact is, I have never repudiated these views and I insist on them even more intensely than before, in the face of the obvious American tendency to turn psycho-analysis into a mere housemaid of Psychiatry, (Jones 1953, Vol. 3, pp. 300–1; see also Freud 1913, p. 210; 1915–16, p. 21; 1927a, p. 252)

9. Freud was vehemently against seeing psychoanalysis as medical. He proposed that the curriculum of his ideal institute 'must include elements from the mental sciences, from psychology, the history of civilization and sociology, as well as from anatomy, biology and the study of evolution' (Freud 1927a, p. 252).

10. More on how this book came to be written and some of the pitfalls encountered can be found in Kirsner 1999.

Chapter 1

1. Two other institutes are directly affiliated with the International Psychoanalytic Association. Comprised mainly of psychologists and social workers, the Institute for Psychoanalytic Training and Research (IPTAR) and the New York Freudian Society were directly affiliated with the Institute of Psychoanalysis (IPA) in 1989.

   The American Academy of Psychoanalysis (originally formed as a group to reform the APsaA but now a group in its own right) and the National Association for the Advancement of Psychoanalysis (NAAP, a group of non-medical analysts) are centred in New York with most of their members working in the New York area. Indeed other psychoanalytic institutes are a phenomenon of New York City where there are thousands of analytically trained practitioners. Important and well-respected institutes outside the APsaA in the New York area include the William Alanson White Institute with a Sullivanian focus, the National Psychological Association for Psychoanalysis (NPAP) founded by Theodor Reik, and the Association for the Advancement of Psychoanalysis, the Horneyan Institute and the Center for Modern Psychoanalysis run by Hymie Spotnitz. Other institutes include the Postgraduate Center for Mental Health, the New York University Post-Doctoral Program, the Adelphi University Post-Doctoral Program, the Washington Square Institute, the New Jersey Institute for Psychoanalytic Studies, the Westchester Institute for Psychoanalytic Studies and two self psychology institutes, The Training and Research Institute for Self Psychology (TRISP) and the New York Institute for Psychoanalytic Self Psychology.

2. Both other major APsaA institutes in New York – the Columbia and NYU Institutes – were also under the direction of small ruling cliques with their share of arrogant leaders, although there were important differences too.

   In the view of long-time leading NY Institute member Norman Margolis, because there was some limited input at the NY Institute,

   > the educational program available to our members was ... unique among the analytic institutes, and thus it always puzzled me why the NY Institute and NY Society was seen to be so 'undemocratic'. Certainly the NYU Institute and the Columbia Center in NY were run as monolithic bureaucracies, and only a few, even if on the faculty, had anything to say: and the non-faculty members had zero to say – nothing, even indirectly. (Margolis pers. comm. 1996)

3. For the history of the NY Society and Institute until 1945, see Oberndorf 1953; Quen and Carlson 1978; Wangh 1962; Lorand 1969; Rubins 1978; Frosch 1991; Hale 1995, Ch. 8. The tensions went well beyond Janet Malcolm's 1981 portrait of the NY Society and Institute.

Malcolm's depiction, however, inspired recognition by many analysts (American Psychoanalytic Association 1981, p. 4). Ernest Wolf reported that he knew many analysts who were 'scared to death' during their analytic training at the NY Institute (Wolf interview 1981). See also Galenson interview (1994) and, most importantly, the site visit reports of the APsaA (American Psychoanalytic Association 1976b, p. 6; 1983; 1992).

4. As well as the Columbia Center (discussed below), the other APsaA-affiliated Institute is the Psychoanalytic Association of New York (known as the 'Downstate Institute') that split off from the NY Institute in 1949 in relatively amicable circumstances, remains a mainstream Freudian Institute with no significant ideological differences from the NY Institute. It was founded by Sandor Lorand who was being edged out of teaching at the NY Institute since he was disliked by the Viennese inner group because he was a Hungarian, followed Ferenczi and, they believed, had trouble with his analysands (see Frosch 1991). It was originally located at the State University of New York, Downstate Division, in Brooklyn from 1950 until 1979 when it moved to Bellevue Hospital and the NYU Medical Center Department of Psychiatry (see Lanes and Corbin 1981). It was established because some analysts wanted to teach more than they could do at the NY Institute, combined with the wish of then Head of Department of Psychiatry and Dean of the Medical School of New York University who was interested in having more psychoanalytic influence in his department. Its chief innovation of encouraging teaching among recent graduates and younger analysts led to vitality and productivity with many papers written by these graduates. The Downstate Institute has had a particularly high number of its members become prominent within the APsaA. These include Mark Kanzer, Shelley Orgel and Harold Blum.

5. The Columbia University Center for Psychoanalytic Training and Research was formed first as a Clinic by Sandor Rado, David Levy, Abram Kardiner and George Daniels. Its members today include Otto Kernberg, Roy Schafer, Robert Michels, Arnold Rothstein and Arnold Cooper. The Columbia Center provides a repository for those seeking less orthodox approaches than the NY Institute, leaving the other two institutes with less internal opposition. Some of the more liberal NY Institute graduates have joined Columbia – a number of analysts are members of more than one APsaA Institute but devote most of their energies to one of them. In contrast to most institutes that are freestanding, the Columbia Center is an integral part of a university as it is an important division of the Columbia University Department of Psychiatry. It was the first APsaA-affiliated Institute to be established within a university and medical school (Glick 1992). Inevitably, the links with the Department of Psychiatry, the Medical Center and Columbia University profoundly influenced the Columbia Center's intellectual and institutional life. Set up on the basis of 'academic freedom', the Columbia Center was established within the university

to guarantee free inquiry and provide the opportunity for collaboration between psychoanalysts and academics from other disciplines. The founders together with the university environment promoted a special respect for academic freedom and scientific rigor as well as a focus on interdisciplinary studies and research. Structuring the institute so that it was connected with the university provided the institutional basis for what a recent Columbia Center Director, Ethel Person, called Columbia's 'iconoclastic identity for contesting psychoanalysis as Holy Writ' (Person 1990, pp. 9–10).

6. See also Karl Menninger's letter to Franz Alexander, April 13, 1938, in K. Menninger (1988, p. 264); Jacobs (n.d).; Talan (1998).
7. Also quoted by Quinn (1987, p. 329). Quinn gently observed that this statement 'seems to have been wishful thinking on the part of the committee, since in fact such non-M.D.s as Erich Fromm and Otto Rank practised with impunity after coming to the United States' (ibid.).
8. The leaders of American psychoanalysis even went so far as to lie to the International Psychoanalytic Association by claiming – falsely – that there was a New York law allowing only physicians to practice analysis (see Oberndorf 1927, pp. 202–3). A search of the statutes of the period does not reveal the existence of any such law, and there was no evidence of such a law in the US.
9. This directive expressed professional rivalry and jealousy, quite typical reactions of people in a group receiving immigrants. In their psychoanalytic study of migration, Grinberg and Grinberg found that sometimes in the receiving group, 'latent paranoia may increase, and the immigrant may be perceived in a persecutory way as an intruder who seeks to deprive the local people of their legitimate rights to work and to enjoy their possessions and property' (Grinberg and Grinberg 1984, p. 35). But in this case, the psychological fears were not irrational but somewhat justified by the course of events.
10. Bertram Lewin, an American, was an exception. However, he had some training in Europe.
11. The Americans included Lehrmann, Hogendorf, Lawrence Kubie and Sally Barnett (Arlow interview 1994).
12. These included Siegfried Bernfeld in San Francisco, the Sterbas in Detroit, Franz Alexander in Chicago, Edith Buxbaum in Seattle, David Rapaport at the Menninger Clinic and Sandor Feldman in Rochester.
13. The Berlin Institute in particular set the model for training in many places. New York analyst Abram Kardiner asserted in 1963:

> My criticism of the Berlin School and all of its ilk for what happened between 1921 and today is that they consolidated an arbitrary system into a monolithic unbreakable structure which has to remain as it is or fall totally. There is no leeway within it for any kind of development. (Kardiner 1963)

14. Gay comments that the Kris and Nunberg families 'established dynasties of analysts' (Gay 1988).

15. In case this period is seen as exclusively rosy, Diana Trilling's account of her analyses in the 1940s as well as that of her husband Lionel, paint a darker side of that time. A president of the NY Society, Bertram Lewin – a 'Giant' – referred Diana to a known morphine addict, Ruth Mack Brunswick. Brunswick, who remained a training analyst, would go to sleep during the sessions they had (Brunswick cancelled half of them), carry out personal business on the telephone (including shopping), and discuss the virtues of Lend-Lease and a second front. In Diana Trilling's opinion Lionel Trilling's analyst, Rudolph Loewenstein – another 'Giant' – harmed Lionel and their marriage. After Brunswick died, Diana consulted Marianne Kris who did not defend Brunswick or the NY Society and also felt that Loewenstein (with whom she was close) was the wrong analyst for Lionel. Psychoanalysis, Kris felt, owed the Trillings restitution and she did not accept payment from Diana for several years until Kris felt it may have interfered with the treatment (Trilling 1993).

    Diana and Lionel's son, James Trilling (1999) wrote about his parents' great commitment to psychoanalysis. Unfortunately, although both blamed their own mental disorders upon neuroses of unconscious origins, both would be seen differently today. Lionel would be viewed as having Attention Deficit Disorder (ADD) while Diana would be diagnosed as having panic disorder with agoraphobia. Neither of these ailments is optimally treated with psychoanalysis.

16. William Menninger, a psychoanalyst and psychiatrist, had headed psychiatry as a brigadier-general and presided over a major shift from diagnosis and discharge to treatment. This 'encapsulated the more general shift in the twentieth century from a purely "descriptive" psychiatry, which classified the mentally ill without helping them, to a "dynamic" psychiatry that was of positive benefit' (Starr 1982, p. 345). Chicago analyst Maxwell Gitelson described dynamic psychiatry as 'a mixture of Meyerian psychobiology, educational and social psychology, and American cultural values, to which psychoanalytic personality theory has been added' (Gitelson 1963, p. 354). Most psychiatrists around 1930 were employed at state hospitals but the '1930s and 1940s saw a shift in both professional views and professional practice, as more urban, psychoanalytically-oriented practitioners won a middle-class clientele and a wider popular and intellectual audience' (Starr 1982, p. 345).

17. William Menninger, an analyst, was a major influence on a generation of psychiatrists. As chief of psychiatry in the Office of the Surgeon-General during World War II he selected analysts as teachers for the young MDs who were drafted and trained in the burgeoning specialty of psychiatry (Charles Brenner, cited in Coser 1984, pp. 47–8).

18. This situation was described humorously by Jacob Arlow at the NY Society's fiftieth anniversary (Arlow interview 1994).

19. These included Charles Fisher was involved and then David Kairys, Edward Joseph and Stuart Asch when M. Ralph Kauffman was Head of the Department of Psychiatry at Mt Sinai.
20. These included Sandor Abend, Robert Kabcenell, Ernest Kafka, Bennett Simon, Ted Jacobs, Martin Willick and Bill Grossman. Others such as Joel Kovel and Eugene Goldberg followed later. Martin Wangh and Eleanor Galenson were influential in sending residents to the NY Institute (Kovel pers. comm. 1995; Galenson interview 1994).
21. During a time of major destructive interfactional struggles within the NY Institute, Janet Malcolm erroneously constructed the central polarity to be one between Brenner and Stone. They were, however, on the same side politically without major differences in their approaches to psychoanalysis within the classical tradition. However, despite the fact that Malcolm ignored the struggles as a fundamental issue and constructed a mistaken dichotomy, she quotes but does not take up a simplistic statement by 'Aaron Green', the analyst, that none the less refers to the real problems of NY Institute. 'Green' said:

    The real issue was that there is a clique of people at the Institute who fill all the important posts and decide who is to become a training analyst, and there is another clique of people who don't have power and who want it. That's what practically every controversy at our institute is about. (Malcolm 1981, p. 66)

22. Brenner later challenged the classical concepts of *The Ego and the Id* (Brenner 1994). He suggested discarding the structural theory of the mind and replacing it with one that he believed better fitted the clinical data.
23. Bertram Lewin – who was particularly close to Isakower as well as to Ruth Eissler, Annie Reich and Edith Jacobson – was popular with everybody. As such, he was the only American who bridged the divide for some time.
24. Manny Furer recalled from discussions with Greenacre that she kept far away from Institute politics 'because first of all she thought it was a waste of time. And secondly she told me that since she did not pay much attention to politics, her judgements in that regard to political things at the Institute were way off base' (Furer interview 1996).
25. Each year two meetings took place in one evening. A society meeting would meet and collect its members' annual dues. Then that meeting would be dissolved, and within two or three minutes the Institute officers would appear on the platform and what had become a meeting of the Institute would receive the money from the society (Arlow interview 1994). This, for example, amounted to $15,000 in 1971 (Brill Archives).
26. Dues increased from $250 in 1966 to $450 in 1976. The 1976 site visitors noted that the NY Institute 'was supported to a large extent financially by the dues of members who carried no direct educational responsibilities and to some extent conflict seems to be an inevitable

result of this kind of situation' (American Psychoanalytic Association 1976a).
27. He was also able to be humorous about himself. On one occasion Isakower was the only male on a committee that he described as the Seven Snow Whites and the Dwarf. Having spent some time in Liverpool, he liked the Beatles and followed their career (Jacobs n.d., pp. 23-4).
28. Similarly, Isakower's development of the concept of the 'Isakower phenomenon' for understanding a patient's dream through the analyst's reaction to it is totally dependent on the analyst's feelings where only some analysts apparently have the ability to apprehend (Balter et al. 1980).
29. Shades of such notions persist at the NY Institute (Calder interview 1996).
30. Arlow related this to an anthropological perspective:

> This phantasy is built into a mythology, the central figure of which is the training analyst. He is the hero who having undergone trials and tribulations has this magical power in his possession. Training analysts, as a group, in the phantasy of the candidates, constitute a council of elders. (Arlow 1970, p. 27)

31. None the less, many New York analysts did vote in APsaA elections. Since New York analysts represented about a quarter of the APsaA membership, many APsaA posts went to New Yorkers (though not the power group members).
32. The tragic story of Victor Rosen, a powerful analyst, a president of the APsaA, who married one of his patients and finally committed suicide, together with that of another New York analyst, David Rubenfine, who also married a patient, the comedienne Elaine May, are recounted by Farber and Green (1993, pp. 201-14). These scandalised the NY Institute, and both were forced to leave psychoanalysis. However, some leading members of the NY Institute tried to help both of them.
33. This was one of the findings of a survey of members by Francis Baudry included in the Report of the Meeting of Board of Trustees of February 24, 1983, in NYPS/I (1983a, p. 11).
34. In chronological order, the EC Chairmen were Heinz Hartmann, Ruth Loveland, Sara Bonnett, Otto Isakower, Phyllis Greenacre, Robert Bak, Martin Stein, Marianne Kris, Nicholas Young, Peter Richter, Irwin Solomon, John Donadeo, Joan Erle and Manny Furer.
35. These were, in chronological order, Jacob Arlow, Isidor Silbermann, Arnold Eisendorfer, Leo Stone, Burness Moore, Arnold Pfeffer, Ken Calder and George Gross.
36. In 1970-71 the Chairman of the EC initiated a change whereby the Chairman would no longer be solely responsible for appointing the Instructors' Advisory Committee, which was responsible for evaluating colleagues proposed by faculty members for faculty membership. This was turned over to the faculty who could nominate any training analyst

to a slate from which five members would be elected with two alternates (Margolis pers. comm. 1996; NYPS/I 1981, p. 5; Stone 1976, p. 5).

37. In 1945 the NY Society and Institute established the rule that appointment to training analyst status required not only five years since graduation but also the publication of two scientific papers. In the course of pointing out how this publication requirement was ignored, Sandor Lorand recalled the general method of appointing training analysts: 'Younger analysts were appointed on the basis of being known by the members of the Educational Committee and being recommended by them' (Lorand 1969, p. 594)

38. No doubt the inner group organised the structure of elections so carefully and minutely that the membership rightly felt effectively disenfranchised. However, Norman Margolis challenged the idea that the EC was a self-perpetuating hierarchy.

> The EC is *elected* by the general membership, not by the faculty alone. It is true that the slate for the EC (consisting of eight people) is chosen by a (democratically chosen) faculty committee (the Instructors' Executive Committee). But the choice offered is large. If the membership at large were as discontented as the Group II [opposition] members contended, some of those whom they saw as villains would simply not be elected and/or reelected. Their election is the only reason they had access to leadership, or, as Group II people would say, 'power'. (Margolis pers. comm. 1996)

39. For example, they did nothing with the recommendations of the Long Range Planning Committee or the Ad Hoc Committee on Community Affairs and Public Information (Leo Stone, in NYPS/I 1978b, p. 25).

40. 'It was often said that the best candidates go to the NY Institute and that was true. It has changed with time' (Calder interview 1994c). John Gedo recalled that the NY Institute may have had the best candidates in the early fifties, by 1960 the competence of candidates was about the same in most institutes (Gedo pers. comm. 1995).

41. The Board of Directors was responsible for society affairs and finances and was elected from the larger pool of society members.

42. This was a supreme example of problems that have been endemic to psychoanalytic institutes. Otto Kernberg noted a 'corruptive' practice in psychoanalytic institutes. 'It is an open secret that the appointment of training analysts is politically motivated, that the actual qualifications of the training analyst may be less important than his or her reliability with regard to local politics' (Kernberg 1986, p. 805).

43. Roose's position was supported by a letter by David Kairys (May 5, 1975).

44. Dues increased from $250 in 1966 to $450 in 1976. The 1976 site visitors noted that the NY Institute 'was supported to a large extent financially by the dues of members who carried no direct educational responsibilities and to some extent conflict seems to be an inevitable

result of this kind of situation' (American Psychoanalytic Association 1976a).
45. The Group I members (inner group) who met with the site visitors were Norman Margolis, David Milrod, Peter Richter, Irwin Solomon and Nicholas Young (American Psychoanalytic Association 1976a).
46. According to Furer:

> The institute is governed by three bodies. The EC (and its standing committees on admissions, student progress, and curriculum) is responsible for undergraduate education. The committee is composed of seventeen members some of whom are training analysts, some not. The Board of Trustees, our legal entity, is responsible for financial administration and has a fiduciary relationship to the whole. The faculty has largely an advisory function. However, with its intimate connections with the EC, its share in policy making is significant. Its relationship with the EC is typical of the interconnections that characterise the functions of the governing bodies of our institution'. The society on the other hand consists of graduates and is governed by an elected Board of Directors. The society owns the building, is in charge of the scientific programme and funds the Institute's educational programme through tuition and supervisory fees together with dues and assessments. Society members are on that account members of the Institute. Furer saw this 'complex arrangement of discrete, shared, and sometimes overlapping responsibility among the several agencies' providing for a 'separation of powers and a system of checks and balances. (Furer 1990, p. 7)

47. Furer accepted the analogy, with the proviso that he is not a Likudnik! (Furer interview 1996).
48. These younger analysts included Sander Abend, Martin Willick, Mike Porder, Albert Sax, William Grossman, Ernest Kafka and Arnold Richards. (Richards interview 1996; Furer interview 1996; Calder interview 1996).
49. The younger group included Lester Schwartz, Albert Sax, Ernest Kafka, Mike Porder, Willick and Joan Erle, and replaced the older generation which included some of the Europeans such as Robert Bak, as well as Phyllis Greenacre, Martin Stein, Irwin Solomon, John Donadeo, David Milrod and Lili Bussel (Calder interview 1992; Richards interview 1992).
50. The same response is reflected in a recent *New York Times* article on responses from the analytic community to the desperate decline of psychoanalysis: 'In a field notorious for its insularity and resistance to outside critique, the threat of extinction has inspired a new vigor, a frenzy of self-examination and the urge to reach out and connect with the world at large' (Goode 1999).
51. Arnold Rogow found that while more than half the psychiatrists he surveyed in 1966 earned $20,000–$40,000 per year, whereas over half of the analysts earned $40,000–$60,000 (Rogow 1970, p. 93).

52. Under Arnold Richards the Extension Division offers courses mainly to mental health professionals interested in psychoanalysis, and reaches out to the community providing grand rounds, speakers, case discussions for Outpatients' Departments, and lectures and services for Psychiatry and Psychology Departments and hospital chaplains. It is an important means of getting better known in the community where the prestige of psychoanalysis has been in steep decline. It is designed to provide outreach to potential candidates for psychoanalytic training at the NY Institute, to help eliminate distortions about the NY Institute and provide them with an impression of the faculty. Where there is a small number of applicants and a large membership the competition for teaching is especially great. So the Extension Division provides an opportunity for many analysts to teach and gain experience (Richards interview 1992; Cohen interview 1992).
53. Candidate numbers had dropped from fifteen in 1988–89 to six in 1990–91 which included three non-medical candidates (American Psychoanalytic Association 1992). Candidates are encouraged to find low fee cases from psychotherapy cases in practice. Training cases come from outside the Treatment Center.
54. The Columbia Center was quite differently organised from the NY Institute. Columbia has been criticised by many for the fact that it is not autonomous. As part of the psychiatry department of the university its director is chosen by a university selection committee rather than by the psychoanalytic faculty and the setting is not so much independent clinical practice but the politics of the university (see American Psychoanalytic Association 1979).
55. Freud was seized by Ernest Jones's idea of a 'secret council composed of the best and most trustworthy among our men to take care of the further development of psychoanalysis and defend the cause against personalities and accidents when I am no more' (Freud to Jones, in Jones 1953, Vol. 2, p. 153). A major problem with this approach is epitomised in a letter Karl Abraham wrote to Freud discussing the works of Ferenczi and Rank: 'I promise you, dear Professor, *in advance*, that it will be done on my part in a non-polemic and purely factual manner and only with the wish to serve you and your work, which is identical with your person' (K. Abraham, in Freud and Abraham 1963, p. 351 (emphasis added); see also Roustang 1982). The desire to serve is accompanied by a promise in advance which will prevent subsequent changes of opinion and critical questioning. What happens to psychoanalysis when the leader is the ultimate theoretical referent, the paradigm of all analysts, the settler of disputes within the society? If one is ready to submit 'in advance' to the leader's judgements, this maintains the transference and faith and provides a vehicle for transmission.
56. Arlow pointed out in relation to the division into the two groups of elevated and degraded teachers in psychoanalysis,

The displacement from father to analyst to Freud is missed. The 'enemy of analysts', really a repudiated aspect of the self, is attacked and in the name of defending Freud, the unresolved transference bond to the father-analyst is pursued with a vigor and intensity that reveal its unconscious origin. (Arlow 1970, pp. 15–16; see also Arlow 1972, pp. 563–4)

Chapter 2

1. A Boston analyst even wrote a novel including these events (Buttenwieser 1981).
2. Those young doctors who went to European psychoanalytic institutes were doing what medical graduates of the time usually did. Since residencies had not yet been established in the 1920s, it was customary for American medical graduates to spend a year studying in Europe where the specialties were more developed. American doctors could go to Vienna to study their preferred specialty, enrol in the American Medical Association of Vienna, study and receive a certificate of achievement (Lewin 1961, p. 101; Murray 1961, p. 122).
3. As set forth in its constitution, the mission of the BPSI is

   the study and advancement of psychoanalysis in its scientific, therapeutic and cultural aspects. The functions of this society and institute shall include the maintenance of adequate qualifications for the practice of psychoanalysis; the official recognition of those who have these qualifications; the conduct of a professional school or institute to supervise the education of psychoanalysts and other professional people associated with psychoanalysis, the establishment and maintenance of clinical facilities; the representation of psychoanalysis in the community; and the development of the relationship of psychoanalysis to medicine and other sciences. (BPI 1942)

4. According to Gifford,

   Ever since the late forties and fifties, Boston had an unusually high proportion of analysts who were part-time in various kinds of teaching in academic and research pursuits outside the institute and most of them had no difficulty with this double role; analysis was part of one's life and one followed three to four analytic patients but your daily work was in a hospital or medical school. At that time there was an attraction to being an analyst and head of department at the same time. There was Myerson at Boston University, Fox at the Brigham. There were strong analytic traditions at Massachusetts General, Beth Israel and McLean. At present, heads of department are not chosen among analysts. (Gifford interview 1981)

   By contrast, in New York relatively few analysts held academic appointments at hospitals such as Columbia and Mt Sinai.

5. Levin and Michaels reported that as

   a consequence of the active role of psychoanalysts in residency training programmes, the resident psychiatrist in a large medical centre generally comes into professional contact with analysts and candidates and is apt to be supervised by them. He is therefore likely to become psycho-analytically oriented to some degree even if he does not undergo training at an institute. (Levin and Michaels 1961, p. 275)

6. The relationship between psychoanalysis and therapy to the Boston medical scene was the subject of a major published symposium (G. Gifford 1978).
7. According to Rosett, compared with New York analysts, Boston analysts tended to subscribe more to the Puritan tradition and consume a little less conspicuously. In Cambridge there is even what Gifford termed 'the cult of seediness'. Analysts are influenced by the academic values that pervade the Boston area. Rosett claimed that Boston analysts are more interested in study groups and being recognised in the academic world than in New York (Rosett interview 1981). However, this is debatable. Analysts in the New York Psychoanalytic Institute have placed high value on study groups within the institute while placing less emphasis on outside involvements including academic positions. As a part of the university, Columbia has always placed great emphasis on participation in academic affairs.
8. The society's tasks are restricted to the monthly Scientific Meetings together with the Library and extension courses, As society rather than institute activities these activities have normally been accorded second-rate status.
9. Elliott Jaques described some useful ways of understanding organisations. The *assumed* organisation is the patterns of connections that are assumed to be the way the organisation operates by the members of the organisation. The *extant* organisation is the way the organisation operates shown by systematic research of the organisation. The *manifest* organisation is the structure that appears on the organisation chart or constitution. Jaques defines the *requisite* organisation as '[t]he pattern of connections which ought to exist if roles in the system are to work efficiently and operate as required by the nature of the work to be done and the nature of human nature' (Jaques 1989, Glossary).
10. Analysts who led psychiatry departments in Boston over these decades included George Gardner at Children's Medical Center and the Judge Baker Guidance Center, Alfred Stanton at McLean Hospital and Elvin Semrad at Boston State Hospital and Massachusetts Mental Health Center (Gifford 1984, p. 7).
11. This was only the beginning of the major decline in psychoanalysis, which became a major issue in the 1980s and still more critical in the 1990s.

12. The APsaA affiliated institutes in the metropolises of New York, Chicago and Los Angeles were better off in this regard. While New York had three institutes, the population served by Manhattan was immense. Chicago had only one institute and Los Angeles two, serving far bigger populations than did the BPSI.
13. The medical restriction was part of a restraint of trade that kept the numbers down. Now that psychoanalysis is less popular, medical candidates do not generally apply. Bob Gardner and John Gedo, who maintain a 'little Englander' position, hold that analysis is best off as a small specialty (Gedo pers. comm. 1994). As Gedo has argued, 'The crux of our profession's vulnerability to the unfavorable social milieu is our unverbalized insistence on two mutually exclusive goals: on one hand, on continually increasing our numbers on the other, on continuing to participate in the uninterrupted, progressive enrichment of the American upper bourgeoisie' (Gedo 1991, p. 161).
14. Mann stated his general goals as dean for the coming academic year noting four areas of responsibility: the institute, the society, the BPSI's relationship with universities and their resident training programmes and its relationship to the community at large (Mann pers. comm. 1995).
15. Mann spent about twenty-five hours a week on his duties and interviewed fifty-five candidates. He found the demands of the deanship 'constant, varied and interesting' (Mann pers. comm. 1995).
16. The other members of that committee were Bob Gardner, Helen Tartakoff, Arthur Valenstein, Edmund Payne and, from the Board of Trustees, Miles Shore and Irving Rabb (Myerson 1973a).
17. This helps to free the analysis from academic considerations and the judgement about graduation. This is now policy in all APsaA institutes.
18. Friedman considered also proposing that the training analyst system be reviewed but decided against it since few analysts would publicly challenge that system. Friedman's view was that the two-tier system should be replaced by one where any qualified analyst could conduct training analyses. This would result in a more liberal system free from the present centralised power system.
19. Such issues included the 'hyphenated' society/institute structure and access to training analyst status. Even in small institutes things can be just as bad. Discontents and splits have been endemic to psychoanalysis right from the beginning of the history of the analytic movement when numbers were very small indeed. PINE has not succeeded because of its small size any more than the BPSI has because of its large size.
20. Gardner has had an abiding interest in education, especially in one-to-one teaching settings (see Gardner 1994).
21. Gifford wrote a little later about this period:

> I thought of the proposed new institute as a tiny balloon, taking off from the flight-deck with five men in a basket. I sincerely hoped that the nucleus of the dissenting group would take off in a five-man

submarine headed in the opposite direction, leaving the rest of us to conduct business as usual, whether we wished them Good Riddance or Pax Vobiscum. (Gifford 1975b)

22. At variance with the BPSI position, Gifford supported PINE's accreditation. He wrote to Edward Weinshel, Chairman of the Board on Professional Standards, conveying his middle position shared by half a dozen other BPSI colleagues. 'I personally believe that the more quickly PINE can be approved, the sooner some kind of uneasy peace will be restored and discussions can begin on some form of future coexistence' (Gifford 1975c).

23. McLaughlin stated that he 'had no friends at PINE who had any significance to me at that time. Bob Gardner later on became a friend, mainly in consequence of having taken that position' (McLaughlin interview 1994a).

24. In Buttenweiser's novel *Free Association*, set during the split, a protagonist is told that there is a chance the analysts who walked out would form their own institute. 'The American will never allow them', she scoffed. 'This city is already overrun with institutes. They're a glut on the market. No, they'll be back, begging to be reinstated' (Buttenwieser 1981, p. 205).

25. The attempted secession in Washington took place after the BPSI–PINE split. It failed both because of hindrance from the APsaA's Board on Professional Standards together with local problems of the timing of accreditation of training analyst status by the Pittsburgh Psychoanalytic Institute which offered to sponsor the secessionists (McLaughlin interview 1994a). In fact, Stanley Goodman, Chairman of the Board on Professional Standards at the time of the Washington events, was adamant, according to Arnold Goldberg, that the APsaA would never again allow the kind of arrangement granted PINE, which meant that the APsaA did not allow the Washington secession. Goldberg said that some of the Washington analysts became like wandering Jews without a home (Goldberg pers. comm. 1994). That the Washington secessionists did not succeed and were greatly hurt provides evidence that if it had not been for the Ad Hoc Committee's recommendations, PINE would not have been accepted by the APsaA.

There have been no splits since the 1970s partly because the APsaA slowly allowed more heterodoxy such as object relations theory and self psychology and there became less reason to split on ideological grounds. Moreover, the waning eminence of psychoanalysis has meant there is less reason to fight for turf since the turf is less prized (McLaughlin interview 1994a).

26. The committee was well aware that if they did not try to stop PINE, as a new institute its natural course would bring it under the purview of an enhancing committee, the APsaA's Committee on New Training Facilities (CNTF) rather than the more inspector-general Committee on Institutes). The committee knew that the CNTF would not impede the development of the new institute. According to McLaughlin, one

reason for letting PINE take its course was that 'PINE would get a very close scrutiny and supportive evaluation because that was the manner of working of the CNTF' (McLaughlin interview 1994a).
27. Arvidson did not restrict his analytic practice to working on the couch and would at times spend time with his patients outside the consulting room (visiting their homes, having dinner). Arvidson saw analysts as too concerned with ritual and not with helping their patients. Far from seeing himself as outside the analytic field, Arvidson viewed his approach as analytic innovation, as primarily seeking the truth. He was appalled by the politics at the BPSI and felt disappointed that PINE was not different. Arvidson eventually left PINE in 1981 (Arvidson interview 1982).
28. Gardner reassured Gifford that nobody (including Arvidson) thought Gifford a spy. Gifford was 'a temporary object of victimisation' that had nothing to do with him personally. 'In my view, it would be best to take the event as a moment of melodrama' and Gardner hoped Gifford would 'let it pass' (Gardner 1976).
29. As a 1981 site visitor to the BPSI, John Gedo concluded that

> the departure of a significant portion of the senior faculty had provided many worthy younger members with an opportunity to step forward to fill teaching and administrative roles suitable for them. Thus, contrary to the anxieties of those who had fought the establishment of PINE, the split had actually benefited both groups. (Gedo 1997, p. 129)

30. The 1981 site visit report noted that many BPSI analysts were not primarily committed to a psychoanalytic career. Gedo noted that as he understood the reasons for the split, 'it was precisely that those who left were unhappy with allowing the parent institution to compromise its commitment to psychoanalysis proper in the manner that still commonly prevailed'; a point that the PINE analysts lamented when they left the BPSI (Gedo 1997, p. 129). From his experiences with Gardner in the same group of the Center for Advanced Psychoanalytic Study that meets annually in Princeton, Gedo recalled Gardner being far more interested in clinical than in administrative/political matters in psychoanalysis, and regards Gardner's clinical acumen as 'unmatched in contemporary psychoanalysis' (ibid., p. 92).
31. There were also deeply dissatisfied non training analysts who could not have qualified but thought they could have. Others never aspired to training analyst status. These included George Gardner who preferred to administer a department of psychiatry and those such as Peter Knapp who opted for research, or those interested in scholarship such as Sanford Gifford.
32. In Myerson's opinion, the appointment of training analysts provided 'the issue' (Myerson interview 1982; Gifford interview 1992). According to Gardner, the meetings organised by Leonard Friedman to review and revise the constitution were

the platform on which the acrimony built up. They built up over probably different views of optimum size, different views of committee representation and most centrally and painfully they began to touch on the issue of who had been appointed a training analyst and who hadn't. That's always the latent issue and that burst out and I suspect that behind the other issues that this was one of the most painful issues. (Gardner interview 1981)

33. The PINE society arose also from the strangeness of the idea of community outreach activities being conducted through the institute and through interest from the APsaA in forming a society so that PINE could have a seat on its Executive Council which represents affiliated societies (Pyles interview 1992). As PINE was set up as an institute, the PINE society – the Psychoanalytic society of New England, East (PSNE) – is clearly quite secondary and does not support the institute financially. It acts principally as a scientific meeting place for institute members and graduates.
34. These include the Advanced Training Program in Psychoanalytic Psychotherapy, the Extension Division's Program in Psychoanalytic Studies, seminars in psychotherapy, lectures and seminars.

Chapter 3

1. Carl Sandburg was the 'white-haired poet' who called Chicago the 'city of big shoulders' in his poem, 'Chicago'.
2. The institute's 1932 statement of purpose laid great emphasis on research outside private practice and its achievement through funding from external sources (see statement excerpted in Pollock 1983, pp. 8–10).
3. The ageing of the staff only became a problem from around 1965 (Gedo pers. comm. 1997).
4. However, Alexander's unorthodoxy about role-playing and the corrective emotional experience paled in comparison with his daughter, Lilla van Saher, who became a consort of Jerzy Kosinski, and was hostess both to a modish New York literary salon, and allegedly to men whom she provided with sexual 'punishment' in her work as a dominatrix! (Sloan 1996, pp. 182–3).
5. Bruno Bettleheim's institute was quite separate and independent of this.
6. Kohut told John Gedo that he was the person who actually devised the five-year curriculum (Gedo interview 1996b).
7. A number of institutes have been sponsored by the Chicago Institute. Topeka and Detroit were earlier daughters of the Chicago Institute, Cincinnati was of the same vintage as St Louis and Denver, and Minnesota and Wisconsin are currently struggling to be born (Gedo pers. comm. 1997).
8. Pollock was the protagonist in a research project begun by Franz Alexander on 'psychosomatic specificity', the idea that a specific

conflict precipitated the onset of a specific somatic illness such asthma, ulcerative colitis and peptic ulcer. This project attracted the powerful elite of the Chicago Institute who worked hard to validate Alexander's hypotheses. The project backfired, never proving the hypotheses and was little discussed in Chicago. Other projects such as the Barr-Harris research on bereavement and mourning which was close to Pollock's heart, were not very successful while many other individual projects were not supported by the institute (Moraitis pers. comm. 1990b; Pollock and Pilot 1970, pp. 85–8; Pollock 1977, pp. 141–68).

9. When Gedo discussed his concerns about Pollock being appointed with Heinz Kohut, then a powerful figure in Chicago and American psychoanalysis, was puzzled by Gedo's concerns about Pollock's being appointed. He declined Gedo's suggestion that Kohut would be the only effective block to Pollock because he felt the job would have interfered with his intellectual work. Kohut felt his prestige would be able to keep any director in line (Gedo interview 1994; Gedo 1997, pp. 104–5).

10. Gedo wrote, 'I still believe that if he had devoted himself wholeheartedly to scientific issue within psychoanalysis, he could have made a truly major contribution to the field, But he could never resist the lure of empire building' (Gedo 1997, pp. 41–2).

11. The budget was $62,000 in 1933–34, $311,000 in 1960–61, and $760,000 in 1976–77 (Pollock 1978, pp. 118–19; 1983, pp. 22–7). By comparison, an institute no smaller than Chicago in terms of analytic candidates, the Philadelphia Psychoanalytic Institute, had a budget of $75,000 while PINE, one of the smallest institutes, started with a budget of about $3,000 in 1976 (Gedo pers. comm. 1997).

12. The BPSI–PINE split may appear to be a counter-example. However, among other things, the level of the BPSI's assets was considerably smaller, there was no real distribution of grants, and so on.

13. This situation seems somewhat similar to one described to me by Elliott Jaques who worked as Research Professor of Management Science at George Washington University. George Washington University, founded in 1828, was defined as consisting of the thirty-six original members appointed by the US president at the time. That body was in perpetual renewal. The university is made up of the original thirty-six, and as one disappeared, of whoever then got elected in his place.

> It's an infinitely self-perpetuating body. That is the university – plus somebody called the president of the university who is appointed by the Trustees and is ex officio a member of the Board of Trustees. The Constitution provides for nobody else – no employees of the university and no teaching staff of the university are to be members of the board. In addition, no issues can be put on the board other than by board members on their own behalf or by the president in terms of the teaching staff and so on none of whom are allowed to put anything on the board agenda other than putting it through the

president who decides whether it goes on the agenda or not. The University also has a Senate and guess who the Chairman of the Senate is! The president. So you have the president who is ex officio on the board, he is the Chairman of the teaching staff Senate, and everything has to go through the Senate. They then complain that the president behaves like a monarch. That's supposed to be a personality characteristic, he's an autocratic, authoritarian monarch. What they haven't noticed is that every president has behaved in that way. It has nothing to do with his personality or anything else, it is what the role calls for. He is in a monarchical position. And, therefore, you can predict a lot of behaviours in the University. (Jaques interview 1990)

14. Since only one appointment had been made in the previous year, this figure was a correct representation of the number of training analysts under Pollock (American Psychoanalytic Association 1991). There were eighty candidates at the time (*Chicago Tribune*, June 9, 1989).
15. As John Gedo observed, 'In Chicago being a training analyst does not amount to much as they are as plentiful as blackberries, *not* being a training analyst is absolutely ruinous' (Gedo 1997, p. 79). When there was a such a surplus of training analysts, according to Gedo,

unofficial distinctions inevitably develop among them. There are those who have the title in name only, because the Institute never refers any candidates to them. There are others who might get one or two referrals in a lifetime, crumbs from the table of patronage, so to speak. Then there are the insiders who get the largest number of referrals, and almost all the candidates who look likely they might make an uncomplicated analytic course. Needless to say, this group used to include the current director, the dean, and their kitchen cabinet. (Gedo 1997, pp. 86–7)

See Kohut's comparable view in a 1963 letter to Gerhart Piers, in Cocks (1994, p. 90).

16. Although he was later re-elected to Council, Kohut dated the end of his sense of loyalty to the Chicago Institute from this event (see Kohut to Arnold Goldberg, May 5, 1980, in Cocks 1994, pp. 398–400; Richmond interview 1996; Gedo 1997, p. 111.
17. Wealthy and prominent board members during Pollock's directorship included: Edward Neisser, an investment banker, chaired the board 1981–91; George Barr, head of one of the nation's largest producers of aerosol products, who helped found the institute's Barr-Harris Center which helps grief-stricken children; Rhoda Pritzker, a member of one of the richest families in the US; Irving Harris, a prominent investor, rich philanthropist and sometime board president who was interested in social issues; and Anne Lederer who made considerable donations (see below).

18. Tom Nicholson resigned from the board after a long conflict with George Pollock. Irving Harris who gave much money to the University of Chicago reportedly never gave that much to the institute because of his battles with Pollock and withdrew from the institute. Another board member, Jim Moss, clashed with Pollock. Kligerman recalled his experience of the contrast between Pollock's conflicts with the board and what he saw as Alexander's excellent relationship with the board (Kligerman interview 1994).
19. For example, total assets for 1982 were $1,820,453 and for 1983 $1,940,731. Contributions and grants received during 1982 were $391,660 and 1983 $451,809, from a large number of contributors *(Institute for Psychoanalysis* 1983).
20. The situation was even worse than it looked then since candidate numbers were artificially bolstered by the 'geographic programme' which brought in candidates from rather distant cities. The institute also reaped some benefit for a few years of the end of the medical requirement for entrance to an APsaA institute with the resultant larger applicant pool (Gedo interview 1992). However, the poor showing should be understood in the context that the Chicago Institute has been the only APsaA institute in the nation's third largest city.
21. See for example, 'Psychiatrist accused of exploiting rich widow', *Southtown Economist Newspapers,* May 9, 1988; 'Psychiatrist Charged with Exploitation', *Rocky Mountain News,* May 9, 1988; 'Psychiatric Chief Takes Leave after Accusations', *San Diego Union-Tribune,* May 13, 1988. Articles on the subject were carried on the national and state wires of Associated Press. Later articles included: James Warren, Maurice Possley and Joseph Tybor, '"As Will Turns": A Real-world Soap', *Chicago Tribune,* September 6, 1988; Mark Perkiss, 'Judge Declares Mistrial in Lederer Will Dispute', November 2, 1988, Associated Press, Wednesday, a.m. cycle; and 'Settlement Ends Will Dispute', *Law Bulletin,* November 14, 1988.
22. Support revenues from contributions and grants were $391,660 in 1982 and $451,809 in 1983 *(Institute for Psychoanalysis* 1983). The institute consultants found that board support was declining. Contributions and benefit in 1989 was $108,000; 1990, $99,000; 1991, $84,000; 1992 (including a special gift of $40,000), $115,000. The board appeared more willing to support special projects and training programmes outside the core educational programmes (Bartling and Hall 1993, p. 15).
23. Consultants to the Chicago Institute concluded in 1993 that the psychoanalytic profession 'is in a state of decline caused by competitive threats and a poor public image. We see no easing in the pressures that have caused this state of affairs' (Bartling and Hall 1993, p. 18). They neglected to point out the harm that internal issues within the profession played, especially in Chicago where the 'success' of psychoanalysis clearly had a price to pay!

Chapter 4

1. A number of the leaders and members of the Los Angeles Study Group and the later society had been socialists and Marxists back in Europe and some remained so. Otto Fenichel, whose book *The Psychoanalytic Theory of Neurosis* remains a classic, had been the leader of political Freudians and sent *Rundbriefe* to his Marxist colleagues until 1945 (Jacoby 1983, p. x). Fenichel was, according to Jacoby, 'a formidable person, intellect, and presence in psychoanalysis. As the *Rundbriefe* hint, Freud and the Viennese analysts deeply respected Fenichel and even feared him' (ibid., p. 35). Ernst Simmel and Max Eitington who had founded the Berlin Institute wanted, in Jacoby's words, 'to emancipate psychoanalysis from an exclusive reliance on wealthy neurotics'. Simmel had been President of the Society of Socialist Physicians and his activities were permeated with socialist principles. Freud much admired Simmel and frequently visited *Schloss Tegel*. A candidate during the 1940s, Leonard Rosengarten, remembered the monthly meetings of the society (which even included Frankfurt School members, Herbert Marcuse, Max Horkheimer and T. W. Adorno) and of the study group as wonderful, refreshing and stimulating – they were rarely missed (Rosengarten 1986, p. 16; Rosengarten interview 1992). Simmel, Grotjahn and Fenichel analysed a number of later leaders of LAPSI and Fenichel in particular was much admired. Two important examples are Ralph Greenson who had been analysed by Fenichel, and Leo Rangell who had been analysed by Grotjahn.
2. The Topeka and Los Angeles Psychoanalytic societies were close – Ernst Simmel, Otto Fenichel and Charles Tidd were Charter members of the Topeka Psychoanalytic society. Immigrants to LAPSI included Gerald Aronson, Martin Grotjahn, Ernst Lewy, Henry Lihn, Charles Tidd (Rosengarten 1986, p. 23) and the clinical psychologist, Milton Wexler. Many of these analysts were to play important leadership roles in LAPSI and their openness towards lay analysis, interest in psychoanalytic research, and their willingness to challenge dogma had been part of the Topeka experience. Despite the fact that Menninger's was assuredly a medical-psychiatric institution, there were mixed attitudes toward the lay émigrés. While Robert Knight, William Menninger and others had no compunction about excluding lay analysts, Karl Menninger felt that the lay émigrés were often competent leaders and initiators in the psychoanalytic movement and were a decided gain to the country (Friedman 1990, p. 120). Karl Menninger generally encouraged a more open and critical scientific approach to psychoanalysis than was usual; the research group around David Rapaport at Topeka involved medical and lay members and initiated several research projects. Many of the collegial associations and friendships at Topeka continued afterwards as a US-wide network so that the Topeka culture of greater scientific

openness and independence made a contribution to the culture of LAPSI.
3. Immediately, the new institute resolved to restrict its membership to physicians and the word 'Medical' was not dropped from the name for a further twelve years (Gabe, in American Psychoanalytic Association 1975c, pp. 51–2).
4. Before 1946 the other group would ask May Romm, who had been strongly influenced by the heterodox analyst, Sandor Rado in New York, 'Dr. Romm, why don't you go back to New York?' To which she would reply, 'Where is your California medical license?' (Romm, quoted in Frumkes 1975, p. 15). Martin Grotjahn was the only European analyst to be welcomed by the new group.
5. Martin Grotjahn, Milton Miller and Norman Levy of the new group came from the Chicago Alexander influence (Rosengarten 1986, p. 17).
6. Rosengarten (1986, p. 20). Before coming to the Los Angeles Psychoanalytic Institute in 1950, Rosengarten worked as a War Crimes psychiatrist at Nuremberg Prison in Germany after World War II. He interviewed and consulted with all of the important defendants in the war crimes trials, including Hermann Goering and Rudolf Hess *(Los Angeles Times*, May 17, 1997).
7. David Brunswick, Frances Deri, Ralph Greenson, Ernst Lewy and Charles Tidd were from the old group while Martin Grotjahn, Milton Miller and May Romm were the leaders of the new group.
8. Rangell recently spoke of this period perhaps too lyrically. According to Rangell, after the splits of the late 1940s and 'with the settling down to an era of peaceful application of the carved-out theoretical views, we enjoyed the golden years of psychoanalytic living, practice and theory. Nowhere was the period of exhilaration and steady work and progress more visible and enjoyable than in Beverly Hills and West Los Angeles during the fifties and into the sixties' (Rangell 1993). Greenson recalled that after the 1950 split the Los Angeles Institute 'had some kind of peace – for a while. We started to have more peaceful meetings. It was such a relief to get up and have people give a paper, not to think psychoanalysis was in danger and could attack it and even bring up some crazy idea without being accused of something – a heresy. I thought it was a very healthy move' (Greenson 1962, pp. 21–2).
9. In his 1964 Dean's Report for that year, Larry Friedman wrote:

> Every new training analyst is struck by the unhealthy, angry atmosphere of our Education Committee. Some have refused consideration for training analyst, others wish to withdraw on account of it. We spend more time fighting about meaningless procedural matters than discussing training problems. Decisions are frequently not based on merit, but on emotional grounds and constantly shifting alliances. New ideas are treated with suspicion, questioning not only the value of the proposition, not only one's judgement, but also one's personal integrity. The Chairman of the Education

Committee is put on the defensive and automatically judged guilty unless proven innocent. He is reproached for action or damned for omission. It would be difficult to find four people as different as the Deans who have been Chairmen since 1950, yet the problems confronting them were almost the same. (quoted in Leavitt 1986)

In a later report Friedman claimed: 'Continuous membership on the Education Committee for all training analysts, the unjustified and frequently misused "confidentiality" of its proceedings, restricted communication with the rest of the membership, created a blind, rigid, self-righteous attitude within, mistrust and suspicion from without' (quoted in ibid., p. 26).

10. This invaluable collection of documents was originally submitted as an appeal by Bernard Bail and Albert Mason to the IPA, asking for the investigation of problems of discrimination in Los Angeles. This book consists of documents collected principally by Bernard Bail, with much assistance from Albert Mason, Carolyn Hays and a number of others – twenty Kleinians contributed the money for the work (Hays interview 1992). Bail offers separate commentaries. This amounts to an archive of many important events of the period of the 'Freud–Klein troubles' in the 1970s. It includes the 1973 site visit report, attorneys' letters, correspondence, Minutes and transcriptions of faculty and society meetings and other documents pertaining to the dispute. In 1991 Bail republished these documents privately together with some additional material as *The Freud–Klein Controversies (1973–1977) Los Angeles: The Testing Ground and Final Solution*. I refer to many original documents included in this collection for ease of reference as 'Bail 1991b' followed by page numbers. These are original documents, and do not imply authorship by Bail.
11. There were 365 members of the APsaA in 1950 (Lindon 1975, p. 11).
12. One of the candidates concerned verified this to me verbally.
13. Some are collected in Greenson (1992).
14. Captain Newman was reputed to get transferences 'the way a movie star attracts schoolgirls'. Rosten's description of Newman certainly resonated with the way colleagues have described Greenson: detachment, kindliness and wisdom were not characteristic of Newman 'his brusqueness, his off-hand manner, his deflating remarks, his irony and petulance and shifts in mood were difficult to understand' (Rosten 1961, pp. 30–1).
15. As well as his text on technique and practice, Greenson's theoretical contributions to psychoanalysis included his development of the concept of the 'working alliance'. He thought the development of the working alliance the primary factor in treatment and of equal importance to the transference neurosis. Increasingly he focused on the 'real' relationship, which he believed was essential in psychoanalytic treatment: the transference neurosis needed to be replaced by a real

relationship. He did not share the view that interpretation was enough. It needed 'to be supplemented by a realistic and genuine relationship to the person of the analyst, limited though it may be' (Greenson 1971, p. 439).

16. The fact that Otto Fenichel worked in Los Angeles formed a significant part of Rangell's attraction to Los Angeles Rangell felt it was 'like Freud being here. To this day he is for me a clinical and theoretical exemplar' (Wilson 1993a, p. 16). Fenichel died a few months before Rangell arrived in Los Angeles. Through Fenichel's published work, Rangell saw him as the 'leader-model' who most influenced him (Rangell 1988a, p. 60). Rangell identified his views as lying within what used to be mainstream American psychoanalysis based on ego psychology and structural theory. Rangell has been well known as an integrator of theories and has contributed in a large number of areas ranging from the nature of anxiety and intrapsychic conflict to the nature of group behaviour and politics (see Shane 1986, p. 37).
17. This was Rangell's Presidential Address to the IPA in 1973.
18. Rangell asserted his primary interest as lying in the science of psychoanalysis and therefore in 'the science of the politics of psychoanalysis' (Rangell interview 1992).
19. Monroe came to consult Greenson seven times a week at his home, later twice daily at his or her home, even living in Greenson's house for a time (Spoto 1993, p. 553). After her sessions with Greenson, she often stayed at his home for champagne, and dinner (ibid., p. 522). At Greenson's behest, she befriended members of his family who drove her home or to the pharmacy to buy drugs. There was scarcely a part of Monroe's life in which Greenson was not involved: Greenson advised her on a new house, on film contracts, on friends and lovers.

Why did none of Greenson's colleagues stand up to correct Greenson for this astonishing behaviour? Spoto believed an important reason lay in his circulating 'the spurious and unsubstantiated report that Marilyn Monroe was "schizophrenic"' and that he himself was being supervised in caring for her by a man well known in Los Angeles for treating schizophrenics, Milton Wexler' (ibid., p. 555). Greenson regarded her as schizophrenic (ibid., p. 586). Spoto quoted a young colleague of Greenson, saying that at that time

> everyone was experimenting with ways to treat schizophrenics, and Wexler had his own method. Greenson used Wexler as his supervisor, and thus gave his unorthodox treatment of Monroe an apparent legitimacy. One of the techniques was to invite the patient into the home – not only to provide what may have been lacking earlier, but to have a constant connection so the patient would never have undue anxiety on weekends, or [suffer] any separation trauma. (ibid., p. 555)

Peter Brown and Patte Barham's *Marilyn: The Last Take* (Brown and Barham 1992) contains valuable information about Greenson and Monroe, some of which overlaps with Spoto's research. Donald Wolfe's *The Last Days of Marilyn Monroe* (Wolfe 1998) contains some interesting material on Greenson, which linked him, along with his colleague and Monroe's physician, Hyman Engelberg, with the Communist Party. However, Wolfe reached well beyond his evidence in claiming that Greenson was a Comintern spy and part of a communist plot. Many intellectuals were attracted to communism in the 1930s into the 1950s. However, by the 1960s they had moved well away from communism, even if they maintained some leftist sympathies,. Wolfe adduced no evidence that as late as the time he treated Monroe, Greenson maintained any link with the Communist Party or the USSR.

20. Spoto provides only one scenario. There are probably as many unfounded speculations about Monroe's death as there are about John F. Kennedy's. For example, Donald H. Wolfe's book, *The Last Days of Marilyn Monroe* (Wolfe 1998), suggests a not very convincing alternative scenario – but one in which Greenson was certainly not responsible for Monroe's death.

21. Greenson did not apply these ideas to Monroe only. Five years later Greenson wrote about cases of eroticised transference in which he offered himself 'as an obvious auxiliary ego and superego ... I demonstrated to them their errors in thought and judgment and offered a better alternative. I became their mentor and guide' (Greenson 1967, p. 341).

22. As Rangell put it, Wexler was 'the closest link to Greenson – the two were like an inseparable pair. And Greenson was succumbing to Wexler's theoretical considerations which led to the Marilyn Monroe case' (Rangell interview 1992).

23. Did Wexler have a valid point in claiming that he was being investigated without his knowledge? It is important to distinguish the preliminary discussions to determine whether the matter merited being taken further from any proper investigation. The preliminary meetings were not kept secret in any case since Greenson (Wexler's close friend) appeared before it and was not sworn to secrecy. Although it is due process that an accused person should always be informed, Wexler was not an accused person. It could be argued that if somebody makes an accusation against somebody else, that person has a right to be informed. However, times have changed – while this is now current procedure within the APsaA and the American Psychiatric Association, it was not so in the mid 1960s. Wexler cited the Los Angeles County and California Medical Association and based his claim that LAPSI was operating differently from established procedures in other professional organisations.

24. Mandel summed up:

Wexler's main complaint was his not being informed and that informing the person who was under investigation was part of the procedure of other organisations in the area. Because this set up the whole suspiciousness that this was a vendetta secretly undertaken to discredit Wexler, even though it was prescribed by the bylaws. Because then you have somebody who was following the letter of the law and not the spirit of fairness and justice. Leo's defence was that he was doing what the law prescribed. And the charge against him was that there was no prescription that the initial investigation had to have been done secretly. (Mandel interview 1994)

25. Wexler's approach derived from his work at the Menninger Clinic where active involvement with psychotics was advocated. In fact, this was not the first time Wexler had used violence with a patient. He even advocates it in a 1951 paper where he discussed a schizophrenic case, 'Nedda'. A well-known case to LAPSI members, Nedda exemplified Wexler's theory that the missing part of the psychotic patient's ego needed to be provided by the analyst. If there was no ego control, it was up to the analyst to provide substitute until the ego could be rebuilt. Wexler wrote:

> I took a very active role in forbidding any sexual or aggressive provocations, which threatened to disturb the therapeutic relationship. If Nedda threatened to use force against me, I made it clear I would employ an equivalent amount of force against her. When, with rapidly diminishing frequency, I was actually assaulted by her, I did what I could to immobilise her. When the physical provocation was severe enough to arouse in me strong resentment and a wish to put a quick end to her assaultive behaviour, I did more than inhibit her movements. I fulfilled my promise to meet force with force. I can say this about our struggle together: With but one exception, never did any of our vehement verbal and physical battles end without peacemaking and affectionate exchange of devotion; rarely did she omit to thank me for putting an end to the threatening and overwhelming forces which had seized control of her. (Wexler 1951, p. 159)

'Every struggle', Wexler reported, led to 'clinical improvement' and every improvement led to Wexler relaxing his demands on the patient and to 'increased dosages of affection, interpretation, and education' (ibid.). In his advocacy of physical interventions in psychosis Wexler even countered the objection that his approach might hark back to the medieval treatment of psychotics with its whipping posts and dungeons: that treatment might not have been that bad: 'After all, what we know about medieval treatment for psychosis is mainly the savagery of some of its methods and very little of its clinical experience' (ibid., p. 164). Wexler advocated large doses of love as the cure for schizophrenia (ibid., p. 157), and one has to wonder exactly how he might administer this prescription. On Wexler's theory, controlling and fighting with the patient was one form of his administration of

love. By constricting the violence you could try to squeeze the anger out. This would all become part of the distinctly unorthodox, active, interpersonal approach which helped to win Wexler so much favour in Hollywood.
26. This situation strongly resembled the Zilbourg affair in the New York Psychoanalytic Society in the late 1930s. A leading psychoanalyst, Gregory Zilbourg, was investigated for unethical conduct by an Ethics Committee of the society, which recommended sanctions. Zilbourg had taken advantage of a vulnerable but wealthy patient. He received a watch, tickets to a Joe Louis fight, a radio and $5,000 for 'business advice' since Zilbourg needed money to pay his taxes. The committee's decision was reversed by the society after Zilbourg claimed it was all a plot by Franz Alexander with David Levy as his accomplice. Zilbourg threatened suit and so intimidated members of the Ethics Committee that they reversed their vote. The society then voted not to reprimand Zilbourg who remained a member. Out of disgust with the reversal of the decision, George Goldman and David Levy resigned from the New York Psychoanalytic Society and others were most disaffected (Frosch 1991, pp. 1051–3). Levy thereupon became a major force in the formation of the Columbia Psychoanalytic Institute and other members of the New York Society who were disaffected not only by the issue of 'academic freedom' but by the unethical way the Zilbourg case was handled (Daniels 1971–72, 11 (1), p. 12; Bernard 1990).
27. Leo Rangell regarded this as a 'good statement' (Rangell interview 1992) while Morton Shane disagreed, maintaining that there were some good analysts in Los Angeles who helped their patients become more free. For example, Hannah Fenichel analysed independent thinkers such as Bob Stoller and Bernard Brandchaft (Shane interview 1992).
28. Rangell suggested that

> the dynamic of this repeated phenomenon is a repression of the Oedipus complex in theory, and an acting of it out in group life. By banishing the oedipal and elevating another phase, not unlike a screen memory to cover a more affectively charged one in an individual history, the chosen element of psychoanalytic theory is used as a vehicle through which an Oedipal triumph is exacted in object relations. (Rangell 1982, p. 38).

29. Rosengarten interview 1992; Rangell interview 1992. Rangell felt that 'a lot of the people involved in the Reorganization were also involved in destructive subsequent activities that took place in the institute after the Reorganization. The broom that swept did more trouble than the thing it was sweeping' (Rangell interview 1992).
30. The 1980 site visitors lamented that some training analysts reportedly circumvented the 'rule of two' (which replaced the 'rule of three'), claiming that

certain candidates in analysis were no longer in 'training analysis'. That kind of practice or even rumor of this practice is demoralizing to the faculty, and, if true, reflects a less than acceptable level of moral standards for those who would be the major models for the next generation of analysts. (American Psychoanalytic Association 1980, pp. 20–1)

31. While it was the case that many of the Freudians later had few or no candidates, this was also related to the enlargement of the pool of training analysts who were simultaneously appointed in 1967.
32. Juliet Mitchell (1986) provides an overview of Klein's basic ideas together with how they differ from Freud's, as well as a collection of Klein's work.
33. Wallerstein interview 1987. This was echoed across the US. For example, George Moraitis recalled that not one piece of reading on Klein was assigned during his training at the Chicago Psychoanalytic Institute during the 1960s (Moraitis interview 1994).
34. Hilda Rollman-Branch recalled that the group 'started out with the research of two embryologists who had done experiments with non-viable premature fetuses and shown their rooting type of reflexes' (pers. comm. 1992).
35. McGuire supervised Bernard Brandchaft, Arthur Malin, Melvin Mandel, Bernard Bail and Carolyn Hays, and analysed Richard Casady, James Grotstein, Gerald Aronson and Arthur Ourieff.
36. John Lindon was an analyst who became interested in Klein and been in touch with Gwen Evans (Brandchaft interview 1992).
37. Brandchaft recalled McGuire's reactions to Rosenfeld:

    He came to the meeting and was unfavourably impressed with Rosenfeld and what he had to say. On what grounds he didn't say. Except to say that he felt that Herbert was too authoritarian, 'too German', he meant for his taste. That was the beginning of the limitation of McGuire's influence as a dissident in LA. (Brandchaft interview 1992)

38. McGuire's considerable disquiet about the lightning conversions reminded me of Freud warning his audience in his *Introductory Lectures* about the process of acquiring new ideas – even good ones – too quickly (Freud 1916–17, pp. 243–4).
39. Some Kleinians mistakenly regarded the attacks on them as really attacks on Bion. Melvin Mandel, who remained both independent and active in LAPSI, believed that Bion did not have as much effect as some thought. Mandel recalled that the papers Bion presented in Los Angeles 'weren't well received' (Mandel interview 1981). McGuire did not see Bion as evangelical: 'I don't think he had a following about him and his influence wasn't that great. Many found him very difficult to read, listen to and understand' (McGuire interview 1992). Rosengarten recalled that while Bion was 'more important than we knew at the time', Rosengarten had 'not one moment's concern about his presence'

(Rosengarten interview 1992). On the other hand, Kleinian analyst Albert Mason contended that Bion's lectures were always packed and stimulated a good deal of interest and that Bion had a number of analysts in analysis and supervision (Mason pers. comm. 1992).

Whatever the facts of Bion's impact on the larger Los Angeles psychoanalytic scene, there can be no doubt that Bion was a particularly important figure for some analysts. Those who found Bion's impact very important to them felt perhaps that Bion must – or should – have been an equally important figure for their opponents as well. James Grotstein edited a memorial edition to him, revealingly entitled, *Do I Dare Disturb the Universe?*, which included contributions by a number of admiring Los Angeles analysts (Grotstein 1983). The enemy for the more mainstream analysts was not so much Bion as the Kleinian influence.

40. Mason recalled:

    Bion said it would be valuable for me to go with him for two reasons: one is he said, well, I'm seventy and you never know how long I am going to last. And the other was he said, it would be very useful to have someone to supervise the people I am analysing. In fact if he hadn't have been encouraging I wouldn't have come. I certainly wouldn't have come on my own steam at that point. We discussed it for many hours with the Bions. (Mason interview 1992); see also Rodman 1983, p. 3; Mandel 1996a, p. 21).

41. Mason received Full Membership of the British Psychoanalytic Society just before coming to Los Angeles. There was an unfounded rumour that Mason's credentials were questionable, that he was only an Associate Member and not a Full Member of the British Society as he claimed to have been before he came to Los Angeles. The British Institute committee was chaired by Herbert Rosenfeld and contained Joseph Sandler. Mason's paper was a case of homosexuality.

42. Only in the 1980s did Mason become a training analyst at LAPSI. Together with some other Kleinians, he has twice served as president of the Kleinian-oriented Psychoanalytic Center of California, which became directly affiliated with the IPA in 1989.

43. In 1963, one of Bail's patients whom he analysed while she was dying of cancer left him a bequest of $700,000. Bail donated this Walker Bequest to LAPSI. The money was used to buy land and construct the architecturally fine LAPSI building (Rosengarten interview 1992).

44. Brandchaft became the leader of the West Coast self psychologists and later distanced himself from the Chicago self psychologists, becoming involved in the 'intersubjective' approach within self psychology with Bob Stolorow when he moved to Los Angeles. He has always been a controversial figure with an independent mind who is liked and respected by many but regarded as a mystery by others.

45. Albert Mason did not feel it was as paralysed as Mandel thought (Mason interview 1992), and for Bernard Bail, 'There was no disruption at all' (Bail pers. comm. 1990).
46. The committee consisted of Justin Krent (chairman), George Allison, Lili Bussel, Homer Curtis, Leon Ferber, John Francis, Shelley Orgel, William Robbins and Ernest Ticho.
47. Rosengarten also felt that the site visitors had an agenda, that they were looking for trouble at LAPSI (Rosengarten interview 1992). Grotstein recalled that the APsaA's site visit 'descended in here like the Gestapo'. Grotstein recalled that three members of the Site Visit Committee separately asked him why he had moved to Los Angeles from London: 'They had me confused with Albert Mason, but the question was tell-tale – they were looking for trouble' (Grotstein interview 1981).
48. Rosengarten recalled that all the LAPSI officers felt that Krent did not listen and was particularly unfair and harsh to LAPSI (Rosengarten interview 1992). According to James McLaughlin (interview 1994b), Krent had a 'narrow gauge view' of psychoanalysis and would not have been happy with what was happening in LAPSI.
49. As Bail put it, 'The institute was put on probation by The American, and in the meantime I held this suit over their heads until this thing was going to be satisfactorily solved' (Bail interview 1981).
50. This bears a strong similarity to the APsaA's concerns about the Columbia Institute gaining affiliation during the 1940s. The APsaA were not troubled about the society (the Association for Psychoanalytic Medicine) becoming affiliated as that institute would be teaching secessionist ideas under the APsaA aegis (Bernard 1990).
51. This was published in 1974 in the *International Journal of Psychoanalysis* and republished in Greenson (1978).
52. The grant came from 'The Foundation for Research in Psychoanalysis in Beverly Hills, California' (Greenson 1974 [original article], p. 47n), the fund that Greenson operated himself. He was Chairman of its Scientific Advisory Board (Greenson 1972, p. 417; see also Greenson 1968, p. 370n) – scarcely an independent grant-making body implying impartiality! This project involved collaborative work with Milton Wexler, Nathan Leites, Alfred Goldberg, Thomas Mintz and Sidney Fine (Greenson 1974 [original article], p. 47n). This is one of numerous instances when Greenson acknowledges the assistance of a grant that he awarded himself!
53. Designed by Charles Moore and featured in Fodor's *Travel Guide to Los Angeles*, the building is known colloquially in psychoanalytic circles, as the 'Fairbairn Pentagon' as its twenty-two tenants are members of LAPSI. Working in the building allows for easy mingling with colleagues and some concentration of power within the institute within the building itself.
54. Rollman-Branch confirmed that Ourieff and she spearheaded the movement towards reconstituting the new institute.

I thought for a long time that it would have been the best thing if we had had two institutes, one that is more Kleinian and the other that is more American, more general, and also eclectic. It seems to have been borne out that mine was not a bad idea because now the Kleinians have founded their own institute even though many of them have kept their membership of the Los Angeles Institute. I think the division would not have been a bad idea about twenty years ago and would have saved all of us a lot of time and anguish ... It was Romi Greenson's decision not to split at that time and the fact that one or two people followed him away from the duly constituted group that brought it to an end. (Rollman-Branch pers. comm. 1992)

55. Those selected were: Gerald Aronson, Neal Peterson, Robert Rodman and Donald Siegal. Seymour Bird later replaced Rodman (Shershow 1993, p. 22).
56. The other members were Maurice Friend, Frances Gitelson, James McLaughlin, Nathan Segal and Stanley Weiss.
57. Fleming introduced the concept of a sliding scale of increasing APsaA involvement where shutting the institute down was the last option only after other educational options failed (McLaughlin interview 1994b).
58. A major difference in McLaughlin's experience with the BPSI and LAPSI lay in the degree of *ad hominem* attack which was as markedly present in LAPSI as it was absent at BPSI (McLaughlin interview 1994b).
59. James McLaughlin felt that the outcome in Los Angeles would have been very different without Mandel (McLaughlin interview 1994b).
60. These included Don Segal, Ernest Schreiber, John Lindon and Arthur Malin (Shane interview 1992).
61. Strangely, this is precisely what the Kleinians could have done at the time if they had only known they could. In an interview published in 1992, Robert Wallerstein, a recent IPA President, revealed that the rule whereby the APsaA would have autonomy together with the exclusive franchise for psychoanalysis in the US was discussed at the 1938 IPA Congress and postponed to the next Congress which would have been in 1940. However, the war intervened and that Congress was postponed. After the war the 1938 Rule was simply taken for granted under an arrangement which had to be made since the Americans threatened to secede from the IPA unless the 1938 'Rule' was effected (Mayer, 1992, p. 21). The 'Rule' was operative from 1938 until it was overturned twenty-nine years later by a change in the bylaws at the IPA Montreal Congress (even though it did not require any bylaw change since it was not 'legal' in the first place) (Wallerstein interview 1992; see Wallerstein 1998b for more on this issue). Robert Knight implied as much in his 1952 Presidential Address to the APsaA when he noted that the American declarations to the IPA

were received with some astonishment and condescension by the latter at the 1938 Congress in Paris, and were referred to committee without official action. The outbreak of World War II prevented the further working out of the relationship between the American and the IPA until the Zurich Congress in 1949. An amicable meeting of American and European analysts the summer before prepared the way for new statutes of the International Psychoanalytic Association which were adopted in Zurich and which accepted by implication the 1938 resolutions of The American' (Knight 1953, p. 291).

It was assumed from the allegedly 'amicable' meetings that it was enacted but it was not enacted in the statutes at all.

Albert Mason said that if this had been known, 'we'd have formed a Kleinian institute' (Mason interview 1992). The basically Kleinian institute, the Psychoanalytic Center of California, was directly affiliated to the IPA in 1989.

62. The 1980 site visitors were Edwin Wood (chair), Eugene Baum, Carl Davis, Richard Greenberg and Roy Lilleskov.
63. Some LAPSI members were concerned that an overriding interest in 'getting the institute to function' minimised the strong personal and theoretical differences that existed, with the result that educational excellence and personal honesty were seriously compromised (American Psychoanalytic Association 1980, p. 16). Moreover, besides wondering about the stability of the changes, the 1980 site visitors were concerned that the leadership was centred on four or five strong people and wondered about how continuity of leadership would be achieved. In transition to new leadership the site visitors thought that dissentions which were 'manifestations of forces kept just below the surface in an effort to maintain a sense of unity' would resurface (ibid., pp. 11–12).
64. The 1987 site visitors concluded:

> In a sense LAPSI may be entering a new phase of its history, having weathered the storms of the 60s and 70s through the arduous efforts of its current leaders. Directions and approaches developed in a context of containing a potentially divisive theoretical diversity and achieving continuation of the educational programs of the institute, may now be open for reassessment in relation to the current state of The Los Angeles Psychoanalytic Society and Institute. (American Psychoanalytic Association 1987, p. 33)

65. LAPSI led the successful fight for 'delinkage' between membership in the APsaA and certification as an analyst by the APsaA (which was a prerequisite for membership). Many component organisations of the APsaA felt that graduation from an accredited institute should be sufficient to become a member of the national organisation and that certification should be a subsequent process if it should existed at all. Many at LAPSI, Chicago and other institutes felt the certification process was unfairly administered, involving discrimination by the

conservative axis (epitomised by the New York Psychoanalytic Institute) against unorthodox approaches such as self psychology. After a considerable battle, delinkage was finally overwhelmingly approved by the APsaA in 1992 (Bergman 1992, p. 1).

66. The 1994 site visitors continued, 'This course is thoughtfully placed in the body of knowledge being presented and it is skilfully instructed.' The candidates

> are exposed to these views without being proselytized. This, of course, is a goal of education and is particularly successful in an institute which justly prides itself on presenting various schools of psychoanalytic thought. Our Subcommittee, however, encourages LAPSI to stay aware of the possible negative side effects where the timing of presenting the various models are ill matched to a particular class. (American Psychoanalytic Association 1994, pp. 4–5)

See Fisher et al, pp. xx–xxxi, for a positive account of LAPSI's pluralistic training in the 1980s.

67. LAPSI's class sizes were not affected and 'good quality of care is still one of our strongest sources of referral' (American Psychoanalytic Association 1994, pp. 24–5).

68. The *well reasoned* differences concerned the nature of psychoanalysis, the frequency of sessions, whether the curriculum should be founded on classical, including ego psychological, approaches, the merits of certification and the criteria for becoming a training analyst. The *emotion-laden factors* involved certification and the APsaA. The site visitors acknowledged that past certification procedures were authoritarian and resulted in LAPSI being disadvantaged. However, the certification procedures were now changed and most applicants from LAPSI were now accepted for certification. Moreover, LAPSI members needed to recognise that the nature of the APsaA site visits had 'dramatically changed' over the past fourteen years. 'The authoritarian, policy function of the 1960s and 1970s has yielded beginning in the 1980s to become collegial, consultative, joint problem solving undertakings' (American Psychoanalytic Association 1994, pp. 24–5).

69. At about $100 per session, with four-times-a-week analysis, training analysts earn $400 per week per analysand. With a maximum of three LAPSI candidates, this could mean $1,200 per week. In 1994, 45 per cent of training analysts were being trained by thirteen analysts over seventy years old, 32 per cent by eight analysts between sixty and sixty-nine, while 19 per cent were trained by ten analysts under sixty (Cohen 1994, p. 8; American Psychoanalytic Association 1994, p. 12).

Conclusion

1. Anointment can be seen as an important aspect of the discipleship in psychoanalysis that François Roustang has explored so ably (Roustang 1982).

2. Even in 1924 there were only forty-one members of the Vienna Psychoanalytic Society (Federn and Freud 1972, p. 29).
3. A study of analytic process by analysts from the Columbia Psychoanalytic Institute indicated scant agreement among analysts about the nature and definition of such a fundamental issue as analytic process (AP). They believed that the ambiguity surrounding this term was scarcely unique to that term. 'It would seem that when analysts speak to each other using the term, AP, the communication is illusory – sabotaged by the erroneous belief that they share an understanding' (Vaughan et al. 1997, pp. 965–6).
4. Wilfred Bion put it aptly:

> Freud talks about 'paramnesia' as being an invention which is intended to fill the space where a fact ought to be. But is one right to assume that a paramnesia is an activity which is peculiar only to patients and to pathological existence? I think psychoanalysis could be a way of blocking the gap of our ignorance about ourselves, although my impression is that it is more, We can produce a fine structure of theory in the hope that it will block up the hole for ever so that we shall never need to learn anything more about ourselves either as people or organizations. I suggest that we cannot be sure that these theories which are so convenient and which make us – both as individuals and as a group – feel better because they appear to make an inroad into the enormous area of ignorance, are therefore final. One would like to say, 'Thus far and no further', but if one carries on this same procedure then one is back again in contact with this vast area of ignorance. (Bion 1980, p. 30)

BIBLIOGRAPHY

Alexander, F., French, T. et al. (1946) *Psychoanalytic Therapy: Principles and Application*. Lincoln: University of Nebraska Press, 1980.

Algren, N. (1963) *Chicago: City on the Make*. New York: McGraw Hill.

American Psychoanalytic Association (1938) 'Information to be Supplied to Psychoanalysts Who Desire to Emigrate to the USA'. Brill Archives.

American Psychoanalytic Association (1974) Report of Committee on New Training Facilities to the Board on Professional Standards, American Psychoanalytic Association, December 12, 1974.

American Psychoanalytic Association (1975a) 'Report on the BPSI Situation'; Chronology BPSI–PINE Split, April 23. Typescript.

American Psychoanalytic Association (1975b) Minutes of the Report of Committee on New Training Facilities to Board on Professional Standards, Minutes of Annual Meeting, April 30–May 4. *J. Amer. Psychoanal. Assn.* 23: 873–5.

American Psychoanalytic Association (1975c) Oral History Workshop, #3, Los Angeles. May. Transcript.

American Psychoanalytic Association (1976/1988) *By-laws of The American Psychoanalytic Association Inc.* New York: American Psychoanalytic Association.

American Psychoanalytic Association (1976a) Board on Professional Standards: Committee on Institutes. 'Final Report of the Site Visit to The New York Psychoanalytic Institute, February 24–28, 1976'. Typescript.

American Psychoanalytic Association (1976b) 'Summary of the Minutes of the Board on Professional Standards'. May 5. Typescript.

American Psychoanalytic Association (1977) 'Los Angeles Society and Institute': Report to Board on Professional Standards of the Final Report of the Ad Hoc Committee for Los Angeles to Board on Professional Standards. Bulletin of Fall Meeting (1976). *J. Amer. Psychoanal. Assn.* 25: 498–502.

American Psychoanalytic Association (1979) Site Visit for Columbia Institute. Typescript.

American Psychoanalytic Association (1980) 'Los Angeles Psychoanalytic Society and Institute: Report of the Site Visit Subcommittee of the Committee on Institutes of The American Psychoanalytic Association, March 12–15, 1980'. Typescript.

American Psychoanalytic Association (1981) 'The Impossible Profession'. Interview with Janet Malcolm, *APsaA Newsletter*. March, p. 4.

American Psychoanalytic Association (1983) Board on Professional Standards: Committee on Institutes, 'Report on The Site Visit to The New York Psychoanalytic Institute'. March 29-April 2. Typescript.
American Psychoanalytic Association (1984) *Standards for Training in Psychoanalysis*. New York.
American Psychoanalytic Association (1987) 'Report of the 1987 Los Angeles Psychoanalytic Society and Institute: Site Visit Subcommittee'. Typescript.
American Psychoanalytic Association (1989) 'At the Meetings. Los Angeles Conducts Poll Regarding Membership'. *American Psychoanalytic Association Newsletter*, 23 (1): 12.
American Psychoanalytic Association (1991) Board on Professional Standards: Committee on Institutes. "Preliminary Site Visit Report, Chicago Institute for Psychoanalysis, February 6–10, 1991'. Typescript.
American Psychoanalytic Association (1992) Board on Professional Standards: Committee on Institutes. 'Report of The New York Psychoanalytic Institute and Society Site Visit' to the March 17–21'. Typescript.
American Psychoanalytic Association (1994) 'Los Angeles Psychoanalytic Society and Institute: Report of the Site Visit Subcommittee of the Committee on Institutes of The American Psychoanalytic Association, February 23–27, 1994'.
Arlow, J. (1962) 'The Future of an Idea', in M. Wangh, ed. *Fruition of an Idea: Fifty Years of Psychoanalysis in New York*. New York: International Universities Press, pp. 44–5.
Arlow, J. (1969) 'Myth and Ritual in Psychoanalytic Training', in *Three Institute Conference on Psychoanalytic Training*. Pittsburgh Psychoanalytic Institute, Pittsburgh, pp. 104–20.
Arlow, J. (1970) 'Group Psychology and the Study of Institutes'. Address to Board on Professional Standards. Typescript.
Arlow, J. (1972) 'Ten Years of COPE: Perspectives on Psychoanalytic Education'. *J. Amer. Psychoanal. Assn.* 20: 556–66.
Arlow, J. (1985) 'Issues in the Evaluation of Psychoanalysis: Criteria for Change', in C. Settlage and R. Brockbank, *New Ideas in Psychoanalysis*. Hillsdale NJ: The Analytic Press, pp. 5–18.
Arlow, J. (1989) 'Personal Memoir', in *The Psychoanalytic Core: Essays in Honor of Leo Rangell. M.D.* Madison CT: International Universities Press, pp. 9–13.
Arlow, J. (1990) 'Comments on the Psychoanalytic Curriculum'. Typescript.
Arlow, J. (1991) 'Jacob Arlow Addresses The Graduating Class of the San Francisco Psychoanalytic Institute – June 16, 1990'. *The American Psychoanalyst*. 25 (1): 15, 16, 20, 21.
Arlow, J. (1993) Discussion of 'The Mind of the Analyst'. *Int. J. Psycho-Anal.* 74: 1147–55.
Arlow, J. (1998) 'Comments on the Cleveland Dispute'. *The American Psychoanalyst*. 32 (3): 36–37.
Arlow, J. and Brenner, C. (1964) *Psychoanalytic Concepts and the Structural Theory*. New York: International Universities Press.

Arlow, J. and Brenner, C. (1988) 'The Future of Psychoanalysis'. *Psychoanalytic Quarterly*. 57: 1–14.
Arvidson, R. et al. (1974) Letter of Arvidson, Daniels, Gardner, Silverman and Stock to Arthur Valenstein, May 28.
Asch, S. and Marcus, E. (1988) 'The Current Status of Psychoanalysis in Medical Student Education in The United States: A Preliminary Overview'. *J. Amer. Psychoanal. Assn.* 36: 1033–57.
Atkin, S. (1962) 'The Fruition of an Idea', in M. Wangh, ed., *Fruition of an Idea: Fifty Years of Psychoanalysis in New York*. New York: International Universities Press, pp. 23–29.
Atkin, S. (1978) 'The New York Psychoanalytic Society and Institute: Its Founding and Development', in J. Quen and E. Carlson, eds, *American Psychoanalysis: Origins and Development*. New York: Brunner-Mazel, pp. 73–86.
Bail, B. (1991a) *History of Object Relations in L.A.* Videotape, Burbank.
Bail, B. (1991b) *The Freud-Klein Controversies (1973–1977) Los Angeles: The Testing Ground and Final Solution*. Beverly Hills: privately published.
Balint, M. (1948) 'On the Psychoanalytic Training System'. *Int. J. Psycho-Anal.* 29 153–74.
Balter, L., Lothane, Z. and Spencer Jr, J. (1980) 'On the Analyzing Instrument'. *Psychoanalytic Quarterly*. 49: 474–504.
Banham, R. (1973) *Los Angeles: The Architecture of Four Ecologies*. London: Penguin Books.
Bartling, L. and Hall, W. (1993) 'Institute for Psychoanalysis: Diagnosis Report for Board Development Project'. Typescript, January.
Basch, M. (1986) 'Can this be Psychoanalysis?', in A. Goldberg, ed., *Progress in Self Psychology*. Volume Two, New York: The Guilford Press, pp. 18–30.
Bergman, R. (1991) 'New Training Group formed in Los Angeles'. *The American Psychoanalyst*. 25 (2): 25–6.
Bergman, R. (1992) 'Delinkage Approved: Bylaw Amendment Passes, 792-111'. *The American Psychoanalyst*. 26 (2): 1–2.
Bernard, V. (1990) 'Start of Columbia Psychoanalytic Center'. Videotaped Interview with Viola Bernard by Ian Alger, May 14. Transcript.
Bernfeld, S. (1962) 'On Psychoanalytic Training'. *Psychoanalytic Quarterly*. 31: 453–82.
Bettelheim, B. (1983) *Freud and Man's Soul*. New York: Knopf.
Bion, W. (1980) *Bion in New York and Sao Paolo*. Pertshire: Clunie Press.
Bion, W. (1992) *Cogitations*. Francesca Bion, ed. London: Karnac Books.
Blum, H., Weinshel, E. and Rodman, F., eds (1989) *The Psychoanalytic Core: Essays in Honor of Leo Rangell. M.D.* Madison CT: International Universities Press.
Bollas, C. and Sundelson, D. (1995) *The New Informants: The Betrayal of Confidentiality in Psychoanalysis and Psychotherapy*. New York: Jason Aronson.
Boston Psychoanalytic Society (1974) Minutes of Small Discussion Group, Committee of the Whole, Boston Psychoanalytic Society.
Boston Psychoanalytic Society (1942) Constitution. Boston: BPSI.

Boston Psychoanalytic Society and Institute (1974) Telegram to Edward Weinshel, December 8.
Boston Psychoanalytic Society and Institute/Psychoanalytic Institite of New England East (1995) Boston Psychoanalytic Society and Institute Inc. and Psychoanalytic Society of New England, East, Inc. Letter to members, July.
Brandchaft, B. (1973) Discussion of Greenson's 'Transference: Freud or Klein'. Audiotape of discussion at the Los Angeles Psychoanalytic Society and Institute, September 20.
Brauer, L. (1998) '1996 Survey of Practice Highlights'. *The American Psychoanalyst.* 32 (2): 20, 24.
Brenner, C. (1973) *An Elementary Textbook of Psychoanalysis.* New York: International Universities Press. Revised edition. Original edition 1955.
Brenner, C. (1979) 'Working Alliance, Therapeutic Alliance, and Transference', in *Psychoanalytic Technique and Theory of Therapy, J. Amer. Psychoanal. Assn.* 27, Supp.: 137–58.
Brenner, C. (1986) 'Reflections', in A. Richards and M. Willick, eds, *Psychoanalysis: The Science of Mental Conflict: Essays in Honor of Charles Brenner.* Hillsdale NJ: The Analytic Press, pp. 39–44.
Brenner, C. (1994) 'The Mind as Conflict and Compromise Formation'. *Journal of Clinical Psychoanalysis* 3: 473–88.
Brent, S. (1962) *The Seven Stairs.* Boston MA: Houghton Mifflin.
Brickman, H. (1993) 'The Southern California Psychoanalytic Institute: A Brief History', *The American Psychoanalyst.* 27 (2): 10, 12.
Bromberg, W. (1982) *Psychiatry Between the Wars: A Recollection.* Westport CT: Greenwood Press.
Brown, P. and Barham, P. (1992) *Marilyn: The Last Take.* New York: Dutton.
Burnham, D. (1978) 'Orthodoxy and Eclecticism in American Psychoanalysis: The Washington-Baltimore Experience', in J. Quen and E. Carlson, eds, *American Psychoanalysis: Origins and Development.* New York: Brunner-Mazel, pp. 87–108.
Buttenwieser, P. (1981) *Free Association.* Boston: Little, Brown and Company.
Calder, K. (1980) 'Dr. Calder Assumes the Presidency'. *Newsletter of The New York Psychoanalytic Society and Institute.* 17 (3): 1.
Calder, K. (1991) Oral History Workshop #35, 'Psychoanalysis in New York'. American Psychoanalytic Association Meeting. Typescript, December 19.
Campbell, L., Lymmberis, M., Campbell, B., Donovan, W. and Decordoba, P. (1982) 'The CAPE Survey: Psychoanalytic Training from the Trainee's View'. *Journal of CAPE* (2) 2.
CAPE News (1976) 'Situation in L.A. Institute Critical'. 6 (1): 1, 4–6.
Chicago Tribune (1987) 'Dialogue vs. Drugs: Psychiatry's Mood Swings between the Lab and Couch', May 10.
Chicago Tribune (1989) 'Psychoanalysis Benefit on Edge, But Never Mind', *The Chicago Tribune,* June 9.
Chicago Tribune (1996) Obituary: Dr Charles Kligerman, April 17.
Cocks, G., ed. (1994) *The Curve of Life: Correspondence of Heinz Kohut 1923–1981.* Chicago IL: University of Chicago Press.

Cohen, S. (1994) 'LAPSI's Organizational Consultation'. Presented to LAPSI, October 29.
Colby, K. and Stoller, R. (1988) *Cognitive Science and Psychoanalysis*. Hillsdale NJ: The Analytic Press.
Coleman, D. et al. (1975) Letter from Coleman, Galenson, Joseph, Marcus Schlossmann, May 8, 1975 for May 12 meeting of the Board of Trustees, Brill Library.
Cooper, A. (1981) 'Research in Applied Analysis'. *Bulletin of the Association of Psychoanalytic Medicine*. 20 (2): 37–43.
Cooper, A. (1984) 'Psychoanalysis at One Hundred: The Beginnings of Maturity'. *J. Amer. Psychoanal. Assn.* 32: 245–68.
Cooper. A. (1987) 'The Changing Culture of Psychoanalysis'. *Journal of The American Academy of Psychoanalysis*. 15: 283–91.
Cooper. A. (1990) 'The Future of Psychoanalysis'. *Psychoanalytic Quarterly*. 59: 177–96.
Cooper. A. and Michels, R. (1978) 'Psychoanalysis and Future Growth', in J. Quen and E. Carlson, eds, *American Psychoanalysis: Origins and Development*. New York: Brunner-Mazel, pp. 189–209.
Coser, L. (1984) *Refugee Scholars in America: Their Impact and Their Experiences*. New Haven CT: Yale University Press.
Daniels, E. (1971) 'Annual Report of the President, April 1, 1970–March 31, 1971'. The Boston Psychoanalytic Society and Institute.
Daniels, G. (1971–72) 'History of the Association for Psychoanalytic Medicine and The Columbia Psychoanalytic Clinic'. *Bull. Assn. Psychoanal. Med.* 11 (1): 12–15; 11 (2): 26–31; 11 (3): 47–53.
Davidson, L. (1983) 'The Cultural School – A Survey of its Contributions'. *Academy Forum*, 27 (3): 11–12.
Decker, H. (1978) 'Psychoanalysis and the Europeans', in J. Quen and E. Carlson, eds, *American Psychoanalysis: Origins and Development*. New York: Brunner-Mazel, pp. 1–19.
Deutsch, H. (1983) 'On Supervised Analysis'. Introduction by Paul Roazen. *Contemporary Psychoanalysis* 19: 53–70.
Eckhardt, M. (1978) 'Organizational Schisms in American Psychoanalysis', in J. Quen and E. Carlson, eds, *American Psychoanalysis: Origins and Development*. New York: Brunner-Mazel, pp. 141–161.
Edelson, M. (1988) *Psychoanalysis: A Theory in Crisis*. Chicago IL: University of Chicago Press.
Eisenstein, S. (1975) 'The Birth of our Institute'. *25th Anniversary Issue. Bulletin of the Southern California Institute and Society*. 42 (April): 1–12.
Eisold, K. (1994) 'The Intolerance of Diversity in Psychoanalytic Institutes'. *Int. J. Psycho-Anal.* 75: 785–800.
Eissler, K. (1965) *Medical Orthodoxy and the Future of Psychoanalysis*. New York: International Universities Press.
Engle, R. (1996) 'Boston Split Throws Organizational Questions into Sharp Relief'. *The American Psychoanalyst* 30 (1): 31–2.
Fairbairn, W. R. D. (1952) *Psychoanalytic Studies in the Personality*. London: Tavistock.

Farber, S. and Green, M. (1993) *Hollywood on the Couch: A Candid Look at the Overheated Love Affair between Psychiatrists and Moviemakers*. New York: W. Morrow.

Federn, P. and Freud, E. (1972) Supplement, *Journal of the History of the Behavioral Sciences*, 8 (1).

Fermi, I. (1971) *Illustrious Migrants: The Intellectual Migration from Europe (1930–41)*. 2nd edn. Chicago IL: University of Chicago Press.

Fine, R. (1979) *A History of Psychoanalysis*. New York: Columbia University Press.

Fischer, N. (1982) 'Beyond Lay Analysis: Pathways to a Psychoanalytic Career'. *J. Amer. Psychoanal. Assn.* 30: 701–15.

Fisher, D. J. (1991) *Cultural Theory and Psychoanalytic Tradition*. New Brunswick: Transaction.

Fleming, J. (1987) 'The Training Analyst as Educator' (1973), in S. Weiss, ed., *The Teaching and Learning of Psychoanalysis: Selected Papers of Joan Fleming. M.D.* New York: The Guilford Press, pp. 62–80.

Fleming, J. and Benedek, T. (1987) 'The Experiential Nature of Psychoanalytic Learning' (1966) in S. Weiss, ed., *The Teaching and Learning of Psychoanalysis: Selected Papers of Joan Fleming. M.D.* New York: The Guilford Press, pp. 1–20.

Fox, R. (1991) 'Psychoanalytic Training and the Development of an Analytic Career: A Proposal for Revising the Structure of Psychoanalytic Education'. *Los Angeles Psychoanalytic Bulletin*, Spring: 21–4.

Freud, A. (1966) 'The Ideal Psychoanalytic Institute: A Utopia', in A. Freud, *Problems of Psychoanalytic Training. Diagnosis and the Technique of Therapy (1966–1970)*. New York: International Universities Press, 1971.

Freud, A. (1983) 'Some Observations', in E. Joseph and D. Widdocher, eds, *The Identity of the Psychoanalyst*. International Psycho-Analytical Association Monograph Series, Number 2, New York: International Universities Press, pp. 257–63.

Freud, S. (1893–95) in J. Breuer and S. Freud, *Studies on Hysteria*, in *The Standard Edition of the Complete Psychological Works of Sigmund Freud*. Translated by James Strachey, London: Hogarth Press and the Institute of Psycho-Analysis [hereafter *S.E.*], 24 vols, 1953–73, vol. 2.

Freud, S. (1900) *The Interpretation of Dreams*. *S.E.* 4–5.

Freud, S. (1905) 'Fragment of an Analysis of a Case of Hysteria'. *S.E.* 7: 7–122.

Freud, S. (1909) 'Analysis of a Phobia in a Five-Year-Old Boy'. *S.E.* 10: 3–147.

Freud, S. (1911) 'Formulations on the Two Principles of Mental Functioning'. *S.E.* 12: 218–26.

Freud, S. (1913) 'On Psycho-analysis'. *S.E.* 12: 207–11.

Freud, S. (1914) *On the History of the Psycho-Analytic Movement*. *S.E.* 14: 7–66.

Freud, S. (1915–16) *Introductory Lectures on Psycho-Analysis* (Parts 1 and 2). *S.E.* 15.

Freud, S. (1916–17) *Introductory Lectures on Psycho-Analysis* (Part III). *S.E.* 16.

Freud, S. (1919) 'Lines of Advance in Psycho-Analytic Therapy'. *S.E.* 17: 157–68.

Freud, S. (1921) *Group Psychology and the Analysis of the Ego*. *S.E.* 18: 69–143.

Freud, S. (1922) 'Two Encyclopedia Articles'. S.E. 18: 235–59.
Freud, S. (1923a) *The Ego and the Id*. S.E. 19.
Freud, S. (1923b) Preface to Max Eitington's *Report on The Berlin Psycho-Analytical Policlinic (March 1920 to June 1922)*. S.E. 19: 285.
Freud, S. (1925) 'The Resistances to Psycho-Analysis'. S.E. 19: 213–22.
Freud, S. (1926a) *Inhibitions. Symptoms and Anxiety*. S.E. 20: 87–175.
Freud, S. (1926b) 'Psychoanalysis'. S.E. 20: 259–74.
Freud, S. (1927a) 'Postscript' to *The Question of Lay Analysis*. S.E. 20: 251–8.
Freud, S. (1927b) *The Future of an Illusion*. S.E. 21: 5–56.
Freud, S. (1930a) Preface to *Ten Years of the Berlin Psycho-Analytic Institute*. S.E. 21: 257.
Freud, S. (1930b) *Civilization and its Discontents*. S.E. 21: 59–145.
Freud, S. (1933) *New Introductory Lectures on Psycho-Analysis*. S.E. 22.
Freud, S. (1937) 'Analysis Terminable and Interminable'. S.E. 23: 216–53.
Freud, S. (1938) *An Outline of Psycho-Analysis*. S.E. 23: 144–207.
Freud, S. (1963) in *Freud. Psychoanalysis and Faith: Letters of Freud and Pfister* (1928), New York: Basic Books.
Freud, S. (1974) *The Freud/Jung Letters; The Correspondence Between Sigmund Freud and C. G. Jung*. William Mcguire, ed. Princeton NJ: Princeton University Press.
Freud, S. and Abraham, K. (1963) in H. Abraham and E. Freud, eds, *A Psychoanalytic Dialogue: The Letters of Sigmund Freud and Karl Abraham (1907–1926)*. New York: Basic Books.
Friedman, L. (1974) Memo to Charles Magraw, January 18.
Friedman, L. (1990) *Menninger: The Family and the Clinic*. New York: Knopf.
Frosch, J. (1991) 'The New York Psychoanalytic Civil War'. *J. Amer. Psychoanal. Assn.* 39: 1037–64.
Frumkes, G. (1975) 'Comments on the Formation and Early History of the Southern California Psychoanalytic Institute and Society'. *25th Anniversary Issue. Bulletin of the Southern California Institute and Society*, 42, April: 14–16.
Furer, M. (1990) 'The New York Psychoanalytic Society and Institute: 1990'. *The American Psychoanalyst*, 24 (2): 7, 8.
Furer, M. (1996) 'Annual Report of the Educational Committee', *Newsletter of the New York Psychoanalytic Society and Institute*, 33 (3), July.
Gardner, H. (1993) *Frames of Mind: The Theory of Multiple Intelligences*. New York: Basic Books.
Gardner, M. R. (1974) Letter to Sanford Gifford. October 21.
Gardner, M. R. (1976) Letter to Sanford Gifford, February 17.
Gardner, M. R. (1994) *On Trying to Teach: The Mind in Correspondence*. Hillsdale NJ: The Analytic Press.
Gardner, M. R. and Kaplan, S. (1974) 'Synopsis of Proposed Developments in the society/institute', Memo to Charles Magraw, January 22.
Gay, P. (1988) *Freud: A Life for Our Time*. New York: Norton.
Gedo, J. (1979) 'A Psychoanalyst Reports at Mid-Career'. *Am. J. Psychiat.* 136: 646–9.

Gedo, J. (1984) *Psychoanalysis and its Discontents*. New York: The Guilford Press.
Gedo, J. (1986) *Conceptual Issues in Psychoanalysis: Essays in History and Method*. Hillsdale NJ: The Analytic Press.
Gedo, J. (1991) *The Biology of Clinical Encounters: Psychoanalysis as a Science of Mind*. Hillsdale NJ: The Analytic Press.
Gedo, J. (1997) *Spleen and Nostalgia: A Life and Work in Psychoanalysis*. New York: Jason Aronson.
Gifford, G., ed. (1978) *Psychoanalysis. Psychotherapy and the New England Medical Scene. 1894–1944*. New York: Science History Publications/USA.
Gifford, S. (1973) Letter to Paul Myerson, October 16.
Gifford, S. (1974a) Paper for Third Floor Discussion Group of the BPSI. Unpublished typescript, February 1.
Gifford, S. (1974b) Letter to Peter Reich, November 20.
Gifford, S. (1974c) Letter to Robert Gardner, October 23.
Gifford, S. (1975a) Letter to Arthur Valenstein, January 18.
Gifford, S. (1975b) Notes for the Visiting Committee. James McLaughlin Chairman. January 24.
Gifford, S. (1975c) Letter to Edward Weinshel, April 25.
Gifford, S. (1975d) Notes of PINE meeting at Rolf Arvidson's house, November 2.
Gifford, S. (1976) Letter to Bob Gardner, February 13.
Gifford, S. (1978) 'Psychoanalysis in Boston: Innocence and Experience. Introduction to the Panel Discussion – April 14, 1973', in G. Gifford, ed., *Psychoanalysis. Psychotherapy and The New England Medical Scene, 1894–1944*. New York: Science History Publications/USA, pp. 325–45.
Gifford, S. (1984) 'The First Fifty Years: 1933–1983'. *BPSI Newsletter*, 1 (1): 5–8.
Gifford, S. (1994) 'Between the Wars: Psychoanalysis in Europe (1918–1938)'. *Psychiatric Clinics of North America*, 17 (3): 649–65.
Gifford, S. (1995) for *Psychoanalysis in The United States*. Edgar Wallace IV, ed. Typescript.
Gill, M. (1983) 'The Point of View of Psychoanalysis: Energy Discharge or Person?' *Psychoanalysis and Contemporary Thought*, 6: 523–51.
Gill, M. (1984) 'Psychoanalysis and Psychotherapy: A Revision'. *Int. Rev. Psycho-Anal.* 11: 161–79.
Gill, M. (1991) 'Psychoanalysis and Psychotherapy'. Letter to the Editors, *Int. J. Psycho-Anal.* 72: 159–61.
Gitelson, M. (1963) 'On the Present Scientific and Social Position of Psychoanalysis', in M. Gitelson, *Psychoanalysis: Science and Profession*. New York: International Universities Press, 1973, pp. 342–59.
Glick, R. (1992) 'Columbia University Center for Psychoanalytic Training and Research'. Memorandum, July 14.
Goldberg, A., ed. (1985) *Progress in Self Psychology*. Volume 1. New York: The Guilford Press.
Goldberg, A., ed. (1986) *Progress in Self Psychology*. Volume 2. New York: The Guilford Press.

Goldberg, A. (1988) *A Fresh Look at Psychoanalysis: The View from Self Psychology*. Hillsdale NJ: The Analytic Press.
Gooch, J. (1990) 'The Psychoanalytic Center of California from Conception to Birth'. *Newsletter of the Psychoanalytic Center of California*, 3 (2): 5-6.
Goode, E. (1999) 'To the Couch: A Revival for Analysis'. *The New York Times*, January 12.
Goodman, S., ed. (1977) *Psychoanalytic Education and Research: The Current Situation and Future Possibilities*. New York: International Universities Press.
Gopnik, A. (1998) 'Man goes to see a Doctor: Six Years on the Couch, and the Author's Shrink did most of the Talking'. *The New Yorker*, August, 24-31: 84-9, 120-1.
Greenson, R. (1962) 'Interview with Ralph R. Greenson' by R. Stoller, Committee for The History of the Society, transcript, LAPSI Library, December 12.
Greenson, R. (1965) 'The Working Alliance and the Transference Neurosis', in *Explorations in Psychoanalysis*. New York: International Universities Press, 1978, pp. 199-224.
Greenson, R. (1967) *The Technique and Practice of Psychoanalysis: Volume 1*. New York: International Universities Press.
Greenson, R. (1968) 'Dis-Identifying From Mother: Its Special Importance to the Boy'. *Int. J. Psycho-Anal.* 49: 370-4.
Greenson, R. (1969) 'The Origin and Fate of New Ideas in Psychoanalysis', in *Explorations in Psychoanalysis*. New York: International Universities Press, 1978, pp. 333-57.
Greenson, R. (1971) 'The "Real" Relationship between the Psychoanalyst and his Patient', in *Explorations in Psychoanalysis*. New York: International Universities Press, 1978, pp. 425-41.
Greenson, R. (1972) '"The Voice of the Intellect is a Soft One": A Review of the *Writings of Anna Freud* Volume IV (1946-1956)'. *Int. J. Psycho-Anal.* 53: 403-17.
Greenson, R. (1973) 'Transference: Freud or Klein'. Audiotape of Paper Delivered to the Los Angeles Psychoanalytic Society, Los Angeles Psychoanalytic Institute, September 20.
Greenson, R. (1974) 'Transference: Freud or Klein'. *[Int. J. Psycho-Anal.* 55: 37-48], in *Explorations in Psychoanalysis*. New York: International Universities Press, 1978, pp. 519-39.
Greenson, R. (1978) *Explorations in Psychoanalysis*. New York: International Universities Press.
Greenson, R. (1992) *On Loving. Hating and Living Well: The Public Psychoanalytic Lectures of Ralph R. Greenson. M.D.* R. Nemiroff, A., Sugarman, and A. Robbins, eds. Madison CT: International Universities Press.
Greenson, R. and Wexler, M. (1969) 'The Nontransference Relationship in The Psychoanalytic Situation', in Greenson, *Explorations in Psychoanalysis*. New York: International Universities Press, 1978, pp. 359-86.

Grinberg, L. and Grinberg, R. (1984) 'A Psychoanalytic Study of Migration: Its Normal and Pathological Aspects'. *J. Amer. Psychoanal. Assn.* 32: 13–38.
Grinker, R. (1965) 'Identity or Regression in American Psychoanalysis?'*Arch. Gen. Psychiatry.* 12: 113–25.
Grinker R. (1975) *Psychiatry in Broad Perspective.* New York: Behavioral Publications.
Grinker R. (1979) *Fifty Years of Psychiatry: A Living History.* Springfield IL: Charles A. Thomas.
Grinker R. (1995) 'The History of Psychoanalysis in Chicago: 1911–1975'. *Annual of Psychoanalysis,* 23: 155–95 (Original typescript 1975).
Grob, G. (1983) *Mental Illness and American Society. 1875–1940.* Princeton NJ: Princeton University Press.
Grosskurth, P. (1986) *Melanie Klein: Her World and Her Work.* New York: Knopf.
Grotstein, J., ed. (1983) *Do I Dare Disturb the Universe: A Memorial to Wilfred R. Bion.* Caesura Press, 1981. Reprinted By H. Karnac (Books) Ltd. As Maresfield Reprints.
Grotstein, J. and Rinsley, D., eds (1998) *Fairbairn and Origins of Object Relations.* New York: Other Press.
Grünbaum, A. (1984) *The Foundations of Psychoanalysis: A Philosophical Critique,* Berkeley: University of California Press.
Gunther, M. (1988a) 'Survey of Chicago Institute for Psychoanalysis Committee Appointments 1975–1987'. Unpublished, October.
Gunther, M. (1988b) 'Cassandra Papers, Chicago Institute for Psychoanalysis: Statistical Analyses of Teaching Assignments and Courses (1975–1988)'. Unpublished, December.
Guntrip, H. (1961) *Personality Structure and Human Interaction: The Developing Synthesis in Psycho-Dynamic Theory.* New York: International Universities Press.
Gutman, S. (1985) 'The Psychoanalytic Point of View: Basic Concepts and Deviant Theories: A Brief Communication'. *Int. J. Psycho-Anal.* 66: 169–70.
Hadda, J. (1991) 'A Report from a Participant Observer'. *The American Psychoanalyst,* 25 (2): 25, 27.
Hale, D. (1988) 'Prominent Psychoanalyst under Fire takes Leave from Chicago Institute'. Associated Press, May 12, Thursday, a.m. cycle.
Hale, N. (1971a) *Freud and the Americans: The Beginnings of Psychoanalysis in the United States. 1876–1917.* New York: Oxford University Press.
Hale, N., ed. (1971b) *James Jackson Putnam and Psychoanalysis: Letters between Putnam and Sigmund Freud. Ernest Jones. William James. Sandor Ferenczi. and Morton Prince. 1877–1917.* Cambridge MA: Harvard University Press.
Hale, N. (1978) 'From Bergasse XIX to Central Park West: The Americanization of Psychoanalysis'. *Journal of the History of the Behavioral Sciences* 14: 299–315.
Hale, N. (1995) *The Rise and Crisis of Psychoanalysis in the United States: Freud and the Americans 1917–1985.* New York: Oxford University Press.
Harrison, S. (1970) 'Is Psychoanalysis "Our Science"? Reflections on the Scientific Status of Psychoanalysis'. *J. Amer. Psychoanal. Assn.* 18: 125–49.

Hartmann, H. (1964) *Ego Psychology and the Problem of Adaptation* (1939). New York: International Universities Press.
Hauser, S. (1992) 'The Fund for Psychoanalytic Research: Recent Work and Future Visions'. *The American Psychoanalyst* 26 (2): 21–2.
Hendrick, I. (1955) 'Presidential Address: Professional Standards of The American Psychoanalytic Association'. *J. Amer. Psychoanal. Assn.* 3: 561–99.
Hendrick, I. (1961a) 'The Birth of an Institute', in I. Hendrick, *The Birth of an Institute*. Freeport ME: The Bond Wheelwright Company, pp. 1–94.
Hendrick, I., ed. (1961b) *The Birth of an Institute*. Freeport ME: The Bond Wheelwright Company.
Hicks, R. (1993) 'Four Decades of Psychoanalysis in San Diego'. *The American Psychoanalyst* 27 (2): 13, 24.
Holt, R. (1989) *Freud Reappraised: A Fresh Look at Psychoanalytic Theory*. New York: The Guilford Press.
Holt, R. (1992) 'The Contemporary Crises of Psychoanalysis'. *Psychoanalysis and Contemporary Thought*. 15: 375–403.
Holzman, P. (1976) 'The Future of Psychoanalysis and its Institutes'. *Psychoanalytic Quarterly* 45: 250–73.
Holzman, P. (1983) Discussion of Wallerstein, *Bulletin of the Menninger Clinic* 47: 518–21.
Holzman, P. (1985) 'Psychoanalysis: Is the Therapy Destroying The Science?' *J. Amer. Psychoanal. Assn.* 33: 725–70.
Hunter, V. (1994) *Psychoanalysts Talk*. New York: The Guilford Press.
Institute for Psychoanalysis (1983) *Annual Report*. Chicago: Institute for Psychoanalysis.
Jacobs, T. (n.d.) 'Dreams and Responsibility: Notes on the Making of an Institute'. Typescript.
Jacoby, R. (1983) *The Repression of Psychoanalysis: Otto Fenichel and the Political Freudians*. New York: Basic Books.
Jahoda, M. (1969) 'The Migration of Psychoanalysis', in D. Fleming and B. Bailyn, eds, *The Intellectual Migration: Europe and America (1930–1960)*. Cambridge: Harvard University Press.
Jaques, E. (1976) *A General Theory of Bureaucracy*. London: Heinemann.
Jaques, E. (1989) *Requisite Organization: The CEO's Guide to Creative Structure and Leadership*. Arlington VA: Cason Hall and Co.
Jaques, E. (1990) *Creativity and Work*. Madison CT: International Universities Press.
Jaques, E. (1995) 'Why the Psychoanalytical Approach to Understanding Organizations is Dysfunctional'. *Human Relations*, 48: 343–49.
Jaques, E. (1996) *Requisite Organization* (2nd edn). Falls Church VA: Cason Hall.
Jaques, E. and Cason, K. (1994) *Human Capability*. Arlington VA: Cason Hall.
Jeffrey, W. (1989a) 'After the *Anschluss:* The Emergency Committee on Relief and Immigration of The American Psychoanalytic Association'. *The American Psychoanalyst*, 23 (2–3): 19–20.

Jeffrey, W. (1989b) 'New York's Three Institutes: Four Decades of Coexistence'. *The American Psychoanalyst*, 23 (4): 6–8, 23.
Jeffrey, W. (1996) 'As LAPSI Celebrates 50th, LA Seeks Concord'. *The American Psychoanalyst*, 30 (4): 26–8.
Jones, E. (1953–57) *Sigmund Freud: Life and Work*. 3 Volumes. London: Hogarth Press.
Kairys, D. (1964) 'The Training Analysis: A Critical Review of the Literature and a Controversial Proposal'. *Psychoanalytic Quarterly*, 33: 485–512.
Kandelin, A. (1966) 'California's First Psychoanalytic Society'. *Bulletin of the Menninger Clinic*, 30: 351–7.
Kaplan, J. (1997) 'The Final Analysis'. *New York Magazine*, October 20, pp. 26–33.
Kardiner, A. (1963) Interview with Blumer Swerdloff. Columbia University Oral History Project.
Kavka, J. (1984) 'Fifty Years of Psychoanalysis in Chicago: A Historical Perspective', in G. Pollock and J. Gedo, eds, *Psychoanalysis: The Vital Issues:* Volume 2. New York: International Universities Press, pp. 465–93.
Kernberg, O. (1980) *Internal World and External Reality: Object Relations Theory Applied*. New York: Jason Aronson.
Kernberg, O. (1982) Book Review of *Advances in Self Psychology*. Arnold Goldberg, ed., *Am. J. Psychiatry*, 139: 374–75.
Kernberg, O. (1986) 'Institutional Problems of Psychoanalytic Education'. *J. Amer. Psychoanal. Assn.*, 34: 799–834.
Kernberg, O. (1996) 'Thirty Methods to Destroy The Creativity of Psychoanalytic Candidates'. *Int. J. Psycho-Anal.*, 77: 1031–40.
Kirsner, D. (1982) 'Self-Psychology and the Psychoanalytic Movement: An Interview with Dr. Heinz Kohut'. *Psychoanalysis and Contemporary Thought*, 5: 483–95.
Kirsner, D. (1986) 'The Other Psychoanalysis'. *Psychoanalysis and Contemporary Thought*, 9: 299–330.
Kirsner, D. (1999) 'Life Among the Analysts'. *Free Associations*, 416–36.
Klein, M. (1927) 'Symposium on Child Analysis', in *Love, Guilt and Reparation and Other Works*. London: Hogarth Press, 1975, pp. 139–69.
Knight, R. (1953) 'The Present Status of Organized Psychoanalysis in the United States'. *J. Amer. Psychoanal. Assn.*, 1: 197–221.
Knight, R. (1995) 'Folklore: Judy Collins' Dance Card is Filled with a New Album, Novel and 23-City Tour'. *Chicago Tribune*, June 25.
Kohut, H. (1974) Letter to the Author: Preface to *Lehrjahre Aur Der Couch* by Tilmann Moser in P. Ornstein (ed.), *The Search for the Self: Selected Writings of Heinz Kohut: 1950–1978*, Volume 2. New York: International Universities Press, 1978, pp. 724–36.
Kubie, L. (1962) 'Psychoanalysis and the American Scene', in M. Wangh, ed., *Fruition of an Idea: Fifty Years of Psychoanalysis in New York*. New York: International Universities Press, pp. 62–76.
Kurtzweil, E. (1995) 'USA', in P. Kutter, ed., *Psychoanalysis International: A Guide to Psychoanalysis Around The World*. Vol. 2, Frommann-Holzboog, pp. 186–234.

Lachmann, F. (1992) 'Three Self Psychologies or One?', in A. Goldberg, ed., *The Evolution of Self Psychology. Progress in Self Psychology, Volume 7*. Hillsdale NJ: The Analytic Press, pp. 167–74.

Lanes, S. and Corbin, E. (1981) 'History of the Division of Psychoanalytic Education', in *Clinical Psychoanalysis*. Downstate Psychoanalytic Institute Twenty-Fifth Anniversary Series, Volume III, New York: Jason Aronson, pp. 295–309.

Langer, W. and Gifford, S (1978) 'An American Analyst in Vienna during the Anschluss: 1936–1938'. *Journal of the History of the Behavioral Sciences*, 14: 37–54.

Laplanche J. and Pontalis, J-B. (1973) *The Language of Psycho-Analysis*. London: Hogarth Press.

Law Bulletin (1988) 'Settlement ends Will Dispute', November 14.

Lear, J. (1998) *Open Minded: Working Out the Logic of the Soul*. Cambridge: Harvard University Press.

Leavitt, M. (1986) '10/40 Celebration: The Founders'. *Los Angeles Psychoanalytic Bulletin*, Special Anniversary Issue, December: 25–32.

Levenson, E. (1983) *The Ambiguity of Change: An Inquiry into the Nature of Psychoanalytic Reality*. New York: Basic Books.

Levenson, E. (1991) *The Purloined Self: Interpersonal Perspectives in Psychoanalysis*. New York: Contemporary Psychoanalysis Books.

Levin, S. and Michaels, J. (1961) 'The Participation of Psycho-Analysts in The Medical Institutions of Boston'. *Int. J. Psycho-Anal.*, 62: 271–7.

Lewin, B. and Ross, H. (1960) *Psychoanalytic Education in the United States*. New York: Norton.

Lewin, B. (1961) 'The Organization of Psychoanalytic Education', in I. Hendrick, ed., *The Birth of an Institute*. Freeport ME: The Bond Wheelwright Company, pp. 95–118.

Lewy, E. (1963) 'Interview with Ernst Lewy' by A. Kandelin. Committee for The History of the Society, Transcript, LAPSI Library, February 24.

Lichtenberg J. and Kaplan, S., eds. (1983) *Reflections on Self Psychology*. Hillsdale NJ: The Analytic Press.

Lifson, L. (1987) 'Analysis of a Psychoanalytic Society: Boston 1984'. *The American Psychoanalytic Association Newsletter*, 21 (3): 6, 7, 10, 11.

Lindon, J. (1975) 'An Unfinished Saga: The American Psychoanalytic Association'. *25th Anniversary Issue. Bulletin of the Southern California Institute and Society*. 42, April: 8–12.

Loewenstein, R. (1962) 'Europe's Coming to America', in Wangh, M., ed., *Fruition of an Idea: Fifty Years of Psychoanalysis in New York*. New York: International Universities Press, pp. 44–5.

Lorand, S. (1969) 'Reflections on The Development of Psychoanalysis in New York from 1925'. *Int. J. Psycho-Anal.*, 50: 589–95.

Los Angeles Times (1997) Obituary for Rosengarten, May 17.

Lothane, Z. (1981) 'Listening with The Third Ear as an Instrument in Psychoanalysis'. *Psychoanalytic Review* 68: 487–503.

McDaniel, C. G. (1979) Associated Press, May 6, Sunday, a.m. cycle.

McDougall, J. (1995) *The Many Faces of Eros: A Psychoanalytic Exploration of Human Sexuality*. Norton: New York.

Magraw, C. et al. (1974) Charles Magraw and sixty other members of BPSI, Letter to Edward Weinshel, December 10.

Mahler, M. (1969/74) Interview with Blumer Swerdloff. Columbia University Oral History Project.

Malcolm, J. (1981) *Psychoanalysis: The Impossible Profession*. New York: Knopf.

Malin, A. (1991) 'A Letter to the Editor'. *Los Angeles Psychoanalytic Bulletin*. Fall: 57–9.

Mandel, M. (1986) 'Political History of LAPSI'. *Los Angeles Psychoanalytic Bulletin*. Special Anniversary Issue, December: 43–53.

Mandel, M. (1991) 'A Splitting Revisited'. *The American Psychoanalyst*. 25 (2): 25–6.

Mandel, M. (1996a) 'Oral History Workshop #42, May 2, American Psychoanalytic Association Meeting, Los Angeles. Transcript.

Mandel, M. (1996b) 'In L.A., A Federation of Four IPA Institutes works toward Unity and Inclusion'. *The American Psychoanalyst*, 30 (2): 15–16.

Marcuse, H. (1965) 'Repressive Tolerance', in R. Wolf, B. Moore Jr and H. Marcuse, *A Critique of Pure Tolerance*. Boston MA: Beacon Press, 1969, pp. 81–117.

Marmor, J. (1975) 'Comments on the formation and Early History of the Southern California Psychoanalytic Institute and Society'. *25th Anniversary Issue. Bulletin of the Southern California Institute and Society*, 42, April: 16.

Maroda, K. (1989) Commentary on 'Writing About Psychoanalysis'. *J. Amer. Psychoanal. Assn.*, 37: 564–6.

Mason, A. (1973) Discussion of Greenson's 'Transference: Freud or Klein'. Audiotape of paper delivered to the Los Angeles Psychoanalytic Society, Los Angeles Psychoanalytic Institute, September 20.

Mason, A. (1981) 'Notes on Wilfred Bion', in L. Wolberg and M. Aronson, eds, *Group and Family Therapy*. New York: Brunner-Mazel, pp. 9–16.

Mason, A. (1985) 'A Postscript'. *Los Angeles Psychoanalytic Bulletin*, pp. 11–16.

Masson, J. (1990) *Final Analysis: The Making and Unmaking of a Psychoanalyst*. New York: Addison-Wesley.

Mayer, E. (1992) 'A Conversation with Robert Wallerstein'. *The American Psychoanalyst*. 26 (1): 21–2.

Menninger, K. (1988) *The Selected Correspondence of Karl A. Menninger 1919–1945*. H. J. Faulkner and V. D. Pruitt, eds. New Haven: Yale University Press.

Menninger, W. (1948) *Psychiatry in a Troubled World: Yesterday's War and Today's Challenge*. New York: Macmillan.

Michaels, J. (1961) 'Chairman's Remarks', in I. Hendrick, ed., *The Birth of an Institute*. Freeport ME: The Bond Wheelwright Company, pp. 155–9.

Michels, R. (1976) 'Professional Ethics and Social Values'. *Int. Rev. Psycho-Anal*. 377–84.

Michels, R. (1988) 'The Future of Psychoanalysis'. *Psychoanalytic Quarterly*, 57: 167–82.

Michels, R. (1991) Oral History Workshop #35. 'Psychoanalysis in New York'. American Psychoanalytic Association Meeting, December 19.
Mitchell, J. (1986) *The Selected Melanie Klein*. Harmondsworth: Penguin Books.
Modell, A. (1994) 'Arnold Modell'. Interview with Virginia Hunter, in V. Hunter, *Psychoanalysts Talk*. New York: The Guilford Press, pp. 349–70.
Molino, A., ed. (1997) *Freely Associated: Encounters in Psychoanalysis with Christopher Bollas, Joyce McDougall, Michael Eigen, Adam Phillips and Nina Coltart*. London: Free Association Books.
Moritz, L. (1990) 'Three Nonmedical US Institutes Accredited By IPA'. *The American Psychoanalyst*, 24 (1): 16–19.
Murray, J. (1961) 'Concluding Remarks', in I. Hendrick, ed., *The Birth of an Institute*. Freeport ME: The Bond Wheelwright Company, pp. 119–25.
Myerson, P. (1973a) *President's Newsletter*, 11, May 24. Boston Psychoanalytic Society and Institute.
Myerson, P. (1973b) *President's Newsletter*, 12, September 3. Boston Psychoanalytic Society and Institute.
Myerson, P. (1973c) Myerson, *President's Newsletter*, 13, November 26. Boston Psychoanalytic Society and Institute.
New York Psychoanalytic Institute (1975) Minutes of Board of Trustees, NY Institute, May 12. Brill Library.
New York Psychoanalytic Institute (1985a) *The Newsletter. Special Supplement*, July.
New York Psychoanalytic Institute (1985b) 'Report of the Meeting of the Educational Committee of March 5, 1985', in New York Psychoanalytic Institute 1985a, pp. 11–13.
New York Psychoanalytic Society (1946) *Bylaws of the NY Society* (adopted March 26).
New York Psychoanalytic Society and Institute (1976) 'History of the Society and Institute, II: Dr. Samuel Atkin at Cornell', *Newsletter of the New York Psychoanalytic Society and Institute*, 13, 4, October.
New York Psychoanalytic Society and Institute (1978a) *Newsletter of the New York Psychoanalytic Society and Institute*, Special Edition, January.
New York Psychoanalytic Society and Institute (1978b) *Newsletter of the New York Psychoanalytic Society and Institute*, 15, June.
New York Psychoanalytic Society and Institute (1980) *Newsletter of the New York Psychoanalytic Society and Institute*, 17, 1.
New York Psychoanalytic Society and Institute (1981) 'Interview with Dr Irwin Solomon', *Newsletter of the New York Psychoanalytic Society and Institute*, 20, 2, May 1981.
New York Psychoanalytic Society and Institute (1983a) 'Report of Meeting of the Board of Trustee Meeting, January 20, 1983. *Newsletter of the New York Psychoanalytic Society and Institute*, 20, 3, p. 10.
New York Psychoanalytic Society and Institute (1983b) 'Report of the Meeting of Board of Trustees of February 24, 1983', *Newsletter of the New York Psychoanalytic Society and Institute*, 20, 3, pp. 11–12.

New York Psychoanalytic Society and Institute (1983c) 'Interview with Dr Arthur Root', *Newsletter of the New York Psychoanalytic Society and Institute*, 20, 3.
New York Psychoanalytic Society and Institute (1985) Board of Trustees meeting, September 19, 1985, *Newsletter of the New York Psychoanalytic Society and Institute*, 22, 6.
New York Psychoanalytic Society and Institute (1986a) *Newsletter of the New York Psychoanalytic Society and Institute*, 23, 1, January.
New York Psychoanalytic Society and Institute (1986b) *Newsletter of the New York Psychoanalytic Society and Institute*, 23, 2.
New York Psychoanalytic Society and Institute (1986c) *Newsletter of the New York Psychoanalytic Society and Institute*, 23, 3.
New York Psychoanalytic Society and Institute (1991) *Newsletter of the New York Psychoanalytic Society and Institute*, 28, 3.
Oakley, C. and Oakley, H. (1998) From Chris and Haya Oakley's Founding Statement for 'The Site for Contemporary Psychoanalysis', in *The THERIP Newsletter*, Spring, London.
Oberndorf, C. (1927) 'Discussion on Lay Analysis'. *Int. J. Psycho-Anal.*, 8: 201–7.
Oberndorf, C. (1953) *A History of Psychoanalysis in America*. New York: Harper & Row.
Orgel, S. (1982) 'The Selection and Function of Training Analysts in North American Institutes'. *Int. Rev. of Psycho-Anal.*, 9: 417–34.
Orgel, S. (1990) 'The Future of Psychoanalysis'. *Psychoanalytic Quarterly*, 59: 1–20.
Ornstein, P., ed. (1978) *The Search for The Self: Selected Writings of Heinz Kohut: 1950–1978*. Volumes 1 and 2. New York: International Universities Press.
Ostow, M. (1979) Letter to the Editor, *Int. J. Psycho-Anal.*, 60: 531–32.
O'Sullivan, J. (1998) 'Far Too Long on the Couch'. *Independent*, August 4, p. 13.
Paul Weiss et al. (1970) Memorandum about a business meeting in 1970 from Paul Weiss Goldberg Rifkind and Stafford, March 30. Brill Library.
Perkiss, M. (1988) 'Judge Declares Mistrial in Lederer Will Dispute', Associated Press, November 2, Wednesday, a.m. cycle.
Person, E. (1990) 'The Columbia University Center for Psychoanalytic Training and Research'. *The American Psychoanalyst*, 24 (2): 9–11.
Peterfreund, E. (1983) *The Process of Psychoanalytic Therapy: Models and Strategies*. Hillsdale NJ: The Analytic Press.
Peterfreund, E. (1985) 'The Heuristic Approach to Psychoanalytic Therapy', in J. Reppen, ed., *Analysts at Work*. Hillsdale NJ: The Analytic Press, pp. 127–43.
Peterson, F. (1933) Editorial, *JAMA* 100, 15, April 15, p. 1176.
Pollock, G. (1977) 'The Psychosomatic Specificity Concept: Evolution, Re-Evaluation'. *Annual Psychoanal.*, 5: 141–68.

Pollock, G. (1978) 'The Chicago Institute for Psychoanalysis From 1932 to the Present', in J. Quen and E. Carlson, eds, *American Psychoanalysis: Origins and Development*. New York: Brunner-Mazel, pp. 109–26.
Pollock, G. (1982) 'Heinz Kohut: 1913–1981'. *Psychoanalytic Quarterly*, 51: 284–5.
Pollock, G. (1983) 'The Presence of the Past'. *The Annual of Psychoanalysis*, 11: 3–27.
Pollock, G. and Pilot, M. (1970) 'Psychosomatic Specificity Hypothesis Testing'. *Bull. Menninger Clin.*, 34: 85–8.
Post, S. (1986) 'Psychoanalytic Rapprochement: A Correspondence'. *Academy Forum*, 30, p. 21.
Psychoanalytic Institute of New England East, Inc. (1974) Statement to BPSI Candidates and Members.
Pulver, S. (1978) 'Survey of Psychoanalytic Practice 1976; Some Trends and Implications'. *J. Amer. Psychoanal. Assn.* 26: 615–31.
Quen, J. and Carlson, E., eds (1978) *American Psychoanalysis: Origins and Development*. New York: Brunner-Mazel.
Quinn, S. (1987) *A Mind of her Own: The Life of Karen Horney*. New York: Summit.
Rado, S. (1963) Interview with Blumer Swerdloff. Columbia University Oral History Project.
Rangell, L. (1974) 'A Psychoanalytic Perspective Leading Currently to the Syndrome of the Compromise of Integrity'. *Int. J. Psycho-Anal.*, 55: 3–12.
Rangell, L. (1980) *The Mind of Watergate: An Exploration of the Compromise of Integrity*. New York: Norton.
Rangell, L. (1982) 'Transference to Theory: The Relationship of Psychoanalytic Education to the Analyst's Relationship to Psychoanalysis'. *The Annual of Psychoanalysis*, 10, pp. 29–56.
Rangell, L. (1988a) 'A Look Around'. *Los Angeles Psychoanalytic Bulletin*. Special Issue Honoring Leo Rangell, M.D. Winter: 55–60.
Rangell, L. (1988b) 'The Future of Psychoanalysis: The Scientific Crossroads'. *Psychoanalytic Quarterly*. 57: 313–40.
Rangell, L. (1988c) 'Let Them be Known by their Deeds and Character, Not by their Charisma'. *Los Angeles Times*, August 4.
Rangell, L. (1993) 'From Anxiety to Integrity: The Paradigmatic Journey of Psychoanalysis'. Simmel-Fenichel Lecture of the Los Angeles Psychoanalytic Society and Institute. Typescript, March 5.
Rankin, Z. (1992) 'A Look at the Two Women who were the Movie Star'. *The Houston Chronicle*, September 20.
Richards, A. (1986) 'Introduction' to *Psychoanalysis: The Science of Mental Conflict: Essays in Honor of Charles Brenner*. Hillsdale NJ: The Analytic Press, pp. 1–27.
Richards, A. (1990) 'The Future of Psychoanalysis'. *Psychoanalytic Quarterly*, 59: 347–69.
Richards, A. (1995) 'A. A. Brill: The Politics of Exclusion and the Politics of Pluralism'. Presented at the New York Psychoanalytic Society as the 47th A. A. Brill Lecture, November 28.

Richards, A. and Willick, M., eds (1986) *Psychoanalysis: The Science of Mental Conflict: Essays in Honor of Charles Brenner.* Hillsdale NJ: The Analytic Press.
Rieff, D. (1992) *Los Angeles: Capital of the Third World.* New York: Simon and Schuster.
Rieff, P. (1966) *The Triumph of the Therapeutic.* New York: Harper & Row.
Ritter, J. (1997) 'Analysts Honor Self-psychology's Chicago founder', *Chicago Sun-Times,* November 17.
Riviere, J. (1937) 'Hate, Greed and Aggression' in M. Klein and J. Riviere, *Love. Hate and Reparation.* London: Hogarth Press.
Roazen, P, and Swerdloff, B. (1995) *Heresy: Sandor Rado and The Psychoanalytic Movement.* Northvale NJ: Jason Aronson.
Rodman, F. (1982) 'Interview with Ivan McGuire, M.D.'. *Los Angeles Psychoanalytic Bulletin,* 1 (2): 2–19.
Rodman, F. (1983) 'Interview with Dr. Albert Mason'. *Los Angeles Psychoanalytic Bulletin,* 1, (4): 2–16.
Rodman, F. (1989) 'Leo Rangell and the Integrity of Psychoanalysis', in H. Blum, E. Weinshel, and F. Rodman, eds, *The Psychoanalytic Core: Essays in Honor of Leo Rangell, M.D.* Madison CT: International Universities Press, pp. 15–43.
Rodman, F. and Wilson, S. (1988) 'Interview with Leo Rangell, M.D.'. *Los Angeles Psychoanalytic Bulletin. Special Issue Honoring Leo Rangell. M.D.,* Winter: 6–20.
Rogow, A. (1970) *The Psychiatrists,* New York: G. P. Putnam's Sons.
Roose, L. (1975) 'Minority Report of ad hoc Committee Concerned with the Composition of the EC, April 23, 1975'. Brill Library.
Rosen, V. (1962) 'The Relationship Between the Institute and the Community', in M. Wangh, ed., *Fruition of an Idea: Fifty Years of Psychoanalysis in New York.* New York: International Universities Press, pp. 47–84.
Rosenfeld, H. (1974) 'A Discussion of the Paper by Ralph R. Greenson on 'Transference: Freud or Klein''. *Int. J. Psycho-Anal.* 55: 37–48.
Rosengarten, L. (1986) 'The Early Years'. *Los Angeles Psychoanalytic Bulletin.* Special Anniversary Issue, December: 10–24.
Rosten, L. (1961) *Captain Newman. M.D.,* London: Victor Gollancz.
Rothstein, A. (1980) 'Psychoanalytic Paradigms and their Narcissistic Investment'. *J. Amer. Psychoanal. Assn.,* 28: 385–95.
Roustang, F. (1982) *Dire Mastery: Discipleship From Freud to Lacan.* Trans. N. Lukacher, Baltimore MD: Johns Hopkins University Press.
Rubin, L. (1991) 'Interview with Charles Brenner – Part 2'. *Boston Psychoanalytic Society and Institute Inc. Newsletter,* 7 (2): 4–7.
Rubins, J. (1978) *Karen Horney: Gentle Rebel of Psychoanalysis.* New York: The Dial Press.
Scott, G. (1997) 'Pills are Replacing Psychiatrists in Era of HMOs'. *The Plain Dealer,* May 13.
Shakow, D. (1962) 'Psychoanalytic Education of Behavioral and Social Scientists for Research'. *Sci. Psychoanal.,* 5: 146–61.

Shane, E. (1987) 'Board Approves Waivers for Non-Medical Training' in *The American Psychoanalytic Association Newsletter*, 21 (2): 1.

Shane, E. (1988) 'Robert S. Wallerstein: Researcher, Educator and Organizer' (Interview). *The American Psychoanalytic Association Newsletter*, 22 (3): 1, 4, 5, 6, 7, 10, 11, 12, 14, 15.

Shane, E. (1992) 'Self Psychology Expanding: A Consideration of Recent Books by Michael Basch, Arnold Goldberg, and Robert Stolorow, Bernard Brandchaft and George Atwood', in A. Goldberg, ed., *The Evolution of Self Psychology. Progress in Self Psychology*. Volume 7. Hillsdale NJ: The Analytic Press, pp. 157–66.

Shane, M. (1986) 'Theoretical History: 1955 to the Present'. *Los Angeles Psychoanalytic Bulletin*. Special Anniversary Issue, December: 33–42.

Shane, M. and Shane, E. (1992) 'Transference, Countertransference and The Real Relationship', in A. Sugarman, R. Nemiroff and D. Greenson, eds, *The Technique and Practice of Psychoanalysis: Volume 2: A Memorial Volume to Ralph R. Greenson*. Madison CT: International Universities Press, pp. 285–303.

Shershow, L. (1986) '10/40 Celebration: The Founders'. *Los Angeles Psychoanalytic Bulletin*. Special Anniversary Issue, December: 4–9.

Shershow, L. (1993) 'The Los Angeles Psychoanalytic Institute: Cycles of Growth'. *The American Psychoanalyst*, 27 (2): 9, 24.

Shorter, E. (1997) *A History of Psychiatry*. New York: John Wiley and Sons.

Sicherman, B. (1978) 'The New Psychiatry: Medical and Behavioral Science, 1895–1921', in J. Quen and E. Carlson, eds, *American Psychoanalysis: Origins and Development*. New York: Brunner-Mazel, pp. 20–37.

Sigg, B. (1990) *Les murs de la psychanalyse: conditions de la pratique*. Paris: Messidor/Editions Sociales.

Slavin, J. (1989) 'The Process of Establishing a Psychoanalytic Training Program. Remarks to Symposium of Philadelphia Society for Psychoanalytic Psychology'. September. Typescript.

Slavin, J. (1990) 'Sources of Legitimacy and Authority in Psychoanalytic Training: an Inquiry Into the Symbolic Meaning of the IPA'. Paper presented to the Spring Meeting of the Division of Psychoanalysis, American Psychological Association, New York City, April. Typescript.

Sloan, J. (1996) *Jerzy Kosinski: A Biography*. New York: Penguin Books.

Smith, D. (1986) 'What Would Freud Think? The Uproar in the Shrine of Psychoanalysis'. *New York*, March 31, pp. 38–45.

Spoto, D. (1993) *Marilyn Monroe: The Biography*. London: Chatto and Windus.

Starr, P. (1982) *The Social Transformation of American Medicine*. New York: Basic Books.

Stepansky, P., ed. (1988) *The Memoirs of Margaret Mahler*. New York: The Free Press.

Sterba, R. (1982) *Reminiscences of a Viennese Psychoanalyst*. Detroit MI: Wayne State University Press.

Sternshein, I. (1971) 'Final Report of the Self-examination of New York Society and Institute' issued in May 1971, Dr. Irving (Chairman)'. Brill Library.
Stoller, R. (1983) 'Judging Psychotherapy'. Typescript.
Stoller, R. and Geertsma, R. (1963) 'The Consistency of Psychiatrists' Clinical Judgments'. *The Journal of Nervous and Mental Disease*, 137 (1): 58–66.
Stolorow, R., Brandchaft, B. and Atwood G. (1987) *Psychoanalytic Treatment: an Intersubjective Approach*. Hillsdale NJ: The Analytic Press.
Stone, L (1976) 'Outline of the (Internal) History of the NY Institute April, 1966-October, 1975'. *Newsletter of the New York Psychoanalytic Society and Institute*, 1 (1) Interim Newsletter.
Strozier, C. (1985) 'Glimpses of a Life: Heinz Kohut (1913–1981)', in A. Goldberg, *Progress in Self Psychology*, Volume 1. New York: The Guilford Press, pp. 3–12.
Sugarman, A, Nemiroff, R. and Greenson, D., eds (1992) *The Technique and Practice of Psychoanalysis: Volume 2: A Memorial Volume to Ralph R. Greenson*. Madison CT: International Universities Press.
Sutherland, J. (1989) *Fairbairn's Journey into the Interior*. London: Free Association Books.
Szasz, T. (1989) Letter to Dr. Karl Menninger, *Bulletin of the Menninger Clinic*, 53: 351–2.
Talan, J. (1995) 'Is the Hour Up? In an Age of Managed Care and Miracle Drugs, the Value of Traditional Long-term Psychotherapy is being, well, Re-analyzed'. *Newsday*, January 31, p. B23.
Talan, J. (1998) 'Evolution of a Psychiatric Hospital – Piecing Together History from Mount Sinai Archives'. *Newsday*, February 17.
Thomä, H. (1993) 'Training Analysis and Psychoanalytic Education: Proposals for Reform'. *Annual of Psychoanalysis*, 21: 3–75.
Tidd, C. (1962) 'Interview with Charles Tidd', December 12, by R. Stoller, Committee for The History of the Society, transcript, LAPSI Library, March 4.
Timms, E. and Segal, N., eds (1988) *Freud in Exile: Psychoanalysis and Its Vicissitudes*. New Haven CT: Yale University Press.
Trilling, D. (1993) *The Beginning of the Journey: The Marriage of Diana and Lionel Trilling*. New York: Harcourt Brace and Company.
Trilling, J. (1999) 'My Father and the Weak-Eyed Devils'. *American Scholar*, 68, 2, pp. 17–42.
Trilling, L. (1951) *The Liberal Imagination*. London: Mercury Books, 1964.
Valenstein, A. (1974) *President's Newsletter* 15, May 31.
Valenstein, A. (1975) Letter to BPSI members by Arthur Valenstein, March 31.
Van Der Heide, C. (1963) 'Interview with Carel Van Der Heide' by A. Kandelin, Committee for the History of the Society. Transcript, LAPSI Library, May 21.
Vaughan, S., Spitzer, R., Davies, M. and Roose, S. (1997) 'The Definition and Assessment of Analytic Process: Can Analysts Agree?'. *Int. J. Psycho-Anal.*, 78: 959–73.

Viederman, M. (1992) 'A Conversation with Roger Mackinnon'. *The American Psychoanalyst*, 26 (4): 24–6.
Wallerstein, R. (1972) 'The Future of Psychoanalytic Education'. *J. Amer. Psychoanal. Assn.*, 20: 591–606.
Wallerstein, R. (1977) 'Psychoanalysis as a Profession and Psychoanalysis as a Science: A Stocktaking', in *Psychoanalytic Education and Research: The Current Situation and Future Possibilities*. New York: International Universities Press, pp. 307–26.
Wallerstein, R. (1980) 'Psychoanalysis and Academic Psychiatry: Bridges'. The *Psychoanalytic Study of the Child*, 35: 419–48.
Wallerstein, R. (1981) 'The Psychoanalyst's Life: Expectations, Vicissitudes, and Reflections'. *International Review of Psycho-Analysis*, 8: 285–98.
Wallerstein, R. (1983) 'The Topeka Institute and the Future of Psychoanalysis'. *Bulletin of the Menninger Clinic.* 47, 6, November: 497–524.
Wallerstein, R. (1986) *Forty-Two Lives in Treatment: A Study of Psychoanalysis and Psychotherapy*. New York: The Guilford Press.
Wallerstein, R. (1988) 'One Psychoanalysis or Many?'. *Int. J. Psycho-Anal.* 69: 5–21.
Wallerstein, R. (1989) 'The Psychotherapy Research Project of the Menninger Foundation: an Overview'. *Journal of Consulting and Clinical Psychology*, 57: 195–205.
Wallerstein, R. (1991a) 'The Future of Psychotherapy'. *Bulletin of the Menninger Clinic*, 55: 421–43.
Wallerstein, R., ed. (1991b) *The Doctorate in Mental Health: An Experiment in Mental Health Professional Education*. Lanham: University Press of America.
Wallerstein, R. (1998a) 'The IPA and the American Psychoanalytic Association: A Perspective on the Regional Association Agreement'. *Int. J. Psycho-Anal.*, 79: 553–64.
Wallerstein, R. (1998b) *Lay Analysis: Life Inside the Controversy*. Hillsdale NJ: Analytic Press.
Wallerstein, R. and Weinshel, E. (1989) 'The Future of Psychoanalysis'. *Psychoanalytic Quarterly*, 58: 341–73.
Wangh, M., ed. (1962) *Fruition of an Idea: Fifty Years of Psychoanalysis in New York*. New York: International Universities Press.
Warren, J., Possley, M. and Tybor, J. (1988) '"As Will Turns": A Real-world Soap', *Chicago Tribune*, September 6.
Weiss, G. (1975) 'Scientists and Sectarians: The Case of Psychoanalysis'. *Journal of the History of Behavioral Sciences*, 11: 350–64.
Weiss, S., ed. (1987) *The Teaching and Learning of Psychoanalysis: Selected Papers of Joan Fleming. M.D.* New York: The Guilford Press.
Wexler, M. (1951) 'The Structural Problem in Schizophrenia: Therapeutic Implications'. *Int. J. Psycho-Anal.*, 32: 157–66.
Wexler, M. (1965) 'Working Through in the Therapy of Schizophrenia'. *Int. J. Psycho-Anal.*, 46: 279–86.
Wilson, S. (1983) 'Interview with Bernard Brandchaft, M.D.' *Los Angeles Psychoanalytic Bulletin*, 2 (3): 2–19.

Wilson, S. (1993a) 'A Conversation with Leo Rangell'. *The American Psychoanalyst*, 27 (2): 15–18.
Wilson, S. (1993b) 'Ralph Greenson: Psychoanalytic Explorer'. *The American Psychoanalyst*, 27 (2): 19–21.
Winer, J. (1998) 'Position Paper for Discussion on March 31, 1998'. Chicago Institute for Psychoanalysis. Unpublished paper.
Wolfe, D. (1998) *The Last Days of Marilyn Monroe*. New York: William Morrow and Co.
Wyman, H. and Rittenberg, S. (1994a) 'Otto Isakower'. *Journal of Clinical Psychoanalysis*, 3: 166–7.
Wyman, H. and Rittenberg, S., eds (1994b) 'The Analyzing Instrument of Otto Isakower, M.D, Evolution of a Psychoanalytic Concept'. Special Edition of *Journal of Clinical Psychoanalysis*, 3.
Young-Bruehl, E. (1988) *Anna Freud: A Biography*. New York: Summit Books.

INTERVIEWS CITED

Altschul, Sol, Chicago, June 8, 1981.
Arlow, Jacob, New York, July 8, 1992.
Arlow, Jacob, Great Neck, July 8, 1994.
Aronson, Gerald, Beverly Hills, July 24, 1992.
Arvidson, Rolf, Cambridge, December 7, 1982.
Atkin, Samuel, New York, March 19, 1981.
Atkins, Norman, Los Angeles, June 24, 1992.
Atkins, Norman, Los Angeles, July 18, 1994.
Bail, Bernard, Beverly Hills, February 12, 1981.
Basch, Michael, Chicago, July 1, 1992.
Brandchaft, Bernard, Los Angeles, February 15, 1981.
Brandchaft, Bernard, Los Angeles, July 13, 1992.
Calder, Ken, New York, July 9, 1992.
Calder, Ken, New York, July 5, 1994a.
Calder, Ken, New York, July 7, 1994b.
Calder, Ken, New York, July 11, 1994c.
Calder New York, September 18, 1996.
Cohen, Sandra, New York, July 24, 1992a.
Cohen, Sandra, New York, July 29, 1992b.
Friedman, Leonard, Welseley, April 28, 1981.
Furer, Emanuel, New York, September 17, 1996.
Galenson, Eleanor, New York, July 5, 1994.
Gardner, M. Robert, Cambridge, April 13, 1981.
Gardner, M. Robert, Cambridge, July 16, 1992.
Gardner, M. Robert, Cambridge, October 14, 1996.
Gedo Chicago, June 30, 1994.
Gedo, John, Chicago, October 29, 1992.
Gedo, John, Chicago, October 4, 1996a.
Gedo, John, Chicago, October 5, 1996b.
Gifford, Sanford, Boston, April 19, 1981.
Gifford, Sanford, Cambridge, December 8, 1982.
Gifford, Sanford, Boston, July 15, 1992.
Gifford, Sanford, Boston, October 21, 1996.
Gill, Merton, June 30, 1992.
Goldberg, Arnold, Chicago, June 22, 1981.
Goldberg, Arnold, Chicago, June 30, 1992.
Goldberg, Arnold, Chicago, June 28, 1994.
Goldberg, Arnold, Chicago, October 4, 1996.
Grinker Sr, Roy, Chicago, June 26, 1981.

INTERVIEWS CITED

Grotstein, James, Beverly Hills, February 12, 1981.
Grotstein, James, Beverly Hills, July 24, 1992.
Gunther, Meyer, Chicago, June 30, 1992.
Hays, Carolyn, Beverly Hills, June 18, 1992.
Hoffer, Axel, Brooklyn, August 20, 1992.
Holzman, Philip, Cambridge, April 28, 1981.
Jaques, Elliott, Melbourne, Australia, November 17, 1990.
Kleinman, Edward, Beverly Hills, June 22, 1992.
Kligerman, Charles, Charles, Chicago, June 17, 1981.
Kligerman, Charles, Chicago, July 1, 1992.
Kligerman, Charles, Chicago, June 30, 1994.
Kovel, Joel, New York, May 22, 1981.
Leavitt, Maimon, Beverly Hills, June 15, 1992.
McGuire, Ivan, Westwood, June 16, 1992.
Mandel, Melvin, Pacific Palisades, February 14, 1981.
Mandel, Melvin, Pacific Palisades, June 14, 1992.
Mandel, Melvin, Pacific Palisades, July 18, 1994.
Mason, Albert, Beverly Hills, July 5, 1990.
Mason, Albert, Beverly Hills, August 11, 1992.
Mason, Albert, Beverly Hills, March 31, 1993.
McLaughlin, James, Pittsburgh, July 2, 1994a.
McLaughlin, James, Pittsburgh, July 3, 1994b.
Moraitis George, Chicago, August 14, 1984.
Moraitis George, Chicago, July 4, 1992.
Moraitis, George, Glencoe, October 2, 1996a.
Moraitis, George, Glencoe, October 3, 1996b.
Myerson, Paul, Boston, December 1, 1982.
New York analyst, New York, May 21, 1981.
New York analyst, New York, July 8, 1992a.
New York analyst, New York, July 24, 1992b.
New York analyst, New York, July 11, 1994.
Ourieff, Arthur, Los Angeles, June 16, 1992.
Pappadis, Tom, Chicago, June 28, 1994.
Peterfreund, Emanuel, New York, January 23, 1983.
Pyles, Robert, Boston, July 17, 1992.
Rangell, Leo, Brentwood, August 11, 1992.
Richards, Arnold, New York, July 9, 1992.
Richards, Arnold, New York, September 18, 1996.
Richmond, M. Barrie, Chicago, October 4, 1996.
Rosengarten, Leonard, Beverly Hills, June 19, 1992.
Rosett, Henry, Newton MA, April 20, 1981.
Schwaber, Evelyn, Brookline, July 19, 1992.
Shane, Morton, Los Angeles, June 23, 1992.
Shershow, Lee, Beverly Hills, June 19, 1992.
Silverman, Samuel, Brookline, October 17, 1996.
Slight, David, Chicago, June 12, 1984.
Tobin, Arnold, Chicago, July 1, 1992.

Valenstein, Arthur, Cambridge, October 15, 1996.
van Dam, Heiman, Westwood, August 10, 1992.
Wallerstein, Robert, San Francisco, June 26, 1987.
Wallerstein, Robert, San Francisco, August 4, 1992.
Weil, Lottie, New York, July 11, 1994.
Weinstein, Lisa, New York, July 10, 1992.
Wolf, Ernest, Chicago, June 10, 1981.
Zaleznik, Abraham, Cambridge, April 27, 1981.

Personal Communications Cited

Bail, Bernard, September 27, 1990.
Brenner, Charles, May 1997.
Calder, Ken, April 22, 1991.
Calder, Ken, December 2, 1995.
Calder, Ken, January 4, 1996a.
Calder, Ken, February 1, 1996b.
Calder, Ken, May 15, 1997.
Calder, Ken, October 16, 1998.
Gedo, John, July 1, 1994.
Gedo, John, November 24, 1995.
Gedo, John, December 10, 1997.
Gifford, Sanford, January 18, 1995a.
Gifford, Sanford, March 31, 1995b.
Gifford, Sanford, April 19, 1995c.
Gifford, Sanford, August 3, 1995d.
Gifford, Sanford, July 12, 1997.
Goldberg, Arnold, July 5, 1994.
Goldberg, Arnold, December 29, 1997.
Grotstein, James, March 17, 1992.
Kovel, Joel, August 31, 1995.
Lothane, Zvi, March 12, 1997.
Mann, James, February 20, 1995
Margolis, Norman, May 17, 1996.
Mason, Albert, April 13, 1994.
Moraitis, George, September 30, 1990a.
Moraitis, George, December 1990b.
Moraitis, George, April 16, 1991.
Moraitis, George, November 10, 1997.
Moraitis, George, January 2, 1998.
Richards, Arnold, April 12, 1996a.
Richards Arnold, May 28, 1996b.
Rollman-Branch, Hilda, April 24, 1992.
Segal, Hanna, January 6, 1993.
Shane, Morton, April 28, 1992.
Winer, Jerome, August 26, 1998.

Index

Abbatte, Grace 36
Abend, Sander 63
Adato, Carl 94
Adler, Alfred 69
Albert Einstein College of Medicine 23–4
Alexander, Franz 110–11, 112, 113–15, 119, 121–2
 influence of 141–3
 petition to IPA 216
Algren, Nelson 108, 126
Altschul, Sol 119
American Academy of Psychoanalysis 7
American Psychoanalytic Association (APsaA) 7–8, 15–16, 34
 Ad Hoc Committee (LAPSI) 207–16, 220, 226
 Advisory/Consultative Committee to LAPSI 221–2
 and affiliation 93, 222, 226
 Board on Professional Standards 93–7, 184, 187, 200, 207, 227
 and Boston Psychoanalytic Society and Institute 73, 89
 and Chicago Psychoanalytic Institute 134–5
 Committee of New Training Facilities 95
 democratisation 225, 232
 discrimination 188, 216–19
 Emergency Committee on Immigration 17, 18
 and foreign psychoanalytic societies 19
 and Kleinian movement 19, 179, 181–8, 194, 200, 212, 226
 and lay analysts 140–1
 and New York Psychoanalytic Institute 34, 47–51, 52–8
 recommending Boston split 94–7, 98
 regulation 19
 and splits 96, 141
 and training standards 213, 226, 240
 see also Los Angeles Psychoanalytic Society and Institute
'analysing instrument' 30–2
'analytic family' 159
Anchluss 18
'Anna O' 6
Annual of Psychoanalysis 117, 136
Aristotle 6
Arlow, Jacob 2–3, 5, 18, 34
 and ego psychology 24–5
 and NYPI 24–5, 28, 29, 43, 59, 60
 on 'secret knowledge' 31–2, 33–4
Aronson, Gerald 155, 167, 169, 189, 203
Arvidson, Rolf 85–6, 96, 99, 101, 103, 104
Atkins, Norman 145, 147, 151, 154–8, 168, 195
authoritarianism 14, 15, 25, 48–9, 71, 234–5

Bail, Bernard
 and IPA report 217–18
 and Kleinianism 164, 168–9, 173–4, 176, 189, 192
 removal from teaching 194–5, 216
 threatened lawsuit 186, 188, 194, 195–8, 199
Bak, Robert 20, 23, 26, 41, 63

INDEX

Balter, Leon 32
Banham, Reyner 229, 231
Basch, Michael 126, 135
Baudry, Francis 54
Berenson, Marvin 169
Beres, David 28, 34
Berlin Psychoanalytic Institute 73, 110, 111, 112, 141
Bernfield, Siegfried 242
Beth Israel Hospital 97
Beverly Wilshire Hotel 170
Bibring, Edward 76, 86, 97
Bibring, Grete 76, 86, 89, 96–7, 99
Bion, Wilfred 170, 172–3, 177, 216, 221, 245
Bleuler, Eugen 234
Blitzsten, N. Lionel 110, 114, 115, 122, 193
Bollas, Christopher 233, 237, 251
Bornstein, Berta 33
Boston 73–4, 77
Boston Psychoanalytic Society and Institute (BPSI) 11, 225
  and American Psychoanalytic Association 73, 89
  autocracy 75, 102
  betrayal 98
  Boston Five 86, 89, 91–2, 96–7, 101, 103–4
  Committee of Training Analysts 75, 85
  Committee of the Whole 84, 85, 86, 91
  community involvement 74, 101, 102, 107
  Coordinating Committee 80
  deanship 78–83
  and democracy 75, 80, 83–4, 87–8, 91, 102
  divisions 76, 82–3
  Education Committee 73, 74, 76, 78, 80–2, 84, 93
  educational philosophy 100–1, 106, 107
  and fear 79
  history of 72–8
  orthodoxy 76–7
  power structure 74–5, 104
  power struggle 78, 88, 102
  and psychiatric hospitals 74, 78
  reformist movement 82–6, 100
  size 77, 78, 100, 102
  society/institute discord 87
  split 72, 75, 84–98, 100–7, 232
  standards 87, 88, 100–1
  Students' Committee 84
  training analysts 76, 80, 81, 83, 85, 88, 91, 98
  and training programmes 73, 79
  'two institutes in one society' 85–6, 92–4, 105
  unrest 82–6
  see also Psychoanalytic Institute of New England East
Boston University 78
Brandchaft, Bernard 230
  and division 147, 193
  and Greenson 189, 190
  and history of LAPSI 139–40
  and ICP 220, 224
  and Kleinianism 167–8, 169–70, 172, 173, 176
  leaving Kleinian camp 174–5, 218
  petition to IPA 216, 218
  and rejection of Susanna Isaacs 202
  and removal of Bail 195–6
  and Reorganisation 161, 164
  and self psychology 174, 215
Brenner Amendment 42, 43–7
Brenner, Charles 16, 24–5, 28, 34, 40, 41, 47–8, 60
Brent, Stuart 114
Breuer, J. 6
Brill, A.A. 15, 16, 141
Brill Archive 29
British Institute of Psychoanalysis 166, 173, 183
British Psychoanalytic Society 172
Brunswick, David 202
Buchbinder, Gilda 132
Burnham, Donald 107
Bussel, Lili 26, 63

Calder, Ken 31, 34
  and fairness 46
  and history of NYPI 70
  on NYPI meetings 36–7
  and power group 29
  on shortage of patients 61
  and training analyst selection 27–8, 62, 63
California Graduate Institute, Psychoanalytic Department 219
Cambridge 77
Casady, Dick 169
Chicago 108, 118–19, 126
Chicago Psychoanalytic Institute 11
  APsaA site visit (1991) 134–5
  authoritarianism 109, 112, 113–14
  and Berlin Institute 110, 111, 112
  Board of Directors 112
  board members as patients 109, 111, 127, 136
  Board of Trustees 75, 108–9, 111–12, 115, 121, 126–7, 135
  and child psychiatry 114, 115
  committee appointments 122–3
  Committee on Committees 134–5
  corruption 109, 111, 115, 127, 130
  decision-making 123–4
  decline 128
  and democracy 113, 118, 123, 134, 136–7, 232
  director's power 108–9, 112, 119, 120–1, 123, 124–5
  early history of 110–11
  funding 111, 118, 119–20, 127, 128, 135, 136
  Graduate Clinic 115
  independence 111–12
  intellectual activity 136–8
  Library 117
  luncheon tradition 112, 124, 128
  machine politics 108, 118–26
  master's degree programme 136
  organisation 108–9, 112–13, 117–18, 119–21
  PhD programme 117
  Piers regime 115–16
  Pollock regime 116–18
  Psychoanalytic Education Council 112, 117, 121, 123
  relationships with universities 136, 137
  reorganisation 134–8
  repressive tolerance 120
  stability of 119–20, 122
  staff 112–15, 117–18
  successful treatment 34
  support for research 125–6
  Teacher Education Programme 115
  and training analyst status 113, 116, 124–5, 128, 138
Chicago Psychoanalytic Literature Index 117
Chicago Psychoanalytic Society 117, 120, 133
Cleveland Psychoanalytic Institute 2
cognitive-behavioural therapies 62
Cohen, Sandra 67
Cohen, Susan 223
Columbia Institute 15, 65, 66
Columbia Presbyterian Medical Center 17
'convoying' 26, 28, 42, 71, 159
Coriat, Isador 73
corrective emotional experience 142
Coser, Lewis 17
Council for the Advancement of Psychoanalytic Education (CAPE) 207
Curtis, Homer 179

Daley, Richard (Sr) 119
Dam, Heiman van 144, 155, 158–9, 162
Daniels, Ed 79, 86, 99, 103
death drive 166, 167

INDEX 315

denial 166
Deri, Frances 167
Deutsch, Felix 76, 97
Deutsch, Helene 76, 97, 241
dynamic psychiatry 21

Eckstein, Rudolf 155, 203
education *see* psychoanalytic training; training analysis; training analysts
ego psychology
  and Europeans 17
  influence of 24, 115
  and LAPSI 181, 183, 193, 221, 222
Eisenstein, Sam 186–7
Eisold, Kenneth 2
Eissler, Kurt 20, 26, 27, 35, 44, 67
Eissler, Ruth 20, 26, 27, 28, 60
'elite 16' 203–6, 214, 226
Ellsberg, Daniel 228
Engle, Ralph 80, 98
Ennis, Jerome 63
envy 167
Erle, Joan 63
European immigrants
  attitude to Americans 26, 27, 32–3, 34, 35, 36, 142
  and competition 17–18, 19
  dominance of 20, 21, 25–6
  in LAPSI 141, 144
  left-wing intellectuals 20
  and medical licences 18–19
  paranoia 36, 70
  and psychoanalytic epicentre 240
  see also Kleinians/Kleinianism; New York Psychoanalytic Institute
Evans, Gwen 169

Fairbairn, W.R.D. 159, 160, 165–6, 169, 170, 221
Federation of Independent Psychoanalytic Societies (FIPAS) 225
Fenichel, Otto 141, 147, 149, 151

Ferber, Leon 200
Ferenczi, S. 69, 190, 234, 245
Fielding, Lewis 203, 228
Fine, Dr 195
Fleming, Joan
  and Boston split 94, 97, 98
  and Chicago Psychoanalytic Institute 115, 116
  and LAPSI 184, 207, 208, 209, 214
Foundation for Research in Psychoanalysis, (Greenson) 150–1
Fox, Richard 224
Foxman, Dr 195
free association 6, 9
Freeman, Marvin (later Judge) 161, 197–8
French, Thomas 115, 116, 141–2
Freud, Anna 21, 27, 142, 175, 181
  Anna Freudians 188, 193
  and Greenson 150–1, 188–9, 190–1
  see also Freud-Klein controversy
'Freud Seminar' 73
Freud, Sigmund 1, 6, 9, 28, 35, 71, 142, 181
  analytic abilities 245
  and authoritarianism 14, 69, 234
  Brill's lectures 15
  colleagues and friends 20, 27, 76–7
  'Committee' 234–5
  idealisation/denigration model 236–7
  ideas challenged 24–5
  language 6–7
  and lay analysts 5, 6
  and orthodoxy 235
  plagiarised 190
  and religion 6
  and role of psychoanalysis 5, 6
  scientific approach 3, 250
  training analysis 239
  and truth 9–10, 234, 238, 240

Freud-Klein controversy 175–7, 179, 181, 188–206, 221
  and American Psychoanalytic Association 187, 212
  and Greenson 151
  and Rangell 158
  reasons for 148, 151, 160, 170
  see also American Psychoanalytic Association; Greenson-Mason debate; Kleinians/Kleinianism; Los Angeles Psychoanalytic Society and Institute
Freudian school 7, 139
Friedman, Lawrence 160, 203
Friedman, Leonard 81–2, 83–5, 87, 92, 104
Furer, Manuel 26–7, 43, 58–9, 63, 64, 69

Galenson, Eleanor 23, 24, 37, 40, 42, 43, 44
Gardner, Bob 84–6, 89, 99, 103
  and PINE 91, 92, 93, 95–6, 100–2, 106
Gedo, John
  on Boston split 96, 100
  and Chicago Psychoanalytic Institute 34, 113, 126, 135, 137–8
  on George Pollock 116, 131
  on LAPSI 224
  on NYPI 71
  on Piers Gerhart 115
Gifford, Ingrid 99
Gifford, Sanford
  on Bibring-Deutsch rift 97
  and Boston split 72, 78, 104–5
  on deanship termination 82–3
  institutionalisation of psychoanalysis 240
  and PINE 92, 93, 95, 99–100
Gill, Merton 126
Gilman, Leonard 206
Gitleson, Maxwell 114
Glover, Edward 168
Goldberg, Alfred 189, 203

Goldberg, Arnold 106, 125, 126, 136, 137
Goldberg, Eugene 40
Goodman, Stanley 184, 186
Gopnik, Adam 246
Greenacre, Phyllis 26–7
Greenson, Ralph (Romi) 148–54, 230
  and 1950 split 144
  and Anna Freud 150–1, 188–9, 190–1
  anti-Kleinian movement 168, 171, 188–93
  and 'elite 16' 203, 204, 205
  on hostility at LAPSI 143
  personal attack on 190–2
  plagiarism 190–1
  and removal of Bail 195
  and Reorganisation 162
Greenson-Mason debate 188–93
  see also Freud-Klein controversy
Grinker Sr, Roy 114, 116, 120, 234
Gross, George 56, 59, 62
Grotjahn, Martin 144
Grotstein, James
  on Greenson 150, 153, 188, 211
  and Kleinianism 169, 173, 174, 175, 177
  Kleinians as outcasts 215
  on Mandell 211
  on Ourieff 186
  and PCC 224
  petition to IPA 216, 218
  on Rangell 153
  as training analyst 164
group therapy 142
Gunther, Meyer 121–2
Guntrip, Harry 166

Hall, Larry 94
Hartmann, Heinz 20, 24, 25–6, 34, 115, 181, 228
Harvard Medical School 78
Hays, Carolyn 169, 173–4
Hazen, Lita Annenberg 151
Heide, Carel van der 143, 144
Heiman, Paula 170

Hendrick, Ives 73, 97
Holt, Robert 4
Holzman, Phillip 188
Horney, Karen 111, 119
Horowitz, William 169
Human Rights Commission 52

identification 69–70, 166, 167, 192
Innsbruck Congress (1927) 241
Institute for Contemporary Psychoanalysis (ICP) 216, 220, 222
integrity, and internal conflict 152
International Psychoanalytic Association 15
  and European lay analysts 19
  and Kleinians 167, 172, 198
  petition to 216–19
  report 217–19
  and standards 239–40
  and Susanna Isaacs case 202
Isaacs, Susanna 201–3, 216
Isakower, Otto 20, 25, 26, 30–3, 34, 35–6
'Isakower phenomenon' 30

Jacobs, Theodore 30
Jacobson, Edith 20
Jaques, Elliot 50, 245
Jones, Ernest 110, 234–5
Joseph, Betty 173, 196
Joseph, Edward 34, 38, 39
Journal of the American Psychoanalytic Association 8
Jucovy, Milton 39
Jung, Carl 69, 73
Jungian school 7

Kabcenell, Bob 62–3
Kafka, Ernie 60
Kairys, David 43
Kaplan, Sam 85
Kavka, Jerome 114
Kernberg, Otto 4, 28, 146, 167, 221, 244, 248
Khan, Masud 170

Klein, Melanie 69, 139, 164, 165, 191, 245
Kleinians/Kleinianism 7, 11, 21, 151, 165–78, 219
  and American Psychoanalytic Association 19, 179, 181–8, 194, 200, 212, 226, 227
  British Kleinians 169, 196
  defining 197
  and discrimination 186, 196, 199–200
  fanaticism 178
  fear of 203–4
  and Freudians' guilt 215
  and Greenson 188–93
  investigations into 189
  and Kohut 215
  and labels 193
  LAPSI reaction to 168–78
  leaving LAPSI 214–15, 219
  militancy 176
  in US 167
  see also European immigrants; Freud-Klein controversy; Los Angeles Psychoanalytic Society and Institute
Kleinman, Edward, 187, 192
Kligerman, Charles 112–13, 118, 119, 121, 128–9, 132
Klumpner, George 126, 133
Knight, Robert 3, 37, 140
knowledge
  and qualification 14, 233, 235, 238, 246–7, 248
  real and presumed 13, 249–50
Kohut, Heinz 69, 106, 221
  analytic abilities 245, 246
  at Chicago Psychoanalytic Institute 114–115, 119, 125, 126
  critical function 228
  and Kleinians 215
Kohutian movement 229
Kovel, Joel 24
Krent, Justin 179
Kris, Ernst 20, 24, 25–6, 28, 115, 181

Kris, Marianne 20, 25
Kris Study Group 28
Kronold, Ed 26, 32, 44
Kubie, Lawrence 18

Lacan, J. 1, 69, 236–7, 245, 249
language, as therapeutic instrument 6–7
lay analysis 18–19, 35, 140–1, 142
Lear, Jonathan 6
Leavitt, Maimon
　and Ad Hoc Committee 213–14
　and 'elite 16' 203, 205
　and Kleinians 193, 215
　and LAPSI Reorganisation 161, 162, 163, 165
　and site visit (1973) 179, 183
　and Wexler affair 154, 155
Lederer, Anne 130–1
Lederer, Francis 130
Levenson, Edgar 6, 245
Lewin, Bertram 18, 30, 241
Lewis, Harvey 167, 168
Lindon, John 169
Loewenstein, Elizabeth Gleerd 26
Loewenstein, Rudolph 20, 24, 25–6, 33, 115, 181
Loomie, Leo 34
Los Angeles 139, 229, 230, 231
Los Angeles Institute and Society for Psychoanalytic Studies 219
Los Angeles Psychoanalytic Society and Institute (LAPSI) 11, 229–30
　Ad Hoc Committee (APsaA) 207–16, 220, 226–7
　Admissions Committee 180–1
　appeal to IPA 216–19
　assignment of supervisors 181–2, 185
　and Bail 193–201
　Board of Directors 163
　British Kleinians 169–71, 172–3, 174–5, 189, 196, 201–3
　bylaws 162–3, 164, 197
　Candidates' Evaluation Committee 180
　child analysis 201
　Committee of Child Analysis 144
　Committee on the Unification of the Institute (CUI) 206–16, 226
　consequences of conflict 220–5, 232
　Coordinating Council 163, 165, 180, 181–2, 184–5
　corruption 163, 179
　Curriculum Committee 193–4
　and democracy 162, 164, 180, 225
　Denver workshop 209
　destructive atmosphere 209–10, 212
　disaccreditation 211–12
　discrimination 186, 196, 198, 201–3, 216–18
　dissatisfaction of training analysts 160
　and dissolution 96, 207–8
　early history 140–4
　Education Committee 143, 144, 145, 147, 158, 160, 162, 163
　effect of student movement 228
　'elite 16' 203–6, 214, 226
　Ethics Committee 156
　and external events 228
　graduation delay 224
　and Greenson 149–50
　Greenson-Mason debate 188–93
　Greenson-Rangell conflict 143–4, 147–8, 152–3, 154–8
　ideological differences 141–2
　impact of ICP 222–3, 224
　impropriety 148
　indemnification 198, 203
　internal conflict 141–5, 178–80, 204
　internal Site Review Committee 184–5
　investigation of 160, 161–5
　IPA report 217–18
　Joint Committee on Mutual Problems of the Society and Institute 161

Kleinian influence 151, 159, 164, 165–78, 181, 183–4, 203
lack of charismatic leaders 228–9
lack of intellectual leadership 224–5
'lost generation' 221, 223
morale 223
openness 225, 231
projection 209–10, 213
and Rangell 151
reasons for conflict 225–31
relationship with American Psychoanalytic Association 197–8
Reorganisation 160–5, 177, 178, 180, 182, 228
repression 145–6
riotous meetings 208
site visits
 (1964) 145–6, 164, 170
 (1973) 178–88, 214, 216, 219
 (1980) 221
 (1987) 221
 (1994) 222
size 224
split (1950) 141–4, 147, 204
split (1964) 154
standards 158–60, 181–2
Susanna Isaacs case 210–3
training analysis 158, 178
training analyst appointments 144, 147–8, 160–5, 180–2, 199, 212, 219, 226
training analysts 158–60
training v. research 142
UCLA residents 177
uniqueness 230–1
Wexler affair 154–8
see also Freud-Klein controversy; Kleinians/Kleinianism
Los Angeles Psychoanalytic Study Group 140
Lothane, Zvi 31, 32

McDougall, Joyce 233, 236, 244
McGuire, Ivan 144, 146, 169–71, 172, 174

McLaughlin Committee 94–9
McLaughlin, James 94–9, 208, 209, 210, 213
Macy Foundation 110
Magraw, Charles 90
Mahler, Margaret 17, 19, 20, 25, 37, 241
Malcove, Lillian 26, 36, 63
Malin, Arthur 169, 177
Mandel, Melvin 221, 230
 and Bail's lawsuit treat 197
 and CUI 206–11, 213–14
 and 'elite 16' 204, 206
 and IPA report 218
 and Kleinianism 167, 168, 171, 175–7, 227–8
 and LAPSI openness 231
 and LAPSI Reorganisation 161, 164, 165
 on LAPSI split 144, 215–16
 and promotions 199–200
 and Wexler affair 155, 156
Manhattan 22
Mann, James 77, 78–82, 80, 84, 88, 98
Marcuse, Herbert 120
Margolis, Norman 44–5, 48–9, 62, 63–4
 and Brenner Amendment 46
 on elections at NYPI 41
 on European immigrants 20
 and training analyst status 38–9, 42
Marmor, Judd 142, 147
Mason, Albert 173, 174, 175, 177
 and 'elite 16' 205
 and Greenson 188–93
 and IPA report 217–18
 and PCC 224
 petition to IPA 216
 on removal of Bail 194
 and Susanna Isaacs case 201, 202
Masson, Jeffrey 246
Meltzer, Donald 173, 174, 175
Menninger Clinic 141
Menninger, Karl 140
Menninger, William 21

Monroe, Marilyn 149, 153–4
Moore, Burness 34, 39, 40
Moraitis, George 123–4, 127, 128, 131–3, 134, 136
Mt Sinai School of Medicine, CUNY 17, 23
Myerson, Paul 74–5, 80–3, 85, 87, 96, 103

National Association for the Advancement of Psychoanalysis 7
National Institute of Mental Health (NIMH) 22, 23, 77
New Haven group 151
New York, and European immigrants 17–20
New York Psychoanalytic Institute 11, 151, 233
  Admissions Committee 23
  and Albert Einstein College of Medecine 23–4
  and American Psychoanalytic Association 34, 47–51, 52–8
  anointment 13–14
  attitude to Columbia Institute 66
  beginnings of 15–16
  bequests 35–6, 54
  Board of Directors 46
  Board of Trustees 38, 39, 40–1, 46, 48, 54–5, 58–9, 63–4
  and change 14, 37, 58–65, 68
  and commitment 65–8
  community relations 35
  Concerned Analysts 40, 43–4
  Concerned Members 46–7, 48, 51
  conference of refugee analysts 19
  and conformity 24, 26, 53
  and decline of psychoanalysis 71
  and democracy 43, 44–5, 49, 59, 71, 232
  Directorship of Treatment Center 56
  divisions 21, 26
  Educational Committee (EC) 14, 36, 37–8, 39, 40, 43, 62

  elections 39, 41–2
  and European immigrants 20, 21, 228
  Europeans and Americans 26, 27, 32–3, 34, 35
  Extension Division 64, 68
  faculty autonomy 46–7, 48, 49, 64
  favouritism/cronyism 13, 27, 28, 30, 49, 50
  Fellowship Programme 68
  financial crisis 29, 36, 48, 51, 55
  internal conflict 36–7, 40–2, 43–6, 47–51
  and intimidation 53
  lack of good will 56–7
  law suits against 51–2
  membership contributions 29, 48, 56
  morale 54, 55
  nepotism 13, 42, 54
  new ideas 68
  new type of candidate 68–9
  and New York Psychoanalytic Society 29
  Nominating Committee 41
  and nonmedical candidates 60–1, 68
  and orthodoxy 24–5, 66
  and patients' fees 34
  polarisation 47–9, 54, 57
  politicisation 55, 62–3
  postgraduate training centre 23
  power structure 14, 27, 43, 47
  and prestige 13, 22
  and psychoanalysis as intuition 31–2
  Psychoanalytic Foundation 51
  rebels 26, 43–4
  and reform 39–40
  reputation of 62
  resignations 54, 55
  ruling clique 15, 20–6, 29–34, 37–8, 40, 57–8
    opposition to 38, 40–1, 43–5, 47, 59–60

self-scrutiny committee 39–40, 43
site visits
  (1976) 47–51
  (1983) 52–8
  (1992) 65, 68
size 13
splits 13, 15, 21, 89, 228
study groups 28, 53, 60, 67
and tradition 67
training 14, 23–4, 26–7, 30, 37–8, 50
Treatment Center 34, 56
and trust 64
voting system 45–6
younger leadership 59–60, 63
see also authoritarianism; European immigrants
New York Psychoanalytic Society and Institute 16–17
separation of 50
New York Psychoanalytic Society (NY Society) 15–16, 18–19
New York University Institute 15
Nunberg, Hermann 20, 26, 27
Nuremberg Psychoanalytic Congress (1910) 15

Oberndorf, Clarence 15
object relations theory 11, 151, 160, 164, 166, 169, 170, 193
  see also Kleinians/Kleinianism
Oedipus complex 166
Oliver Cromwell Hotel 16
Ourieff, Arthur 207, 230
  and Bail's lawsuit threat 197
  and 'elite 16' 203–4
  and Kleinians 169, 172, 183–6, 188, 194–5, 202, 215
  and LAPSI Reorganisation 161, 164, 177
  and object relations theory 193
  and removal of Bail 194

Pappadis, Tom 136
Patterson, Dr 195
personality 166

Peterfreund, Emanuel 28
Peterson, Neal 206
Peto, Andrew 23
Philadelphia Institute 96
Piers, Gerhart 112, 115–16
Piggott, John 161
Plato 6
Pollock, George 109–10, 111, 116–18, 128–9
  and American Psychoanalytic Association 121, 128
  and directors' tenure 112
  lawsuit 130–4
  power of 127
  reappointment of 129
  resignation 132–4, 135
  withdrawal 129
Porder, Mike 60, 62, 63
postmodernism 1
psychiatry, and psychoanalytic training 21–2
psychoanalysis
  and American culture 106–7
  and biological psychiatry 229
  boom in America 22
  as a cause 20–1
  commercialisation of 127
  competition for 61–2, 77
  critical 9–10
  decline in popularity
    effect on institutes 42, 60–1, 78, 117, 127–8, 135
    reasons for 1, 77, 233, 246, 248–9, 250–1
  definitions of concepts 243–4, 248
  deinstitutionalisation 248–9
  and dogma 7, 9, 70–1
  failed analyses 246
  false expertise 233, 237, 246
  fees 61, 69
  and Freud 1, 4
  history of 2
  humanistic discipline 233
  and idealisation 236
  institutionalisation 240, 246
  as intuition 31–2

psychoanalysis *continued*
　and medical science 6, 250
　and new psychotherapies 229
　and omnipotence 33–4, 250
　and philosophy/religion 5, 250
　professionalised 9, 10, 238
　and psychotherapy 142
　and research 248, 249
　role of 4, 5–6
　and sceptical inquiry 250–1
　and science 3, 233, 235, 237, 242–3, 250
　science or art 238, 243–4
　success of 21–4
　and truth 236
　see also knowledge
psychoanalysts
　competence 245–7
　and medical qualification 15
　skills 6
　see also European immigrants; qualification; training analysis; training analysts
Psychoanalytic Center of California (PCC) 216, 219
Psychoanalytic Institute of New England East (PINE) 72, 74, 89–90, 95–9
　and American Psychoanalytic Association affiliation 91, 93, 96, 105
　criticisms of BPSI 95
　and democracy 75, 91
　dual membership with BPSI 85–6, 92–4, 105–6
　formation of 86, 89, 92–4
　'institute without walls' 41, 106
　McLaughlin Committee 94–100
　position statement 90
　resignations 99
　and standards 101
　and younger generation 103
　see also Boston Psychoanalytic Society and Institute (BPSI)
psychoanalytic institutions 7–9, 10–12
　closed 2, 3, 5, 235
　conflicts 232

　and conformity 10
　and democracy 14, 15, 29, 43
　and free inquiry 2, 10
　free-standing 1, 3, 8, 234
　governance of 8
　models of 4, 28
　and power 75–6
　and received truth 10, 28
　size 90–1
　and societies 75–6, 87
　splits 2–3, 11, 89
　suspicion of 3
　and training 8, 236
　training analyst problem 232, 242
　umbrella organisations 7–8
　and university culture 248
psychoanalytic training 3–4, 91, 233–6
　anointment 113, 233, 234, 239, 240, 244, 249
　in city hospitals 23
　and conflict 237, 238
　and indoctrination 4, 9, 227
　informal 16
　as initiation 34
　mystification 236, 239
　and personal analysis 239, 244, 247–8
　and psychoanalytic procedure 241–2
　regulation 19
　standards 237, 244
　see also training analysis; training analysts
psychopathology, and developmental failure 150
psychosis, treatment of 160, 166, 167
psychotherapy 10, 35, 142
psychotropic drugs 61, 77, 246
Putnam, James Jackson 15, 72–3
Pyles, Robert 87, 100

qualification 249
　and knowledge 14, 233, 235, 238, 246–7, 248

Rado, Sandor 14, 15
Rangell, Leo 2, 18, 144, 148, 151–4, 230
  on analytic process 159
  on cause of split 139, 140, 141
  and indoctrination 227
  and Reorganisation 162
Rank, Otto 73
Reich, Annie 20, 25, 63
Reiser, Mort 32
research grants 22
Richards, Arnold 25, 59, 60, 62, 63, 64, 65, 68
Richmond, Barrie 133
Richter, Peter 26, 44, 63
Rie, Oscar 20
Ritvo, Samuel 216
Rockefeller Foundation 110
role-playing 114
Rollman-Branch, Hilda 150, 161, 167, 187, 193, 195
  and 'elite 16' 203–4
Romm, May 142–3, 147
Roose, Lawrence 46
Root, Arthur 57, 58
Rosen, Victor 32, 34, 35
Rosenbaum, Milton 23
Rosenfeld, Herbert 169–71, 173, 175, 190
Rosengarten, Leonard
  and CUI 206–9, 211
  and 'elite 16' 205
  on Greenson 150
  on LAPSI conflict 143, 145, 168, 200, 229
  and rejection of Susanna Isaacs 202
  and training analyst appointment 160, 161, 164, 226
Rosenwald Foundation 110
Ross, H. 115, 241
Rosten, Leo 149
Rothstein, Arnold 64
Russian Psychoanalytic Association 3

San Francisco Psychoanalytic Society 140–1

Sarlin, Charles 155
Schafer, Roy 66
Schilder, Paul 73
Schlesinger, Nathan 126
Schloss Tegel 141
Segal, Hanna 170, 173, 191, 196, 216, 218
Seidenberg, Henry 132
Seitz, Phillip 116
self psychology/psychologists 125, 126, 136, 137, 174, 215, 220
Semrad, Elvin 32
Shane, Estelle 220, 224
Shane, Morton 167, 176, 186, 203, 205–6, 220, 224
Shapiro, Louis 115, 126
Shershow, Lee 177, 194, 208, 214, 222
Shorr, Jay 57
Silbermann, Isidor 41
Silverman, Sam 76–7, 86, 91
Simmel, Ernst 141, 147, 149
Society for Psychoanalytic Medicine of Southern California 141
sodium pentathol 149
Solnit, Albert 151
Solomon, Irwin 26, 37, 44, 63
Solomon, Rebecca 44
Southern California Institute 143–4, 186, 188
Southern California Society and Institute, (SCPI) 219–20
splitting 166, 167
Spoto, Donald 149, 153
Stein, Martin 26, 30, 34, 41–2, 44, 63
Stekel, William 149
Sterba, Richard 169
stereotyping 28
Stern, Alfred K. 110, 111
Stock, Malvina 85, 86, 96, 103
Stoller, Robert 169, 224
Stolorow, Robert 220
Stone, Leo 34
Sullivan, Harry Stack 193
Sundelson, D. 233, 237

'syncretism' 241
'Syndrome of the Compromise of
  Integrity' 152

'talking cure' 6
Tartakoff, Helen 89, 96–7, 99
Tedesco, Dr 195
Thomä, Helmut 5
Thorner, Hans 173
Tobin, Arnold 133
Tolpin, Marain and Paul 126
Topeka Institute 140
training analysis 4–5, 69
  alternatives 247–8
  and fees 61–2
  misuse of 179
  problems of 28, 159–60, 239, 241
  reporting on analysands 83–4, 146, 159
  separated from institute 247–8
  and theory 159
  see also psychoanalytic training; transference
training analysts
  and anointment 5, 25
  appointment 37–9, 50, 52–5, 98–9, 180, 185
  and Boston split 102–4
  and Brenner Amendment 42, 43–4, 48
  changes in 58–9, 62–3, 83–4
  'Concerned Analysts' 40, 48
  convoying 26, 28, 42, 159
  reward system 124–5
  and ruling clique 14
  and younger analysts 116, 117
  automatic status 220, 226
  European immigrants 20
  pledge 199
  power of 76, 81, 85, 88, 185, 240–1, 242
  and prestige 61–2, 224, 226
  and reputation 52–3
  'rule of three' 164
  self-nomination 55, 58, 59, 64

standards 85, 88, 158–60, 165, 185, 238
'training analysts' war' 219–20
training grants 22
transference
  and 'corrective emotional experience' 114
  Freudian and Kleinian approaches 189–90
  infantile 166–7
  and Kleinianism 176
  in training analysis 28, 49, 69, 104, 159, 227, 244
Trilling, Lionel 6
truth 14, 28, 29, 70, 236
Tufts University Medical School 78

Valenstein, Arthur 79, 86, 88, 89–90, 93, 96–7, 103
Vatz, Jack 162
Veterans Administration 22, 78

Waldhorn, Herb 42
Wallerstein, Robert 118, 167
Walsh, Maurice 154
war neuroses 144, 149
Warburg, Bettina 18
Washington Institute 96
Weil, Fred and Anna-Marie 26
Weimar Congress 15
Weinshel, Edward 184, 186, 187, 188, 207
Wexler, Milton 150, 154–58, 189
Widlocher, Daniel 216
Willick, Martin 63
Winer, Jerry 136–7
Winnicott, D.W. 166, 169, 170, 201, 221, 245
Winston, Lisa 66
Wolf, Ernest 126

Young, Nicholas 26, 41, 44
Young-Bruehl, Elizabeth 150

Zalcznik, Abraham 72, 96, 99, 102–3